"*Understanding Police Operational Performance* provides a clear understanding of the history of policing coupled with key organizational areas worth examining to ensure best practices. This book is a must read at a pivotal time in American policing for local leaders, police executives, and community members. Critical topics such as police staffing, operations, organizational culture and management practices your local police should be continually examining are clearly described with citations for further exploration. As a police consultant who has conducted organizational assessments throughout the United States, *Understanding Police Operational Performance* succinctly identifies the key areas communities and police executives need to have ongoing dialogue on what public safety looks and feels like in their community."

Jackie Gomez-Whiteley, *Police Chief (Ret.), Principal &*
Founder of Meliora Public Safety Consulting, LLC

"... practitioners, administrators and students who read these pages will benefit from the authors' vast experience and bring new and thoughtful ideas and practices to policing resulting in better outcomes ..."

Thomas Belfiore, *Former Police Commissioner, Westchester*
County Department of Public Safety – Division of County Police;
Former Chief Security Officer, Port Authority of New York and New Jersey

"The team of James McCabe, Paul O'Connell, Carol Rasor-Cordero and Demosthenes Long is the gold standard in the analysis of police operations. They offer practical and realistic analysis of resource allocation, the 'right sizing' of law enforcement agencies, best practices, policies and procedures, department budgets, internal and external surveys, community engagement and partnership, crime reduction, ethics, communication and cultural issues. A must read for policing professionals."

Edmund Hartnett, *NYPD Deputy Chief (retired),*
Former Police Commissioner Yonkers NY

"This book is of great value for agencies considering self-evaluation and consultant management studies. The topics are relevant, well researched and well written by four pracademics with substantial experience in the field and as police agency evaluators. With hundreds of police management studies under their belts, I highly recommend *Understanding Police Operational Performance*."

Stephen A. Morreale, *D.P.A., Worcester State University, DEA (retired)*

Understanding Police Operational Performance

Understanding Police Operational Performance provides a roadmap for police agencies to implement performance-improvement strategies that work. This book provides an easy-to-read, comprehensive overview of the key indicators of successful internal operations of police agencies in the United States, and equips readers with the tools needed to bring police organizations to top performance.

Ideal for law enforcement professionals, as well as city or county administrators and policymakers, this book offers practical advice for planning and conducting an evaluation of the various components of a police organization. It is also appropriate for use in law enforcement, criminal justice, and political science courses.

James E. McCabe is a Professor of Criminal Justice at St. John's University. He is a retired Inspector from the New York City Police Department and is an expert on police organizational behavior, leadership, and the impact of police operations on public safety and neighborhood satisfaction with police services.

Paul E. O'Connell is a Professor Emeritus at Iona University and a leading expert on the application of Compstat model Police Management principles to public administration organizations. O'Connell conducts research, publishes scholarly papers, and lectures widely on the topics of police performance measurement, integrity management, and law enforcement training systems.

Demosthenes Long is a Professor of Criminal Justice and Security at Pace University. Prior to joining the faculty at Pace University, Long had a 31-year career in public safety with 21 years with the New York Police Department, retiring at the rank of Assistant Chief, and served for five years as the First Deputy Commissioner of the Westchester County Department of Public Safety.

Carol Rasor-Cordero is a Professor of Criminal Justice and Public Safety Administration at St. Petersburg College. A retired Captain from the Pinellas County Sheriff's Office in Florida, she served in various divisions over her 25-year career and has conducted research examining the relationship between personality preferences in law enforcement/corrections leaders and exemplary leadership practices.

Routledge Series on Practical and Evidence-Based Policing

Books in the Routledge Series on Practical and Evidence-Based Policing disseminate knowledge and provide practical tools for law enforcement leaders and personnel to protect and serve the public and reduce crime. With an aim to bridge the "translation gap" between frontline policing and academic research, books in this series apply sound scientific methods as well as practical experience to make everyday police work safer and smarter. These books are an invaluable resource for police practitioners, academic researchers, public policymakers, and students in law enforcement and criminology programs to guide best practices in all aspects of policing.

Twenty-One Mental Models for Policing
A Framework for Using Data and Research for Overcoming Cognitive Bias
Renée J. Mitchell

Public Corruption in the United States
Analysis of a Destructive Phenomenon
Jeff Cortese

The Wicked Problems of Police Reform in Canada
Laura Huey, Lorna Ferguson & Jennifer L. Schulenberg

Human Rights Policing
Reimagining Law Enforcement in the 21st Century
Peter Marina & Pedro Marina

Interviewing Vulnerable Suspects
Safeguarding the Process
Edited by Dr Jane Tudor-Owen, Dr Celine van Golde, Dr Ray Bull & David Gee MBE

Reframing Police Education and Freedom in America
Martin Alan Greenberg & Beth Allen Easterling

Gold Medal Policing
Operational Readiness and Performance Excellence, 2nd Edition
Judy M. McDonald

Understanding Police Operational Performance
James E. McCabe, Paul E. O'Connell, Demosthenes Long, and Carol Rasor-Cordero

Understanding Police Operational Performance

James E. McCabe, Paul E. O'Connell,
Demosthenes Long, and
Carol Rasor-Cordero

Routledge
Taylor & Francis Group

NEW YORK AND LONDON

Designed cover image: Olivier Le Moal

First published 2025
by Routledge
605 Third Avenue, New York, NY 10158

and by Routledge
4 Park Square, Milton Park, Abingdon, Oxon, OX14 4RN

Routledge is an imprint of the Taylor & Francis Group, an informa business

ISBN: 9781032500034 (hbk)
ISBN: 9781032490748 (pbk)
ISBN: 9781003396437 (ebk)

DOI: 10.4324/9781003396437

Typeset in Sabon
by Newgen Publishing UK

Contents

Chapter 1

Why Assess?

The Value-Added of Conducting Periodic Assessments

Perhaps the single most difficult question that an American police chief could be confronted with today is *"Hey chief, what's the plan?"* Prior to the mid-1990s, American police chiefs were not in the habit of responding to questions like "What are your department's current strategic objectives?" or "Exactly how far has your department gotten in accomplishing its stated goal of reducing domestic violence incidents by 20%?" even if they were posed by the city/town manager, community leaders or other important stakeholders. Years ago, police departments did not have a business-like approach to their work and police chiefs were not held personally accountable for assessing organizational "performance." Assessment was reserved for private corporations, not police departments. After all, what are they going to do, close down the local police department on account of poor performance? We are the police – a monopoly – the only game in town.

For this reason, police departments across America traditionally were quite content with the status quo. Rather than approaching their work in a businesslike fashion, police departments were satisfied with maintaining a responsive or reactive posture towards their work. If you brought a problem to their attention, they would address it. Little effort was expended in identifying potential problem areas. Why look for problems if they don't yet exist?

American police departments were originally designed in the mid-nineteenth century as hierarchical, paramilitary, bureaucratic organizations that would approach their work in a methodical, inflexible, un-creative, inefficient, and relatively unresponsive fashion. They "adopted the quasi-military organization model characterized by a rigid rank hierarchy of authority, impersonality, and an authoritarian command system. This model [was] intended to foster strict and unquestioned discipline for rapid mobilization in emergency and crisis situations. This traditional approach to police administration is largely grounded in the work of O. W. Wilson who sought to divorce police operations from political influences and rationalize haphazard management practices. Wilson advocated a pyramidal hierarchy to attain proper direction, coordination, and control, and the principles of management derived from Fayol's administrative management theory" (Jermier and Berkes, 1979, p. 2) (citations omitted). This highly formalized approach to management included "an emphasis on mistake avoidance, caution and systematic rule application" (Davies and Thomas, 2003, p. 682). Bureaucracies have widely been criticized for being "inflexible, inefficient, uncreative and unresponsive in times of rapid change" (Perrow, 1972, p. 6). Describing the NYPD prior to 1994, Silverman (1999) states that the department was addicted to formal rules and procedures, subject to an occupational culture that had proven itself to be particularly resistant to change. Like most departments, it was characterized by strict hierarchical structures, organizational rigidity, and a culture that was generally unreceptive to change. This is certainly not a recipe for success.

DOI: 10.4324/9781003396437-1

The single most quoted measure of police performance for the better part of the twentieth century was police "response times." If a chief could demonstrate that the average time of response to a call for service was dropping, he/she was considered to be a superior manager. Unfortunately, during the 1970s and 1980s, crime rates rose to unprecedented levels. The increase of both violent and property crime continued into the 1990s unabated, yet police managers pointed to diminishing response times as an indicator of police "effectiveness." They simply weren't measuring what mattered most.

Additionally, the information technology (IT) capabilities of most American police departments were quite limited through the 1970s and early 1980s. Prior to the advent of the desktop computer, forward-thinking chiefs and field commanders who wanted to access real-time data concerning their department's operations had to wade through reams of original paper records or hard copy data printouts. Data requests typically had to be forwarded to specialists who were often not even department employees. These data centers typically responded to data requests one or more weeks later, well after the window of opportunity for effective action had closed. Many chiefs simply chose not even to make such requests.

Things began to change in the early 1990s. Chiefs and field commanders could review the current operations of their units and personnel with the push of a button or click of a mouse. Finally, police managers had the ability to move their resources and deploy their personnel more effectively, based upon timely and accurate data.

Additionally, with the enactment of the Government Performance and Results Act (GPRA) in 1993, the federal government now began to challenge public administrators to account for themselves and the work of their agencies. No longer would an agency's budget be granted automatically, in a *pro forma* manner. Public administrators in the federal system now needed to justify their efforts; to demonstrate specifically where the money had been spent, how it had been spent and, most importantly, whether or not that agency's efforts were having any success. The GPRA required agencies to actually establish performance goals and plans, to measure results and to periodically report on their progress. For the first time, agencies were required "to provide evidence of their performance relative to targets and to report their results annually to the public" (Heinrich, 2007, p. 258). Not surprisingly, this dramatically transformed the way business was conducted in the federal system. It did not take long for states and municipalities to follow suit by creating new demands for accountability and evidence of performance.

The economic downturn of 2008 placed additional pressure upon state and municipal public officials to ensure that limited resources were being expended judiciously. Suddenly, gone were the days when the mayor or city manager would blindly fund a police department without knowing exactly where and how the money was spent. In the old days, the city manager would ask the chief, "*I see that you put in a request for 10 more patrol officers. Why do you need them?*" The typical response: "*If I tried to explain it to you, you wouldn't understand; you're a civilian.*" By 2008, such a response was no longer tolerated. Due to new public expectations and fiscal realities, public officials now needed to account for every dollar that was spent, and they were no longer willing to give police departments a pass. Accountability and fiscal transparency is required and made part of the ongoing business model of American police departments.

This new fiscal environment led to an entirely new way of doing business for police departments. American police chiefs were now being asked where their department's money was being spent, how exactly it was being spent, and whether these expenditures were making a positive difference. Police chiefs were now held strictly accountable for the efforts of their personnel and, more importantly, they would now be asked to identify exactly what "success" looked like for their agencies. They were asked to describe where their department's work was being performed, why it was being performed, etc. Often, these answers were not readily available. Someone needed to search through department records and call for service data to answer these questions. Forward-thinking chiefs quickly realized, *"We shouldn't have to be searching through past records all the time. We need to monitor this information on the fly!"* In other words, they recognized the need for ongoing, internal operational monitoring and analysis (i.e., assessments) of their departments' operations. New skills and an entirely new mindset were required.

Ongoing Performance Assessment: A Critically Important Part of Any Manager's Job

Assessment is generally defined as the act of evaluating or judging the amount or quality of something. All organizations perform assessment. Indeed, assessment is a natural human function that individuals also perform. Continually.

Consider your car. During an average trip to work or to the store, you perform a variety of immediate assessments that assist you on your journey. You continually check: the speed limit; your speed; total distance to destination; current fuel level; amount of fuel required; the location of nearby gas stations; and whether there is enough fuel for the return trip.

This is what assessment looks like.

When we use the word *assessment* in this text, we are referring to an overall qualitative and quantitative evaluation or estimation of the quality of *all* a particular department's operations and services. Assessments can be comprehensive or discreet. Assessments utilize performance metrics from a variety of sources, to evaluate the work of all operational units, as well as the department itself. Good assessment entails triangulation, viewing the department or unit from a number of different perspectives. Thus, the evaluation of a school resource officer (SRO) or unit should include input from stakeholders outside of the department, such as school administrators, teachers, parents of schoolchildren, etc. The evaluation of an enforcement initiative should also include input from stakeholders as well.

All police organizations get assessed. Average departments get assessed periodically. Good departments get assessed frequently. Excellent departments are assessed continually.

Assessment matters. It is a tool that is relatively new to the field of policing. Granted, state and national accreditation (i.e., by state-wide standards and training councils, CALEA, etc.) have been available for many years, but that is a very specific type of assessment performed every few years by external agents who in essence provide an overall grade (of pass or fail) to a department. It is a retrospective analysis and appraisal of what has already occurred or, at best, an "as-is" or "dip stick" measure of a department's current operations. Police managers typically find these exercises to be burdensome and somewhat uncomfortable. Much effort and a considerable amount of anxiety goes into preparing a department for a site visit and review.

Police departments across the United States are now also required to accumulate and report out data regarding certain activities such as police use of force, and vehicle stops. Police in Connecticut, for example, are required to submit a written report for every traffic stop and vehicle pursuit they conduct. This certainly is a form of organizational assessment, but it is relatively limited in scope.

There are other types of assessment, however: internal ones that are performed far more frequently; ongoing review of real-time performance data by the managers themselves, who are seeking answers to address issues and make appropriate and effective management decisions. A good manager consults an array of performance metrics each day in order to identify and select an appropriate tactical response to the issues of the day and to provide quality assurance.

Assessment fosters organizational learning. That is what this book is about.

Incorporating Ongoing Assessment into the Practice of American Policing

When internal performance measurement and assessment was introduced to American policing in the 1990s, the "performance management (PM) movement" was officially begun (Heinrich, 2007). Police officials began to critically reevaluate their profession and their management practices. It was naïve to assume that one particular metric or measure could accurately capture the wide range of services provided by the police. For example, would it be fair to simply tally the number of arrests made by a particular department? What exactly would that prove? Is a department with a large number of arrests a good or effective department? What about another agency where officers are so highly skilled in community relations and interpersonal communications that it is no longer necessary for them to make large numbers of arrests? Would it be fair to simply tally the total number of arrests made? Clearly, policing entails far more than simply making arrests. While not particularly complex (from a statistical and analytical standpoint), real assessment is more nuanced.

Police officers today are charged with ensuring the public's safety, which includes such varied functions as crime prevention, community outreach, respecting civil rights, ensuring the free flow of vehicular and pedestrian traffic, etc. Additionally, police departments, like other public agencies, must focus upon budgeting, planning, and the training, supervision, and professional development of personnel.

How should a police chief respond when asked, *"Did your department have a good year?"* It begs the question, what exactly would a good year or month actually look like? What characteristics would the community and the workforce have if things were going well? What measures would indicate organizational effectiveness? Which ones are truly accurate and meaningful? Which should be actively tracked?

Here is a central point; there is no one measure of organizational success. Police departments must intelligently review their operations and derive a small set of key performance measures that are of importance to the agency. Look at your department's mission or vision statement. Exactly what is it that you are telling the world you are going to accomplish? Reduce crime? Enhance traffic safety? Work in partnership with the community? Are you in fact doing this, each and every month? Can you produce any evidence to this effect?

Police managers must have the ability to regularly produce evidence of "success." This comes in many forms. Ideally, a department will cull data from its own information systems, or elsewhere (such as the results of a community safety survey conducted by the city or a local community college). With proper analysis, combined with pre-existing knowledge and experience, data speaks. The good news is that often, the data is already there, contained in the department's computer-aided dispatch (CAD) and records management (RMS) systems. There is no need to expend a great deal of time and effort assembling new data. The key is to access and use this information to report out (to public officials and stakeholders) and to guide operations.

Data overload is a concern. Peter Senge (1990) suggests that "the fundamental 'information problem' faced by managers is not too little information but too much information. What we most need are ways to know what is important is not important, what variables to focus on and which to pay less attention to – and we need ways to do this which can help groups or teams develop shared understanding" (p. 128) see also, Gleick, 2011). Even the casual student of modern policing recognizes that all police departments possess an incredible volume of information. If you begin wading through all of it, you will understand none of it. You are likely to become lost relatively quickly. So, what to do?

Answer: Police managers must narrow their attention to only that information which matters.

But how do you discern which information matters? The answer lies within the department. The typical chief and his/her command staff know their department intimately. They are the ones who know what issues matter most.

For example, a department with 35 sworn personnel located in the Northeastern United States might record 3–5 UCR robberies per year over a ten-year period. Should the number of robberies each month be a major focus for this department? Would an increase from 3 to 4 robberies per year be cause for great alarm in this department? Granted, all American police departments must actively track robberies and report them via the UCR as indeed. They are in many ways the bellwether of violent crime in any community. But perhaps the bulk of this department's work efforts each month relate to some other issues and operations.

It is highly likely that this community might include a large number of "snowbirds," residents who travel south each winter for many weeks at a time to escape the cold weather. This department likely performs "residence checks" each night, for homeowners who have requested additional attention to their homes while they are away. How many are typically performed each January and February? Where are they most frequently performed? Does the total number of checks have any relationship to reports of vandalism, theft, and burglaries in those areas of town? It is not uncommon for small departments in this country to receive no calls for service at all during the overnight shift on cold winter nights. Residents and town officials might ask, "you had two uniformed officers on patrol all night, what exactly did they do for those ten hours?" This is a very legitimate question and a chief need to formulate reasonable responses to questions such as this. It only makes sense to capture information regarding the work that is actually being performed.

Let's review. Thus far, we have established the answers to two central questions:

1) Q: *Who* should perform this assessment?

    A: The chief and his/her command staff.

2) Q: *When* should this assessment be made?

    A: In addition to period assessments which are made for the purpose of "reporting out" (to public officials or external bodies), all police departments should assess their operations on a *monthly basis* (i.e., ongoing, internal assessments).

The next question is, *what* needs to be assessed? We believe that the department itself is in the best position to decide this, but the approach should be balanced between operational measures, such as crime and traffic, as well as community measures such as citizen satisfaction and service delivery metrics. Narrowly constructing the measures can lead to an over-reliance on one at the expense of the other. Throughout this book, you will see many common practices and content areas that should be examined for most departments. These are useful to consider, but they should not be understood as an inflexible array of performance indicators that need to be tracked in every department. On the contrary, an effort must be made to determine what matters most for the particular department. This could actually vary quite a bit from month to month.

Any and all performance targets or benchmarks must be derived with the active input of key stakeholders. If external benchmarks are imposed prior to an assessment of what constitutes normal operations for the organization, the likelihood of success will be greatly diminished. Comparisons with "peer" departments and the use of external benchmarks is generally not recommended.

Newly developed performance assessment systems must run for a time before baselines are established. That is, equivalent units must be identified, and data must be acquired and analyzed over time so that "apples to apples" comparisons can be made. Once seasonal or geographic variations are identified, we can understand average performance, and reasonable and challenging targets may be set. There should be far less concern about having the department compete against other departments. The key is to have the department compete against itself, month-to-month, year-to-year.

O'Connell and Straub (2007)[1] suggest that timely and accurate data must be obtained and combined into a user-friendly data dashboard. This dashboard would consist of a small set of key performance indicators to provide an accurate and ongoing assessment of the department's most critical operations. The data dashboard would have two key functions: 1) providing essential data that can be used for "reporting out" to public officials and members of the community; and 2) providing police managers with essential information that allows them to assess the ongoing operations of the department. No longer can a department simply point to average response times or the aggregate number of arrests made. American police departments are now held accountable for developing a user-friendly system that can accurately reflect organizational performance and "effectiveness."

Initially, police departments, like other public agencies, struggled mightily with the concept of organizational *outcomes*. You see, outcomes are distinguishable from simple organizational outputs. The best way to understand this distinction is to consider a narcotics enforcement unit. If that unit is asked to demonstrate effectiveness, it is likely that supervisors would simply report out the total number of drug arrests made, as well as the total number and aggregate weight of all illegal narcotics seizures. But is it enough to simply state that "*We seized 50 pounds of cocaine last year?*" This is just an output. We need to consider *outcomes* as well. What impact have our efforts made? Are we making any difference at all? Consider the question, "*Well then, how much more illegal cocaine is out there on the streets?*" What percentage of the amount available on the street does this 50-pound seizure represent?" Most agencies would be unable to answer this.

It is one thing to demonstrate *how much* work you have done. It is another thing entirely to demonstrate *how well* you did it!

If we consider this question carefully, we will see that there are in fact other ways to measure the relative effectiveness of this unit. Useful information is also available from outside the department.

Consider the following. The emergency rooms of all public hospitals maintain records of fatal and nonfatal drug overdoses. Wouldn't that suggest whether or not illegal drug use in the community was on the rise? Similarly, all police departments perform laboratory analysis of suspected illegal narcotics that are seized. Once it is determined that a substance is indeed cocaine, wouldn't the relative purity of that substance suggest to a professional whether or not the availability of that product was rising or falling? (e.g., If a particular sample was found to have a very high concentration of pure cocaine, and if price on the street was low, it would suggest a high level of availability; alternatively, low purity would suggest that the narcotics unit was indeed having an impact on the flow of illegal drugs in that locale.)

Selecting outcome measures is difficult though, particularly for police organizations. As Burt Perrin (2006) explains, it entails an entirely new way of thinking:

> Implementing an outcome focus represents a fundamental shift in the nature of thinking, acting and managing within the public sector, away from a focus on process and on what one needs to do, to a focus on benefits.
>
> (p. 7)

Thus, a variety of performance measures can and should be used to provide an accurate picture of how well organizational outcomes are being achieved. For example, if a desired *outcome* for a department is stated as "enhancing the safety and security of local residents," that agency should collect data concerning: 1) the number of crime prevention/security surveys performed; 2) the number of arrests and criminal convictions obtained; 3) the number of weapons seized; 4) the results of citizen satisfaction surveys, etc., whereby the rate of reported crime can be examined relative to population density (Tran et al., 2004).

All managers within a police department must have easy access to key performance indicators. In this way, any significant variations or fluctuations in productivity can be detected immediately and corrective actions can be taken promptly. Trends and patterns can be readily identified and acted upon before they become major problems. You cannot wait until the end of the year to learn that your organization has failed in several key areas of its mission. Police managers now utilize timely and accurate data on a daily basis. Ongoing organizational assessment has become an essential part of the job.

The Right Data and an Opportunity to Think

All members of professional trades understand and appreciate the wisdom of the old adage, "measure twice, cut once." Carpenters and seamstresses alike are taught to pause and measure, prior to acting. In other words, take a moment to assess where you are in time and space, and consider all your options prior to moving forward in a thoughtless or undisciplined manner. This strategy is quite useful for managing any organization. Consider the example of an ice cream shop. At any given time, a thoughtful owner should know the answers to the following questions: how much inventory do we have? What is our busiest day of the week, busiest week of the year? How many employees do we schedule for next Tuesday?; What flavor is our biggest seller?; etc. If the establishment has been in business for several years, the owner will undoubtedly learn the answers to these questions through observation, trial, and error. Over time, the owner will intuitively answer these and similar questions as they arise in the ordinary course of business. This information forms the basis of a solid business plan.

Why haven't police chiefs sought answers to such questions as: What is our slowest month, in terms of calls for service? Which intersection has experienced the most traffic accidents over the past five years? or how are the probationary officers in field training performing relative to their peers in prior groups? Is the community satisfied with the services we are providing? What is the level of fear in the community? Do the officers have the right equipment and training? Shouldn't the police chief possess all (or at least most) of the necessary operational information at his/her fingertips, without having to go back and look for it? Why can't the police chief operate more like the owner of the ice cream shop?

Clearly, most competent chiefs are able to obtain answers to the above questions and have been doing so for many years. The question is not whether this information exists. The question is whether or not this information is continually available to the chief, and whether or not there is a practice of consulting this information on an ongoing basis in order to "steer the ship." There is a vast difference between merely having access to information and actually *using* it.

Some police departments possess and use performance information. Some are much better at doing so than others. The following chart reflects the various levels/stages of sophistication that departments exhibit regarding the practice of acquiring, analyzing, and using performance information:

Stage I: The organization has the ability to know where work is occurring but cannot measure the relative effectiveness of its efforts (i.e., outcomes). Organization is primarily concerned with service delivery in the form of timely response to calls for service (a reactive orientation towards its work). The organization may or may not possess all necessary management information. Organizations primarily use performance data to report on actions and decisions that have already been made. It does not regularly attempt to obtain and proactively use timely and accurate information to support management decisions in any comprehensive way.

Stage II: The organization has a knowledge inventory and essentially "knows what it knows." It attempts to obtain and use performance data for decision support (both strategic and tactical decisions) in some circumstances. Organization has small pockets of analytics, but information silos and an overall lack of coordination and systems thinking prevents these data centers from effectively communicating and coordinating with one another. The organization may or may not have one designated or de facto person serving as chief information officer (CIO).

Stage III: The organization moves beyond mere knowledge inventory, routinely using information via sense and respond mechanisms to inform most management decisions (via "gap analysis" and cost–benefit analyses) and it engages in systems thinking. The organization is adept at double loop learning and can effectively pivot, as necessary. The organization has a designated or functioning CIO, clearly articulated performance goals with supporting data, and uses a live feed of performance metrics to obtain an accurate view of both the internal and the external work environments.

Today, it is likely that most American police departments would be properly categorized as being Stage II. Hopefully, there are not many Stage I departments remaining, as this low level of information management/use sophistication represents a very real liability risk to the municipality, the department, and its employees.

Every American police department performs crime analysis in one form or another (some at a rudimentary level, others in a sophisticated fashion). There are also budgetary reviews, assessments of personnel, traffic analysis, etc. that take place in all departments. But, many times, these are done separately, in an *ad hoc* fashion. These reviews are typically performed only after a problem has been detected. In many instances, this amounts to "too little, too late."

All police organizations must develop their sense and respond capabilities. They need to be agile and develop the ability to quickly identify patterns and emerging problems, then formulate effective interventions. In other words, as opposed to merely accumulating information, they need to *use* data to learn from their experiences. This knowledge improves effectiveness.

There is an ancient Taoist saying attributed to Lao Tzu that, *"The wise man knows what he does not know."* Similarly, "the historian Arthur Schlesinger once wrote, "ignorance of the present, ignorance of the future, these are pardonable. But ignorance of how ignorant we are is unpardonable." It is impossible to adequately lead a police department without continually asking questions. "Great leaders combine self-confidence with reasonable doubt, a skepticism that starts the questioning. Organizations that have acquired the learning habit are endlessly questioning the status quo, are forever seeking new methods or new products, forever testing, and then reflecting, consciously or unconsciously pushing [forward]" (Handy, 1995, p. 49). There is great wisdom here. No one person has all the answers, all the time. Not even police chiefs. They need to rely heavily upon subordinates to provide accurate information, new perspectives and their best personal judgments and opinions.

Assessment is not a solitary endeavor. It is a team effort.

Thus, in every American police department:

- field training officers assess the progress of probationary officers;
- training officers consider which in-service topics should be delivered to patrol officers during the upcoming training cycle;
- the Special Operations Lieutenant meets with the crime analyst to assess the relative effectiveness of the directed patrols that have recently been implemented on the south end of town;
- the department's (or the City's or Town's) civilian IT specialist considers whether a software upgrade is needed for one of the department's various information systems;
- the dispatch supervisor examines why the average response time for priority 2 calls for service has risen 30% since April;
- the community affairs officer reviews end of course surveys completed by graduates of the most recent citizens' police academy class; and
- all supervisors at or above the rank of sergeant meet on a monthly basis to review and assess the performance of all major units, as well as the operations of the department as a whole.

Effective policing is really all about ongoing assessment; *learning* what is working and what is not. Good departments learn well. Poor departments often suffer from learning disabilities. Good organizational learning requires timely and accurate data and open discussions. No important decisions should be based merely upon anecdotes or past practices.

All managers need the confidence and humility to pause before any major decision point and ask themselves, "What are we missing here? Is there anything that we have failed to consider before moving forward?" Granted, this skill is typically lacking in many managers in any industry. Also, there is an adrenaline bias in most organizations. This occurs when leaders are "seemingly hooked on the daily rush of activity and firefighting within their organizations. It is as though they are afraid to slow down and deal with issues that are critical but don't seem particularly urgent" (Lencioni, 2012, p. 3). Perhaps the hierarchical paramilitary structure of police departments make it harder for ranking officers to pause and consider available options, as this might show weakness or vulnerability to peers and subordinates. Even in the corporate world, "leaders who pride themselves on expertise and intelligence often struggle to acknowledge their flaws and learn from peers. They aren't as easily open and transparent with one another, which delays recovery from mistakes and exacerbates politics and confusion" (Lencioni, 2012, p. 9). Nevertheless, this is a critically important step in managing an organization as dynamic as a police department. The chief will ultimately remain the chief after these open discussions are concluded. The final decision always rests with him/her. But in the meantime, the wise leader seeks and considers the counsel of individuals who actually perform the work and have a "street-level view" of exactly what is occurring and why. Subordinates are more likely to follow through if they believe they contributed to the solution.

When this approach is taken, subordinates will recognize the authority of competence and good performance, as opposed to the mere authority of rank.

Police Organizational Learning Challenges

Open communications and thoughtful reflection can be hampered, however, by groupthink. This psycho/sociological phenomenon exists in all human organizations, including police departments. In fact, it is quite possible that the rank structure of American police departments actually enhances its effect. It is believed that the quasi-military command model of American policing "highlights the extraordinary emphasis placed upon a 'conformance to authority' syndrome and the encouragement of a 'keep your mouth shut and listen ethos'" (Jermier and Berkes, 1979, p. 2).

The concept of "groupthink" was first proposed by Janis (1972) as "an explanation for poor decision-making processes and outcomes in groups" (Chapman, 2006, p. 1391). It occurs when members of a group prematurely seek concurrence, "before a problem or proposed solution has been sufficiently analyzed or evaluated" (p. 1393). That is, they engage in behaviors that deter imaginative thinking and open discussion and increase the likelihood of poor decision-making. These behaviors include: "incomplete survey of alternatives; incomplete survey of objectives; failure to examine risks of the preferred choice; failure to reappraise initially rejected alternatives; poor information search; selective bias in processing the information at hand; and failure to work out contingency plans" (p. 1393). As a result, the group can assume an overly optimistic or pessimistic view of current organizational challenges and opportunities, thereby leading to poor decisions.

It is natural for members of a decision-making group to seek unanimity and endeavor to gain commitment to group decisions. It is also common for individuals within the group to seek the protection afforded by diffused responsibility for poor decisions (Chapman, 2006). Unfortunately, these tendencies are rarely recognized during the course of decision-making.

The group can rapidly become insulated and isolated from the experiences, views, and opinions of their colleagues outside the group. In turn, the relative distance between the group and the rank-and-file members of the organization (who actually perform the day-to-day work of the organization and have a clear view of current conditions) widens considerably, hampering any ability to obtain an accurate picture of the organizational landscape and current environmental conditions.

Many managers hesitate to take risks, or to deviate from conventional wisdom. Police managers have historically been quite guilty of this. Groupthink must therefore be addressed and eliminated in modern police departments as it is fatal to organizational learning.

Another persistent threat to quality decision making is the tendency for human organizations to engage in *satisficing*. Simon defines satisficing as a decision-making process through which an individual seeks and chooses an approach or solution that is merely sufficient, rather than one that is perfect (Simon, 1973). Individuals compare the benefits of obtaining additional information against the additional cost and effort of continuing to search. In fact, in many organizations, "problems are considered resolved when a good enough solution has been found, that is the manager satisfies as she looks for a course of action that is satisfactory" (Choo, 1998, p. 49).

The consequences of putting time and effort into finding optimal solutions can be costly; therefore, "decision makers must be willing to forgo the best solution in favor of one that is acceptable" (Stroh et al., 2002, p. 94). In so doing, information seekers "... satisfice... and choose the one [solution] that produces an outcome that is 'good enough'" (Stroh et al., 2002, p. 94). The very abundance of information makes it crucial for information seekers to decide what information is enough to meet their objectives. Users may unfortunately stop looking for information prematurely if the information systems are blocked, unusable, or simply unavailable.

Perhaps the most common pathology affecting decision quality is the personal and collective risk aversion that exists in most bureaucracies. Well-developed organizational cultures tend to develop a cohort of risk-averse high-ranking decision makers (i.e., careerists) who have a continuing desire to compel people outside the organization "to think that the organization is under control" (Holgersson et al., 2008, p. 85). In addition to risk, top administrators typically fear the appearance of incompetence and embarrassment. In other words, perception is everything. In order to preserve the status quo, or to make it appear so, managers will unconsciously develop a world view that diminishes actual threats to the organization. This is a protective public relations stance rather than a candid assessment of current status and it severely hampers open communications within the organization. Few middle managers wish to tell their supervisors that the emperor is actually wearing no clothes.

Simply put, when groupthink occurs, individuals are unlikely to give voice to their true thoughts and concerns. Rather, through the desire for harmony or conformity within the group, individuals will simply serve as "yes men/women" and echo the opinions of their superiors. Why rock the boat, when I can simply go along with the crowd and support the boss's position?

Rooney and McKenna (2008) note that, "the [true] organizational challenge is to be able to get outside a limiting discourse and accepted practice, particularly when doing so assists in achieving excellent new practice" (p. 714). They raise a hopeful note by their suggestion that "there still must be a role for frank and fearless advisors who reach beyond the narrow vocabularies of managerialism so detrimental to wisdom" (p. 714).

Possible Solutions

Persistent issues and attitudes that retard organizational learning can be altered if addressed properly. Indeed, the problem of groupthink has been referred to as only "a temporary derangement" (Chapman, 2006, p. 1397). Chapman recommends that organizations protect themselves from this pathology by "instituting impartial leadership and more systematic ways of evaluating choice alternatives" (p. 1398).

In public service organizations, the implementation of "impartial leadership" might unfortunately prove to be difficult. The civil service rank system poses a true challenge, due to the fact that decision-making authority will always be directly linked to one's relative position within the hierarchy of these organizations. However, dramatic operational changes can be and, in fact, have been made in these organizations. Perhaps the most dramatic example of such a change is the COMPSTAT model of police management. We will address this model in depth in the following chapters.

Evidence-based decision-making is still relatively rare in public service as "It is costly in both time and resources for governments to seek information pertaining to a particular program or practice, and policy makers rarely have the opportunity to await 'systemic evidentiary support' before acting. Governments are faced with short decision contexts and settings of incomplete information" (Hall and Jennings, 2008, p. 696). Sherman (1998) offers evidence-based practice, however, as an entirely new paradigm for policing. He identifies it as a particularly effective means of providing "systematic feedback to provide continuous quality improvement" (p. 6).

Evidence-based practice, which utilizes honest and open discussion, is the antithesis of groupthink. By pausing to acquire evidence upon which to base the decision, the organization will necessarily slow down and provide the "think time" that is required to make optimal decisions (Forrester, 2011).

A wise manager understands that every workday is an opportunity to learn and that there are myriad sources of available information. The average American police department currently possesses a great deal of tacit knowledge, stored within the experiences of seasoned professionals. This institutional knowledge must be accessed and leveraged. Patrick Lencioni (2012) explains, "The healthier an organization that is, the more of its intelligence it is able to tap into and use. Most organizations exploit only a fraction of the knowledge, experience, and intellectual capital that is available to them. But the healthy ones tap into almost all of it" (p. 11). Police departments need to get better at accessing this abundant source of information. Additionally, modern police departments need to avail themselves of multiple data streams that convey real-time assessments of the internal and external work environments.

In other words, police organizations need to learn how to learn. Unfortunately, many departments have suffered from significant learning disabilities for many years.

Proactively Managing the Organizational Learning Process

The concept of the *learning organization* was first developed by Chris Argyris in the 1970s (Argyris and Schon, 1974) and was further refined by Senge during the 1990s. The term generally refers to "an organization that is continually expanding its capacity to create its future" (Geller, 1997, p. 3).

> All organizations learn, but not always for the better. A learning organization is an organization that has an enhanced capacity to learn, adapt, and change. It's an organization in which learning processes are analyzed, monitored, developed, managed, and aligned with improvement and innovation goals. It's the vision, strategy, leaders, values, structures, systems, processes, and practices all work to foster people's learning and development and to accelerate systems level learning ... In any organization, learning occurs at multiple levels: individual, group, and organizational. Although individuals and teams or groups are the agents through which organizational learning occurs, learning organizations focus primarily on systems – level organizational learning.
>
> (Gephart and Marsick, 1996, pp. 36–37)

Learning organizations develop a culture of learning. They continually monitor and assess their ability to *learn how to learn*.

In the field of policing, this mindset is often the exception rather than the rule; most bureaucratic organizations favor the familiar and the status quo. Individuals working within these bureaucracies "have a limited capacity to accept change because it disorients them" (Boyne et al., 2004, p. 464). Bureaucracies are generally not known for embracing the concepts of inquiry and experimentation, which serve as the foundation of the learning organization:

> Most organizations exhibit a deterioration in vital signs that is inconsistent with – in fact, often destructive to their ambitions and purposes. As organizations grow older and larger, people often develop a sense of resignation in response to seemingly insurmountable obstacles or to lack of support from their superiors in the daily hassle of getting things done. As organizations become more complicated and demanding, people strive to carve out private patches of turf where they can exercise responsibility, protect themselves, and keep the world at bay. When it comes to their identity, therefore, employees lose their sense of teamwork and alignment with the entire enterprise and begin to seek the safety of their particular profession, union, function, team, or location. People in mature organizations tend to avoid conflict for fear of blame or of having someone take their disagreement personally. Alternatively, they may take part in a succession of routine collisions that lead to stalemate rather than resolution. As for learning, larger, and older organizations tend to be less receptive to new ideas than their younger counterparts. In place of inquiry and experimentation, ideas get studied to death in hopes of ferreting out possible weakness before making a commitment. The precondition for action is certain knowledge.
>
> (Pascale et al., 1997, p. 130)

Argyris and his colleagues identified two distinct types of organizational learning, "single-loop" and "double-loop" learning, which they distinguish as follows:

> Single-loop learning involves improving the organization's capacity to achieve known objectives. It is associated with routine and behavioral learning. Under a single-loop, the organization is learning without significant change in its basic assumptions. Double-loop learning re-evaluates the nature of the organization's objectives and values and beliefs surrounding them. This type of learning involves changing the organization's culture. Importantly, double-loop consists of the organization's learning how to learn.
>
> (Luthans, 2005, p. 112)

The key for any organization is to move toward a system of double-loop learning. Single-loop learning simply "produces behavioral changes that are adaptive in a particular instance, but do not produce significant value changes" (Van Wart, 1998, p. 577); on the other hand, double-loop learning "produces values change from which behavioral changes flow" (p. 577). Here, "decisions are based on the rethinking of existing competencies/methods, which have proved inadequate ... Existing knowledge is challenged in this type of learning is closely related to continuous improvements in TQM [total quality management] and business excellence" (Eskildsen et al., 1999, p. 524). Double-loop learning is different because it entails thoughtful consideration of underlying assumptions, understandings, and practices. It is a far more critical and reflective approach to organizational problem-solving. It goes beyond merely adapting to changing conditions, it examines underlying conditions that might be unnecessarily restricting organizational progress.

Argyris (1993) argued that single-loop learning is associated with sophisticated defensive routines that produce "skilled incompetence." That is, it develops "the behavior patterns that over protect us from threat or embarrassment as well as significant learning" (cited in Van Wart, 1998, p. 578). He argued that double-loop learning is more difficult, but it can be taught to individuals and to groups (i.e., to police organizations), and "can replace more limited and more defensive single-loop learning in entire organizations" (p. 577).

Senge further developed these concepts by distinguishing between adaptive and generating learning (Luthans, 2005, p. 112). Adaptive learning consists of merely adapting to environmental changes as they occur. Generative learning involves "creativity and innovation, going beyond just adapting to change to being ahead of and anticipating change" (p. 112). It is associated with a spirit of continual feedback, experimentation, and reassessment of core beliefs and assumptions. Under this view, failure is viewed as an opportunity for feedback, and not merely as a setback. Organizations that are adept at this skill continuously learn from their experiences and widely disseminate this learning. In other words, it becomes part of the organization's normal functioning (MacDonald, 1995; Snyder and Cummings, 1998).

Information must be treated as intellectual capital that can be acquired, channeled, and leveraged to continuously improve the efficiency and effectiveness of the organization's processes (Hayward, 2004). If it is managed appropriately, this "evidence" can be readily accessed and will contribute to the generation of organizational knowledge and wisdom as well as the "continuous process of reformulating and refining theory" (Chaiklin, 2004, p. 96). What is absolutely necessary is a system designed to maintain strategic focus, ensure data quality, provide continual monitoring, and the dissemination of necessary information.

Police agencies must therefore seek to become both "learning" and "knowing" organizations.

A knowing organization is well prepared to sustain its growth and development in a dynamic environment. By sensing and understanding its environment, the knowing organization is able to prepare for adaptation early. By marshaling the skills and expertise of its members, the knowing organization is able to engage in continuous learning and innovation. By applying learned decision rules and routines, the knowing organization is primed to take timely, purposive action. At the heart of the knowing organization is its management of the information processes that underpin sense making, knowledge building, and decision-making.

(Choo, 1998, p. xi)

Strategic management (which will be discussed at length in Chapter 12) is built upon the concept of organizational learning. However, in many respects, the learning organization is simply an ideal. It implies a system whereby employees are provided with all necessary information, without even asking (Lee, 2000). It suggests an organizational culture that:

- supports and rewards learning and innovation
- promotes inquiry, dialogue, risk-taking, and experimentation
- allows mistakes to be shared and viewed as opportunities for learning, and
- values the well-being of all employees (Gephart and Marsick, 1996, p. 39; see also Luthans, 2005).

As Handy (1995) notes:

The learning organization is built upon an assumption of competence. [This] means that each individual can be expected to perform to the limit of his or her competence, with the minimum of supervision. This idea is at the core of the concept of the professional. For too long organizations have operated on an assumption of incompetence. Characteristics of this assumption are controls and direct tubes, rules and procedures, layers of management and pyramids of power – all very costly. By contrast, the assumption of competence promotes flat organizations, with fewer checkers checking checkers. Flat organizations are far more responsive, efficient, and cost-effective.

(p. 46)

In this type of organizational culture, "imposed authority no longer works. Instead, authority must be learned from those over whom it is exercised. This organization is held together by shared beliefs and values, by people who are committed to each other and to common goals" (p. 48).

Martha Gephart and Victoria Marsick (1996) suggested that learning organizations are "people-centered," providing "a caring community that nurtures, values and supports the well-being, development and learning of every individual" (p. 38). Police administrators will likely struggle with this concept, particularly since paramilitary organizations are not run as democracies and are not designed primarily for valuing the well-being of all employees. They have "ranks, levels of command in uniforms" and are designed primarily for the rapid execution of orders from above (Bennett and Hess, 2001, p. 3). Rarely, if ever, willfully supervisors solicit attitudes or opinions from their subordinates regarding their professional development or the overall quality of their work life. If this is done at all, it happens within the context of annual performance reviews. It does not occur frequently. Charles McClintock (2004) suggested that the goal of becoming a learning organization is a difficult one to achieve: "the notion of the continuously changing and learning organization is often a fiction that is not feasible, given the limits of human dynamics, resources, or political restraints" (p. 598).

Nevertheless, becoming a "learning organization" is not an either/or opposition. Organizations can take a variety of affirmative steps to help move in the direction of becoming one (Senge, 1990). In this sense, we are dealing with a continuum; all organizations can measure their relative ability to perform generative learning. Gephart and Marsick (1996) described five distinct phases that organizations pass through on their way to becoming a learning organization:

1) the *forming* organization
2) the *developing* organization
3) the *maturing* organization
4) the *adapting* organization, and
5) the *learning* organization. (p. 44)

Using this hierarchy, it is likely that most U.S. police agencies are currently either *maturing* or *adapting* organizations. This is certainly acceptable, as long as the agency is moving forward towards the goal of becoming a true learning organization (see also, Yang et al., 2004). If a department is not regularly assessing its most essential functions, in an open and honest manner, no real learning will occur. Once again, it is not enough to simply measure and *assess* operations. This performance information must be actively *used* and the organization needs to *learn* how to make necessary adjustments and become more efficient and effective in the future.

All police organizations can make substantial progress and achieve success by increasing the overall amount of individual, team, and strategic learning that takes place within the organization. The key here is to create an atmosphere where the more adaptive and flexible double-loop learning can take place. As Richard Pascale and Jerry Sternin (2005) state, the goal is to "make it safe to learn" (p. 74). An essential part of the learning process is to determine what works and what doesn't. Handy (1995) suggests that "because experiments can fail, forgiveness is essential. Instead of failures, unsuccessful experiments must be viewed as part of the learning process, as lessons learned. One can also learn from successful experiments. That form of learning needs are not forgotten but to be celebrated" (p. 47).

Whether management recognizes it or not, learning is continually taking place within their organizations. The problem occurs when management is not cognizant of this process, when learning is haphazard and when lessons are not used as the basis for intelligent management decisions. Police managers must be tuned into knowledge gaps (essentially being aware of what they are unaware of) and must utilize their internal systems of assessment, communication and training to help foster an atmosphere where true organizational learning can occur.

To summarize, ongoing assessment and organizational learning are synonymous. All modern police departments need to master this skill in order to succeed. The following chapters in this text will explore specific content areas and operations of modern police agencies and will suggest the most effective means of assessing performance and utilizing the resulting information to achieve continuous improvement.

Note

1 The author wishes to gratefully acknowledge the collaboration and assistance of Frank Straub Ph.D. in developing many of the concepts contained in these chapters that previously appeared in O'Connell and Straub (2007) and in a previously unpublished white paper entitled *Reflection, Collective Wisdom and the Need for Robust Discourse in Public Service Decision-Making* (2017).

References

Argyris, C. (1993). *Knowledge for action: A Guide to Overcoming Barriers to Organizational Change*. Josey-Bass.

Argyris, C., & Schon, D. A. (1974). *Theory in Practice: Increasing Professional Effectiveness*. Jossey-Bass.

Bennett, W. W., & Hess, K. (2001). *Management and Supervision in Law Enforcement*. Wadsworth.

Boyne, G. A., Gould-Williams, J. S., Law. J., & Walker, R. M. Walker. (2004). Toward the self-evaluating organization?: An empirical test of the Wildavsky model. *Public Administration Review*, 64(4), 463–473.

Chaiklin, H. (2004). Problem Formation, Conceptualization, and Theory Development. In Roberts, A. R. and Yeager, K. R. (eds.). *Evidence-Based Practice Manual: Research and Outcome Measures in Health and Human Services*. 95–101. Oxford University Press.

Chapman, J. (2006). Anxiety and defective decision making and elaboration of the groupthink model. *Management Decision*, 44(10), 1391–1404.

Choo, C. W. (1998). *The Knowing Organization*. Oxford University Press.

Davies, A.& Thomas, R. (2003). Talking cop: Discourses of change and policing identities. *Public Administration*, 81(4), 681–699.

Eskildsen, J. K., Dahlgaard, J. J., & Norgaard, A. (1999). The impact of creativity and learning on business excellence. *Total Quality Management*, 10(4), 523–531.

Forrester, D. P. (2011). *Consider: Harnessing the Power of Reflective Thinking in your Organization*. Palgrave MacMillan.

Geller, W. A. (1997). Suppose we were really serious about police departments becoming "learning organizations"? *National Institute of Justice Journal*, 234, 2–8.

Gephart, M. A., & Marsick, V. J. (1996). Learning organizations come alive. *Training and Development*, 50(12), 34–45.

Gleick, J. (2011). *The Information: A History, A Theory a Flood*. Pantheon Random House.

Hall, J. L., & Jennings, E. T. (July 2008). Taking chances: Evaluating risk as a guide to better use of best practices. *Public Administration Review*, 68(4), 695–708.

Handy, C. (1995). Managing the Dream. In Chawla, S. and Rensch, J. (eds.). *Learning Organizations: Developing Cultures for Tomorrow's Workplace*. Productivity Press.

Hayward, R. (2004). Informing health choices: Reflections on knowledge integration strategies for electronic health records. In A. R. Roberts & K. R. Yeager (Eds.), *Evidence-based practice manual: Research and outcome measures in health and human services* (pp. 29-46). New York: Oxford University Press.

Heinrich, C. J. (2007). Evidence-based policy and performance management: Challenges and prospects in two parallel movements. *The American Review of Public Administration*, 37(3), 255–277.

Holgersson, S., Gottschalk, P., & Dean, G. (2008). Knowledge management in law enforcement: Knowledge views for patrolling police officers. *International Journal of Police Science and Management*, 10(1), 76–88.

Janis, I. L. (1972). *Victims of Groupthink: A psychological study of foreign-policy decisions and fiascoes*. Houghton Mifflin Company.

Jermier, J., & Berkes, L. (1979). Leader behavior in a police command bureaucracy: A closer look at the quasi-military model. *Administrative and Science Quarterly*, 24(1), 1–23.

Lee, J. (2000). Knowledge management: The intellectual revolution. *IIE Solutions*, 30(10), 34–37.

Lencioni, P. (2012). *The Advantage: Why Organizational Health Trumps Everything Else in Business*. Josey-Bass.

Luthans, F. (2005). *Organizational Behavior*. McGraw Hill-Irwin.

MacDonald, S. (1995). Learning to change: An information perspective on learning in the organization. *Organization Science*, 6(5), 557–568.

McClintock, C. (2004). Integrating Program Evaluation and Organization Development. In *Evidence-Based Practice Manual: Research and Outcome measures in Health and Human Services*. 598–606. Oxford University Press.

O'Connell, P. E., & Straub, F. (2007). *Performance-Based Management for Police Organizations*. Waveland Press.

Pascale, R., Millemann, M., & Gioja, L. (November/December 1997). Changing the way we change. *Harvard Business Review*, 75(6), 127–139.

Pascale, R. T., & Sternin, J. (2005). Your company's secret change agents. *Harvard Business Review*, 83(5), 72–81.

Perrin, B. (2006). *Moving from Outputs to Outcomes: Practical Advice from Governments Around the World*. IBM Center for the Business of Government. Retrieved from www.businessofgovernment.org/sites/default/files/PerrinReport.pdf

Perrow, C. (1972). *Complex Organizations*. Scott, Foresman & Company.

Rooney, D., & McKenna, B. (2008). Wisdom in public administration: Looking for a sociology of wise practice. *Public Administration Review*, 68, 709–721.

Senge, P. (1990). *The Fifth Discipline: The Art and Practice of the Learning organization*. Doubleday.

Sherman, L. W. (1998). Evidence-based policing. *Police Foundation, Ideas in American Policing*, July, 1–15.

Silverman, E. (1999). *NYPD Battles Crime: Innovative Strategies in Policing*. Northeastern University Press.

Simon, H. A. (1973). Organization man: Rational or self-actualizing? *Public Administration Review*, 33(4), 346–353.

Snyder, W. M., & Cummings, T. G. (1998). Organization learning disorders: Conceptual model and intervention hypotheses. *Human Relations*, 51(7), 873–896.

Stroh, L. K., Northcraft, G. B., & Neale, M. A. (2002). *Lawrence Organizational Behavior: A Management Challenge*. Erlbaum Publishers.

Tran, A., Gardon, J., & Polidori, L. (2004). Application of Remote Sensing for Disease Surveillance in Urban and Suburban Areas. In Roberts, A. R. and Yeager, K. R. (eds.). *Evidence-Based Practice Manual: Research and Outcome Measures in Health and Human Services.* 368–378. Oxford University Press.

Van Wart, M. (1998). *Changing Public Sector Values.* Garland.

Yang, B., Watkins, K. E., & Marsick, V. J. (2004). The construct of the learning organization: Dimensions, measurement, and variables. *Human Resource Development Quarterly*, 15(1), 31–55.

Chapter 2

Patrol Allocation and Deployment

Introduction

Understanding patrol operations in any police department is undoubtedly the most important process police managers undertake. It is arguably the least understood, and most neglected part of police management. Traditionally referred to as the "backbone" of a police department, the reality is far different. This irony is not lost on the hundreds of thousands of uniform patrol officers in the United States that believe their department pays lip service to this message. Those officers often believe patrol is under-resourced and there are never enough officers on patrol to deal with unrelenting demand. Ask any officer on patrol and they will likely tell you they are the last ones considered in important decisions. Patrol resources are routinely sacrificed to support other areas of operation in the department.

And yet, patrol officers are the most visible representatives of the department. They are synonymous with the public image of the police in any community. Officers on patrol are expected to act as guardians, warriors, legal and medical experts, marriage counselors, and social workers. They are available 24 hours a day, 7 days a week, and can be summoned at a moment's notice from any location. Ask any police chief how many officers she needs on patrol, and the answer will likely be "more." Ask a member of the community what kinds of services they expect from the police on patrol in their community and the answers will be as numerous as the people you ask.

The need to assess patrol operations is critical. The next two chapters explore this issue from two different perspectives. Chapter 4 looks to provide an approach to the assessment of the allocation and deployment of patrol resources. Allocation refers to the process of determining how many officers are needed on patrol to meet the needs of the community. Deployment refers to the process of distributing these officers across time and space to maximize their effectiveness (achieving the goals of the department and community), and efficiency (proper use of resources).

Patrol Allocation

Town Managers/Administrators, and Police Chiefs around the country wrestle with three very serious questions: How many officers does my police department really need? How many should be assigned to patrol (allocation)? And lastly, once the proper allocation for patrol is determined, then how should they be scheduled and assigned to work (deployment)?

The number of officers assigned to a police department, and the allocation and deployment of these officers on patrol, are arguably the most critical decisions a police department and a community can make. For many communities, the police department represents the

DOI: 10.4324/9781003396437-2

largest budgetary expense. Communities faced with difficult budgetary decisions often look at public safety agencies for potential cutbacks. To be sure, no one wants to cut public safety resources and risk harm to the community. On the other hand, some communities are growing at a rapid pace and are finding it difficult to provide sufficient services to the growing populace. In addition, in the middle, there are numerous communities looking to make the "right" decisions in the interest of "good government." Collectively, the decisions to be made are critical ones, and providing the right level of police staffing, in the right amounts, at the right times and days, leads to the right delivery of services and effective policing.

With these issues in mind, decision-makers need to ask the more difficult question: Is there an objective standard for making this determination? And are there metrics to making staffing decisions that are more than speculation? The answer is a resounding "YES!"

Most police departments generally make uninformed decisions regarding patrol allocation. These decisions are based usually on past practices, budgets, collective bargaining agreements, or just haphazardly. Informed patrol allocation relies on empirical data and a firm understanding of workload demands and striking the right balance between patrol operations and the rest of the department. This chapter provides some empirical support and guidance to make this most important decision.

Determining the number of police officers needed for any given community is often an exercise in great speculation. After education, one of the greatest expenses on any local government's budget is public safety (Huddleston, 2005). And yet, the impact of having too few or too many police officers allocated to a police department is often neither recognized nor fully understood. When the police are absent, as in a strike, the consequences are known and the complete absence of the police has a direct impact on crime (Ayres, 1977; Bopp et al., 1977; Giacopassi and Sparger, 1981). However, under normal conditions, the size of police departments varies by jurisdiction, and personnel deployment does not appear to be related to factors such as population, crime, geography, etc. (Edwards, 2011). Some studies, however, suggest that staffing could very well be related to certain community characteristics (Maloney and Moty, 2002; Hollis and Wilson, 2015).

In 2011, the U.S. Department of Justice, Office of Community Oriented Policing Services (COPS Office) issued a report detailing the impact that the downturn of the economy had on local law enforcement. Local communities, still reeling in the aftershock of the "Great Recession," experienced budget shortfalls in the face of declining tax revenue. Many communities were hard-hit financially and were forced to make tough decisions regarding the size of their workforce and the quality and nature of their work (Wilson, 2012). They looked to leverage technology, consolidate services with other agencies, civilianize, enlist volunteers, cut services, or simply eliminated positions (U.S. Department of Justice, COPS, 2011)

The overall number of law enforcement employees decreased 12.2 percent from a high of 1,024,228 in 2008 to 899,212 in 2014, or a reduction of just over 125,000 positions. In percentage terms, civilian workers were the hardest hit group of employees. Civilian police employee positions fell 14.7 percent from a high of 318,104 in 2007 to a low of 271,263 in 2014. In absolute terms, the U.S. experienced the loss of more than 80,000 sworn police positions (11.3 percent) in the six years after the "Great Recession." However, in conjunction with this decrease in personnel, crime rates also fell. Violent crime rate in the communities covered by this survey fell 23.6 percent from a high of 479 per 100,000 population in 2006 to a low of 366 per 100,000 in 2014. Property crime experienced a similar reduction, declining 24.4 percent between 2005 and 2014 (U.S. Department of Justice, 2014).

These data suggest that the downsizing of American police departments in the aftermath of the "Great Recession" did not necessarily translate into an increase in violent and property crime rates. The data also suggest that staffing with fewer police officers is not related to more crime; in fact, just the opposite occurred. However, making the decision on how many police officers are necessary to meet the public safety needs of a community is still an unsettled issue. While the police do more than just respond to crime, the experience of the last decade has opened a discussion on how many officers a community needs and what those officers should be doing during their shifts. Police managers are now routinely asked to justify requests for additional staffing, as well as current staffing levels. However, this calls for facts, not opinion. As Brotheim (2003) noted, "as requests for staffing projections increase in this age of tighter municipal budgets, law enforcement agencies are faced with an ever-growing demand to accurately and consistently foresee staffing needs and to present a methodology for the projections and requests" (p. 9). Throughout most of the United States, a weakened economy resulted "in a lower municipal tax base which, in turn forced police agencies to justify their workforce size in an effort to reduce costs and substantive expenditures to the local constituents" (Srinivasan et al., 2013, p. 702).

Several other recent industry-wide challenges such as increased retirements and turnover, generational preferences and expectations, competition among employers and military call-ups have significantly affected both the pool of qualified police applicants and the number of active-duty officers available for assignment (Wilson and Heinonen, 2011; Wilson, 2012). It is agreed that these factors have profoundly affected a department's ability to maintain appropriate staffing levels.

Police managers cannot afford to rely solely on anecdotal evidence, intuition, or historical precedent when staffing their departments (Wilson and Weiss, 2014). They require new skills and more quantitative methods of allocating personnel to address actual workload.

Historic Staffing Models

In the early years of policing, the "father of modern law enforcement," August Vollmer, recognized the need to more efficiently allocate personnel to patrol. Vollmer suggested that the police should be assigned to specific territorial areas, known as beats, for continuous periods throughout the day. Also, it was recognized that police resource allocation needed to change in response to changing political, social, and demographic conditions in the community (Fritsch et al., 2009). This early work generated a patrol allocation system that was distributed by beats, with equal numbers of officers assigned to these beats on three shifts regardless of demand. Known as "allocation by geography," police departments sought to examine the physical characteristics of the community to design appropriate beats for officer assignment.

In the 1940s, O.W. Wilson first implemented a "hazard formula" to efficiently allocate personnel. The LAPD weighted several types of crimes and calculated a score for each patrol area. This was an improvement on the static geographic approach as it sought to incorporate criminal events in determining the impact on police demand in a specific area. Similarly, the early "queuing models" sought to include the impact of calls for service on the demand for police resources in specific beat areas. The queuing model relied on the data from past calls for service from the public and predict the future demand and accounted for seasonal variations and changing community characteristics. Police resources were then determined based upon the length of time a call could be delayed (queued), and therefore, resources assigned to ensure a minimum acceptable queuing delay (Fritsch et al., 2009).

These models were again improvements over the original beat allocation approach, but still had limitations. Based upon these early approaches, police allocation evolved into more elaborate and sophisticated methods relying on quantitative analysis of workload demands. The Patrol Car Allocation Model (PCAM) of the 1970s included measures of workload demand, uncommitted time, response time, and queuing time to determine the number of patrol cars needed for a police department. In the 1990s, Northwestern University's Traffic Institute developed the Patrol Allocation Model (PAM). The PAM was designed to determine the number of patrol officers needed based upon established performance object-ives, such as workload, response time, etc. Several years later, building off the PAM, the Allocation Model for Police Patrol (AMPP) was designed, computerizing workload and staffing calculations used in the PAM (Northwestern University, 1993).

Each of these early models in their own way contributed to the development of the sci-ence behind police patrol allocation. Although they have limitations in their approach the value comes from the use of data to determine resource allocation. Most modern police departments employ some form of computer-assisted dispatch (CAD) system to manage workload demands from the public. These CAD systems are rich sources of data that can be used, like in all the models mentioned above, to understand workload and therefore predict the amount of patrol resources needed to meet that demand. Police departments, however, seldomly leverage these data available to them, and as the next section illustrates, rely on many other methods to determine patrol staffing needs.

Prevailing Staffing Models

Wilson and Weiss (2014) provide a comprehensive overview of the various staffing models employed by local police departments in the United States. Five common methods have been traditionally used to determine police staffing models in the United States: 1) Crime trends; 2) a per-capita approach; 3) minimum-staffing levels; 4) authorized/budgeted levels; and (least commonly); 5) workload-based models.

As the police professionalized during the early twentieth century, the primary goal of police operations became crime reduction (Kelling and Moore, 1988). Crime levels and trends became the primary driver for police staffing. As crime levels rose, more police offic-ers were hired to address it. This approach seems appropriate. It is a particularly inefficient approach to staffing.

Crime Trends. Consider the following: When the police are ineffective at combating crime more police are added. When the police are effective at combating crime, fewer officers are needed. This model provides incentives for poor performance and disincentives for superior performance. Additionally, we know that crime rates are influenced by many factors other than merely the level of police response. In fact, many criminologists dis-count the role of the police entirely when it comes to crime rates in a particular com-munity (Greene and Taylor, 1991; Felson, 1993). Therefore, using crime rates to staff a police department should not be the recommended approach. Fortunately, this model of staffing is rarely used.

Pre-Determined Minimums. Another extremely popular approach to staffing is based upon predetermined minimum-manning levels for patrol. Generally determined by past prac-tice, policy, supervisory judgment, or a combination of the three, personnel staffing is set at a certain level. Typically, this approach is also used to determine the number of officers required to work each shift. Departments establish "hard" and "soft" minimums. Hard minimums cannot be breached without calling other officers in to work on an overtime basis. Soft minimums occur where supervisors use discretion to drop staffing below a

predetermined level, when circumstances allow. However, departments often memor-
ialize these staffing levels in collective bargaining agreements. Staffing levels therefore
becomes part of the labor-management context and are thereby difficult to modify. These
hard minimums memorialized in collective bargaining agreements are often the drivers of
high overtime expenditures for police departments. Under these conditions patrol vacancies must be filled and this often requires calling other officers in on overtime. This is
undoubtedly the most disadvantageous and inefficient approach to patrol staffing.

Police Per-Capita. Equally popular is the per-capita approach to police staffing. Departments
across the country look to officer-to-population ratios as a simple method to determine
appropriate staffing. Although the International Association of Chiefs of Police (IACP)
does not recommend this method, it nonetheless published a directorate on just this very
topic. A recent IACP "Perspectives" article presents Bureau of Justice Statistics (BJS) data
on local police department officer-to-population ratios. The source is a 2003 BJS study
that reports the average ratio of full-time officers per 1,000 residents. Departments are
categorized by size of population served, ranging from 250,000 or more, to communities
of 1,000 to 2,499 residents. According to the article, the ratio of full-time officers per
1,000 residents ranges from 2.6 per 1,000 to 1.8 per 1,000, with an average ratio of 2.5
full-time officers per 1,000 residents (IACP, 2005). Many communities rely on this IACP
model to make staffing decisions. As easy as it is to comprehend and apply, this model is
equally flawed and unreliable.

Authorized Budget. The authorized/budgeted approach to staffing is a variant of the
minimum-manning model. In this approach, the city or town establishes a predetermined
level of staffing that fits within the budget of the community. This is a "What can we
afford?" model, as opposed to one that is based on actual community needs. Again, this
is a common approach to police staffing, and it bases the determination of personnel
levels on the community's budgeting process. It is also a simple approach whereby the
previous year's budget is examined considering the current financial situation and staffing decisions are made. The danger here is that staffing decisions can become politicized
or predicated on an artificial figure. The ability of a community to pay for services in
previous years, or a change in political administrations, is not necessarily a sound foundation on which to make police staffing decisions.

Workload. Lastly, and least common, are staffing decisions that are made based upon
actual workload. As discussed above, a number of pioneering queuing and optimization
models for patrol resource allocation were developed but unfortunately, are not widely
used (Srinivasan et al., 2013, p. 703). Operations research methods have proven to hold
promise (Curtin et al., 2010) but unfortunately, research indicates that these methods
have been underutilized for police staffing (Wilson and Heinonen, 2011). Police departments lack the resources and/or expertise to utilize these methods.

Recently, professional organizations such as the International City/County Management
Association (ICMA), the International Association of Chiefs of Police (IACP), and the
Commission on Accreditation for Law Enforcement Agencies (CALEA) have been advocates of this approach, as it relies on actual levels of demand for police services and matches
that demand with the supply of police resources. Typically, this approach relies on an examination of calls for service received by a department; these calls are modelled to understand
demand and supply. This approach also has shortcomings though, in that it relies exclusively on demand through 911 calls and ignores other elements of community demands
placed on a department. To overcome these shortcomings, workload demands should be

modelled and then placed in context with other operational demands facing the department. The result is a comprehensive assessment of workload through both calls for service and other sustained operational commitments placed on the department. This approach, however, requires a complex data analysis that is beyond the capacity of many police departments. Nonetheless, it offers the most accurate and reliable predictor of police staffing levels (Northwestern University Traffic Institute, 1993; Wilson and Weiss, 2012; McCabe, 2013).

Communities make personnel staffing decisions in a manner that reflects strategic and operational preferences. The breadth and scope of police services and the mix of equipment, personnel, and technology deployed in a particular community is discretionary to the management of that community (Edwards, 2011). The substantial flexibility inherent in these choices, therefore, leads to broad variation in staffing levels in local police departments. However, it is incumbent upon police managers and town/city administrators to look objectively at the allocation of police patrol personnel. A critical assessment of this important function mandates that police departments engage in a rigorous approach capitalizing on the best available data to make these decisions. The best approach relies on the combination of both science and art. Meaning that performance-based, workload models, need to be integrated with a fulsome discussion with community stakeholders regarding the desired level and mix of services their police department will provide. This approach starts with an analysis of workload data captured by the police CAD system and translating those data into understandable measures to make allocation decisions. The next section illustrates this approach and provides an explanation of a simple rule for patrol allocation.

Establishing a Benchmark for Patrol Allocation

In 2006 the Bureau of Justice Statistics published a report from the 2003 Law Enforcement Management and Administrative Statistics (LEMAS) series about local police. Data from this report showed the percentage of full-time sworn personnel that were assigned to respond to citizen calls for service. These include all uniformed officers whose regular assigned duties included responding to community calls for service, or more commonly called patrol personnel. The definition provided by LEMAS would support a wide range of police assignments, such as traffic officers, community policing officers, and numerous others that regularly respond to community requests for service; therefore, it is difficult to interpret the exact nature of officers in these assignments. Nonetheless, Table 2.1 shows a breakdown of the percentage of officers in these calls for service capacity compared to the population of the community served.

The data in Table 2.1 illustrates that as the size of the service population decreases, the greater the percentage of sworn officers assigned to call-response function. Similarly, the smaller the police department, the greater percentage of officers in that department will be assigned to patrol. The largest communities, with more than 500,000 population assign less than 60 percent of their officers to patrol functions, and the smallest assign almost all their officers in this capacity.

The 2022 "Benchmark City Survey" report is another useful resource to evaluate patrol resource allocation. The Benchmark City Survey was originally designed in 1997 by a group of Police Chiefs from around the country. These Chiefs sought to establish a measurement tool to help ensure their departments were providing the best service possible within their respective communities. The survey provides a wide range of information about each Department. With that information, the participating agencies can set better goals and objectives, and then compare their performance in the various areas. The Overland Park,

Table 2.1 Percentage in CFS Assignment by
Population of Community Served

Population Served	Number	Percent
1,000,000 or more	57,530	59
500,000–999,999	26,940	54
250,000–499,999	19,914	62
100,000–249,999	31,170	62
50,000–99,999	34,125	68
25,000–49,999	34,716	71
10,000–24,999	46,344	79
2,500–9,999	40,953	88
Under 2,500	17,159	96
All sizes	308,849	68

Kansas Police Department has taken the lead in compiling the survey results. The average size of the 25 departments participating in this survey is 250 sworn officers, which is larger than the average police department in the U.S. Also, the average service population for these departments is approximately 189,000, which again would put these departments on the higher end of the scale of community size. However, the data reported by the Benchmark City Survey provides another opportunity to explore patrol resource allocation.

According to the data reported by this consortium, the percentage of first-responders ranges from a low of 37.3% of the Coral Springs, FL police department, to a high of 81% in the Boca Raton, FL police department. The overall average of first-responders in the group of 30 departments is 58.5%, and non-first-first responders at 41.5%. A first-responder is defined as a commissioned police officer below the rank of first-line supervisor whose primary responsibility is handling dispatched calls for service (Overland Park, KS, 2022).

The International City Manager Association's Center for Public Safety Management (CPSM) is also an advocate for using a benchmark. This is an approach that gives police managers a simple and effective mechanism to assess patrol allocation and deployment. This rule has two parts. The first part involves patrol allocation and suggests that approximately 60 percent of the total number of sworn officers assigned to a police department should be assigned to patrol. This organization does not offer an empirical justification for this standard, but the simplicity and ease with which it can be applied is appealing (McCabe, 2013).

Combining all these approaches creates the opportunity to assess patrol resource allocation. Police managers are encouraged to examine the allocation of resources to the patrol function considering these various approaches. Using the sliding scale presented in Table 2.1 and the positions of the different professional groups, departments should look in the range of 60 percent as the goal for patrol resource allocation. Each community has different needs, which will be reflected in the style of their police department, but some form of standard should be applied. It is important at this point to consider which sworn personnel are included in the definition of "patrol" officers.

The Benchmark City departments use the definition "first responder," and limit the definition to personnel with the *primary* responsibility for handling calls for service from the public. Departments with K9 officers, and traffic officers, or school resource officers need to consider whether to include personnel in these functions in the group of first responders. Undoubtedly, officers in uniform working in the community on a regular basis regardless of specific function will respond to calls for service as required. For example, a school resource officer will likely respond to calls for service at their assigned schools, or to and from those locations, or even times when school is not in session. Similarly, K9 officers, while assigned with the dog, should not be primarily assigned to handle calls for service, but are on patrol and back-up officers and provide valuable support to patrol operations. Including these officers as "first responders" should be done carefully and on a case-by-case basis.

Therefore, to assess the appropriate allocation of resources to patrol operations it is recommended that police managers make two separate calculations. First, identify all the sworn officers assigned primarily to handling calls for service on patrol, and compare this to the overall number of sworn officers in the department. This identifies the basic commitment to patrol operations and should be no less than 60 percent of all sworn personnel. If this figure is less than 60 percent it is likely that the department is over-specialized and either not enough resources are allocated to patrol, or there are too many specialized units in the department. Again, personnel staffing decisions in a police department should reflect the overall mission of the organization and meet the needs of the community they serve. Having patrol personnel allocated at a level of less than 60 percent does not mean that the department is operating ineffectively or inefficiently. It does indicate that there might be an opportunity to re-examine the process by which personnel are assigned, and the value-added benefit of specialized units.

The next step is to identify sworn personnel that have ancillary patrol functions that do have the responsibility for responding to calls for service, perhaps as a secondary or support function. Personnel on patrol in this category would include traffic officers, community resource officers, school resource officers, and officers in administrative positions that might be assigned to the patrol division. In other words, they are under the "patrol" umbrella but not with a specific primary responsibility to handle calls for service from the public. Adding these personnel to the personnel assigned to the basic patrol function should position the department well over the 60 percent threshold. If the department is much higher or lower, percentage-wise, in this area compared to the range of percentages presented in Table 2.1, then an assessment should be made of tasks and responsibilities of the various units and personnel to determine if adjustments should be made.

To illustrate this patrol allocation approach, the fictitious community of "Anytown" will be used. Table 2.2 is the table of organization for the AnyTown Police Department. Anytown has 32 sworn officers. The ATPD has one chief, two lieutenants, six sergeants and 23 sworn

Table 2.2 Table of Organization – Anytown PD

	Chief	Lt.	Sgt	PO
Executive	1			
Admin and Training			1	
Operations				
Patrol		1		
Nights			1	5
Days			1	5
Evenings			1	6
Special Operations		1		
Detectives			1	3
Traffic			1	2
SRO				2
	1	2	6	23

Table 2.3 Table of Organization – Hometown PD

	Chief	Asst. Ch.	Lt.	Sgt	PO
Executive	1				
Support		1	1	1	
Admin				1	
Training				1	
Lab					1
Operations		1			
Patrol					
Day Command			2		
0700x1700				2	14
1100x2100				2	14
SRO					3
Night Command			2		
1700x0300				2	14
1900x0500				1	4
2100x0700				2	14
Investigations			1		
Detectives				1	6
Special Enforcement				1	4
Career Criminal Team				1	8
Violence Offender TF				1	4
	1	2	6	16	86

officers (non-sworn personnel are not shown). The basic patrol function works eight-hour shifts and the officers are assigned evenly among these shifts. There is a sergeant assigned to supervise each shift as well as a patrol lieutenant to manage operations. There are a total of 32 sworn officers working in the ATPD, and 20 of them, or 62.5%, are assigned to the basic patrol function. These sworn personnel include the supervisors (lieutenants and sergeants assigned to the day and night shifts). Based upon the benchmark recommended, the ATPD had about the right number of sworn personnel assigned to basic patrol. Adding the sworn personnel that have ancillary patrol functions, the traffic, and school resource officers, brings the patrol percentage up to 75% of the overall department. Therefore, the allocation of sworn officers assigned to patrol ranges from 62.5 to 75 percent. Depending upon the scope and breadth of the support provided to patrol by the ancillary functions, the ATPD should carefully examine whether there are sufficient resources allocated to patrol to provide basic coverage to the community. A better understanding of whether the ATPD is meeting this basic responsibility is covered later in this chapter under the discussion of workload demand.

The next example is of a larger police department. The Hometown Police Department has a service population of 68,000 and a total of 111 sworn officers assigned. The basic patrol function is organized into several 10-hour shifts with officers assigned evenly to the four primary patrol squads, plus one overlapping squad. Again, there are lieutenants and sergeants assigned to the various shifts. This department does not have any sworn personnel assigned to ancillary patrol functions.

The HTPD allocates 74 sworn officers, or 66.7% of the department, to patrol. Based upon the various benchmarks discussed above, it appears that the HTPD is allocating personnel to patrol as expected.

This simple calculation provides police managers with a benchmark to assess their department. There are several factors that must be considered when using it, however. First, is that it is not a "bright-line" benchmark. This means that it does not serve as an absolute criterion and must be taken in context with other factors that influence allocation decisions. Second is that consideration must be taken with regards to including or excluding other sworn personnel resources that are not primarily assigned to handle calls for service but are on patrol. The number of officers in this category will obviously alter the ratio of patrol to non-patrol personnel. Lastly, the actual workload experienced by patrol personnel needs to be considered. If patrol resources are overwhelmed by work, for example, but meet the expected allocation level, the patrol function could be understaffed. Conversely, if there are more than enough resources to handle the workload and the patrol function is properly allocated, then this could signal that the police department is overstaffed. It is critical, therefore, that the second part of the allocation formula be considered, which involves the calculation of actual workload from CFS. To have a proper allocation of personnel to patrol, the workload from calls for service, on average, should not be greater than 60 percent of the available number of officers on patrol to handle that workload. This is much more difficult to assess, and often overlooked by police managers.

Patrol Workload – Demand for Services. The three-digit telephone number "9-1-1" has been designated as the universal emergency number for people throughout the U.S. since the late 1960s. The catalyst for the development of a nationwide emergency phone number was the National Association of Fire Chiefs, and the 1967 Presidential Commission on Law Enforcement and Administration of Justice recommended that a single phone number be established for police emergencies. Since then, the flood gates have opened and the use of 9-1-1 has exploded into an easily accessible means of summoning emergency personnel on a 24x7 basis around the country. Approximately 96 percent of the geographic U.S. is covered by some form of Public Safety Answering Points (PSAP).

The use, or misuse, of 9-1-1 calls for service is an area of police management that is often ignored, or at best misunderstood. As the discussion above illustrates, police departments allocate more than 60 percent of their personnel resources to handle calls for service from the community. However, the type and nature of these calls is not generally managed. In other words, police managers around the U.S. are unaware of the types of calls their officers are responding to, and generally have little knowledge of how much time and effort goes into servicing these calls from the community. It is critical that police managers rigorously assess this aspect of operations and get a firm handle on the amount and type of work being generated by this function (NIJ, 1967).

With the implementation of community policing as an operational philosophy for American police departments, the tension between handling calls for service through 9-1-1 and the need to have time to engage in problem-solving became clear. Often, police officers on patrol are directed to calls that are not related to underlying crime and disorderly conditions in a community. Police emergencies take on many different forms, and the community is encouraged to report traffic accidents, noise complaints, and a whole host of incidents through 9-1-1. In New York City during the early 1990s, the NYPD discovered that officers on patrol dedicated more than 87% of their time to addressing calls for service from 9-1-1. The Police Commissioner at the time, Lee P. Brown, was committed to bringing community policing to New York City and reasoned that the officers on patrol were dedicating far too much time to calls for service. There was a recognition at the time that there needed to be more time on patrol for the officers to engage in other community policing activities, such as problem-solving, and that handling calls for service interfered with the ability to do problem-solving. The solution for the NYPD was to manage the response to calls for service by minimizing the sheer volume of calls and to structure patrol resources more efficiently to meet the overwhelming demands for service. The goal for the NYPD in 1991, to have sufficient time for patrol officers to engage in community policing activities, was to reduce the time dedicated to calls for service from the community to less than 60 percent of the amount of time available for patrol (Webber, 1991).

The implementation of community policing in the NYPD never developed beyond the tenure of Commissioner Brown. His successor, William Bratton, implemented a revolutionary management process called Compstat, which essentially displaced community policing priorities. Nearly 30 years after the implementation of Compstat, the NYPD implemented a different policing philosophy called Neighborhood Policing. This philosophy included some of the principles from community policing and required that officers have sufficient time away from handling calls for service to engage with the community. The NYPD determined that officers on patrol should not be committed to work from calls for service more than 5 hours out of each 8.5-hour patrol shift. The goal for NYPD patrol managers, therefore, was to ensure that at least 58.8% of the average officer's patrol shift be "uncommitted" time, or time not engaged in handling calls for service. To accomplish this goal, NYPD patrol managers needed to staff enough officers on patrol to meet the workload demands *and* have ample time left over for the officers to engage in neighborhood policing activities. The experience of the NYPD created another useful metric to assess patrol resource allocation (Beck et al., 2022).

The International Association of Chiefs of Police (IACP) recommends a similar metric. According to the IACP, patrol activities can be categorized into three broad areas: operational time, administrative time, and uncommitted time. Operational time is the amount of time consumed by patrol officers to answer calls for service from the public. This includes the total of criminal, traffic, disorder, back-up activity, generated by a call from the public or an incident an officer comes upon during their shift. In general, IACP recommends that not more than 30 percent of the available amount of time in the average officers' shift should be committed to operational time.

In addition to operational time, the IACP recognizes administrative time as a necessary part of an officer's shift. This time would include report writing, court attendance, administrative briefings, or meetings with supervisors, etc. IACP suggests that administrative time also accounts for approximately 30% of an officer's average day.

The remaining balance of a patrol officer's average day, according to the IACP, should be "uncommitted" time. This uncommitted time allows officers to engage in a wide range of activities associated with their primary duties and responsibilities. During this uncommitted time officers might interact with members of the community, investigate crime-prone or crash-prone locations, engage in proactive enforcement, or simply remain available in the event of a sudden emergency. This is a key measure from a police management perspective. Understanding discretionary, or uncommitted time, and how it is used, is vital. Yet most police departments do not compile such data effectively. To be sure, this is not easy to do, and some departments may require improvements in management information systems (Vose et al., 2020).

Essentially, uncommitted time on patrol is the amount of time available each day where officers are not committed to handling CFS, and workload demands from the public. It is "discretionary" and intended to be used at the discretion of the officer to address problems in the community and be available in the event of emergencies. When there is no discretionary time, officers are entirely committed to service demands, do not get the chance to address other community problems that do not arise through 911, and are not available in times of serious emergency. The lack of discretionary time indicates a department is under-staffed. Conversely, when there is too much discretionary time officers are idle. This is an indication that the department is overstaffed.

Staffing decisions, particularly for patrol, must be based on actual workload. Once the actual workload is determined, the amount of discretionary time is determined and then staffing decisions can be made that are consistent with the department's policing philosophy and the community's ability to fund the staffing. It is necessary to look at workload to understand the impact of this style of policing in the context of community demand.

From an organizational standpoint, it is important to have uniformed patrol resources available at all times of the day to deal with issues such as proactive enforcement and community policing. Patrol is generally the most visible and most available resource in policing and the ability to harness this resource is critical for successful operations.

From an officer's standpoint, once a certain level of CFS activity is reached, the officer's focus shifts to a CFS-based reactionary mode. Once a threshold is reached, the patrol officer's mindset begins to shift from a proactive approach, looking for ways to deal with crime and quality-of-life conditions in the community, to a reactive approach where they are continually waiting for the next call. After this threshold is reached and the officer's shift becomes "saturated" with work, officers cease proactive policing and engage in a reactionary style of policing. The outlook becomes "Why act proactively when my actions are only going to be interrupted by a call?" Any uncommitted time is spent waiting for the next call. It is important, therefore, for police managers to calculate the amount of uncommitted time available to officers on patrol. Resources can then be allocated to balance the amount of committed to uncommitted time to reach an appropriate ratio.

This "Rule of 60" is an informal standard that accounts for workload and discretionary time and suggests that no more than 60 percent of time should be committed to calls for service. In other words, it is suggested that no more than 60 percent of available patrol officer time be spent responding to the service demands of the community. The remaining 40 percent of the time is the "discretionary time" for officers to be available to address community problems and be available for serious emergencies. This standard for patrol deployment does not mean the remaining 40 percent of time is downtime or break time. It is simply a reflection of the point at which patrol officer time is "saturated" by CFS. Therefore, workload can be measured by the "saturation index" (SI), or amount of time committed to service demands from the community.

Based upon the experience of the NYPD and the model advocated by the IACP, it is believed that the appropriate amount of uncommitted time should be at least 40% of the average patrol shift, or no more than 60% of the average officers' shift be dedicated to workload from calls for service and administrative requirements. This 60% threshold, once calculated, can be integrated with the other criteria to create a simple but powerful standard for patrol allocation.

Approximately 60% of all a police department's sworn personnel should be assigned to the patrol function, and no more than 60% of the average shift should be dedicated to operational and administrative demands. Calculating these 60% thresholds will allow police managers to assess patrol operations and make informed and empirical decisions about personnel allocation.

Departments must be cautious in interpreting the SI too narrowly. For example, one should not conclude that SI can never exceed 60 percent at any time during the day, or that in any given hour no more than 60 percent of any officer's time be committed to CFS. The SI at 60 percent is intended to be a benchmark to evaluate overall service demands on patrol staffing. When SI levels exceed 60 percent for substantial periods of a given shift, or at isolated and specific times during the day, then decisions should be made to reallocate or realign personnel to reduce the SI to levels below 60. Lastly, this is not a hard-and-fast rule, but a benchmark to be used in evaluating staffing decisions.

Case Study – Anytown Police Department

A hypothetical example using a fictitious police department will illustrate the application of these two patrol resource allocation principles.

To understand the demand for police services faced by the patrol function, we return to the fictitious Anytown PD (ATPD). This department will serve as a model for the step-by-step process necessary to calculate workload demands from ICAD data.

The first step is to extract all the CFS from the CAD system. It is recommended that an entire year of CAD data be used for analysis. Typically, CAD data can be exported in excel files which can be manipulated to create the data needed to understand workload.

After the raw data is collected, several steps need to be taken to convert the raw data into data useful for analysis. First, CFS not involving patrol officers need to be excluded from the analysis. Therefore, any CFS handled by personnel assigned to non-patrol officers should be eliminated from the analysis. Next, it is recommended that any CFS with a duration of one minute or less should be excluded from the analysis. An assumption can be made that any CFS of such a short duration was not handled at all and simply canceled by the person calling or reassigned to another unit on patrol. After these steps are taken there will be a useful dataset on patrol-based workload.

With the CFS available for analysis, several calculations will be necessary to convert these data into workload measures useful for analysis. The first step is to calculate the total amount of time expended on each CFS. To do this the start time of the CFS should be subtracted from the end time, which results in total time expended. Once the total time expended is determined, it is necessary to exclude the amount of time that is incurred past the expiration of the officer's shift. For example, if a CFS was received at 2:00 p.m. by an officer on patrol working on the day shift, and that CFS ended at 3:15 p.m., 15 minutes of the amount of time on this call needs to be excluded from the workload. The assumption being made here is that after 3:00 p.m. a new shift began, a new supply of personnel was available for work, and the officer assigned to the CFS that began at 2:00 p.m. was still working, except on overtime. The goal here is to understand the relationship between demand and staffing; therefore, since the overtime staffing needs to be excluded from the analysis the overtime workload needs to be excluded as well. This will make for simpler comparisons of the workload and the officers needed to meet it. Essentially, once the officer passed their ordinary shift end time, both their work and their presence as part of the workforce is excluded from the analysis. This step provided a more accurate understanding of the workload demands in the context of staffing supply.

The next step in the analysis is to collapse CFS categories into larger units that permit a better understanding of the data. In 2022, the ATPD assigned 133 separate CFS categories to describe the calls they handled. These 133 incidents were collapsed into 17 categories. Using these major categories of CFS, the next step is to distinguish CFS that come directly from the public through the 9-1-1 system from those that are initiated by the officer. Research shows that public-initiated CFS are likely to last longer, and require more than one officer to handle, compared to officer-initiated activities like car stops and location checks (McCabe, 2013). Once the categories are organized appropriately, calculations can be made to determine the average amount of time spent on CFS, and the average number of

Table 2.4 Breakdown of CFS for the Anytown Police Department

Category	Public-initiated			Officer-initiated		
	Minutes	*Calls*	*Units*	*Minutes*	*Calls*	*Units*
Accident	45.2	1,945	1.6	39.2	140	1.6
Alarm	16.8	1,124	2.3	3.4	3	1
Animal	27.9	435	1.3	10.3	14	1.1
Assist citizen	27.5	1,352	1.5	13.4	575	1.1
Assist other agency	31.4	642	1.9	21.1	127	1.4
Check/investigation	35.6	3,464	2.1	52.1	285	1.5
Crime–persons	85	332	3	70.8	178	2.8
Crime–property	56	2,413	2.1	57.5	134	1.9
Disturbance	38.4	22	2.5	31	5	2
Juvenile	36.7	202	1.9	29.4	35	1.7
Miscellaneous	30.6	949	1.4	15.4	3,922	1.1
Park complaint	18.7	681	1.2	10.5	60	1
Prisoner–arrest	95.5	149	2.7	88.5	234	2.3
Prisoner–transport	107	172	2.1	108.2	122	2
Suspicious person/vehicle	26.4	3,562	2.1	20.2	1,097	1.9
Traffic enforcement	37.1	591	1.6	13.7	8,633	1.2
Total/Average	**36.7**	**18,035**	**1.9**	**19.9**	**15,564**	**1.3**

units assigned to CFS in these categories, separated by public or officer-initiated responses. Table 2.4 illustrates the results of this process.

Examination of the data presented in Table 2.4 reveals several interesting observations. For the 18,035 CFS from the public handled by the ATPD, there was an average of 1.9 units assigned to the public-initiated CFS and 1.3 units assigned to handle the 15,564 officer-initiated CFS. On average, it took 36.7 minutes for officers to handle a CFS from the public and only 19.9 minutes to handle an officer-initiated CFS. In terms of overall work, the ATPD expended 11,031 hours (18,035 CFS x 36.7 minutes, divided by 60) on CFS direct from the public, and 5,162 (15,564 CFS x 19.9 minutes, divided by 60) hours on officer-initiated work, for a total of 16,193 hours of total work captured by the CAD system.

Several questions should arise when presented with these data. Should the ATPD respond to this number of CFS, or is there an opportunity to handle more or less work? Is the ATPD spending too much time handling CFS? Is the ATPD assigning enough officers to each CFS? What is the response time to these incidents? Are there enough officers on patrol to handle this volume of demand? An appropriate assessment of the patrol function begins with a response to these types of question. These are the basic questions every police department should be asking. The answers permit a proper assessment of the patrol function and a better understanding of workload experience by officers on patrol, and similarly, the level of service expected and provided to the community.

Assessment of CFS Volume. There are no known benchmarks to evaluate the number of CFS handled by the police. The illustration above shows that the ATPD responded to 33,599 CFS in one calendar year (18,035 directly from the public and another 15,564 initiated by the officers). The question should not be whether the sheer volume of CFS is appropriate. If each one of these CFS were a true emergency, then the answer to this question would be yes. However, police managers know that many CFS that come through the 9-1-1 system are not emergencies. Therefore, the assessment should shift to minimizing the number of non-emergency CFS responses to ensure prompt response to actual emergencies. Determining what constitutes an emergency call versus a non-emergency call is a challenging exercise. Police managers should not be put in a position to make this determination unilaterally. These decisions should be made with input from the community with a collective understanding of what is expected of the police. However, there are broad categories of CFS that are known to be non-emergency, even frivolous in nature. Non-injury traffic crashes, routine medical incidents, false alarms, etc. are all categories of CFS that occupy an inordinate amount of police attention.

In our illustration above, the ATPD responded to 3,711 of these types of CFS, or more than 20% of all calls received. Essentially, one in five of all the CFS from the public through 9-1-1 were arguably non-emergency and did not require an immediate police response. Similarly, officers initiated almost 4,000 "miscellaneous" CFS, or almost 1,000 hours of work dedicated to a category of CFS that was beyond clear definition. Therefore, an appropriate assessment of the patrol function would involve an examination of these types of call categories and the number of police responses. Is there an opportunity to reduce some of this workload? Are there other ways of meeting these demands? Each police department will have its own answer, which will reflect the community it serves. The point here is not that there is a preferred mix or concentration of CFS, but there should be an assessment to ensure that patrol resources are expended efficiently.

Assessment of the Response. The next step in assessing patrol is to assess the efficiency and quality of the CFS response. Looking again at the data in Table 2.4, we see that the average amount of time spent on a CFS from the public is 36.7 minutes and is handled by an average of 1.9 units. There are no known benchmarks to evaluate these variables, however the International City Managers Association published a series of measures distilled from studies they did with member communities that suggest an area for comparison. In a white paper published by ICMA (McCabe, 2013), it was reported that the average amount of time committed to a CFS in the 61 communities studied was 28.7 minutes to a CFS from the public and 17.7 minutes for a CFS initiated by the officers. In addition, for the public-driven CFS there was an average of 1.6 units assigned, and 1.2 units assigned for an officer-initiated CFS. Based upon the ICMA standard, the ATPD appears to be expending more officers, and more time, to the average CFS.

There are many factors that influence the amount of time needed to handle a police CFS. Travel time, administrative and legal requirements, the nature and character of the call, the motivation of the officer, the quality of supervision, etc. could all influence the amount of time officers spend on a given CFS. Understanding the drivers behind this time is an important component of patrol assessment. It starts with calculating the time and resources committed to CFS in the first place (as in Table 2.4), then requires a "deeper dive" into what exactly is contributing to that time. Each police department is different, but everyone should engage in this type of process. It starts with processing the raw data captured by the department's CAD system and ends with a thorough assessment of the amount of time and effort spent on the different types of CFS reported to the department.

Assessment of Patrol Resources. The ultimate assessment is to explore the relationship between the workload from CFS and the amount of patrol resources allocated to meet that demand. This is the second part of the rule of 60. This section provides a quantitative assessment of that workload to staffing ratio in the context of the 60 percent rule. Armed with the data that was used to construct Table 2.4, a temporal representation of these CFS can be developed to illustrate the workload across the average day. This temporal workload can then be compared with the number of personnel assigned throughout the day to handle it.

To calculate the number of officers assigned to patrol for these periods it is recommended that a manual count be undertaken. Instead of relying on the number of officers assigned to patrol from staffing rosters, an appropriate assessment would require that the *actual* number of officers that appeared for work during those periods be calculated. On any given shift there will be a difference between the number of officers assigned for duty, and the actual number of officers working. The realities of patrol indicate that officers will be given leave for their normally assigned shift for several reasons, both operational and administrative. Court appearances, sick and vacation leave, training attendance, etc. influence the number of officers that are working on any given day. It is recommended that these natural absences be considered to determine patrol staffing level.

To determine the number of officers working, the department should extract information from their personnel management system on the times and numbers of officers assigned through these months. For the best possible analysis, it is recommended that hourly time increments be used to record the number of officers working. Most records management systems can report on the units assigned to patrol at different times during the day. This exercise would require a query of the system at increments during the days used to draw the comparison. A less precise approach would be to inspect the daily time sheets/rosters/duty assignment logs to identify the number of officers that reported for duty at the beginning of each shift and assuming that they were on duty and working for the entirety of their assigned shift. Understandably, this method is not as accurate as using samller increments but can be used to provide an approximation of staffing levels in a department.

It is assumed that police workload through CFS will be influenced by both the season and part of the week. In the summer months, a typical police department will likely experience its highest demand for services, while also encountering the greatest demand for vacation time by officers on patrol. Winter would present the opposite, with lower levels of workload and requests for time off, on average. In addition, weekday nights are typically slow, from a CFS perspective. Weekdays during the afternoons tend to be busy with school and commuters. The inverse seems to be true for the weekends. Weekend nights and evenings tend to be busy, while mornings and afternoons are slower. The contrasts naturally occurring during these seasonal and weekly periods allow for a multi-layered assessment of workload demands. It is recommended that the workload and staffing assessments be conducted across these various periods: weekdays vs. weekends, and summer vs. winter to explore the variations.

The next several figures represent workload, staffing, and the "saturation" of patrol resources in the ATPD during the summer and winter months (seasons), different parts of the week (weekday/weekend).

The figures represent the manpower and demand during weekdays and weekends during the months of February and July 2022. Examination of these figures permits exploration of the "Rule of 60" as it applies to patrol workload in the ATPD. To comply with this rule, total work should be less than 60 percent of total patrol.

These figures present the relationship between patrol workload demands, the number of police officers assigned to meet that demand, and the relative saturation of those officers' time with workload. As the figures indicate, workload saturation exceeds the 60 percent threshold most of the day. It ranges from a low of approximately 35 percent at 5:00 a.m. to a high of 95 percent at 5:00 p.m., with a daily average of 64 percent.

Figure 2.1 illustrates many interesting facts about patrol deployment in the ATPD during weekdays in February. During this period, it appears that the deployment fluctuates from

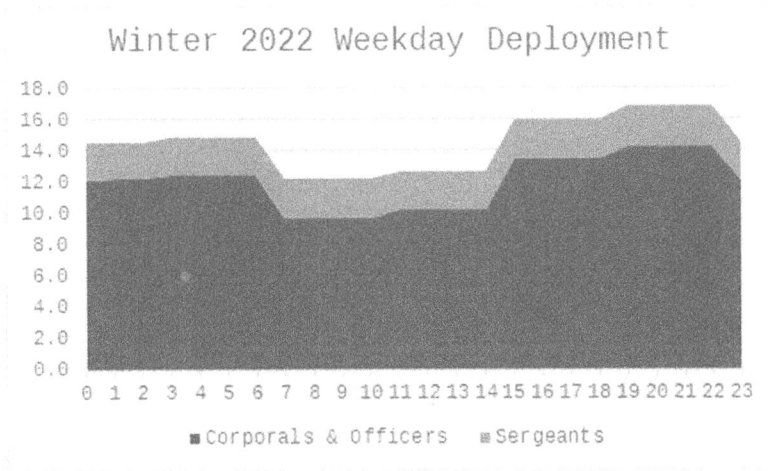

Figure 2.1 Deployment Winter Weekdays.

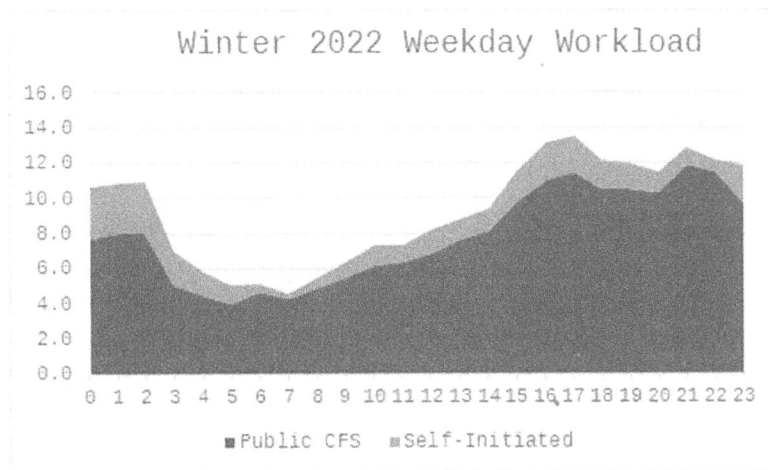

Figure 2.2 Workload Winter Weekdays.

shift to shift, ranging from about 12 officers assigned on the average day for the Night-Shift, 10 on the Day-Shift, to about 14 officers assigned on the average day on the Evening-Shift. Staffing is represented by the top of the shaded area in Figure 2.1.

Workload demand is represented in Figure 2.2 by the shaded area. The darker shaded area represents the workload from 911 CFS from the public, and the lighter shaded area represents ones generated by officer-initiated activity. It also includes the administrative time used in support of those CFS. It also appears that the workload fluctuates during the 24-hour period with total demand very low during the nighttime and early morning hours, and increasing steadily throughout the day, peaking at 4:00 p.m. The workload appears to fall off after 9:00 p.m., and then decreases and remains low during the early morning hours.

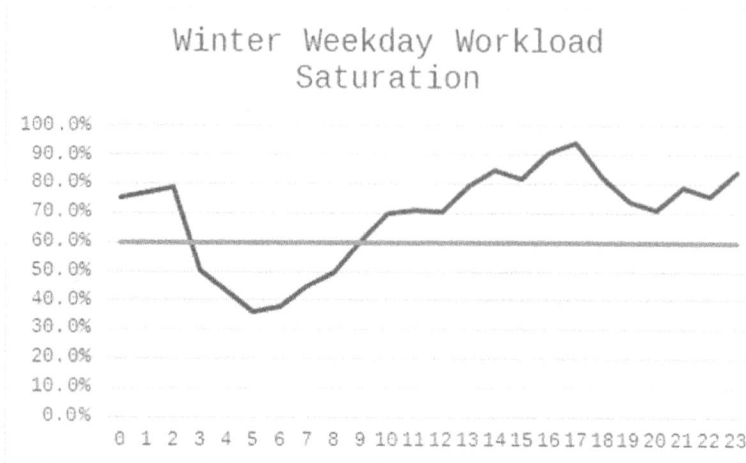

Figure 2.3 Workload Saturation, Winter Weekdays.

It appears that the ATPD struggles to meet workload demands during winter weekdays. The workload saturation index is greater than 60 percent for most of the day. And even during the times of the day when it dips below the 60 percent threshold, the variability of the workload would undoubtedly make an impression on the officers that they were busy all the time. This experience would be reinforced each day because workload increases throughout the day, and only abates after 2:00am. Essentially, the entire patrol function would be under stress to handle CFS during these times.

In general, "right-sizing" the patrol function, balancing workload with personnel, should be approached in three ways. The first way, as discussed earlier in the chapter, is to manage the demand. By examining the types of CFS that officers respond to in the first place, police departments can minimize the work handled. The second approach is to add more personnel to patrol to meet the demand. The challenge for the ATPD is that simply adding more officers to meet the demand in the winter might not be the most effective way to address the situation. The third approach is to configure the shift schedules in such a way to match the number of officers working during the times they are needed. The shift data presented here on the ATPD show three, almost evenly staffed shifts. Perhaps there is an opportunity to reconfigure these shifts to better match the supply of personnel with workload demands. The next part of the chapter explores this important approach.

Patrol Deployment and Staffing

Once there is an understanding of the proper personnel allocation, then it is critical to understand appropriate deployment. Deployment refers to the way the patrol officers are organized and assigned to work. This section of the chapter provides an overview of shift scheduling, and the various ways departments construct shifts to meet service demands. A discussion about the costs and benefits of different shift lengths and the empirical evidence on shift work is also provided. In addition, several illustrations are attempted to model patrol shifts in an efficient way that maximizes staffing resources to provide them at the times they are needed the most. Taking into consideration the demand for police services and the concept of saturation index, appropriate levels of patrol staffing can be determined.

The optimal level of patrol staffing will lead to the modeling of patrol schedules and act as the foundation for the staffing of the entire department.

Continuing with the ATPD example, the main patrol force is divided into three shifts with approximately the same staffing levels on each shift. They have three sergeants, and 16 officers assigned. All shifts have steady hours with rotating days off. Officers and sergeants work five days on, have three days off, work five days, and then have two off. This pattern repeats itself all year.

The available literature on shift length provides no definitive conclusions on an appropriate shift length. A study published by the Police Foundation examined 8-hour, 10-hour, and 12-hour shifts, and found positive and negative characteristics associated with all three options (Amendola et al., 2011). The report, funded by the National Institute of Justice, studied the Arlington, TX and Detroit, MI police departments for a six-month period and collected data related to work performance, officer health and stress, quality of life, and sleep and fatigue. The study concluded that alertness decreased with length of shift, and that the 10-hour shifts had quality of life advantages over both 8-hour and 12-hour shifts. Anecdotal accounts from officers overwhelmingly supported 10-hour shifts and a compressed work-week. Consistent with other studies on shift work, younger and unmarried officers preferred longer shifts and more days off, and older and married officers shorter shifts and more workdays. Each shift length presents advantages and disadvantages; therefore, the length of the shift should be secondary to the application of that shift to meet service demands. A balance needs to be achieved between meeting service demands and the quality of life of the police officers doing the shift work.

The Eight-Hour Shift Model. The eight-hour shift used for the day and evening shifts is common in the mid-Atlantic states and in the northeast. Eight hours easily divided into 24, making three clean and evenly divided shifts to cover the day. The ATPD relies on this shift, but there are some obvious deficiencies. In addition to the difficulty in meeting demand at various times during July weekends, each shift is only supervised by one sergeant. As Table 2.6 shows, there are no sergeants assigned to work during the weekends. This is problematic. Regardless of which shift is selected for staff patrol operations, it is strongly suggested that at least one supervisor be always assigned. Every assessment of shift scheduling must include this element, and proper and continuous supervision of patrol operations is essential. Also, research shows that the rotation of work hours from day to night and back is the most disruptive to employees. This alternating work schedule should be avoided if possible. Similarly, having steady days off has been associated with increased reports of quality of life. These studies assume that the steady days off fall on the weekends, and there is not much evidence to support preferences and improved quality of life associated with days off during the weekdays (Amendola et al, 2011).

Returning the workload demand issues in the ATPD during the summer, it is possible to explore different shifts and deployment. The assessment of patrol operations should naturally involve this type of exercise to match the deployment with the workload. For this illustration both 12-hour and 10-hour shift lengths will be considered.

Twelve-Hour Shift Model. The 12-hour shift is probably the most used shift length in U.S. policing. It too poses advantages and disadvantages. On the positive side, the 12-hour shift requires fewer work appearances for officers and supervisors. Again, fewer appearances presumably translate into a higher quality of life away from work. Under 12-hour shift models, officers are generally required to work less than half the days each year. This is substantially less than the 260 workdays in a typical five-day week. From an operational perspective, the 12-hour shift results in a greater percentage of officers working on any given day, thus more officers to deploy toward crime, traffic, disorder, and community issues at any one time. This shift also affords a tight unity of command with supervisors and officers working together each shift. This promotes better supervision and better esprit de corps among employees.

On the negative side, a 12-hour shift configuration with four equally staffed squads results in a constant and fixed level of patrol staffing throughout the day. Service demands vary, peaking in the evening hours and waning in the early morning hours. With a constant supply of personnel and a variable demand for their services there will be a continual surplus and shortage of resources. Also, with a four-squad configuration a "silo" effect is often created. The natural rotation of this shift configuration creates four separate squads that do not interact often, this creates personnel "silos." Similarly, it is difficult to communicate between the "silos" and between the squads and the executive management of the department.

The following discussion applies this deployment model to the ATPD. This shift model requires a minimum of four sergeants, with at least one supervising each squad. The ATPD has three sergeants, therefore, one additional sergeant will be required. To complete the deployment model the 16 police officers assigned to patrol will be evenly divide among the four squads. Table 2.5 illustrates the personnel distribution pursuant to this model.

The 12-hour shift plan illustrated in Table 2.5 eliminates the variability in assignments and provides for uniform and continuous coverage throughout the week. The major shortcoming in this model is that while personnel availability is uniform throughout the week, demand for services fluctuates. The discussion about workload demands showed that the busiest times of the day for the police in Anytown are in the afternoons and early evenings. Having a constant supply of personnel to meet these variable workload demands is not the most efficient use of personnel. The appropriate deployment of personnel to patrol is accomplished when demand and supply are closely matched. In the Anytown example provided here, the officers working patrol in the afternoon and evenings will be busy, and the officers working early morning hours will be under-utilized. An adjustment can be made to the 12-hour shift plan to accommodate the variability of workload demands. The ATPD could create two additional patrol squads within the 12-hour shift plan and have them overlap the four basic patrol squads illustrated in Table 2.5.

The deployment model illustrated in Table 2.6 shows six patrol squads and uses the same number of sworn personnel in Table 2.5. The four sergeants and 16 officers are now spread out across the six squads. One officer was removed from each of the four basic squads to staff the two additional squads. Sergeants supervise the foundational squads that work throughout the day, and then overlap these squads as two additional squads with officers

Table 2.5 Twelve-hour Shift Configuration

Squad	Shift	Sgt.	PO	Total
A	0600X1800	1	4	5
B	1800X0600	1	4	5
C	0600X1800	1	4	5
D	1800X0600	1	4	5

Table 2.6 Twelve-hour Shift Configuration with Overlap Squads

Squad	Shift	Sgt.	PO	Total
A	0600X1800	1	3	4
B	1800X0600	1	3	4
C	0600X1800	1	3	4
D	1800X0600	1	3	4
E	1200x2400		2	2
F	1200x2400		2	2
		4	16	20

in each to provide support during the busiest times of the day. The time period of Noon to Midnight was selected for this model, but this can be adjusted to any 12-hour period of the day to reflect the needs of the department.

Staffing patrol under the deployment model in Table 2.6 above provides for sworn officers from Noon to Midnight, during the times when service demands are the highest, and then reduces staffing between Midnight and noon when the service demands are lowest. This deployment model would probably make the most sense for the ATPD and address all the operational needs.

For both of the 12-hour shift models it is recommended that a day-off rotation be created that limits the number of consecutive days worked and provides suitable time off during weekends. The most common rotation of days off under the 12-hour deployment model for police departments is known as the "Pitman" schedule. Days off under this plan would rotate on a bi-weekly basis. Each squad would have an alternating rotation of two- and three-day combinations. The four squads work opposite each other. Two share the same work hours, and the other two share the same day-off rotation. The rotation permits each squad to have every other weekend off. This schedule calls for seven 12-hour shifts over the two-week period. This will result in 84 work hours in the two-week period. If the ATPD (and departments use this schedule) work under a 40-hour workweek payroll plan, the department would need to fund four extra hours each period or require officers to use four hours of time off each period. The logistics of the 84-hour period would need to be determined by the department.

The Pitman schedule consists of the rotation of days off shown in Table 2.7.

The 6-squad, 12-hour deployment model presented in Table 2.7 offers an improvement over the plan described in the example of the ATPD. It features many of the important elements of police shift work that an assessment of patrol deployment should consider.

1. Provides supervision throughout the day.
2. Staffs up with personnel resources during the times needed the most and staffs down when personnel are need the least.
3. Provides for an acceptable minimum number of officers on patrol.
4. Has steady start and end times.
5. Minimizes the number of days worked consecutively, and maximizes time off, including weekends.
6. Minimizes the "silo" effect by having overlapping squads that can communicate more effectively and share information.

Table 2.7 Pittman Day Off Rotation

A	DAY	6AM TO 6PM	DDOODDD-OODDOOO
B	NIGHT	6PM TO 6AM	NNOONNN-OONNOOO
C	DAY	6AM TO 6PM	OODDOOO-DDOODDD
D	NIGHT	6PM TO 6AM	OONNOOO-NNOONNN
E	AFTERNOON	12PM TO 12AM	AAOOAAA-OOAAOOO
F	AFTERNOON	12PM TO 12AM	OOAAOOO-AAOOAAA

The next section discusses the 10-hour shift deployment model. This is an equally popular shift schedule in police departments in the U.S. However, it has numerous disadvantages, and if not developed and implemented properly and with careful management, the 10-hour shift plan can be the most inefficient work schedule that a department would consider.

The 10-hour Shift Deployment Model. The 10-hour shift is very popular in policing in the U.S. There is no data available that demonstrates the percentage of police departments using a 10-hour shift. However, there is an abundant amount of anecdotal evidence that support the popularity of the 10-hour shift, particularly in the west and southwestern parts of the U.S. Like all other shift lengths, the 10-hour shift poses advantages and disadvantages. On the positive side, the 10-hour shift requires fewer work appearances for officers and supervisors than the typical 8-hour shift. As reported by Amendola et al. (2011), fewer appearances, and conversely more days off, translates into a higher quality of life away from work. Fewer workdays also translate into less time spent commuting. From an operational perspective, the 10-hour shift results in a greater percentage of officers working on any given day, thus more officers to deploy toward crime, traffic, disorder, and community issues at any one time. This shift also affords a tight unity of command with supervisors and officers working together each shift. This promotes better supervision and better esprit de corps among employees.

On the negative side, 10-hour shifts, in general, are difficult to implement. Since 10-hour blocks of time do not divide evenly into a 24-hour period, adjustments and overlaps are necessary. The way these overlaps are designed is critical to the efficiency of the 10-hour shift length. The typical overlap with the 10-hour shift is found in one of four different ways. First, and the most inefficient, is using three 10-hour shifts and placing the overlaps at various times during the day. With three 10-hour shifts, six hours of overlap are created and departments around the country have distributed these six hours in many ways. Some are more efficient than others. The worst possible approach with three 10-hour shifts is to simply add two hours to each shift. Under such a model, patrol shifts would be deployed from 7:00 a.m. to 5:00 p.m., from 3:00 p.m. to 1:00 p.m., and from 11:00 p.m. to 9:00 a.m. This is a simplistic illustration, and departments around the country have many different iterations of this model with different start and overlap times. Regardless of the exact combination of starts and overlaps, this approach is the most inefficient. Simply adding two hours to the beginning or end of each shift does not properly consider the operational needs of the department in the first place. Unless there are data to support have twice as many officers assigned for two-hour intervals at various parts of the day, this model does little to conform with the main purpose of shift design and deployment, which is to design a schedule to meet operational demands.

The next approach still relies on three 10-hour shifts, but the overlaps are created in such a way as to address some of those operational demands. One of the most common approaches here is to staff a larger block of time to periods of high CFS volume. For example, many departments using this approach will deploy two shifts from 9:00 p.m. to 1:00 a.m., or from 3:00 p.m. to 7:00 p.m. when demand is high. The other overlap times are then used to cover shift changes so that there are always officers on patrol and ready to respond to CFS.

The third way 10-hour shifts are deployed is by adding a fourth shift to the patrol schedule. Adding a fourth shift each day increases the number of overlaps that are available. Now there a 40 hours of shift assignments that need scheduling, therefore generating 16 hours of overlapping shifts. With a fourth shift, a new shift starts essentially every four hours. Under this approach, departments can generate overlapping coverage during extended periods throughout the day and cover 16 hours with double coverage and 8 hours with single coverage of patrol shifts. In addition, the extended overlap greatly minimizes the "end of shift slow-down" that seems to be occurring. Experience with other departments using this type of schedule indicates that shifts transition more smoothly without CFS stacking up or officers requiring time to be out-of-service for administrative functions. Since shifts are doubled for most of the day the perception of a "hand-off" at the end of one shift to the beginning of the next shift does not occur. Adding the fourth shift, therefore, would eliminate those jagged spikes that are present now in the workload saturation figures, ensuring a steadier allocation of personnel throughout the day.

The last type of 10-hour shift that is typically seen in policing is the "power" shift. The power shift is one that is simply added, or laid on top of, an existing shift rotation plan either in 8-hour or 12-hour designs. The 10-hour shift is not part of the rotation, it's just layered on top of the existing patrol schedule and provides operational support during times of high demand. Departments using this approach will typically deploy a power shift from 3:00 p.m. to 1:00 a.m., or 6:00 p.m. to 4:00 a.m. to support the existing patrol shifts. So, for example, the department would deploy three conventional 8-hours shifts that begin at 7:00 a.m., 3:00 p.m., and 11:00 p.m. and then add the fourth 10-hour shift as an overlay to these shifts.

Table 2.8 illustrates an example of how the deployment of patrol personnel under a 4-squad, 10-hour, shift might look in the ATPD. Under this model the officers on patrol are evenly divided into one of four squads. The squads would work shifts from 6:00 a.m. to 4:00 p.m., 10:00 a.m. to 8:00 p.m., 4:00 p.m. to 2:00 a.m., and 8:00 p.m. to 6:00 a.m. This shift alignment would mean that between 10:00 a.m. and 2:00 a.m. two patrol squads would be assigned to work, and between 2:00 a.m. and 10:00 a.m. only one squad would be assigned to work. This alignment provides the advantage of having more officers assigned to work during the busiest times of the day, and fewer when workload demands are less.

Because of the nature of 10-hour shifts and the structure of a conventional work-week, officers working this schedule are given four consecutive workdays followed by three consecutive days off, which are fixed each week. The four-day on, three-day off rotation, produces seven possible combinations of days off/on. The ideal situation would be to have seven officers assigned to each one of the four patrol shifts in this model. This would allow for uniformed coverage during each shift, with four officers assigned to work, and three officers off each day.

Table 2.8 shows teams of officers report for duty at multiple occasions throughout the day. From 10:00 a.m. all the way until 2:00 a.m., there are two teams assigned at the same time, which results in twice as many officers assigned to patrol during these times.

Police departments with fewer than 34 officers assigned to patrol should not consider implementing a 10-hour work schedule. To maximize the benefits of a 10-hour patrol deployment plan there should be a minimum of six sergeants and 28 police officers. Twenty-eight officers would be the required number to staff all day on/off combinations and always

Table 2.8 Shift Deployment Example, 4-Squad – 10-Hour Plan

Hour	1000x2000	2000x0600	0600x1600	1600x0200	Total
12:00 AM		X		X	2
1:00 AM		X		X	2
2:00 AM		X			1
3:00 AM		X			1
4:00 AM		X			1
5:00 AM		X			1
6:00 AM			X		1
7:00 AM			X		1
8:00 AM			X		1
9:00 AM			X		1
10:00 AM	X		X		2
11:00 AM	X		X		2
12:00 PM	X		X		2
1:00 PM	X		X		2
2:00 PM	X		X		2
3:00 PM	X		X		2
4:00 PM	X			X	2
5:00 PM	X			X	2
6:00 PM	X			X	2
7:00 PM	X			X	2
8:00 PM		X		X	2
9:00 PM		X		X	2
10:00 PM		X		X	2
11:00 PM		X		X	2

provide a balanced number of patrol personnel. With 28 officers assigned there would be seven in each shift, four assigned to work and three off every day. Applying these staffing levels to the deployment plan in Table 2.8 would result in four officers assigned from 2:00 a.m. to 10:00 a.m. and eight officers assigned from 10:00 a.m. to 2:00 a.m. If this deployment plan can support the workload from a given community, then it is an efficient use of personnel resources. Police departments with fewer than the needed staff to support the efficient implementation of this patrol deployment model risk inefficiencies and operational shortcomings.

Another danger in implementing the 10-hour deployment plan for patrol is the design of the rotation for days off. Many departments, however, leverage the compressed work week with 10-hour shifts to create overlap days. The overlap day is generated when two-sides of the patrol shift are working at the same time. Instead of evenly distributing the days on/off across seven combinations, departments reduce these combinations to two: Sunday through Wednesday workdays with Thursday, Friday, and Saturday off, and Wednesday through Saturday workdays, with Sunday, Monday, and Tuesday off. This is a very worker-friendly schedule and provides for part of every weekend off. It is also very inefficient.

Many departments that have 10-hour patrol deployment plans rely on these days off/ on rotation. The rationale behind this approach generally considers the overlap day as an opportunity to conduct training or deploy officers to hot-spots and conduct saturation patrol. Patrol operations is the topic in the next chapter, and we will discuss the various approaches to policing; however, there isn't a strong justification to deploying officers to target hot-spots on Wednesdays, unless of course there is justification that Wednesdays in the community are the most problematic day of the week. This is usually not the case. In most instances, the 10-hour deployment plan with two sides, and an overlap day, is designed by convenience and does not really meet the operational needs of a police department. The goal of creating efficient patrol deployment schedules is to meet operational demands with the appropriate level of personnel. While training is an important part of police management, it is not an operational reality. Police departments must consider other methods to accommodate training needs and should develop deployment schedules to address workload demands first and all other things a distant second.

Conclusion

This chapter explored the important issue of patrol allocation and deployments. An historical view of staffing models is presented with a call for departments to rely on workload models to staff patrol. We argue that a simple "Rule of 60" can be applied, which calls for about 60% of all sworn officers in a department assigned to patrol, and that no more than 60% of their available time should be dedicated to work. The chapter also discusses the advantages and disadvantages of various shift lengths. And these issues are illustrated by using two fictitious police departments to model workload and staffing.

References

Amendola, K. L., Weisburd, D., Hamilton, E. E., Jones, G., & Slipka, M. (2011). *The Impact of Shift Length on Policing Performance: Health, Quality of Life, Sleep, Fatigue, and Extra-Duty Employment*. National Institute of Justice.

Ayres, R. (1977). Case studies of police strikes in two cities: Albuquerque and Oklahoma City. *Journal of Police Science and Administration*, 5, 19–31.

Beck, B., Antonelli, J., & Piñeros, G. (2022). Effects of New York City's neighborhood policing policy. *Police Quarterly*, 25(4), 470–496.

Bopp, W. J., Chignell, P., & Maddox, C. (1977). San Francisco police strike of 1975: A Case Study. *Journal of Police Science and Administration*, 5(1), 32–42.

Brotheim, H. (2003). A proven staffing methodology. *Journal of California Law Enforcement*, 37(1), 9–13.

Curtin, K. M., Hayslett-McCall, K., & Fang, Q. (2010). Determining optimal police patrol areas with maximal covering and backup covering location models. *Networks and Spatial Economics*, 10(1), 125–145.

Giacopassi, D. J., & Sparger, J. R. (1981). The Memphis police strike: A retrospective analysis. *American Journal of Criminal Justice*, 6(2), 39–52.

Greene, J. R., & Taylor, R. B. (1991). Community-based policing and foot patrol: Issues of theory and evaluation. In J. R. Green and S. D. Mastrofiski (eds.). *Community Policing: Rhetoric or Reality*. Praeger.

Edwards, D. 2011. *Smarter, Faster, Cheaper: An Operational Efficiency Benchmarking Study of 100 American Cities*. IBM.

Felson, M. (1993). *Crime and Everyday Life: Insight and Implications for Society*. Pine Forge Press.

Fritsch, E. J., Liederbach, J., & Taylor, R. W. (2009). *Police Patrol Allocation and Deployment*. Pearson Education, Inc.

Hollis, M., & Wilson, J. (2015). Police staffing levels: Disaggregating the variation. *Policing: An International Journal*, 38(4), 820–839.

Huddleston, J. R. (2005). *Lincoln Institute of Land Policy Workshop on Curriculum for Graduate Planning Programs: The Nuts and Bolts of Development Finance*. University of Wisconsin-Madison

International Association of Chiefs of Police. (2005). *Research Center Directorate Perspective: Police Officer to Population Ratios*. IACP.

Kelling, G.L., & Moore, M.H. (1988). *The Evolving Strategy of Policing*. Washington, DC: U.S. Department of Justice.

Maloney, M., & Moty, L. (2002). The impact of community growth on the staffing and structure of a midsized police department. *FBU Law Enforcement Bulletin*, 71(1), 8–13.

McCabe, J. (2013). *Police Allocation and Deployment*. ICMA.

National Institute of Justice. (1967). *The Challenge of Crime in a Free Society: A Report by the President's Commission on Law Enforcement and the Administration of Justice*. NIJ.

Northwestern University Traffic Institute. (1993). *Police Allocation Manual: Determination of the Number and Allocation of Personnel for Patrol Services for State Police Departments*. National Highway Traffic Safety Administration. www.nhtsa.gov/people/injury/enforce/pub/stallocm.pdf

Overland Park, KS. (2022). *Benchmark Cities Survey*. Overland Park.

Srinivasan, S., Sorrell, T., Brooks, J., Edwards, D. McDougle, R. (2013). Workforce assessment method for an urban police department using analytics to estimate patrol staffing. *Policing: An International Journal*, 36(4), 702–718.

U.S. Department of Justice, Office of Community Oriented Policing Services. (2011). *The Impact of the Economic Downturn on American Police Agencies*. Washington, D.C.

U.S. Federal Bureau Of Investigation.(2014). *Uniform crime reporting handbook: UCR*. Washington, D.C.: U.S. Dept. of Justice, Federal Bureau of Investigation. https://ucr.fbi.gov/crime-in-the-u.s/2014/crime-in-the-u.s.-2014/cius-home

Vose, B., Miller, J. M., & Koskinen, S. (2020). Law enforcement manpower analysis: An enhanced calculation model. *Policing: An International Journal*, 43(3), 511–523.

Webber, A. M. (1991). Crime and management: An interview with New York City Police Commissioner Lee P. Brown. *Harvard Business Review*, May–June, 1991.

Wilson, J. (2012). Articulating the dynamic police staffing challenges: An examination of supply and demand. *Policing: An International Journal of Police Strategies and Management*, 35(2), 327–355.

Wilson, J., & Heinonen, J. (2011). Advancing police science: Implications from a national survey of police staffing. *Police Quarterly*, 14(3), 277–297.

Wilson, J., & Weiss, A. (2014). Police staffing allocations and managing workload demand: A critical assessment of existing practices. *Policing*, 8(2), 96–108.

Chapter 3

Assessing Patrol Operations

Introduction

Assessing patrol operations is the next important step after making allocation and deployment decisions. With personnel resources properly allocated to patrol and deployed during the times when they are needed most, attention can be turned to the activities the officers are engaged in, whether these activities are being done efficiently, and to what extent, if any, the officers are having an impact on the goals of the department. Essentially, this chapter explores the what, how, and why of patrol operations and explores issues of relevance, efficiency, and effectiveness. In other words, what are patrol officers doing, and are these activities efficient and effective?

Kelling and Moore's seminal work on the evolving strategy of policing describes three commonly accepted eras of policing (Kelling and Moore, 1988). According to their paradigm, policing started in the mid-nineteenth century with the "political" era, evolved into the "reform" era towards the beginning of the twentieth century, and then continued to evolve into the "community policing" era in the late 1960s. These eras were characterized by certain common elements and emerged in response to problems associated with the previous era. For example, the community policing era evolved because the strategic focus of the police in the reform era was disengaged from the community and narrowly viewed their role as crime-fighters. The social upheaval of the 1960s illustrated the problems of an insular and distant crime-fighter and ushered in a new approach to policing.

Since this article was written, events are forcing the police to evolve even further. The crime wave of the 1980s and early 1990s ushered in zero-tolerance and quality of life enforcement strategies. The attacks on September 11 pivoted the police towards intelligence-led policing and counterterrorism. The public outcry regarding police use of force witnessed in Ferguson, Baltimore, and New York, required yet a new evolution in policing towards neighborhood policing. The recent past, since Kelling and Moore's work, has not produced an identified, separate, and distinct, new era, but the recognition that the policing function is rapidly evolving in the United States. The current strategic paradigm of policing likely embraces the characteristics of all the eras, and models the best qualities of each while eliminating the worst.

Similarly, the police function in society has been conceptualized to take on different styles. Wilson's work identified three different styles of policing: service, watchman, and legalistic. These styles were not considered to be unilaterally determined by the department but emerged as a function of the type of community being policed.

DOI: 10.4324/9781003396437-3

Suburban, affluent, homogenous communities, for example, would adopt a service or watchman style. Urban, heterogeneous communities would adopt a more legalistic style (Wilson, 1968).

The confluence of strategy and style has created a wide variety of programs, policies, and tactics implemented by local police departments. Problem-solving, directed, or hot-spot patrol, gang and drug crackdowns, and many others have been part of the police operational arsenal. In addition, while strategy and style imply characteristics of an entire police department, they have implications for patrol operations. Therefore, the strategy and style lead to the policies and tactics that drive patrol operations. An appropriate assessment of the effectiveness and efficiency of patrol operation would therefore consider these factors and use them to guide that assessment. Are we effective? Well, effective at doing what? It depends on the policing style embraced by your community, and the strategic alignment of the department. Understanding these "big ticket" items will allow for a better understanding of what functions patrol officers should be performing: are these functions making an impact on the strategic goals of the department.

The chapter starts with a broad strategic and organizational perspective, and then drills down to the individual patrol officer, looking at activities, supervision, and equipment along the way. Assessment needs to occur at every level and the chapter outlines what should be assessed at these levels, and potential methods and measures to conduct that assessment.

Police Strategy

American policing is a product of its English heritage. In 1829, the London Metropolitan Police Department emerged from an extended period of unrest, disorder, and crime. Robert Peel, the "father" of modern policing, fought for decades to establish an organization that could respond to the growing incidents of social disorder in London. Still today, the officers are known as "Bobbies" or "Peelers" in honor of Peel. The police in London would be different and embrace a mission that focused on crime prevention and not just respond to crime after it happened. Peel also embraced a utilitarian ideal that the police should be a part of the community. To distinguish them from the military "Red Coats," the Bobbies would perform their duties in blue overcoats and be considered part of the fabric of local control of crime and disorder. One of Peel's famous quotes is: "the police are the public and the public are the police" (Patterson, 2023).

This "brand" was central in the development of the American police and contributed to three distinct characteristics of policing. With the high value placed on individual liberty and the rule of law, and the ideal of a limited government, American policing would feature a characteristic of limited authority. The second characteristic is local control. In 2020, the U.S. Department of Justice reported that there are almost 18,000 law enforcement agencies in their Census of State and Local Law Enforcement Agencies. The product of this local control is the third characterisitc, which is a fragmented system of law enforcement that inhibits coordination and national control (D.O.J., 2022).

The first "modern" police department to emerge in the U.S. was the NYPD in 1845. Similar social and political events in New York, and other cities in the U.S., forced them to confront a rising tide of social unrest and disorder. Rapidly increasing urban population, industrialization, civil unrest, and crime, overwhelmed traditional mechanisms of social control, and required the establishment of an organization that could help. These early departments borrowed from the London example and adopted the mission of crime prevention, a quasi-military organizational structure, and the deployment of officers on foot patrol on geographically specific "beats."

From these humble beginnings, American policing evolved over time. Scholars of American policing place this evolution into four eras. The current day function and structure of police departments can be traced back to features that developed during eras, and understanding this history will have importance in understanding the type of patrol that exists today.

The "political" era spanned the period from approximately 1830 to 1900. In these early years, the police were agents of the local political establishment. The term "precinct" as used in political elections became synonymous with the police "precinct" and illustrates how closely politics and the police are related. The police function varied but focused on crime prevention and order maintenance. However, the police also performed any service that was deemed appropriate by the political powers in place. The police patrol on foot and were assigned regularly to the same areas. This allowed them to become intimately familiar with the local conditions and the people that lived and worked on their beats (Kelling and Moore, 1988).

As cities matured and social disorder stabilized, the middle class became prominent. Business and civic groups saw the concentration of police power in the hands of the political establishment as a threat to order. The system was also rife with corruption where the police enforced the law at the behest of the political establishment and not necessarily in the interests of the public. In addition, the decentralized and limited ability of officers assigned to beats was very inefficient. New modes of transportation and communication were emerging and the deployment of officers to foot patrol was no longer the most efficient way to respond to public demands for service.

The original ideals of early American policing remain with us today. The notion of limited and local control of the police is clear. Most police departments in the U.S. feature police commissions, or some other entity, that have ultimate oversight over the department. These governing bodies hire and fire personnel and influence the general approach of the police in their community. In addition, the political era featured a close connection, if not partnership, between the police and the public. This is a prominent feature of modern American policing.

The "reform" era, from 1900 to 1960, ushered in a time of professionalization of the police. With the growing dissatisfaction about inefficiency and corruption, the police rejected politics and patronage and embraced a system of civil service to hire and promote officers. The police function narrowed to crime control and the social service functions were eschewed in favor of crime control with the image of an impartial law enforcer. This era also witnessed the deployment of officers in automobiles. Officers in cars could respond to calls quicker and cover more geography than officers on foot patrol. Later in the era, the 9-1-1 system created a simple method to summon the police. This strategic approach is also called the "traditional" approach to policing. This system, however, removed the officers from close connection with the community and isolated them in cars. This isolation led to a perception of unresponsiveness and distrust. The police response to civil unrest and increases in crime during the 1960s exposed the glaring inefficiencies of this era of policing (Kelling and Moore, 1988).

The President's Commission on Law Enforcement and Administration of Justice report in 1967 called for a sea change in the way police operated. The report concluded that the police needed to be fairer and use force more prudently, particularly with juveniles and minority groups. It also called for a renewed focus on working with the community to fight crime and disorder together. Moreover, it called for greater screening, training, and education for police officers in the U.S. Essentially, the traditional approach to police service delivery from the previous era needed modification to make it more community-centered and less distant.

The President's Commission was the fulcrum that ushered in a new era of policing called the "community policing" era. This era runs from the 1960s to the present day. The hallmarks of the reform era, however, are clearly baked into the operations of current patrol operations. The use of emergency communications and 9-1-1 systems, coupled with the deployment of officers in cars, are a fixture in American policing. The civil service system, hierarchical and quasi-military organization, and crime control functions are common elements of current-day American policing (President's Commission on Law Enforcement, 1967).

The community policing era, however, asks for a renewed connection to the community with an emphasis on sharing the burden of dealing with crime and disorder. The police role would shift from an impartial professional to a partner invested with the support of the community. The "beat" would re-emerge as a mode of deployment. Foot patrol allows for closer proximity to community residents and businesses and this proximity creates a better understanding of the community and permits the police to solve crime and disorder problems more effectively. The community policing era also called for a renewed and broader approach to the police mandate. Not just crime fighters, the police role would expand to resemble the political era functions and include order maintenance and services activities identified by the community in whatever form they might take (Trojanowicz and Bucqueroux, 1990).

Ask any police chief today if their department practices community policing, and the universal answer will be "yes!" Ask the follow-up question and ask the chief to describe exactly what that means and how they do it and you will get 18,000 different answers. Attempts since the 1960s define community policing as a philosophy and a strategy that have identifiable tactics and organizational requirements. Police chiefs cannot say that they do not practice community policing because that would infer that they do not consider the community important. However, the lack of precision in the concept of community policing makes it impossible to implement.

The elements from this era, however, are another enduring part of the police tradition in the U.S. Police–community partnerships are an important ingredient in the police function. The recognition that the police need to work closely with the community as co-producers of crime prevention and order maintenance is clear. Police departments around the country engage communities in meaningful ways with a variety of programs and policies designed with the philosophy of this era in mind.

Since its reemergence as an ideal of American policing in the 1960s, community policing suffered many setbacks. The economic recession in 1973 sent local budgets into a tailspin. The desire to deploy more officers on foot and support community programs took a backseat to the need to balance budgets and maintain minimum functioning. This generally meant that handling calls for service that came from 9-1-1 (reform era function) took precedent over community policing. In 1975, for example, the NYPD laid-off more than 5,000 police officers to accommodate budget cuts that fiscal year. Communities around the country experienced similar financial crises and simply could not afford community policing (Ferretti, 1985).

As communities emerged from the financial distress of the 1970s, crime became a problem. The "war on drugs" started by President Nixon in 1971 didn't really materialize until the early 1980s. The insurgence of illicit drugs into communities and the scale-back of police and enforcement because of fiscal restraints contributed to a rising tide of crime.

By the time communities got "back on their" feet financially in the early 1980s, crime was considered a major problem. President Reagan renewed the "war on drugs," enacting the Comprehensive Crime Control Act in 1984 that significantly expanded penalties for drug possession and established a system of mandatory minimum sentences. Community policing was pushed aside during this time while law enforcement waged war against drugs and crime (Hodge and Dholakia, 2021).

The attacks on the U.S. on September 11, 2001, also influenced the police function. Now police officers in our communities are not just expected to deal with crime and disorder, they are expected to be first responders to terrorism. In addition, departments across the country participate in joint intelligence task forces to process information into intelligence about terrorist activities. In a similar vein, the events at Columbine H.S. and the scourge of school shootings are leaving an indelible mark on the functions of the police. The police need to develop a "warrior" mindset and be capable of responding instantly to terrorist attacks and mass-shooting events. This mindset comes with a price (Council of State Govt., 2022).

Lastly, the police function is experiencing what is being called "The National Police Crisis." Racial profiling, police brutality, and police corruption are again center stage. The American public is witnessed to shocking incidents of police misconduct. Smart-phone videos seem to appear almost daily showing graphic imagery incidents of police shootings and mistreatment of the public (Walker and Katz, 2022).

The first U.S. Department of Justice case involved the Pittsburgh Police Bureau in 1997. Other cities and state agencies around the country were investigated and charged by the Justice Department for various civil rights violations since then. The Obama administration quickened the pace on these investigations and suits by DOJ and now more than 20 major police departments in the U.S. are under some form of federal oversight. It is hard to determine the lasting impact these efforts will have; however, the reforms being mandated include changes to use-of-force policies, racial profiling, and handling complaints from the public, and improved training for the police (Davis et al., 2006).

The present-day police function exhibits features from all these eras. The "reform" era was the most dominant on police organizations and we can see that the elements of rapid response and patrolling geographic beats by officers in cars are the most notable features of American policing. There is no turning back on these things now, and the public expects that they can call 9-1-1 and get a police response in a reasonable time. Community policing as well has an enduring impact on the police function. It is true that no police chief would ever disavow community policing, but operationalizing this important concept is a challenge. Police departments need to embrace this approach and implement community policing in a way that is not marginal to the operation. Community groups need an active voice in police operations and every police department should be engaging in meaningful partnerships with them. Giving the community more than just a voice is an important part of dealing with the "national police crisis" currently gripping police departments.

Since the identification of community policing as an era, other policing strategies have emerged. Data-driven policing, pioneered by the NYPD with Compstat, relies on crime data and mapping technology to hold local commanders responsible for crime in their areas. Similarly, hot-spot and problem-oriented policing are strategies police departments employ to identify and eliminate problem areas in the community. Social media is an important development in policing. It is a tool that departments use to manage operations, interact with communities, and combat crime. The Social Medial the Internet and Law Enforcement (SMILE) conference is a leading platform helping police departments adopt social media tools and policies for outreach, crime prevention, and investigations. Cyber-crime and the criminal threats posed by the internet is a powerful force shaping policing strategies in the U.S.

Understanding the evolution of policing in the U.S. is important to understand patrol operations in any police department. Assessing patrol operations cannot occur in a vacuum and must consider the strategic approach employed by the department. Several questions need to be considered:

- What type of strategy does my department employ? How do you know?
- Is the strategy efficient? Is it effective? How do you know?
- Is this the right strategic approach for my department?
- Is there an opportunity to do things differently?
- What approaches could my department consider?

For assessing patrol operations, in context with the evolving and competing strategies of the police, it is necessary to consider the main strategic dimensions simultaneously. The likelihood is that every police department engages all the different strategic variations at the same time. There are no "purest" organizations. Police departments do not rely only on a traditional approach, or community policing, or data-driven policing. They do all three. The concentration of operations in anyone of these approaches is the important thing to consider. If a department considers itself a community policing department, but patrol officers engage in little or no community policing activities then the department is not aligned. In addition, since all police patrol operations involve the traditional approach, there needs to be an assessment of how efficient the department is at handling CFS.

Layered on top of this assessment, consideration must be given to the relationship between reactive and proactive activities. Patrol work is largely reactive. When someone calls 9-1-1 the officer reacts to this CFS, handles the assignment, and waits for the next CFS. Proactive patrol seeks to prevent crime from happening in the first place. Under a proactive approach, officers can either work with communities to identify areas of concern or rely on criminal intelligence or other sources of information to direct their activities. The question is not whether patrol operations in a police department are either reactive or proactive; it is both. The assessment considers the degree to which patrol operations exist along the spectrum from reactive to proactive and is that the right mix given the strategic goals of the department in general. Sound patrol operations incorporate traditional and community policing approaches in both a reactive and proactive fashion. Essentially, this calls for a balance between assessing what officers are doing when they are called for service (reactive) to what they are doing when they are not being called (proactive). The following sections elaborate on effective patrol strategies across these dimensions.

Reactive Patrol

The largest amount of any police department's overall work is undoubtedly committed to reactive patrol. Chapter 2 argues that no more than 60 percent of all sworn personnel in any given police department should be allocated to patrol operations, and no more than 60 percent of the officers working on patrol should be committed to workload demands from the public. Combining these figures suggests, therefore, that more than on-third of all the work done in a police department could involve reactive patrol. So, if patrol is the "backbone" of a police department, reactive patrol is the cornerstone, upon which the rest of the patrol function is positioned.

Before we can dive into the "nuts and bolts" of assessing reactive patrol, there are many myths that need confronting. While reactive patrol consists of the lions-share of work activities for a police department there are limitations on what it can and cannot do. What we know about patrol comes from groundbreaking research by police scholars in the 70s and 80s. There is an expectation that the police will prevent and solve crime. Research supports this notion, but the impact a police department can have on crime in a community will not come from the activities associated with reactive patrol.

The Kansas City Preventative Patrol Experiment explored the impact that police patrol had on crime, traffic crashes, perceptions of fear, and response times to CFS in Kansas City, MO in the early 70s. The conclusions were startling. It turned out that removing officers from their patrol areas and adding them to adjacent patrol areas, therefore "saturating" those areas with patrol officers, did not significantly influence conditions in the community. Crime did not increase in the areas where the officers were removed, and the perception of crime and the fear of crime did not change. This research was the first to challenge two of the core pillars of reactive patrol: rapid response time and random patrol (Kelling et al., 1974).

The thinking about patrol is that deploying officers to geographic beats will create an "omnipresence" effect in the area. A visible police presence, appearing at random times of the day could create a deterrent effect on crime for the people in that area. Not knowing when the police will be present produces that deterrent effect. The conclusion reached in Kansas City, interpreted eloquently by the late Carl Klockers, is that it makes as much sense to have the police randomly patrol in cars to fight crime as it does to have firefighters patrol randomly in fire trucks to fight fires. Random patrol does not reduce crime or increase the chances of the police making an arrest.

Response time is another "red herring" in the discussion about reactive patrol. Research has consistently shown that response time is not related to reducing crime, increasing the probability of making an arrest, or improving satisfaction with the police response. From a strictly empirical perspective, this makes sense. The average time it takes to dispatch a CFS is around two minutes. In those two minutes from the time a person dials 9-1-1, until an officer is assigned to handle that call, the perpetrator can cover a lot of ground, and this does not consider the delay in time before the victim makes the call in the first place. Even if the officer were around the corner, the lag between criminal event and officer arrival would be too long to matter in the average case. There is a difference, however, between the impact on criminal events and the overall impact on public safety. Looking at response time as simply a function of crime control is narrow-minded, and departments should take a more holistic approach to this issue and look for "reasonable" response times to emergencies. Assuming that response time is not an issue in crime control, the public still should expect a police response in a reasonable amount of time. Defining "reasonable" is a community-to-community process, and while national benchmarks on police response times do exist, assessing police response times needs to include numerous factors.

Another myth regarding the police is that they do an excellent job at solving crimes. Here again, the research shows that the probability of the police "solving" your crime is low; about 20 percent chance overall. The probabilities are different for different crimes. Murder has the highest percentage of crimes solved at around 65 percent, and burglary has the lowest at around 13 percent. The notion that having a police officer respond to a 9-1-1 call will start the process of solving my crime is somewhat misleading. What we also know about solving crime is that the probability significantly increases if the preliminary investigation by the first responding officer is thorough. Even if the overall success of a department is not great in this area, the actions of the first officer on the scene are critical. Locating witnesses, preserving, and collecting evidence, and writing good reports are the hallmarks of a thorough investigation and an important element of reactive patrol (Federal Bureau of Investigation, 2019).

Lastly, the notion that officers on patrol respond to crime and are instrumental in preventing crime from occurring is unfounded. The research shows here that less than 3 percent of all the CFS handled by officers involves a violent crime. Similarly, interceding in an actual crime as it is occurring is even rarer. Most reactive patrol work is involved with order maintenance activities, handling disputes, providing services, responding to accidents and alarms, and preparing paperwork. It can be described as hours of boredom punctuated by moments of terror.

Summing this all up:

1. The number of officers on patrol does not influence crime, traffic safety, and disorder in the community.
2. Random patrolling of "beats" is unrelated to crime control.
3. Rapid response times to CFS are unrelated to crime control.
4. Patrol involves service activities.

Police managers should not expect the reactive patrol function to be a tool in fighting crime. Since the advent of the 9-1-1 system, and the availability of 24-hour, seven-day, emergency response to CFS, police departments saddled with this responsibility need to assess it carefully. It is not a panacea for crime control. It is a necessary function, and one of the most important services provided to a community. In general, the public expectation of police patrol is that officers are available to respond to emergencies, and that they do so in a reasonably prompt manner. Therefore, police departments should be looking at these two pillars: AVAILABILITY and REASONABLE RESPONSE TIME as the measures of success. These two concepts work together. To have patrol officers able to respond promptly there must be enough of them available throughout the day. Ensuring this level of availability means assessing the kinds of CFS they handle in the first place and eliminating the non-emergency and frivolous ones. Preserving emergency resources for emergencies is the most important function of patrol managers as they assess patrol operations. This involves three processes. First, managers need to manage the demand and evaluate the type and frequency of CFS. Second, there needs to be an assessment of the relative efficiency of how these CFS are handled. Third, these needs to be an assessment of the processes by which alternative methods are used to handle non-emergency demands made by the public. To illustrate these processes, we will reintroduce the data used in Chapter 2 from the Anytown Police Department (ATPD).

A. Demand management – answering only emergencies

Table 3.1 illustrates the CFS breakdown for the ATPD. The first step in demand management is to inspect the major categories of CFS presented here and determine the threshold issue of whether a response is required, and if the answer to this question is "yes" then minimize the number of responses to the greatest extent possible.

Table 3.1 shows that the ATPD responded to more than 2,000 traffic crashes in the 12-month period reported here. Automobile accidents are another category of call for which the response by a sworn officer is questionable. It is recommended that police departments consider a policy of responding to and investigating routine traffic accidents (property damage only, no criminality) be minimized or discontinued altogether. Most accidents involve

Table 3.1 Breakdown of CFS for the Anytown[2] Police Department

Category	Public-initiated			Officer-initiated		
	Minutes	Calls	Units	Minutes	Calls	Units
Accident	45.2	1,945	1.6	39.2	140	1.6
Alarm	16.8	1,124	2.3	3.4	3	1.0
Animal	27.9	435	1.3	10.3	14	1.1
Assist citizen	27.5	1,352	1.5	13.4	575	1.1
Assist other agency	31.4	642	1.9	21.1	127	1.4
Check/investigation	35.6	3,464	2.1	52.1	285	1.5
Crime – persons	85.0	332	3.0	70.8	178	2.8
Crime – property	56.0	2,413	2.1	57.5	134	1.9
Disturbance	38.4	22	2.5	31.0	5	2.0
Juvenile	36.7	202	1.9	29.4	35	1.7
Miscellaneous	30.6	949	1.4	15.4	3,922	1.1
Park complaint	18.7	681	1.2	10.5	60	1.0
Prisoner – arrest	95.5	149	2.7	88.5	234	2.3
Prisoner – transport	107.0	172	2.1	108.2	122	2.0
Suspicious person/vehicle	26.4	3,562	2.1	20.2	1,097	1.9
Traffic enforcement	37.1	591	1.6	13.7	8,633	1.2
Total/Average	**36.7**	**18,035**	**1.9**	**19.9**	**15,564**	**1.3**

only property damage to vehicles and the role of an officer is simply report preparation. When injuries occur or vehicles are inoperable and blocking traffic, however, police response is important. Proper training of dispatchers and inquiries by dispatchers during the initial call-taking process can easily triage vehicle accident calls to determine which ones require a police response. Police departments around the country have discontinued assigning police officers to handle routine property damage only accidents. This is a difficult area for police managers to deal with. One the one hand, there is a recognition that the role of the police at the scene of traffic crashes is meaningless. On the other hand, there is a public expectation that traffic crashes require a police response. Balancing reality with public expectations is a challenging task. Assessing these types of CFS is a community function, and not the sole responsibility of the police department. Nonetheless, there is a huge opportunity to minimize responses to routine traffic accidents to preserve time on patrol for officers to do other important functions, which may reduce the accident from occurring in the first place. Therefore, any policy that calls for the indiscriminate dispatch of police officers to routine traffic crashes needs revisiting.

If, after careful consideration, the community still demands a police response in these routine situations alternative methods are available. Police departments across the country are utilizing non-sworn uniformed personnel to handle minor non-emergency calls for service. Individuals in these positions can provide support to sworn officers on patrol. Properly trained and equipped civilian personnel can respond to accident scenes, and other non-emergency CFS, and handle the incidents without the need of a sworn officer.

Alarms

Burglar alarms are another source of wasted patrol resources. False alarms are a source of inefficiency for police operations. The alarm industry is a strong advocate of developing ordinances and procedures to address police response to false alarms and will work closely with any agency exploring this issue. 98 percent of alarm calls that are false are caused by user error, and an alarm management program can address this. According to the data in Table 3.1, the ATPD responded to more than 1,100 alarm CFS. The response to most of these calls is undoubtedly unnecessary, and an inefficient use of police resources.

Many communities in the U.S. have effective Alarm Ordinances that have both registration requirements and penalties for false alarms. In addition, Ordinances often have stipulations for alarm companies and have requirements for their operation. In general, there is usually no charge for the first two alarm responses in a one-year period. Successive false alarm responses by the police incur fees, which usually start at a modest rate and increase in many cases to more than $1,000. Each community has different regulations, but the general approach is to manage and reduce police responses to unnecessary and false alarm CFS.

Similarly, sound assessment of CFS in this category includes analyzing the data on false alarm activations. Undoubtedly, with a greater level of analysis patterns and trends will emerge. Data analysis permits the identification of problematic locations and/or alarm installation companies that are generating many false alarms and work with them to reduce or eliminate future occurrences.

In addition, some communities are enacting a double-call verification protocol. Under such a program, the 911 dispatcher with the alarm company verifies an alarm CFS before an officer is dispatched to respond. In general, responding to false burglar alarms is an inefficient use of police emergency resources. An assessment of patrol operations needs to include an aggressive approach in this area.

Medical Calls

Many police departments assign a police officer to respond to every medical CFS. In medical emergencies, the rapid response of a trained police officer can mean the difference between life and death. For example, it is recommended that officers carry automatic external defibrillators in patrol vehicles. In cardiac CFS, officers can deploy these devices and potentially save lives. The overwhelming number of medical CFS, however, are not life and death. For example, anecdotal accounts of medical CFS by officers on patrol indicate that the role of the officer at these types of CFS is not much more than standing around waiting for the ambulance to leave.

Departments should develop a policy to curtail assigning patrol officers to routine medical CFS. Dispatchers can be trained to triage medical CFS and only assign ones that are appropriate for police officers. Similarly, EMS personnel can be trained to request a police response when one becomes apparent, for example in medical cases that appear to be criminal in nature.

Traffic Enforcement

Table 3.1 shows that the ATPD handled more than 9,000 traffic related CFS, including more than 8,600 traffic stops. This represents almost one-quarter of all CFS (police-initiated and community-initiated combined). It is important to ensure that there is a clear relationship between this level of enforcement and overall traffic safety. This is discussed in detail in Chapter 6 regarding specialized operations. There is an operational assumption that traffic enforcement leads to traffic safety, but this direct connection is not necessarily the case. The point here is that an overwhelming number of CFS and workload is being committed to traffic enforcement without a clear understanding of the outcome of this effort.

Departments and community stakeholders need to evaluate this category of work to consider a more strategic, and ultimately more efficient and effective approach to traffic safety.

Miscellaneous

Table 3.1 reports almost 4,000 "miscellaneous" CFS handled by officers on patrol. The table here collapses many types of CFS into smaller categories for easier discussion. The actual nature of this miscellaneous CFS is undoubtedly broad, and difficult to define, therefore the term miscellaneous applies. Assessment of these types of CFS is critical. If the CFS defies a label it is likely superfluous to emergency operations, but it appears as if these types of CFS are handled every day by officers on patrol in Anytown. What are they? Why are they being dispatched? What are the officers doing in response to these calls? These are the types of questions that need to be answered and are an instrumental part of assessing reactive patrol functions.

Many police departments deploy patrol officers to conduct "patrol checks" during their shifts. Often time departments offer this type of service to residents as an added degree of security while they are away on vacation. In addition, businesses request this type of service. For example, some police departments in the U.S. implement a policy where officers should visit the inside of banks during business hours as a way of deterring bank robbery. From a criminological standpoint, research shows that spending as little as 15 minutes in a crime "hot spot" has a deterrent effect on crime at that location. Therefore, patrol checks, if done correctly, can produce that deterrent effect. Departments need to assess this type of CFS carefully to ensure officers are performing the patrol checks in the right locations, at the right times, for an appropriate length of time. This is discussed later in this chapter under proactive patrol assessment, but the point here is that the data from the CAD system, as illustrated in Table 3.1, needs to be scrutinized very carefully and assessed with an eye towards minimizing non-emergency responses.

B - Assessing CFS Efficiency

Further examination of various elements of the CFS and patrol response data also warrants discussion. Police managers need to leverage the process of collecting and analyzing the data from a department's CAD system in a way to conduct meaningful assessments. As discussed in Chapter 2, those data are extremely useful for understanding the allocation of resources to patrol. The same data that generate the workload figures in that chapter can be used to calculate numerous other variables for assessment. These variables are useful in determining the efficiency of reactive patrol operations. Table reports critical variables that measure patrol efficiency. They are allocation percent, CFS rate, average service times, average number of responding units, total service time, workload saturation, and response time. The table reports the measures for the ATPD along with suggested benchmarks in these areas.

The first data point in the table is the patrol allocation percentage. As discussed in Chapter 2, the patrol allocation in the ATPD is 62.5% for basic patrol resources and this compares favorably with the suggested benchmark of 60%.

The next data point is a variable labeled CFS Rate. The CFS rate is the number of CFS handled by a police department compared to the residential population. The ATPD handled 33,599 CFS in the 12-month period (18,035 from the public, and 15,564 initiated by officers). The service population in Anytown is approximately 37,000 residents. This creates

Table 3.2 CFS Efficiency

Variable Description	Benchmark	Anytown
Patrol Percent	60	62.5
CFS Rate	1	.91
Avg. Service Time Police CFS (min)	15	10.4
Avg. Service Time Public CFS (min)	30	21.2
Avg. # of Responding Units Police CFS	1.2	1.1
Avg. # of Responding Units Community CFS	1.5	1.6
Total Service Time Police CFS (officer-min.)	18	11.4
Total Service Time Community CFS (officer-min.)	45	33.9
Workload Saturation (%)	60	32
Average Response Time (min)	15	8.5
High Priority Response Time (min)	5	6.3

a CFS Rate equal to .91 CFS for every resident. While there is no accepted standard ratio between calls for service and population, studies suggest a CFS-to-population ratio ranging between .4 and 1.0 per persons per year. Lower ratios typically suggest a well-managed approach to CFS. The value of .91 CFS/per thousand/year would suggest that the ATPD is at the higher end of this scale and perhaps responding to more CFS than expected given the size of the community. This would also suggest the need for an appropriate policy for triaging nonemergency calls. As discussed above, a well-managed dispatch system includes a system where CFS are screened, and nuisance calls eliminated before they are dispatched.

Table 3.2 reports average service time for CFS. This is the amount of time, including dispatch and response time, that officers on patrol spend handling CFS. The average service time for a police-initiated CFS is approximately 10.4 minutes; since there is no response time to these types of CFS (the officer is already on scene). For CFS from the public, officers spend on average about 12.7 minutes (21.2 minus 8.5 minutes average response time). Therefore, on the average CFS, the officers on patrol in Anytown spend an average of a little more than 10 minutes with the public. The suggested benchmark is about 15 minutes, which means that the ATPD spends less time than expected handling CFS. The next variable to explore is the number of officers the department assigns to the average CFS. In the ATPD, Table 3.2 reports that 1.6 officers are assigned, which is slightly higher than the suggested benchmark of 1.5 officers per CFS. The number of officers assigned to CFS varies by call type. Reports of crimes in progress will require more than one officer, perhaps many more than one depending on the call. Alarm CFS requires a two-officer response. Routine traffic crashes probably only one officer, as well as many of the other routine non-emergency CFS. The ATPD appears within expected norms here so additional scrutiny is not required. However, if this figure were substantially more or less, this would warrant a much-closed assessment by police managers.

The product of average service time and officers assigned equals "total service time." The ATPD reports a total service time of 33.9 minutes, which is about 25 percent less time than the suggested 45 minutes per CFS. To assess this duration of time many variables need to be considered. Overall, how busy are the officers? Is their shift heavily saturated with workload inhibiting them from spending time with the public? Are they rushing from call to call, or spending too much time handling the work? Is the department more focused on traditional or community policing and should officers be spending more or less time interacting with members of the community? In general, low service times, while not necessarily a problem, can point to other issues in the department. For example, officers are generally concerned about getting tied-up on CFS because they want to remain available to respond to emergencies. When patrol shifts are perceived to be minimally staffed, officers might resist spending much time with callers or being proactive and being too engaged in CFS and other proactive type work. That concern might be manifesting itself here and be responsible for shorter than expected service times. In other words, officers feel the pressure to remain available for emergencies. During routine CFS, this results in completing the assignment quickly and then becoming available again. The quality of these encounters may not be suffering, but the department should be mindful of this situation, and ensure that CFS are being handled as thoroughly and expeditiously as possible.

While response time is not a factor in crime control or caller satisfaction, it is important for police departments to maintain a REASONABLE response time standard. The number of officers on patrol, time of day, traffic volume, population density, and community geography all influence the amount of time it takes to respond to a CFS. There are no requirements in this area, but many police professional groups suggest a range of times that are reasonable. The Benchmark Cities Survey managed by the Overland Park, KS Police Department suggests a target response to "Priority 1" CFS of 5.25 minutes. The definition of priority 1 CFS is likely to be different from agency to agency, however, it is generally assumed to be crimes in progress, and traffic accidents with injuries. The Benchmark Cities survey also reports an average response time of 8.25 minutes to a priority-2 CFS, and a 16.95-minute response to all other calls. The International Association of Chiefs of Police suggests that police departments strive to respond to emergencies in under 5 minutes. Reports from the 10 largest cities in the U.S. show the fastest response time to emergency CFS is in San Francisco with 5.5 minutes to the slowest in Fort Worth at 9.5 minutes on average (Overland Park, KS, 2022). The Center for Public Safety Management suggests an average response time to an emergency of 5 minutes, and 15 minutes for a routine CFS (McCabe, 2013). Table 3.2 reflects this standard.

Compared to the 5–15-minute standard, the ATPD shows a much faster response to routine CFS than expected, but a slightly slower response to emergency CFS. Keeping in mind that each community is different and there are no requirements in this area, departments should assess this carefully. A 6.3-minute average response to an emergency CFS may be appropriate given the resources available and community characteristics. Increasing response time is expensive; therefore, departments must proceed deliberately in this area. If the average time is slower than expected, this requires an analysis of each component of the time (dispatch and travel time) to ensure CFS are being handled as efficiently as possible.

C - Alternatives for Non-Emergency Workload

Research shows that the bulk of reactive patrol work is to non-emergency CFS. Over 85% of all CFS deal with service and order maintenance activities. Proper assessment of this workload suggests that these types of CFS should be eliminated from the workday of officers on patrol. Unfortunately, this is not realistic. Many communities demand that the police respond to every call, no matter how minor, at all hours of the day. In fact, this is the most common position most departments take. It is easier to staff patrol to handle all of the frivolous CFS than to deal with unreasonable community expectations and eliminate these CFS. With this understanding in mind, if police managers cannot prevent the call from being assigned in the first place, then there should be a robust system in place to manage these non-emergency calls when they are made (Neusteter et al., 2019). Typically, these non-emergency CFS management approaches take on one or more of the following methods: deferred response, differential response, and alternative response (Lewin and Acevedo, 1980). Each one of these is discussed below.

Alternative Response – An alternative response is a method of creating different ways for the public to make complaints and interact with the department. Typically, departments around the U.S. use their website and other social media platforms to provide this type of service.

The department website should provide a number of features that would allow the browser to learn about the department's organization as well as link to City services (meeting minutes, online bill paying, etc.). In addition, the website should feature web-based reporting of minor crimes and other incidents online and without the response of an officer. Communities around the country have had success with this additional feature for community members to report minor offenses, such as property damage or lost property; even non-injury traffic accidents can be prepared remotely.

It should be noted that web-based reporting is not a panacea for reducing non-emergency responses. Communities around the country that have developed an online service do not experience a large amount of traffic to the site. Many people prefer to have a police officer respond and take a report directly and are not comfortable reporting crime and disorder remotely. Although this service can alleviate some of the demands from patrol, it will not solve the non-emergency response problem in its entirety. However, assessing patrol operations requires that the department's web presence be scrutinized carefully. Usage data needs to be analyzed and social media platforms need to be active and not passive. A passive approach involves the creation of a website, for example, with that website accepting incoming transactions. The opposite is to push department services outward to the public. Do not wait for responses, actively engage the public with social media and this will become a common form of communication, which will translate into more familiarity with the department services and, therefore, the ability to prepare reports and notify the department about incidents using the online features made available.

Deferred Response – This is a process where CFS are handled later. In addition to the web-based reporting, departments could consider staffing a telephone response program to various categories of CFS. The telephone response or deferred response function could deal with past crimes and routine inquiries to the department, thus eliminating the response of a sworn officer. Nonemergency calls, such as past crimes, minor property damage, and harassment (all of the categories of web-based reporting options) can be handled by this program. Instead of dispatching an officer to these types of calls, or having an officer respond to headquarters off patrol, the information is deferred (delayed) until a staff member becomes available to respond to the call. This staff member could be a civilian staff member assigned to the police headquarters, an officer assigned to limited duty officer (because of injury, for example), or the officer assigned to that zone when they have available time. This process could divert nonemergency calls from the patrol units, and thus provide officers with more time to engage in proactive and directed patrols or traffic enforcement duties.

Differential Response – This is a system where personnel other than patrol officers handle non-emergency CFS. Many departments rely on non-sworn personnel on patrol to deal with such CFS. Traffic Control Officers (TCO) and Community Service Officers (CSO) are examples of non-sworn personnel positions that departments use to handle non-emergency CFS. In general, personnel assigned to these positions work on patrol, in uniform, but have limited power and authority. They are usually responsible for handling traffic crashes, reports of past minor crime complaints, routine animal calls, etc. The rationale is to have a cadre of personnel available for these non-emergency CFS to keep sworn officers available on patrol for emergencies and proactive enforcement.

All three of these processes can provide valuable support for patrol operations. Police managers need to consider these alternative approaches. The first step is to identify opportunities to reduce demand and triage CFS away from officers on patrol. The next step, after demand has been minimized to the greatest extent possible, is to leverage these non-emergency workload systems to further support patrol. Many communities are adopting 3-1-1 non-emergency systems. Communities implementing 3-1-1 systems typically experience about a 20 percent reduction in calls through the 9-1-1 system. In addition, 3-1-1 systems are evolving from simply non-emergency call systems to cloud-based management systems that are becoming the primary way for the public to document and request services from their local government. Conceptually, all police managers need to consider a 3-1-1 type of approach. The point here is that where 3-1-1 is available and in use, demand for emergency police responses is reduced. This preserves scarce resources and creates the opportunity to redirect these resources from frivolous work to work that is central to the police mission in the first place. If 3-1-1 technology is not available or too costly for a particular community, the spirit of the system needs to be implemented. In some form, there needs to be an outlet for the public to report incidents and access police services that do not involve the immediate response of an officer on patrol. This will make patrol operations more efficient, and create time to engage in proactive patrol, which is instrumental in combatting crime, disorder, and traffic problems.

Proactive Patrol

The first priority for managing patrol operations is to control the level of reactive patrol. There is no escaping the workload demands from the public through 9-1-1- and the associated work that this generates. The previous section discussed strategies to do this and the necessity for a rigorous assessment of this facet of police operations. As Chapter 2 discussed, the saturation of available time spent on police work should not exceed 60 percent during any parts of the day. The 60-percent threshold serves as a useful benchmark to assess the relative business of the patrol function due to reactive work. An important question follows from this approach. What do the officers on patrol do with the rest of the time during the day? Arguably, more than half of an officers shift while on patrol should be "uncommitted" time. The expression "uncommitted" is related to reactive work and not intended to imply that the other half of the day is spent doing nothing. Structuring the "uncommitted" time on patrol is critical. Lazy officers will abuse this "uncommitted" time, avoid other work, and only wait to be summoned by CFS. Active officers will use this "uncommitted" time to engage in procative enforcement, community interactions, but if not structured properly will result in a haphazard approach and not necessarily directed at the overall mission of the department.

The patrol function needs a plan. This plan should address both reactive and proactive patrol. The plan should implement strategies to minimize reactive work, and structure the remaining "uncommitted" time to respond to the overall mission of the department. From a partrol perspective, this includes reducing crime, improving traffic safety, reducing disorder, and promoting positive police–community relationships. The strategic planning process identified in this text provides the blueprint for the department-wide apporach. The approach for the patrol function is no different. It starts with a thorough analysis of the available data, the development and execution of effective strategies, and the relentless follow-up of the impact of those strategies to ensure they are working or to make the changes necessary.

It is also important for the department to assess what kind of policing their community demands. As discussed in the beginning of the chapter, the kind of policing in a community is a function of the character of the community. There will always be an expectation that CFS are handled professionally and promptly, but then what? Police departments implemented a wide array of deployment strategies throughout the years. Some strategies recevied attention in the academic literature and mainstream media, and have merit with regards to improving police operations. Successful integration of these strategies, however, into patrol operations is mostly uncommon.

Problem-oriented policing is the philosophical foundation for several patrol strategies. The goal is to identify the underlying problem at a location and then direct police resources to eliminate that problem. This approach appears in "hot-spot" policing, "directed patrol," "saturation patrol," "high-visibility patrol" and used to support the notion of crackdowns and aggressive patrols. Simply stated, each of these strategic approaches uses information to identify problem areas in the community and then brings police resources to bear on these problems. The research on these approaches indicates that there are both positive and negative outcomes with a "problem-oriented" approach. There is support for the idea that police, when properly directed at a problem, can have an impact on eliminating that problem. However, the lasting impact of these efforts is sometimes questionable (Telep and Higdon, 2019).

Aggressive policing, for example, without community support can engender dissatisfaction from the community. The classic case of this is the NYPD's stop, question, and frisk program, which was determined by the court to be unconstitutional. This was intended to be a crime reduction program, but it resulted in the unlawful stops of thousands of people, mostly black and Hispanic. The "crackdown" was designed to remove guns from the street and eliminate gun violence, but generated widespread community distrust and dissatisfaction (*Floyd et. Al*, 2013).

Others argue that short-term police enforcement at target locations will only serve to displace the crime conditions; to other locations or to different times. Either crime will move to another place, or it will reappear after the police efforts end. Without a long-term and systematic approach targeting the underlying conditions that lead to crime, a short-term approach based narrowly on law enforcement will be ineffective.

Then there are the more structural issues with respect to these approaches. The primary responsibility of officers on patrol is to handle CFS from the community. Engaging in problem-solving programs can interfere with meeting this responsibility. When officers experience "uncommitted" time, they resist engaging in other work because it would make them unavailable for CFS. Problem-solving takes time. Officers need to have the ability to have enough time during the day, and regularly during the year, to address problems. The desire to remain available for emergencies is strong and can have a negative impact on efforts to get patrol officers to deal with problems that do not come from 9-1-1. To deal with this reality, the patrol function needs to be managed appropriately so that the time is created to handle long-term problems and that officers are properly supervised to ensure they are focused on addressing them.

The first step in the assessment of proactive patrol is exploring whether or not uncommitted patrol time is being accounted for in the first place. As the text discusses, strategic planning is essential to effective performance. Integrating strategic plans at all levels of the department is critical to full implementation of these plans. From a patrol perspective, this means not only mazimizing the efficiency of the reactive patrol function, but structuring uncommitted time in a way that addresses the strategic priorities of the department. Therefore, when officers on patrol are not assigned to CFS, there needs to be clear answers to the following:

- What are the officers expected to do?
- What direction are they given?
- Are their activities focused on the problems being faced by the department?
- How is it measured?
- What is the coordination between patrol and the other elements of the department?
- Who is responsible for ensuring implementation?

Answers to these questions are important. In police departments where the use of uncommitted time is not planned rigorously, responses are similar to:

- "the officers are expected to patrol their beats and take proactive enforcement;"
- "the officers know their beats and address crime;" and
- "Officers are expected to be visible on patrol."

Basically, these responses communicate a lack of direction and an unsupervised and unplanned approach to proactive patrol. The appropriate use of uncommitted time needs to incorporate several important characteristics.

1. It needs to be feasible. In other words, patrol officers cannot be expected to dedicate large blocks of time to proactive patrol. They need to be ready to respond to emergencies and will resist efforts to mandate proactive work that will interfere with this readiness.
2. Proactive patrol needs to be linked to the mission of the department and the strategic plans developed to carry out that mission. This typically involves crime reduction, traffic safety, community relations, and improving the quality of life in the community by addressing disorder.
3. Proactive patrol needs to be focused. It's not enough to instruct patrol officers to "address traffic safety." They need to be given the information and intelligence that focuses their enforcement at problematic people, places, and things. So instead of "address traffic safety" the direction is "speed enforcement on Main Street between Beech Ave and Elm Ave, between 2:00 p.m. and 4:00 p.m."
4. It needs to be measurable. Police departments are usually focued on measuring the activity officers produce. How many tickets did you write? How many arrests did you make? These are measures of "output" and while appropriate to assess officer activity, they do not measure whether or not the problem that's being addressed is actually solved. Measures of this nature are "outcome" measures and assess the presence or absence of the particular problem. "Have traffic accidents decreased since the enforcement on Main Street began?" "Did the number of car thefts decrease since we started doing 'checkpoints' in the targeted area?" The measures need to be quantitative illustrations of the problems and not measures of the officers activities. An officer can issue 10,000 tickets and if traffic safety doesn't improve then most of those tickets were wasted effort.
5. Proactive policing needs to be broad-based. It cannot focus solely on crime or traffic. It must incorporate the multi-dimensional realities of police work. Therefore, patrol

officers should be expected to use their uncommitted time to address crime, and traffic satety, and community relations, and disorder control, and any other issue determined to be important by the department, all at the same time.

6. It should be community-focused. Patrol officers often focus their non-committed time on enforcement activities. This is a natural part of their professional mandate and should be encouraged. However, making time for the "softer side" of police work is essential. Uncommmitted time should also be structured to include attendance at community meetings and events, interacting with members of the community on an informal basis, and working with juveniles both in and out of school.

7. Proactive patrol should be team-based. If all items 1 through 6 were implemented by officers on patrol, as individuals, it would be less effective than if they worked as a coordinated team. Departments should avoid leaving the decision on how to spend uncommitted time to the sole discretion of the individual officers. Similarly, individual officers should not be held accountable for the success or failure of the strategic plans. In other words, the focused efforts of officers on patrol should be coordinated by the supervisors on patrol, and they should be held accountable for the performance of their squad/shift/team. Individual officers are limited in what they can accomplish by themselves. Supervisors should use the team aspect already present within patrol squads and leverage this to engage in proactive efforts. Supervisors can also monitor the amount of time being spent on proactive patrol and ensure that reactive patrol readiness is not pre-empted.

In order to implement these items successful patrol operations need to engage in the conventional planning process. There needs to be an accurate identification of the problems to be addressed, and there needs to be a plan developed that embraces the seven items listed above. The first step, therefore, involves the collection, analysis, and dissemination of comprehensive intelligence.

Crime Analysis / Criminal Intelligence

Police departments need to develop a thorough and rigorous criminal intelligence function to support criminal investigations and crime reduction initiatives in general. The first order of business to assess patrol operations is to assess the role of the crime analyst or criminal intelligence officer, or even if there is one linked to patrol.

Crime analysis and criminal intelligence are often conflated and thought to be the same thing. To put it in economic terms, crime analysis is analogous to counting your money, and criminal intelligence is how you spend it. Combining the two disciplines can provide a more accurate picture about where and when crime is occurring, and what to do about it. A police department needs to do both and there is an opportunity to enhance proactive patrol with a vigorous approach in this area. The analysis of crime and traffic data should lead to the creation of actionable intelligence and inform departmental planning. The product of these efforts would lead to the identification of problem areas related to crime, traffic, and disorder, along with specific detailed data for patrol officers to orient their work.

Police departments need to designate a specific person or unit, depending upon the size of the department, to do this work. In smaller departments, it would be appropriate for one sworn officer to coordinate the analysis and intelligence function as an ancillary duty assignment. In large departments, this function could be assigned to a team of officers that processes all the crime and traffic data into intelligence as well as developing strategic plans.

Each agency will have their own approach, but there needs to be a connection between this process and the officers on patrol. Armed with crime and traffic intelligence, as well as the identities and concerns of local community leaders, patrol shifts can structure their uncommitted time to support the strategic efforts of the department.

Ultimately, the responsibility for these efforts should fall under the "criminal intelligence officer" (CIO). The CIO would, therefore, be responsible for preparing strategic crime analyses and trend reports, monitoring and tracking high-propensity offenders, developing, and managing crime prevention programs, securing search warrants, training department personnel, making community and media presentations, exchanging crime information with surrounding agencies, and initiating proactive crime-solving strategies. An additional area of responsibility for the CIO could be debriefing prisoners. Every day people are arrested, booked, and processed by the police. These individuals are potentially an enormous wealth of information about the criminal activities in the community. The CIO should have primary responsibility of not only interviewing (debriefing) prisoners, but also teaching other officers how to conduct an effective prisoner debriefing. Additionally, it would be the CIO's job to develop the questions and areas of inquiry to be broached with the arrested individuals. Keep in mind, the debriefing is not an interrogation about the crime the person is arrested for, but about other incidents and events they might have knowledge about. For example, who is selling drugs, where is stolen property "fenced," who is responsible for the most recent robbery or assault, do you know anyone that steals cars, etc. Asking these types of questions can produce valuable information, but if they are never asked, nothing can be learned.

Most departments take a passive approach, with the analyst sifting through data and documents and sending information out to the operational units in the department. A more active approach is preferred. This approach calls for the CIO to do more than simply provide an account of historical records. Data needs to be mined and processed into actionable intelligence to reduce crime and apprehend offenders.

The basic requirement of the CIO is to illustrate the spatial analysis of crime, traffic, and disorder problems by mapping technology. Maps need to be generated using the CFS data, and crash and crime reports, identify problematic locations in the community and the need to develop specific strategies around those locations.

Figures 3.1–3.4 provide an example of data from the Anytown Police Department. The maps show that there are several distinct incident "hot spots" in the community. Retail, commercial, and traffic conditions command a great deal of attention from ATPD. There are numerous discernable hotspots in this area, as well as sizeable concentrations of CFS in other retail and commercial locations throughout the town. Each one of the actual "hot spots" in the community should be the focus of a specific and targeted strategy that aims to eliminate, or drastically reduce, the conditions present at those locations. Undoubtedly, these locations receive the lion's share of attention from patrol officers in the department; proactive patrol is an essential part of the plan to deal with these locations.

Taking a strategic approach to problems at these locations, the ATPD would create a specific plan for each location. All the operational resources, patrol, investigative, etc., should be brought to bear on crime and disorder at this location. Shoplifting could just be a simple juvenile prank, or it could be part of an organized ring of retail and identify theft. Police departments across the country are experiencing a growing trend of gang involvement in retail and identity theft, as well as auto larceny near commercial hubs.

Under the leadership of the patrol supervisors, the officers could be directed to target these locations. They could provide high-visibility patrol in these areas, identify and track

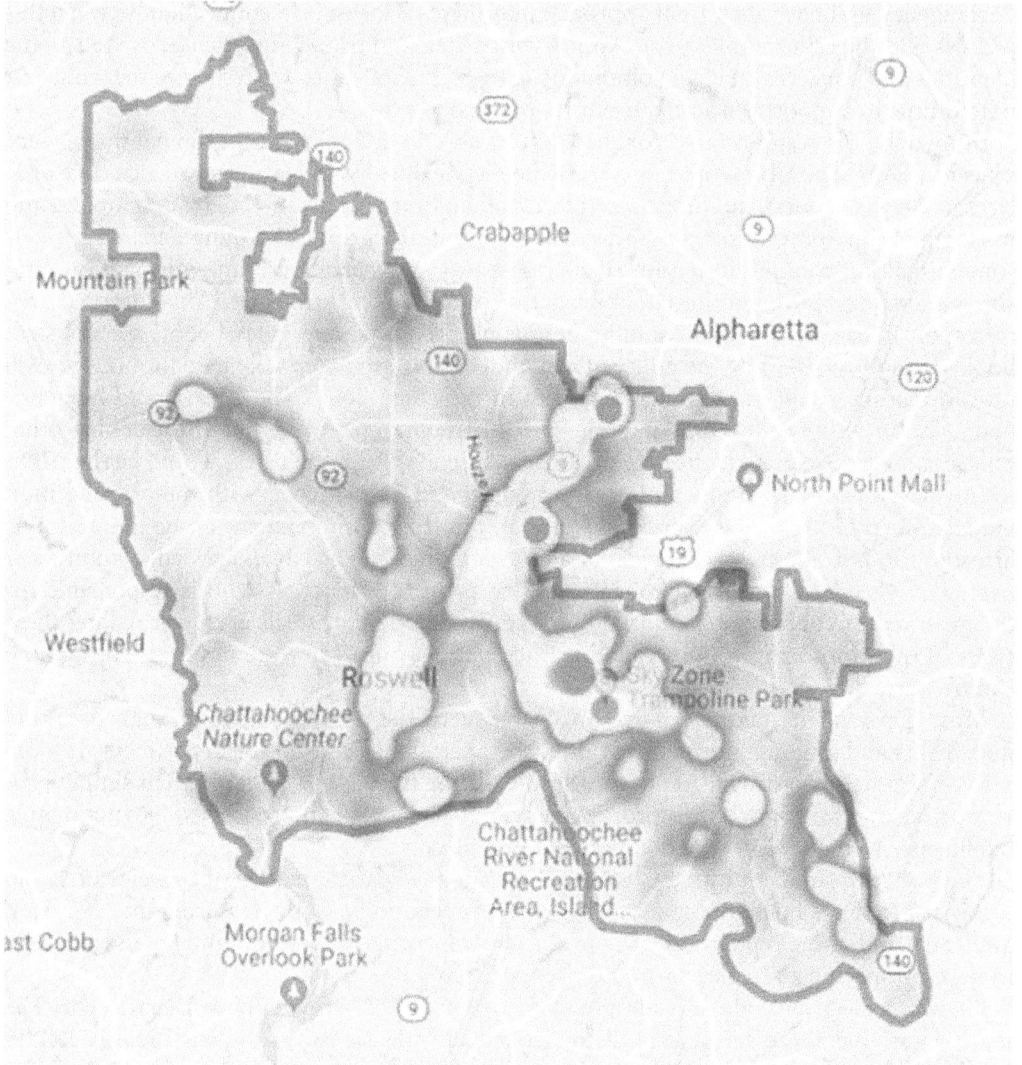

Figure 3.1 Crime Report Map.

recidivist offenders, follow up on open investigations, conduct targeted enforcement on motor vehicles used in these offenses, as well as a variety of tactics identified by the ATPD that might influence crime at these locations. With the appropriate resources, the supervisors could develop and implement tactics, and be held accountable for the success of those tactics. This same approach could be applied to other areas of importance as well, such as safety and security in parks and in the playgrounds, traffic safety, community policing, etc. The maps, therefore, become a tool to focus the department on where the problem areas are, and the commanders become the tool to develop and implement the strategic plan to address these problems.

Ideally, targeted enforcement should be conducted at these locations. Figures 3.1–3.4 show the locations of traffic stops and accidents in Anytown made during the year. The

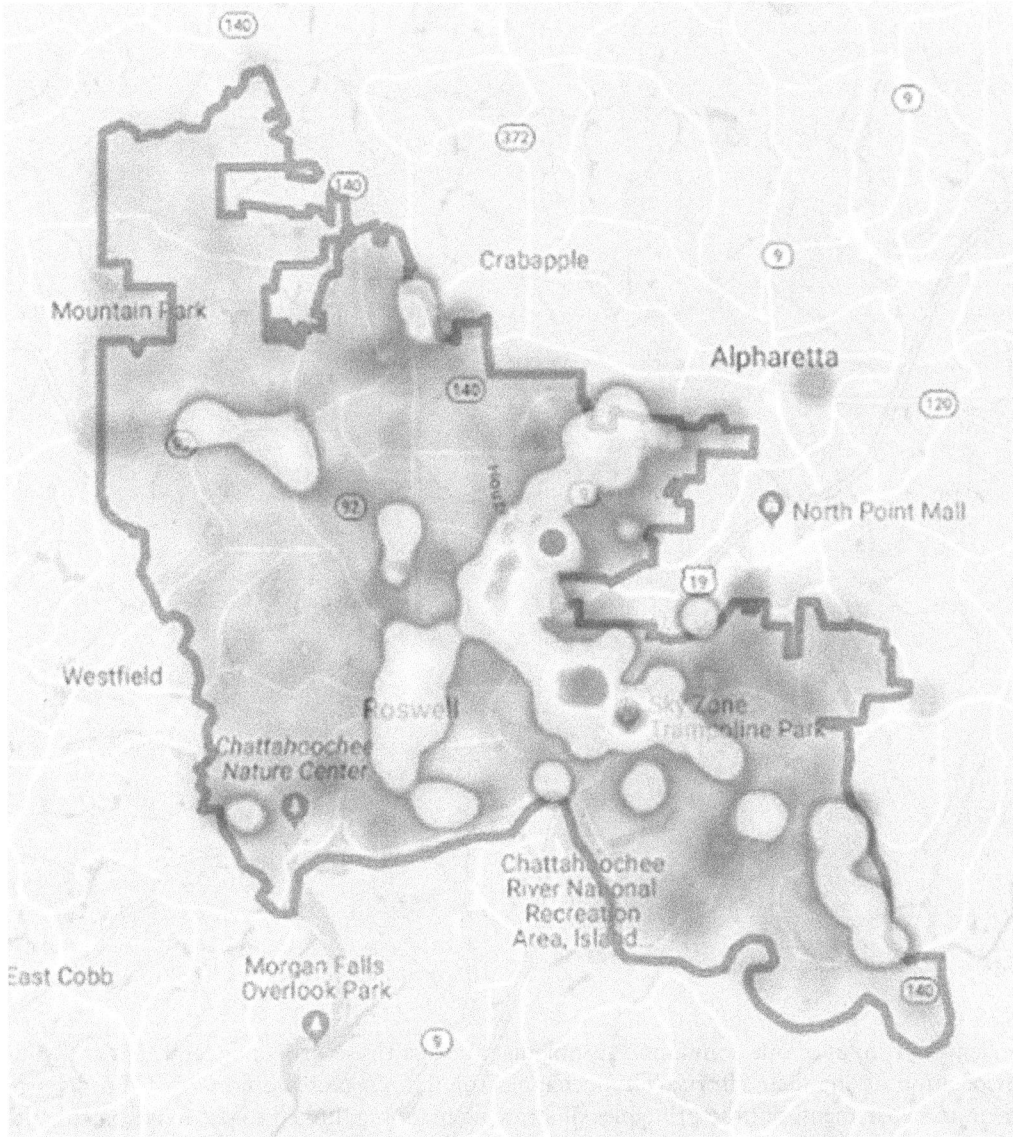

Figure 3.2 CFS Map.

maps indicate that enforcement is being conducted at the most problematic locations. Examining Figures 3.1 and 3.2 together, it appears that the ATPD is conducting the right enforcement at the right locations.

Mapping technology can be instrumental from a community relations perspective as well. Police managers need to explore collecting and disseminating information about community groups and their activities to officers on patrol. The name, contact information, meeting's time/day/location, etc. pertaining to these groups could be collected and mapped. To maintain relationships with these groups, each officer on patrol could be assigned to liaise with groups that exist on their patrol beats. Patrol officers could attend association meetings,

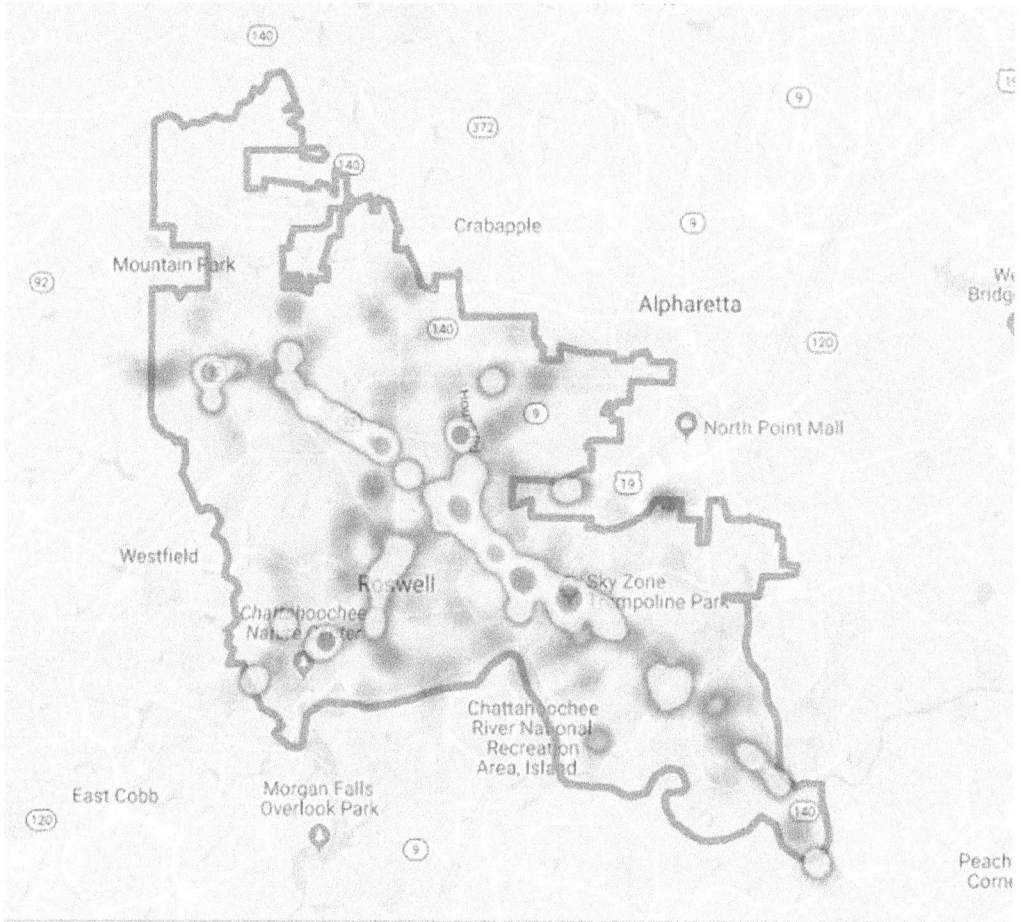

Figure 3.3 Traffic Crash Map.

solicit their input about community problems, address those problems, and report to the association about their efforts. The mechanics of this process would vary from department to department, but the principles of strategic planning, linked to proactive patrol and uncommitted time could be useful.

Example from Rockville, MD Police Department... The method for addressing these problems is by assigning a "Code-18" for the problem identified. When an RCPD liaison receives a complaint from an association a Code-18 is generated. This means that the location and condition are assigned to patrol officers covering that location for a three-week period. Once the Code-18 is assigned, the officers are expected to visit the location at the relevant time and take whatever action necessary to address that condition. In 2017 alone, the RCPD assigned almost 500 Code-18s that resulted in 7,158 checks by patrol, with 47 citations and 85 warnings issued. If the condition still exists after the initial three-week period, the RCPD will extend the Code-18 assignment.

The Code-18 policy is excellent. It creates a system where active participation at neighborhood associations results in a response by the police. This response also engages more than just the chief or command staff; it engages officers on patrol. Undoubtedly, many

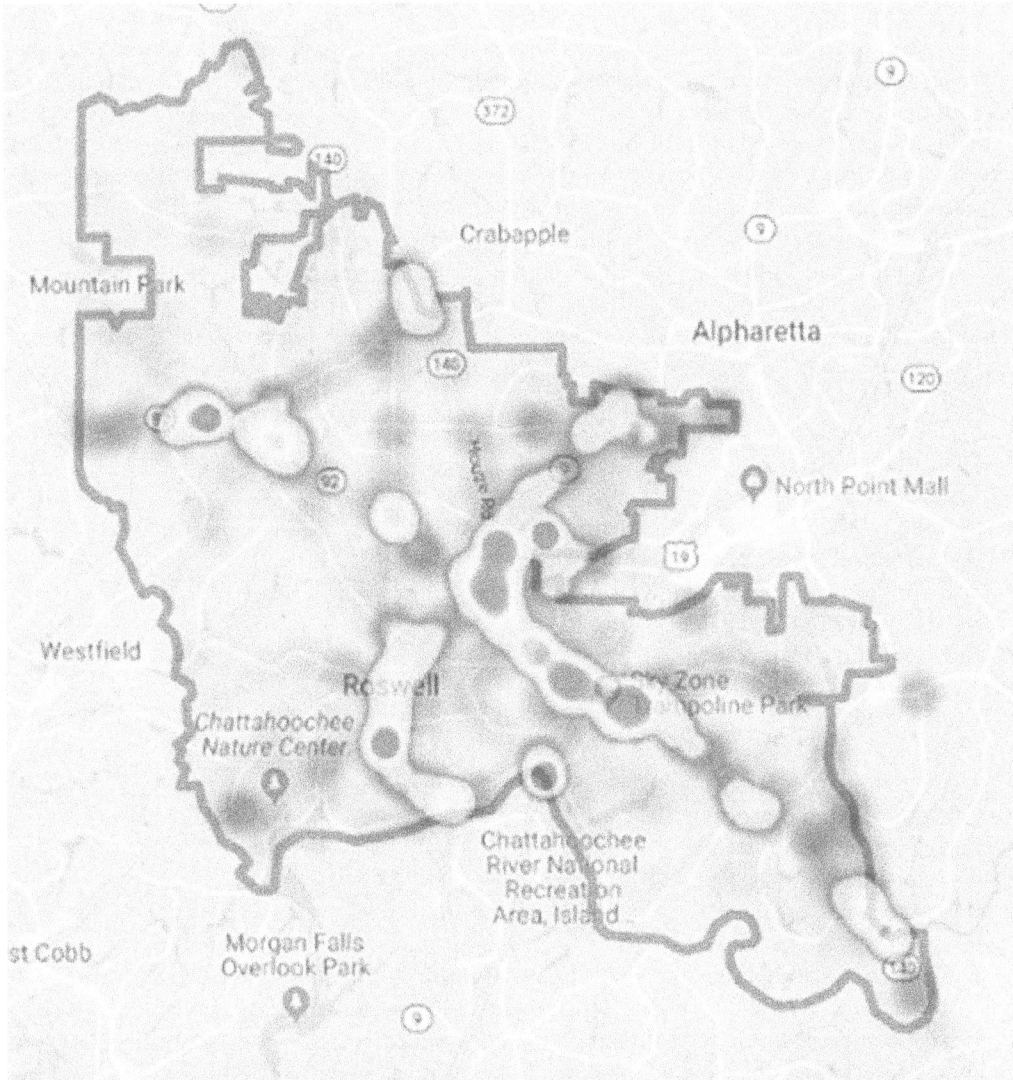

Figure 3.4 Traffic Stop Map.

community problems need more than just proactive patrol to solve. However, the process described here clearly links officers on patrol with the people that live and work on their beats and makes the officers aware of their problems and concerns. Proactive patrol, combined with the larger planning and response efforts by the department produce a more robust, and integrated approach to these problems.

Equipment and Technology

A trip in a modern, well-equipped, police patrol vehicle will introduce to the rider a dizzying display of technology. Undoubtedly, there will be a mobile digital terminal used by the officer to manage CFS. There will be radar and speed detection equipment, in-car audio-visual systems, automatic license plate readers (LPR), hot-spot maps, heavy weapons such as a rifle and/or shot gun, less-than-lethal weapons such as conductive energy devices (CED), beanbag shotguns, rifles, automated external defibrillators (AED), electronic citation readers and printers, and the list goes on. Moreover, that is just in the car. On the officer's belt or ballistic vest, there might be a body-worn camera (BWC), Taser, pepper-spray, firearm, baton, handcuffs. In every department, there will be an assorted mix of all these technologies. Each vehicle will be different, as will each officer "tool belt."

Where do you start to assess the effectiveness of all this technology? The National Institute of Justice published a report in May 2016 that explores the impact of technology on policing (Strom, 2017). RTI International and the PERF conducted the research and presented their findings. They explored the use of technology across the following core policing activities:

- Crime mapping and GIS software
- Predictive analytics
- Data mining
- Case management systems
- Search and data sharing across informational silos
- Software to discover criminal connections
- Software to track and exploit cell phones
- Social media
- Regional and national information sharing
- License plate readers
- Gunshot detection
- DNA
- Mobile biometric devices
- Gun/contraband detection
- Early intervention systems
- Car cameras
- Body-worn cameras

The report concluded that there is little relationship between policing strategy and technology adoption. In addition, police departments are generally not making technology decisions based on their dominant policing philosophy, and that technology acquisition is often ad hoc and not based on strategic planning.[1] These findings probably will not come as a big surprise to most officers working patrol. They are usually on the receiving end of new technology that they do not think they need and did not ask for. The approach to technology for patrol is scattershot and untested, with the decision being made by someone removed from patrol operations.

Assessing technology used on patrol in any police department is much easier than it sounds. There are a few core principles that should be followed. The actual technology selected and implemented is less important than the process behind its selection and the method in which the use of the technology is monitored. For starters, there needs to be a plan. As the NIJ study pointed out, police departments in the U.S. adopt an ad hoc approach to technology. This means technology is purchased and deployed without much connection to the philosophical or strategic priorities of the department. This sounds crazy, but it is reality. Therefore, the first order of business is to develop a plan that explores the questions: what are we trying to accomplish? What equipment do we need to help us reach that goal? What are the advantages and disadvantages of using different technologies? What are the costs?

The best technology for patrol is the ones that helps patrol officers do their jobs better. The only way to know if any technology is better or worse than any other one, is to ask the officers that are using it. This might sound like an obvious thing to do, but it is not common practice. Officers on patrol are usually the last ones to know about technological acquisitions and arrive at work to meet the new system or device that was installed while they were away. This is the exact opposite of the approach that should be taken. Patrol officers (and their operational counterparts in the department) need to be in the initial planning stages of technological adoption. To accomplish this, every police department should have a "technology committee" that assesses the needs for patrol and participates in the acquisition and deployment of patrol technology. This entity would work with a strategic approach and link the mission of the department to the need for technology. This would change the ad hoc approach to a more focused and user-friendly one. This committee should have the responsibility to explore and evaluate technology in the following core areas:

- Deadly weapons (firearms and heavy weapons)
- Less-than-lethal weapons
- Vehicle
- Communications (radio, computer, cellular)
- Management Information Systems (use of the core technologies listed above)
- Tactical (specialized equipment such as "stop-sticks," restraining devices, etc.)

Although the acquisition and implementation of patrol technologies will be different for every department, several critical technologies must be considered for use in all departments.

BWC – The NIJ study found that only one-third of the departments used BWCs. These devices received increased public attention after several critical incidents regarding the police use of force. A PERF study in 2014 found that the use of BWCs has many benefits. They promote trust between the police and the community and are successful in helping resolve civilian complaints. Research has also shown a decrease in use of force incidents by the police and a decrease in civilian complaints. Other studies reported an increase in arrest activity by officers wearing BWCs. There are also problems associated with these devices. There are privacy concerns, and concerns about the method by which police departments release police BWC footage. In addition, studies have shown an increase in officer line-of-duty injuries with the implementation of BWCs (Lum et al., 2019).

It is essential that officers on patrol be equipped with BWCs. It is equally essential that sound policies are created that maximize trust and accountability, increase transparency, and promote operational efficiency. The IACP publishes a "model" policy for BWC and police departments are encouraged to use this policy as the foundation for their own.

The IACP Model BWC Policy is available here: www.theiacp.org/sites/default/files/all/b/BodyWornCamerasPolicy.pdf

LPR – Automatic license plate readers are an essential part of patrol operations, and all departments should deploy them. LPRs can be mobile or mounted on structural objects, such as overpasses or light poles. They can be used in auto-theft prevention and recovery efforts, traffic enforcement, and criminal investigations. The empirical research on LPRs is not conclusive or complete. Several studies show some limited impact that LPRs have on crime, and others note the prohibitive cost of acquisition and maintenance. Nonetheless, these devices, when used integrated into the strategic mission of the department, can substantially increase the effectiveness of patrol operations.

AED – Patrol vehicles should be equipped with automated external defibrillators (AEDs). AEDs are designed to be simple to use for first responders, and their use is taught in many first aid, first responder, and basic life support (BLS) level CPR classes. The deployment of AEDs in marked police vehicles would greatly enhance the life-saving capabilities of the department. These inexpensive (less than $2,000 for each unit) and easy-to-use devices would be a tremendous asset to every police department. Their purchase and deployment are strongly always recommended in vehicles on patrol.

Patrol Supervision

Effective patrol supervision is undoubtedly the most important element for successful patrol operations and is arguably the most important job in policing. The patrol supervisor is the point-person between upper management and the rank-and-file and must be an effective manager and a motivational leader. These skills need to be balanced in the context of supervising tactical operations in a challenging environment, often alone, during all hours of the day and night, and quickly during rapidly unfolding and chaotic situations. Assessment of the patrol supervisor's role, therefore, is perhaps *the* most important responsibility for any police department. That assessment should include a rigorous evaluation of the selection and promotion of first-line supervisors, the process by which they are trained, mentored, and evaluated, and their preparation for handling critical incidents in the community.

Selection and Training

Chapter 9 discusses in depth police training in general. This is particularly important for the discussion in this chapter on patrol operations. It should be obvious that first-line supervisors in any police department should be properly trained. But are they really? How do you know and what standard does your department use to identify, select, and train first-line patrol supervisors? The answers to these questions will dictate the effectiveness of the entire patrol function.

From an operational perspective, the police department must ensure that patrol supervisors are experts at handling "critical incidents" and "high liability" policies. A police critical incident is considered any event that has the potential to result in controversy, conflict, or disruption in the community. These would include the use of deadly force by or against an officer, natural or man-made disasters, serious criminal events such as bank robberies or hostage, and any event that requires the department to act quickly to restore order or respond to unrest. High-liability policies govern incidents that might not be critical or newsworthy but have the potential to expose the department or the public to harm. Police pursuits, use of force, handling complaints from the public, responding to domestic violence incidents, responding to emotionally disturbed persons, etc. These incidents are discussed at greater length in Chapter 13.

It is imperative that patrol supervisors know how to handle these incidents, practice responding to them regularly, and engage in a routine assessment of their actions in an ongoing fashion. To accomplish this routine assessment, police departments should engage in after-action reviews of all critical incidents. This process should be both formal and informal. For serious or major critical incidents, a formal after-action report (AAR) must be conducted. This formal AAR should be assigned to the appropriate individual that had overall responsibility for handling the incident. If there were a chief, commander, captain, etc., as the incident commander, it would fall to that person to initiate and conduct the AAR. Generally, this would take the form of an actual written report on the incident.

The Department of Justice publishes a "Police Critical Incident Checklist" that covers an assessment of the immediate, short-term, and long-term response of police agencies to critical incidents, and provides milestones and actions for successful recovery from these incidents (DOJ, n.d.). Many national and state police accreditation agencies recommend the preparation of AAR as a method of improving operations. It is incumbent, therefore, for police departments to ensure that this formal process is taking place. The Seattle Police Department provides an excellent example of this process.

The Seattle Policy and Form is available here: www.seattle.gov/police-manual/title-14---emergency-operations/14010---after-action-reports

The general format for this process explores three central questions: what happened? What was our response? What would we do differently next time? In addition, while it is critical for police departments to engage in this process for serious events described above, it is critical to develop and foster an informal approach as well. Those three simple questions need to be "baked" into patrol supervision, and need to be asked every day, after every shift, with all the personnel involved, and led by the first-line supervisor. The process by which patrol supervisors do this, or do not do this, will shape the quality of the response to and recovery from critical incidents. Supervisors should be discussing events with their personnel regularly, with formal reporting after serious incidents, and informally after other events. Developing the habit of after-action review will improve overall operations. It is essential that this process occurs and is the hallmark of effective supervision.

High-liability policies are another critical area for patrol supervisors. In 2013, the Police Executive Research Forum published a report in their Critical Issues in Policing Series entitled "Civil Rights Investigations of Local Police: Lessons Learned." That report was the product of discussions that PERF held among police leaders from around the U.S. It centered on the U.S. Justice Department's (DOJ) authority and practice of investigating local police departments for policies and practices that were alleged to violate the U.S. Constitution. DOJ's role in investigating local police is a controversial issue. It was a frequent tactic used by the Obama Administration and appears to have been abandoned under the Trump Administration. Nonetheless, the violations that precipitate a DOJ investigation are violations that also generate civil lawsuits and both real and perceived harm to the community. The way a police department handles these situations can prevent or mitigate exposure to lawsuits, DOJ investigations, and improve overall service delivery. The specific categories of events described by the PERF report are the police use of force, biased-policing and unlawful stops, searches, and arrests, gender bias and the handling of sexual assaults, and policing persons with mental illness. Not covered by the PERF report, but an area where the police have high exposure to liability involves police pursuits of motor vehicles (PERF, 2013).

The combination of critical incidents and high-liability policies creates a list of tasks, duties, and responsibilities that should represent the core of the first-line supervisor's role. Promotion in rank should be based on the knowledge and proper handling of these incidents/events. Training for first-line supervisors should be geared towards the continued successful handling of these incidents/events. And the day-to-day actions of patrol supervisors should include an awareness of these incidents/events occurring, a proper response and oversight, as well as a thorough and rigorous after-action review of how they were handled.

Officer-In-Charge (OIC)

In general, police departments deploy personnel in the rank of Sergeant to supervise patrol operations. There are variations throughout the county, where the first-line supervisor is a lieutenant, in others a corporal. In many others, when supervisors of any rank are absent or unavailable for any reason, they rely on what is known as an "Officer-In-Charge" (OIC) model of supervision. In some cases, the OIC receives supervisory training and may even receive additional compensation for working in an OIC role. On one shift, they are a police officer assigned to patrol, on the next shift, because of the absence of a supervisor they become the OIC, and on the next shift, they return to being a shift officer again.

The notion that effective supervision will be delivered by an OIC that will revert to a patrol officer at the next shift seems unrealistic. Police departments should ensure that a supervisor, sergeant or even commander, if necessary, is assigned to always supervise patrol operations. Having a sergeant assigned to each shift will improve supervision, and command and control of emergency incidents as well as provide greater protection against liability for the community.

Building a Culture of Performance

Patrol supervisors should be expected to be part of the performance culture of the department. As this chapter suggests, their role in fostering a performance-based culture is three-fold. First, patrol supervisors must manage reactive workload demands. Supervisors need to ensure that officers respond to CFS promptly and professionally, and they are instrumental in achieving efficiency in this area. Second, patrol supervisors are critical in identifying, prioritizing, and supervising proactive response to crime, traffic, and disorder in the community. Officers, on their own, are unlikely to use their uncommitted patrol time in a coordinated manner with other officers. This is where the supervisor's role is critical. Balancing the reactive and proactive patrol responsibilities is difficult, but squarely in the realm of the patrol supervisor. Aware of the reactive demand in patrol zones, and the crime, traffic, and disorder conditions in those zones, the patrol supervisor can direct resources to address both. With responsibility for all operations during the shift, the supervisor should be expected to ensure that CFS are being handled properly AND uncommitted time is being spent wisely on the things most important to the department. The third area is dealing with critical incidents and high-liability events.

Effective patrol supervision, therefore, requires achieving several important goals that all police departments share:

- To identify criminal offenders and criminal activity and when appropriate, to apprehend offenders, and participate in subsequent court proceedings.
- To prevent the commission of crimes through proactive techniques by reducing the opportunities for such crimes.
- To create and maintain a feeling of security in the community.
- To ensure safe and expeditious movement of vehicle traffic on public roadways.
- To reduce traffic deaths through engineering, education, and enforcement.
- To provide the public with educational information regarding the police function and crime prevention.
- To ensure officer safety and well-being.

From a performance-based perspective, each of these broad areas of police responsibility should be part of the patrol supervisor's mandate. Each of these measures should be measured, and plans and tactics should be created to achieve success in each area. In addition, the results of these efforts need to be monitored continuously and patrol supervisors held accountable to execute these strategies and tactics effectively. The integration of these many components will create a culture of performance that will contribute to the overall success of the department.

Conclusion

This chapter explores the various issues regarding patrol operations. Building upon the discussion in Chapter 2 about how many officers to deploy on patrol and during what times and locations, this chapter argues that a strategic approach must be taken when dealing with how officers on patrol approach their jobs. Demand for service from reactive calls should be minimized, and pro-active and self-initiated work should be purposeful and driven by data and comprehensive plans. Departments should also embrace techology to leverage performance and view effective supervision as the fulcrum for building a culture of performance.

Notes

1 www.ncjrs.gov/pdffiles1/nij/grants/251140.pdf
2 The AnyTown Police Department is a fictitious name given to an actual department in the U.S. The data that appear above were extracted from the CAD system from this department in the calendar year 2022.

References

Council of State Governments. (2022). *The Impact of Terrorism on State and Local Law Enforcement: Adjusting to New Roles and Changing Conditions*. US Govt. Print. Off.

Davis, R. C., Henderson, N. J., Mandelstam, J., Ortiz, C. W., & Miller, J. (2006). *Federal Intervention in Local Policing: Pittsburgh's Experience with a Consent Decree*. Office of Community Oriented Police Services.

Federal Bureau of Investigation. (2019). *Uniformed Crime Reports: Clearances*.

Ferretti, F. (July 11, 1985). The city layoffs raise questions. *NY Times*. New York.

Floyd v. City of N.Y., 959 F. Supp. 2nd 540.

Hodge, J., & Dholakia, J. N. (2021). *Fifty Years Ago Today, President Nixon Declared the War on Drugs*. Vera Institute of Justice.

Kelling, G., Pate, T., Dieckman, D., & Brown, C. E. (1974). *The Kansas City Preventive Patrol Experiment*. National Policing Institute.

Kelling, G. L., & Moore, M. H. (1988). *The Evolving Strategy of the Police: Perspectives on Policing (No.4)*. Harvard University, Boston.

Lewin, B. Acevedo R., & National Institute of Justice (U.S.). Office of Development Testing and Dissemination. (1980). *Differential Police Response to Calls for Service*. U.S. Dept. of Justice, National Institute of Justice Office of Development Testing and Dissemination: For sale by the Supt. of Docs. U.S. G.P.O.

Lum, C., Stoltz, M., Koper, C., & Scherer, J. A. (2019). Research on body-worn cameras: What we know, what we need to know. *Criminology & Public Policy*, 18(1), 93–118.

McCabe, J. (2013). *Police Allocation and Deployment*. ICMA.

Neusteter, S. R., Mapolski, M., Khogali, M., O'Toole, M. (2019). *The 911 Call Processing System: A Review of the Literature as It Relates to Policing*. Vera Institute of Justice.

Overland Park, KS. (2022). *Benchmark City Survey*.

Patterson, T. (February 9, 2023). Pillars of truth in law enforcement's past. *Law Enforcement Bulletin*.

Police Executive Research Forum. (2013). *Civil Rights Investigations of Local Police: Lessons Learned*. PERF.

Strom, K. (2017). *Research on the Impact of Technology on Policing Strategy in the 21st Century. Final Report*. Research Triangle Park, RTI International.

Telep, C. W., & Hibdon, J. (2019). *Understanding and Responding to Crime and Disorder Hot Spots*. Arizona State University, Center for Problem-Oriented Policing.

Trojanowicz, R., & Bucqueroux, B. (1990). *Community Policing: A Contemporary Perspective*. Anderson Publishing.

U.S. Department of Justice, D.O.J. (2022). *Local Police Department Personnel, 2020*. November 17, 2022.

U.S. Department of Justice, DOJ. (n.d.) *Police Critical Incident Checklist*.

United States. President's Commission on Law Enforcement and Administration of Justice. (1967). *The Challenge of Crime in a Free Society: A Report*. U.S. Govt. Print. Off.

Walker, S., & Katz, C. M. (2022). *The Police in America, 10th Edition*. McGraw Hill.

Wilson, J. Q. (1968). *Varieties of Police Behavior*. Harvard University Press.

Chapter 4

Investigative Operational Performance

Learning Objectives

Upon completion of this chapter, the reader will be able to:

- Understand the emergence of the role of detective and the importance of Criminal Investigative Units in the history of U.S. Police Departments.
- Understand the structure of Criminal Investigation Units and the responsibilities and duties of the detective position.
- Understand what case management is and why solvability factors are essential.
- Understand the rationale for collecting clearance rates from law enforcement agencies.
- Identify how Performance Indicators are used to evaluate detectives and Criminal Investigation Units.

Introduction

Criminal Investigations Operations have always had a mystique and invoked curiosity as professionals focused on solving crime. The public has been fascinated by fictional characters such as Sherlock Holmes, Detective Danny Reagan of *Blue Bloods*, and others portrayed as action-oriented, focusing on critical evidence, using an array of interview and interrogation skills, and putting the apprehension of criminals as the priority of their lives. Television shows do not reflect the reality of being a detective or supervising a detective unit. Most television shows centered around detectives and Criminal Investigations Units are sixty minutes of continuous action, such as dynamic entries into a target location to surprise and overwhelm suspect(s), challenging hand-to-hand combat with a suspect, and sometimes resorting to deadly force. At the end of the sixty minutes, the entire incident is concluded, not revealing the reality that occurred. The investigatory strategies presented by these shows reveal more luck than steps taken during an investigation. Moreover, the detectives are rarely seen writing reports, discussing the evidence with the forensic crime unit, or producing various documents, and supervisors are not sitting at their desks conducting case management, performance measures, or realistic meetings with their detectives. Furthermore, on television shows, if an autopsy is required and the body is decomposing, the detectives are rarely seen putting Vicks ointment in their nostrils or displaying a reaction to the stench of a decomposing body.

While these detective television shows are fascinating and create a cult of viewers interested in criminal investigations, television shows do not reflect reality. There are television shows, such as COPS, which originated in 1989 and is still relevant today, that reflect

DOI: 10.4324/9781003396437-4

primarily the duties of patrol officers during a snapshot of a shift in a particular city/county. This chapter examines the reality of being a detective and the responsibilities of supervising a detective unit/division/bureau.

The Emergence of Detectives and Criminal Investigations Units in American History

American policing has undergone eras of change and reform. The reform era was responsible for the professionalism of policing and a detachment from politics that dominated earlier eras. The reform era timeframe was 1900s to 1970s, and policing focused on criminal apprehension and crime control measures. Technology changed during the reform era, introducing two-way radios, police cars, and a focus on specialization within police departments. Hence, emerged the position of detective. Detectives were viewed as having enhanced investigatory and interview/interrogation skills, and Criminal Investigations Units were held in high esteem within a police department. The Criminal Investigations Units selected the best crime solvers from the Patrol Operations Division. The Patrol Operations Division has always been viewed as the "backbone" of the Police Department, and the Criminal Investigations Division has been described as having the "cream of the crop" of crime solvers.

The Federal Bureau of Investigations is credited with advancing the methods and science that significantly assisted Police Departments with criminal investigations. The Federal Bureau of Investigations monitors a nationwide fingerprint and biometric identification system created by scientific methods such as fingerprints to identify individuals and the national DNA electronic database. The Federal Bureau of Investigations also supports local Police Departments in high-profile criminal investigations.

Advances in the methods and science alone were not enough to increase the solvability of crimes. While detectives had more tools to use in criminal investigations, a valuable resource was being overlooked – the public. Tip lines to enable citizens to report crimes began to emerge in communities. The concept of community policing also emerged and required the police and community to enter a partnership to solve crime. The public had information about crimes, but it was often not utilized as a resource. Yes, neighborhood checks were being used by criminal investigators after a crime occurred. However, the strength of the public's information about crimes must be cultivated by the police department and build trust in the community. Community partnerships with Police Departments began to grow as the Police Departments began to embrace community policing. At the same time, more sophisticated scientific advances for solving crime expanded, such as DNA analysis and growth in computer technology to enable DNA to be collected, stored, and matched with profiles of individuals. The Federal Bureau of Investigations oversees both the CODIS, which is "the acronym for the Combined DNA Index System and is the generic term used to describe the Federal Bureau of Investigations program of support for criminal justice DNA databases and the software used to run these databases. The National DNA Index System or NDIS is considered one part of CODIS, the national level, containing the DNA profiles contributed by federal, state, and local participating laboratories" (n.d.). This technology propelled forward the ability of Police Departments to solve crimes.

Other growth in technologies include electronic networks and databases, automated fingerprint analysis systems (AFIS), computer software to extract information from digital devices, video surveillance, closed-circuit television (CCTV) cameras, drone surveillance, Global Positioning Systems (GPS), and most recently, body cameras. Embracing the community policing philosophy, technology, and enhanced training and education have been forces for continuing professional policing.

The Structure of Criminal Investigation Units and Responsibilities of Detectives

The structure of Criminal Investigation Units varies due to the size of the police department, financial resources, and the types and number of crimes occurring in a particular community. Small police departments with less than ten employees may rely on other larger police departments near them to conduct criminal investigations that the small police department cannot follow up. These small police departments rely on state resources for criminal investigations that would require the skills of a detective and advanced forensic capability. Large Police Departments usually have a Criminal Investigations Bureau or Division of several distinct Criminal Investigations Units.

Criminal Investigation Units can be categorized as being generalized or specialized functions. When a Criminal Investigations Unit is categorized as being generalized, the detectives in this unit have a caseload that reflects a variety of types of crimes. Detectives assigned to specialized units focus on honing their skills to investigate a particular type of crime. Examples of specialized units can include but are not limited to Crimes Against Persons, Crimes Against Property, Homicide, Robbery, Special Victims, Tactical Investigations, Strategic Investigations, Narcotics, Gang Intelligence, Intel and Terrorism, Economic Crime, Environmental Crime, Guns, Burglary, Theft, Motor Vehicle Theft, Major Crimes, and Real Time Crime Center. Police Departments' Criminal Investigations Unit may vary in name or mission, but the units are created to serve the needs of each police department's community and type of crime. Below are the organizational charts for the Sarasota Police Department in Florida and the Portland Police Department in Oregon. This compares what a Criminal Investigations Unit may represent in a smaller department compared to a larger department. What can be seen are many more specialized units within the Portland Police Department (Table 4.1).

In 2023, the Sarasota Police Department hired ten additional police officers, resulting in the full strength of sworn positions increasing to 190 (Warfield, 2023). According to the Sarasota Police Department (2023), the Criminal Investigation Unit has a General Crimes Unit, Crimes Against Children Unit, Economic Crimes Unit, and Narcotics Unit. The General Crimes Unit investigates the following crimes: Homicides, Aggravated Battery, Aggravated Assault, Sexual Battery, Robbery, Home Invasion, Kidnapping, Burglaries, and Grand Thefts. This unit also monitors pawns, secondhand dealers, and scrap metal recyclers. The Crimes Against Children Unit investigates all crimes against children under the age of 18, including locating runaways and sexual offenders/predators in the city limits. The Economic Crimes Unit investigates crimes ranging from organized check fraud to multi-million-dollar fraud cases. The Narcotics Unit investigates street-level narcotics sales, high-level interstate smuggling, drug trafficking cases, prostitution, gambling, and human trafficking. Two additional units support the Criminal Investigations Division: the Victim Advocate Unit and the Criminalistics Unit. The Victim Advocate Unit provides various services to victims and supports them through the criminal justice system. The Criminalistics Unit collects, processes, and analyzes all evidence and crime scenes.

According to the Portland Police Bureau (2023), the department has 811 sworn officers. The organizational chart displays investigations having two components, the Detective Division and the Specialized Resources Division, which includes some investigatory units.

Table 4.1 Sarasota Police Department Table of Organization

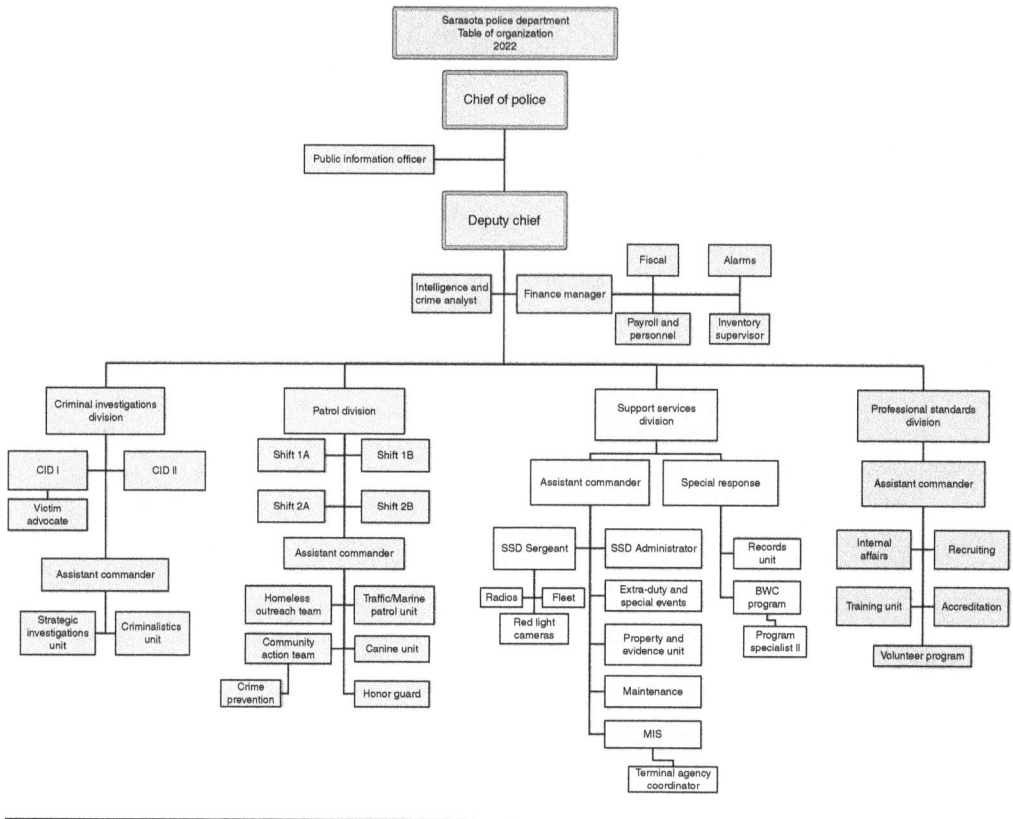

The Detective Division is comprised of the following units: Family Services, Child Abuse Team, CARES Unit, Internet Crimes Against Children, Special Victims, Domestic Violence Reduction, Gun Dispossession, Vulnerable Adults and Elders, Persons Crimes, Bias Crimes, FBI Violent Robbery Task Force, Property Crimes, Polygraph, Court Coordinator, Human/ Sex Trafficking, Forensic Evidence, and Juvenile Identification. The Special Resources Division includes the Narcotics and Organized Crime Unit. Generally, the larger the police department, the more investigatory units will be required to serve the community's needs, especially in areas with high crime rates (Table 4.2).

The responsibilities of the position of detective in police departments may have some variance due to the structure of the Criminal Investigations Unit being organized as general investigations, specialized investigations, task forces, undercover units, and if the detective has ancillary duties not related to their primary duty of being a detective such as being a member of SWAT, Major Accident Reconstruction Team, or assisting the Property and Evidence Unit. However, detectives have core responsibilities and duties every day. In querying Artificial Intelligence through ChatGPT (2023), the following responsibilities of a detective are listed as familiar to most detective positions in Police Departments.

1. Case Investigation: Detectives are responsible for investigating criminal cases, which may include homicides, sexual assaults, robberies, burglaries, fraud, and more. They gather information, interview witnesses, and collect evidence to determine what happened.

Table 4.2 Organizational Chart Portland Police Bureau

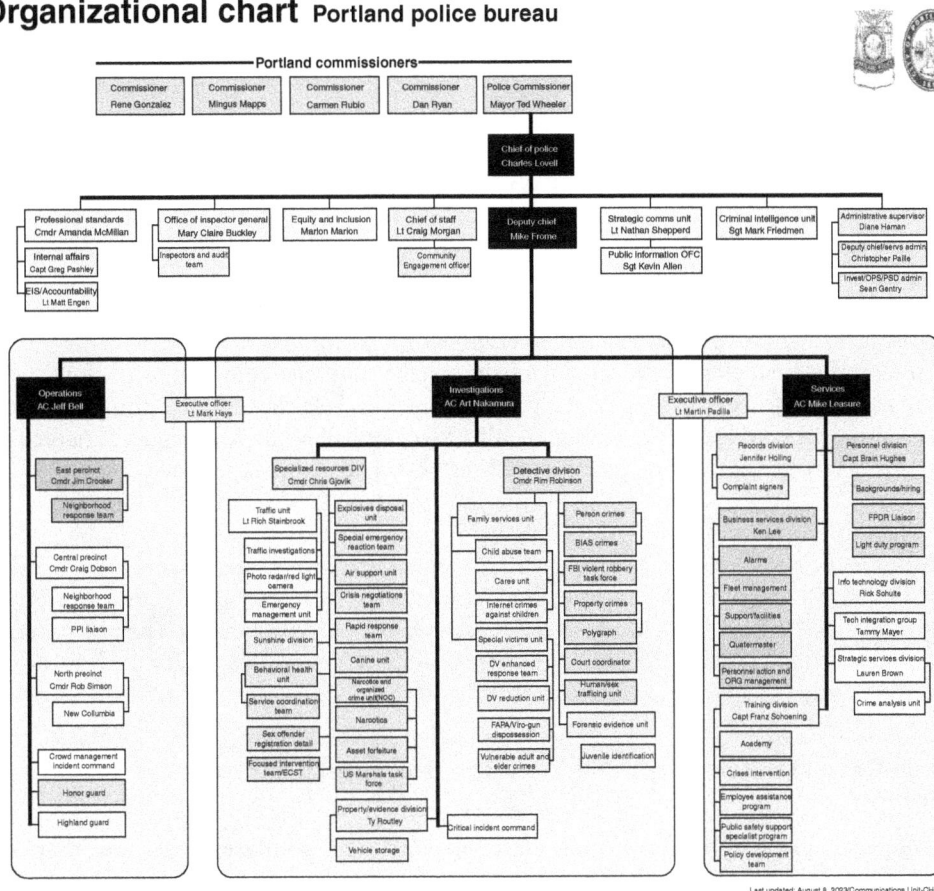

Organizational chart Portland police bureau

Portland commissioners

| Commissioner Rene Gonzalez | Commissioner Mingus Mapps | Commissioner Carmen Rubio | Commissioner Dan Ryan | Police Commissioner Mayor Ted Wheeler |

Chief of police
Charles Lovell

Professional standards
Cmdr Amanda McMillan
- Internal affairs Capt Greg Pashley
- EIS/Accountability Lt Matt Engen

Office of inspector general
Mary Claire Buckley
- Inspectors and audit team

Equity and inclusion
Marlon Marion

Chief of staff
Lt Craig Morgan
- Community Engagement officer

Deputy chief
Mike Frome

Strategic comms unit
Lt Nathan Shepperd
- Public Information OFC Sgt Kevin Allen

Criminal intelligence unit
Sgt Mark Friedmen

Administrative supervisor
Diane Haman
- Deputy chief/servs admin Christopher Palle
- Invest/OPS/PSD admin Sean Gentry

Operations — AC Jeff Bell
Executive officer — Lt Mark Hays

- East precinct Cmdr Jim Crooker
  - Neighborhood response team
- Central precinct Cmdr Craig Dobson
  - Neighborhood response team
  - PPI liaison
- North precinct Cmdr Rob Simeon
  - New Columbia
- Crowd management incident command
- Honor guard
- Highland guard

Investigations — AC Art Nakamura

Specialized resources DIV
Cmdr Chris Gjovik
- Traffic unit Lt Rich Stainbrook
  - Traffic investigations
- Photo red/arred light camera
- Emergency management unit
- Sunshine division
- Behavioral health unit
- Service coordination team
- Sex offender registration detail
- Focused intervention team/ECST

- Explosives disposal unit
- Special emergency reaction team
- Air support unit
- Crisis negotiations team
- Rapid response team
- Canine unit
- Narcotics and organized crime unit(NOC)
- Narcotics
- Asset forfeiture
- US Marshals task force

Property/evidence division
Ty Routley
- Vehicle storage

Detective division
Cmdr Rim Robinson
- Family services unit
  - Child abuse team
  - Cares unit
  - Internet crimes against children
  - Special victims unit
- DV enhanced response team
- DV reduction unit
- FAPA/Viro-gun dispossession
- Vulnerable adult and elder crimes

- Person crimes
- BIAS crimes
- FBI violent robbery task force
- Property crimes
- Polygraph
- Court coordinator
- Human/sex trafficking unit
- Forensic evidence unit
- Juvenile identification

Critical incident command

Services — AC Mike Leasure
Executive officer — Lt Martin Padilla

Records division
Jennifer Holling
- Complaint signers

Business services division
Ken Lee
- Alarms
- Fleet management
- Support/facilities
- Quartermaster
- Personnel action and ORG management
- Training division Capt Franz Schoening
  - Academy
  - Crises intervention
  - Employee assistance program
  - Public safety support specialist program
  - Policy development team

Personnel division
Capt Brain Hughes
- Backgrounds/hiring
- FPDR Liaison
- Light duty program
- Info technology division Rick Schulte
- Tech integration group Tammy Mayer
- Strategic services division Lauren Brown
- Crime analysis unit

Last updated: August 8, 2023/Communications Unit-CHO

2. Crime Scene Analysis: Detectives often arrive at crime scenes to examine the area, document evidence, and ensure the preservation of crucial information. They work alongside forensic experts to gather physical evidence like fingerprints, DNA, and ballistic data.

3. Witness Interviews: Detectives interview witnesses, victims, and suspects to obtain statements and gather information about the crime. They may conduct multiple interviews to establish timelines and corroborate information.

4. Evidence Collection and Analysis: Detectives collect and preserve physical evidence such as weapons, clothing, or other items related to the crime. They may send evidence to crime labs for analysis and maintain a chain of custody to ensure its integrity.

5. Surveillance: In some cases, detectives conduct surveillance operations to monitor the activities of suspects. This may involve tracking individuals, vehicles, or locations to gather evidence or identify criminal patterns.

6. Interrogation: Detectives may interrogate suspects to obtain confessions or additional information about a crime. They must follow legal procedures to ensure the admissibility of any statement in court.

7. Report Writing: Detectives are responsible for documenting their findings and activities in detailed reports. These reports are often used in court proceedings and provide a record of the investigation.
8. Collaboration: Detectives often work closely with other law enforcement agencies, such as the FBI, DEA, or local police departments, to share information and resources in complex cases.
9. Case Management: They manage their caseload, prioritizing investigations based on severity and available leads. Detectives may also coordinate with prosecutors to build solid cases for trial.
10. Testifying in Court: Detectives may be called upon to testify as witnesses, presenting evidence and providing testimony about their investigations and findings.
11. Staying Informed: To stay effective, detectives must stay informed about changes in laws, investigative techniques, and emerging criminal trends.
12. Community Engagement: Some detectives engage with the community to build trust and gather information. This can help solve crimes and prevent future criminal activity.
13. Training and Development: They may also be responsible for training and mentoring junior detectives or officers, passing on their knowledge and experience.

The responsibilities and duties of a detective require an array of diverse skills, including but not limited to oral communication, written communication, interpersonal skills, technical skills, investigatory skills, and physical skills. Detectives must understand and apply constitutional law, state statutes, and policies competently. Detectives must be highly motivated to solve crimes, reflect ethics in their actions, and understand that victimization affects victims differently.

What is Case Management, and Why are Solvability Factors Important?

Case Management systems have some variances but also similarities in how they are performed from one Police Department to another Police Department. Changes in Case Management systems have evolved over the years; however, most police departments utilize a hybrid combination of a paper case file and a newer computerized system (CaseGuard, 2016).

The first step in Case Management is Case Screening. The criminal investigations that a Patrol Officer cannot follow up on due to the complexity of the case, extensive time allocation needed, and the need for specialized skills are the primary reasons why a Patrol Sergeant refers cases to the Detective Sergeant. The Detective Sergeant is responsible for determining which cases should be followed up by the Criminal Investigations Unit. The Detective Sergeant will review the incoming case and determine if the case should be assigned to a detective or suspended due to no workable leads. The Detective Sergeant is also responsible for keeping track of the number and type of investigations assigned to each detective, ensuring that the case is being updated by the detective utilizing a supplemental report, ensuring that the supplemental report is updated promptly, and determining the assignment of the case is based on an appropriate number of solvability factors.

What are solvability factors, and do Police Departments use the same ones? Police Departments identify the solvability factors that are the most important for determining if a case should be assigned to a detective for further investigation. Therefore, it is not unusual for police departments to use a different number of solvability factors to reach the threshold of assigning a case to a detective. These solvability factors are generally listed in a General Order or Standard Operating Procedure for Criminal Investigation Units. For example, the Salisbury University Police Department in Maryland lists the following solvability factors in chapter 42.1.2(C1–12):

1. CAN A SUSPECT BE NAMED? The officer conducting the preliminary investigation shall determine from any pertinent party available whether a full or partial name of a suspect is available. It shall be stated in the officer's report with whom he/she spoke to obtain this information and to whom he/she spoke with negative results.
2. COULD A SUSPECT BE IDENTIFIED BY THE VICTIM/WITNESS IF SEEN AGAIN? The officer shall determine whether the victim/witness can identify the suspect if seen again. This information should be stated in the officer's report.
3. IS THE ADDRESS OF A SUSPECT KNOWN? Often, a victim/witness may not know the suspect's name but could state that they have seen the suspect leave a particular residence or know where he/she lives. This information should be included in the officer's report.
4. IS IT KNOWN WHERE A SUSPECT MAY USUALLY BE FOUND? As in the case of a suspect's address, a person providing information may not know the suspect by name but could state that he/she may usually be found at a particular place – bar, social club, gym, class, or other location.
5. WAS A VEHICLE PLATE NUMBER OBTAINED BY THE VICTIM/WITNESS? Citizens have been trained to look for this feature during moments of suspicious activity. The investigating officer shall closely question pertinent parties when a vehicle is known to be involved. Even partial numbers may assist; consider the witness who cannot provide a complete vehicle tag number.
6. CAN THE VEHICLE BE IDENTIFIED BY THE VICTIM/WITNESS IF SEEN AGAIN? The investigating officer shall determine if the vehicle had distinguishing characteristics such as bumper stickers, dents, bodywork, unusual paint or tires, or extra antennas. This inquiry shall not necessarily be limited to the exterior of the vehicle.
7. WAS ANY TRACEABLE PROPERTY TAKEN? Determine if any property taken had serial numbers, distinguishing characteristics that would make identification easy, or other considerations generally made in tracing stolen property.
8. IS THERE ANY SIGNIFICANT PHYSICAL EVIDENCE AVAILABLE? State what evidence was taken by whom, where it was found, the purpose of taking the evidence, and the significance of the material to the investigation. The officer must evaluate the evidence's importance in solving the crime. If the answer to this solvability question is "yes," the officer must report all the details about the evidence. If the answer is "no," the officer must document the efforts to find significant evidence.
9. IS THERE A SIGNIFICANT "MODUS OPERANDI" PRESENT? Criminals generally commit the same type of crime more than once. They also commit the crime in the same or similar fashion as they had in the past. Therefore, the investigating officer shall cite in the report exactly how the crime was committed and determine if the method has any particular significance about other crimes, known criminals, or unique circumstances.
10. WAS THERE A LIMITED OPPORTUNITY FOR THE SUSPECT TO HAVE COMMITTED THE CRIME? Attempt to determine from the victim if the crime could have been within a specific time frame or if only specific persons could have committed the crime. This factor often has significance concerning people who know the victim's

habits or schedule, who are "casing" a place, or when only certain persons have access to a restricted area.

11. IS THERE A REASON TO BELIEVE THAT THE CRIME WOULD AROUSE SUCH INTEREST THAT PUBLIC ASSISTANCE WILL LEAD TO ITS RESOLUTION? Certain crimes, such as homicide, offenses against children, or a series of rapes, all generate a good deal of public interest. Since police rely on people for information, this increased interest is often beneficial. The investigating officer shall use his/her judgment on the level of interest in a particular offense and answer this question accordingly.

12. IS THERE REASON TO BELIEVE THAT FURTHER FOLLOW-UP INVESTIGATION WILL LEAD TO THE RESOLUTION OF THE CRIME? The investigating officer in a particular case may feel that more work could conclude the case, but for one reason or another, this officer cannot conduct this work at the time. In some cases, the officer may feel that there are steps that he/she can take that may lead to the resolution of the crime, even though no other solvability factor is present. If the officer answers "yes" to this question, he/she must state the basis upon which he/she rests this conclusion and specify what steps should be taken to bring the case to a successful conclusion (2014).

Other departments may utilize a point system for solvability factors. For example, a department may weigh solvability factors and create a cut-off score for referring the case to a detective. An example of this case management system using solvability weights is listed below.

So, how many cases should a detective supervisor assign to a detective? There is no single standard/formula to determine the appropriate caseload for criminal investigators. The investigator's knowledge, skills, and abilities, coupled with the complexity of the investigation, should determine an investigator's caseload. For example, one homicide investigation could occupy the time of several detectives for months. On the other hand, one detective could handle scores of simple theft investigations in a similar period. That said, there is some guidance on this issue from police practitioner organizations. The International Association of Chiefs of Police (IACP) suggests that a criminal investigator's caseload of 120 to 180 cases per year (10 to 15 per month) is manageable. The Detective Sergeant should monitor each detective case using a Report Management System (RMS), excel spreadsheet, or maintain a paper format if technology is not available. The Sergeant Detective and the detective should be able to view how many open cases the detective has and what type of case has been assigned. Also important is the ability of the detective sergeant to monitor the follow-up of cases through supplemental reports. Most Criminal Investigations Units have a timeframe for initiating a supplemental report to indicate that action has been taken by the detective assigned to the case. Detective sergeants must review case closures to ensure all possible investigatory steps have been taken to solve the case. The facts and Uniform Crime Reporting requirements dictate how cases are categorized as closed.

Clearance Rates

Clearance rates have played an essential role in measuring crime in communities. Collecting crime statistics was initiated by The International Association of Chiefs of Police in the early 1920s and was the foundation for the Uniform Crime Reports, which originated in 1930. The program has been maintained by the Federal Bureau of Investigations (FBI). While the Uniform Crime Report program is voluntary for law enforcement agencies, the International Association of Chiefs of Police and the National Sheriff's Association have been instrumental in encouraging 18,000 or more law enforcement agencies to report their statistics to the Uniform Crime Report program. However, the purpose of the Uniform Crime Report program was to generate summary statistics about crime and provide data for public safety measures and social indicators.

Clearance rates have remained consistently low in the United States despite the many advances in crime analysis, crime forensics, surveillance, and investigative technologies (Prince et al., 2021). The Uniform Crime Reporting (UCR) program, maintained by the FBI, collects and publishes crime statistics from law enforcement agencies throughout the United States. For example, official estimates of crime clearance by the Federal Bureau of Investigation's Uniform Crime Reporting program in 2019 (which defines clearances as crimes resolved by arrest or by exceptional means) indicate that of the 1.2 million violent crimes reported to the police, 54.5% were never cleared. Clearance rates are even more abysmal for property crimes. Of the 6.9 million property crimes in 2019, 82.8% were not cleared.

Further, these average clearance rates have remained remarkably stable (and in the case of homicides, have declined) for many decades (Braga et al., 2011; Lum et al., 2018; Scott et al., 2019; Vovak, 2016; Wellford and Cronin, 2000). Researchers have tried to link the relationship between arrest and clearance rates over time but found it difficult because they could not examine specific investigatory activities or strategies that directly contributed to the arrest or clearance rate. Interestingly, early on, researchers from the Rand Corporation (Chaiken, 1975; Chaiken et al., 1977; Greenwood and Petersilia, 1975; Greenwood et al., 1975) discovered that solvability factors are paramount to case clearance and more critical than an investigator's efforts or actions.

The Uniform Crime Report program was initially developed to capture only the most severe offense within an incident. The Uniform Crime Report program provided limited information about crime, and the Federal Bureau of Investigations decided to transition to an incident-based reporting system. This resulted in the birth of the National Incident-Based Reporting System (NIBRS). As of January 1, 2021, NIBRS is the national standard for reporting crime data in the United States. The National Incident-Based Reporting System is a more detailed and comprehensive version of reporting crime. The National Incident-Based Reporting System collects more detailed information on individual incidents, including data about victims, offenders, and circumstances involved in the crime. NIBRS enables users to provide more accurate information because the users can edit data (Tables 4.3 and 4.4). *The Report of the Attorney General under Section 18(A) of Executive Order 14074: Department of Justice Review of the Transition of Law Enforcement Agencies to the National Incident-Based Reporting System (NIBRS)* (n.d.) asserts the following:

> NIBRS is a significant shift-and improvement – in how reported crime is measured and estimated. The broad scope of the information collected in NIBRS greatly improves the nation's understanding of crime and public safety. Compared to the previous crime data collection system, NIBRS collects data about 47 more offenses and more detailed data about each victim, offender, person arrested, and property stolen or damaged for each victim, offender, person arrested, and property stolen or damaged for each crime incident. NIBRS data more accurately reflects the types of crime addressed by police agencies, like simple assault, animal cruelty, destruction of property, intimidation, and identity theft. NIBRS also captures detailed data about a broad array of offenses and the characteristics of criminal incidents, including types and amount of property lost; demographic information about victims, offenders, and persons arrested; and what type of weapon, if any, was

Table 4.3 Case Management Solvability Factors and Solvability Weights

Solvability Factors	Solvability Weights
Estimated time lapse	
Less than 1 hour	3
1–12 hours	2
12–24 hours	1
More than 24 hours	0
Crime discovered on view by officer	5
Witness (depends on credibility)	1 2 3 4 5
Suspect can be identified	7
Suspect can be described	4
Suspect can be located	4
Suspect has been seen in area previously	2
Suspect vehicle can be identified	7
Suspect vehicle can be partially described	2
Stolen property can be traced	5
Stolen property has been recovered	7
Significant or unique M.O.	3
Significant amount of evidence recovered	3
Recovered latent prints	5
Recovered DNA evidence	5
Limited opportunity for offender to commit crime	4
Other consideration/impact	1 2 3 4 5
Total	
Supervisor's Signature:	
Detective Assigned:	

Table 4.4 Key Benefits and Fast Facts of NIBRS

KEY BENEFITS OF NIBRS	NIBRS FAST FACTS
• Detailed, high-quality data that provides a completer and more accurate picture of crime. • Additional context to understand victimization and offending. • Standardized data to compare crime across jurisdictions. • Used for tactical or strategic analysis at the local, state, and national levels	• Includes up to 10 offenses per incident. • Creates profiles of victims and offenders • Provides details on the context of crime. • Offers insight into incidents involving multiple offenses. • Collects data on 71 crimes across 28 offense categories

Source: *The Report of the Attorney General pursuant to Section 18(A) of Executive Order 14074: Department of Justice Review of the Transition of Law Enforcement Agencies to the National Incident-Based Reporting System (NIBRS)*, (n.d.)

used in the incident. NIBRS also provides insight into the circumstances and context for crimes like location, time of day, and whether the incident resulted in an arrest. (pp. 2–3)

NIBRS is a solid enhancement to how data is captured from crime incidents. More data is being mined from each incident report. However, the sophistication of NIBRS makes the police department's reporting more complex. In 2022, the Congressional Research Service reported that in 2021, only 9,881 of the 18,818 law enforcement agencies in the United States submitted NIBRS data. This results in only 53% of the law enforcement agencies utilizing NIBRS in 2021. Below are some of the Key Benefits of NIBRS and NIBRS fast facts.

Performance Indicators and Evaluation of Criminal Investigation Units

When assessing the performance of a Criminal Investigation Unit, consideration must be given to measuring the performance of each detective and then combining the efforts of all detectives to measure the Criminal Investigations Unit at a macro level. This approach is like the pieces of a puzzle being placed together to see the whole picture the puzzle presents. Sworn and civilian members of police departments have annual performance evaluations. For validity, the performance evaluation should be based on a job-task analysis of the position. A job-task analysis enables a job description and performance evaluation to be sculptured from the information. Below is an example of a job description based on a completed job task analysis for a detective position with the Hillsborough County Sheriff's Office in Florida (Hillsborough County Sheriff, 2023) (Table 4.5).

Conducting a job task analysis for each position within a police department enables a customized performance evaluation instrument to be created. This process is time-consuming but will produce an excellent performance evaluation. However, some departments have performance evaluations that are one size fits all and may be used for all governmental positions in the city or county. These performance evaluations generally present a watered-down perspective of the employee's performance. The measured criteria are very generalized and reflect overly broad categories such as attendance, dependability, quality of work, work habits initiative, quantity of work, and relations with other employees. The descriptions of these categories may be limited so that the rater can determine performance standards.

The rating scales may also be overly broad, such as satisfactory or above, needing improvement, or improvement. While rating scales can be more defined, such as superior, exceeds expectations, meets expectations, needs improvement, poor, or not applicable, if the criteria need to be clearly defined, it can be difficult for the rater to evaluate the employee. Nonetheless, conducting annual performance evaluations captures components of a detective's performance.

Another measure of a detective's performance is the number of cases assigned as active cases, closed cases, cleared by arrest, exceptional or unfounded, and the clearance rate. These performance indicators provide a picture of a detective's workload. If the detectives worked on the same types of cases, such as property crimes, comparisons could be made between detectives. Comparisons between detectives should not be made if the detectives work on different types of cases. Comparing homicide statistics to larceny statistics would be comparing apples and oranges. However, comparing the statistics of a detective working the same types of cases over time can provide performance data. Table 4.6 is an example of statistics utilized to track the performance of a detective.

When evaluating the performance of a Criminal Investigations Unit, statistics that reflect the performance of the unit over a period can be captured. Table 4.7 is an example of data that may be captured to enable the supervisor to examine the unit's performance by the categories and changes over time. A supervisor should determine factors that may affect the performance of the unit. The four-year average is compared to 2025, and an underlying factor for the negative percent change may be due to COVID or some other factor. Another consideration for these unit statistics is to provide information to the public on the performance of the Criminal Investigations Unit either through the police

Table 4.5 Law Enforcement Detective Job Description

- **Job Code:** S2728
- **Pay Grade:** SO
- **Pay Scale:** $31.77–$45.70 Hourly; $69,385.68–$99,808.80 Annually.
- **Exempt:** No

OVERVIEW

Perform latent criminal investigations, interrogations, and surveillances for the apprehension and prosecution of law violators. Primary duties include implementation of standard police investigation procedures and techniques to apprehend, indict, and prosecute suspects and to prevent or solve crimes.

DUTIES & RESPONSIBILITIES

Note: Depending on assigned responsibilities, employees may perform some or all the duties below.

- Patrol areas that present special problems to detect planned criminal activity.
- Maintain surveillance of known criminals.
- Conduct criminal investigations.
- Conduct crime scene investigations to gather, preserve, identify, and evaluate physical evidence.
- Photograph the crime scene by taking serial photographs.
- Attend autopsies to collect information.
- Perform chemical and technical laboratory tests such as preliminary tool mark, ballistic, or cast comparisons.
- Process film for print preparation.
- Interview suspects and witnesses; arrest persons suspected of crimes.
- Prepare reports on work progress and submit reports to superior officers.
- Prepare applications for search warrants; serve capiases, court orders, and arrest warrants.
- Testify in court on evidence obtained.
- Investigate auto thefts, forgeries, and other related offenses.
- Transport prisoners to state institutions.
- Perform other related duties as required.

KNOWLEDGE, SKILLS & ABILITIES

- Considerable knowledge of crime detection and criminal investigation.
- Working knowledge of state laws and county laws, ordinances, rules, regulations, and court procedures related to arrest and evidence.
- Working knowledge of basic photography techniques and equipment use.
- Working knowledge of county geography and road network.
- Skill in the use and care of firearms and other law enforcement equipment.
- Skill in collecting and preserving diverse kinds of physical evidence for laboratory testing.
- Skill in mixing chemicals for specific tests.
- Ability to perform both mechanical and chemical tests to identify latent fingerprints.
- Ability to draw crime scene sketches.
- Ability to fingerprint deceased subjects.
- Ability to act quickly and correctly in emergencies.
- Ability to handle confidential information.
- Ability to communicate effectively, both orally and in writing.
- Ability to enforce the law firmly, tactfully, and impartially and to deal courteously with the public.
- Ability to meet such specific physical requirements as may be established by competent authority.
- Ability to safely operate a motor vehicle.
- Ability to use a computer and related software.

Table 4.5 (Continued)

MINIMUM EDUCATION & EXPERIENCE
- A high school diploma or possession of a GED certificate.
- Four continuous years of time-in-grade as a Law Enforcement Deputy with the Hillsborough County Sheriff's Office (HCSO) by the time of the Promotion Application deadline.

Additionally, the following are required:
- Possession of a valid Florida Driver License.
- Promotion Application.
- Eighty hours of subject-specific advanced, specialized training, or career development courses.
- No punitive disciplinary action consisting of a 5-day suspension or greater and/or involuntary or voluntary demotion within the last two years.
- An overall rating of three "fully acceptable" or better on the annual evaluation in the Employee Performance Management System (EPMS) for the three years prior to the Promotion Application deadline.
- A rating of three "fully acceptable" or better in each dimensional category on the annual evaluation in EPMS within the one year prior to the Promotion Application deadline.
- A promotion recommendation from the division/district major (or equivalent authority for those areas without a major).
- Live within Hillsborough County or within Citrus, Hardee, Hernando, Lake, Manatee, Pasco, Pinellas, Polk, Sarasota, or Sumter County if the residence is located within the 60-mile parameter of Falkenburg Road Jail at the time of appointment/employment.

REQUIRED PRE-EMPLOYMENT TESTING
- Successful completion of the Fitness Challenge within one year prior to the Promotion Application submission.

ADDITIONAL JOB REQUIREMENTS
- Attendance at the specified Sheriff's Office work location is required.
- Depending on assignment, employees may be required to possess a valid Florida Driver License at time of employment. Driving history will be thoroughly reviewed and may be grounds for disqualification.
- No visible tattoos on face, head, and neck. Tattoos determined to take away from the professional appearance of the Sheriff's Office must be covered with an appropriate white, black, or neutral covering.
- No illegal drug sale within lifetime.
- No illegal drug use within the past 36 months. No marijuana use within the last 12 months.
- No felony convictions within lifetime.
- No misdemeanor convictions involving perjury, false statement, or domestic violence within lifetime.
- No dishonorable discharge from any branch of the United States Armed Forces, the United States Coast Guard, National Guard, or Reserve Forces.
- Successful completion of a background investigation including criminal, reference, employment, and neighborhood checks; polygraph; medical evaluation; and drug screening.

department's website or annual report. Sharing information promotes transparency with the community.

It is imperative for the supervisor of a Criminal Investigation Unit to constantly assess the unit's training, policies, technology, staffing levels, overtime, opportunities for cost reduction, relationships with other divisions such as patrol and other agencies, work processes, and crime trends to position the Unit to perform at maximum capabilities while limiting unnecessary stress.

The performance evaluation of police departments can also be enhanced by contracting with an external company to evaluate their performance. For example, Certus Public Safety Solutions, LLC provides advanced statistical modeling in assessing workload and

Table 4.6 Clearance Rate Example

Detective	Number of Assigned Cases	Closed Cases	Cleared by Arrest	Cleared Exceptionally	Unfounded	Clearance Rate
#1	19	12	4	0	1	42%
#2	64	39	1	2	5	21%
#3	53	45	8	1	9	40%
#4	100	90	5	0	9	16%
#5	70	52	10	1	5	31%
#6	56	13	6	2	5	100%
#7	63	26	2	2	7	42%
#8	76	62	3	0	10	21%
Total	**501**	**339**	**39**	**8**	**51**	**29%**

Table 4.7 Caseloads 2019–2023

Category	2019	2020	2021	2022	Four-Year Average	2023	Percent Change
New Cases	1,971	2,423	2,442	2,178	2,253.5	1,978	-12.24%
Average Monthly Caseload	56	91	81.7	59.6	72.1	48.6	-32.60%
Cases Filed	462	539	670	581	563	494	-12.30%
Cases Worked	1,857	2,072	2,624	2,224	2,194.3	2,070	-5.70%
Arrest Warrant	209	175	260	211	213.8	265	24.00%
Search Warrants	68	71	46	62	61.8	82	32.70%
Property Recovered	$412,838	$319,436	$632,700	$1,187,382	$638,089	$583,091	-8.60%

performance. Certus Public Safety Solutions, LLC has conducted almost 200 studies of local police departments in the U.S., across 40 states and every region of the country. Certus Public Safety Solutions, LLC provides customized services to police departments to evaluate performance and provide realistic and targeted recommendations to improve organizational performance. An outside perspective on the performance of a police department can awaken a police department or validate a police department's performance measures, strategic planning, and future growth and vision.

References

Braga, A., Flynn, E., Kelling, G., & Cole, C. (2011). *Moving the Work of Criminal Investigators towards Crime Control*. National Institute of Justice. Retrieved September 22, 2023, from https://nij.ojp.gov/topics/articles/harvard-executive-session-policing-and-public-safety-2008-2014

CaseGuard. (March 7, 2016). *Instruction and Introduction of Case Management and Assignment*. Retrieved September 15, 2023, from https://caseguard.com/articles/instruction-introduction-of-case-management-assignment/

Chaiken, J. M. (1975). *The Criminal Investigation Process (Volume II): Survey of Municipal and County Police Departments*. The Rand Corporation.

Chaiken, J. M., Greenwood, P. W., & Petersilia, J. (1977). The criminal investigation process: A summary report. *Policy Analysis*, 3(2), 187–217.

Congressional Research Service. (2022). *NIBRS Participation Rates and Federal Crime Data Quality* [Review of *NIBRS Participation Rates and Federal Crime Data Quality*]. Insight; Congressional

Research Service. Retrieved September 21, 2023, from https://crsreports.congress.gov/product/pdf/IN/IN11936

Federal Bureau of Investigations. (n.d.). *Frequently Asked Questions on CODIS and NDIS.* Retrieved September 15, 2023, from www.fbi.gov/how-we-can-help-you/dna-fingerprint-act-of-2005-expungement-policy/codis-and-ndis-fact-sheet#:~:text=What%20is%20the%20National%20DNA,and%20local%20participating%20forensic%20laboratories.

Greenwood, P. W., Chaiken, J. M., Petersilia, J., Prusoff, L. L., Castro, R. P., Kellen, K., & Wildhorn, S. (1975). *The Criminal Investigation Process (Volume III): Observations and Analyses.* RAND Corporation.

Greenwood, P. W., & Petersilia, J. (1975). *The Criminal Investigation Process (Volume I): Summary and Policy Implications.* RAND Corporation.

Hillsborough County Sheriff (2023). Law Enforcement Detective Details | HCSO, Tampa FL. Teamhcso.com, Hillsborough County Sheriff's Office, teamhcso.com/JobDescription/Detail/S2728. Accessed September 21, 2023.

Lum, C., Wellford, C., Scott, T., Vovak, H., & Scherer, A. (2018). *Identifying Effective Investigative Practices: A National Study Using Trajectory Analysis, Case Studies, and Investigative Data, Final Report to the Laura and John Arnold Foundation.* George Mason University.

Portland Police Department. (2023, August 8). Retrieved September 30, 2023, from www.portland.gov/police/chiefs-office/documents/police-organizational-chart/download

Portland Police Bureau. (2023, August 24). *Police Staffing Numbers.* Portland.gov. Retrieved September 20, 2023, from www.portland.gov/police/open-data/ppb-staffing-report

Prince, Lum, & Koper (2021). *Effective Police Investigative Practices: An Evidence-Assessment of the Research.* Retrieved September 17, 2023, from https://craftmediabucket.s3.amazonaws.com/uploads/2021-Prince-Lum-Koper-Effective-Investigations.pdf

Salisbury Police Department. (2014). *Chapter 42 Criminal Investigations.* Retrieved September 15, 2023, from www.salisbury.edu/police//_files/Chap42.pdf?v=20230624044722

Sarasota Police Department. (2023). *Table of Organization.* Retrieved September 15, 2023, from www.sarasotapd.org/your-spd/chief-s-message/table-of-organization

Scott, T., Wellford, C., Lum, C., & Vovak, H. (2019). Variability of crime clearance among police agencies. *Police Quarterly*, 22(1), 82–111.

The Report of the Attorney General Pursuant to Section 18(a) of Executive Order 14074: Department of Justice Review of the Transition of Law Enforcement Agencies to the National Incident-Based Reporting System (NIBRS). (n.d.). Retrieved September 18, 2023, from www.justice.gov/media/1268971/dl?inline#:~:text=Agencies%20participate%20voluntarily%20and%20submit.

Vovak, H. (2016). Examining the Relationship between Crime Rates and Clearance Rates Using Dual Trajectory Analysis, Unpublished doctoral dissertation, George Mason University, Fairfax, VA.

Warfield, A. (2023, April 3). *SPD Welcomes a Class of 10 New Patrol Officers. Your Observer.* Retrieved September 20, 2023, from www.yourobserver.com/news/2023/apr/03/spd-welcomes-class-of-10-new-patrol-officers/

Wellford, C., & Cronin, J. (2000). Clearing up homicide clearance rates. *National Institute of Justice Journal*, 243, 1–7.

Chapter 5

Professional Standards
The Integrity Function

Introduction

Who is best suited to hold police as an organization and officers individually responsible and accountable for their actions? Stated another way, who should be vested with the authority of policing the police? Sound management suggests that the authority and responsibility to police the police must reside with the police themselves. However, to effectively police themselves, the chief/agency must be empowered and mandated to hold officers accountable for upholding agency standards, espoused values, constitutional/ statutory/caselaw and legislative /administrative mandates. To be successful, the chief/ agency head must be supported by a command staff who shares the same vision of police professionalism and accountability as the chief/agency head. When the leaders of a police agency are unable or unwilling to investigate allegations of police misconduct impartially and hold officers accountable for their actions, then those leaders should be replaced with those that can. Whether the chief is appointed or elected, s/he is accountable to those who placed them in that position. They should be removed from their positions for incompetence, malfeasance, nonfeasance, or misconduct. If removal is not a viable option, the police accountability function can be vested outside of the agency. There are several models to consider. All of the models have value, but none are perfect. The best approach is developing a culture where police leaders themselves hold their agencies and their members accountable.

One oversight model has the department conduct misconduct investigations, but those investigations are subject to review and may require the approval of an outside entity. This adds a layer of bureaucracy to the internal investigations process and negates agency decision making as it relates to investigative findings and proposed discipline when appropriate. The ability to impose discipline can and has changed behavior. Weakening the cheif's ability to discipline their officers also weakens their control of their officers. Here, the power to discipline shifts to the oversight entity that lacks an intimate knowledge of what is actually happening in that police agency and creates an opportunity for inappropriate interference from the oversight agency.

Another model is where the investigative authority is separate from the department, has the support of municipal leaders, and is vested with full authority to investigate complaints of police misconduct. This entity would also have the authority to undertake self-initiated investigations based on emerging or current trends, patterns of problematic behavior. This model, however, is an expensive undertaking. The outside entity must have unfettered access to relevant department databases, documents, reports, and personnel. This means they must

DOI: 10.4324/9781003396437-5

either have direct access to department documents, records, evidence and personnel, or have the power to compel the production of documents, records, evidence, and personnel for examination or interview. Without direct access or the power to compel production, the police department may resist, delay, and deny production of documents or access to personnel for one of many spurious reasons and hinder the mission of the investigating entity. This oversight model, however, strips the agency head of the ability to investigate and correct misconduct, through discipline or other means, of its members.

Except for day-to-day police operations, civilian oversight boards, and local, state, and federal prosecutors can serve as an effective check on police agency heads' ability and effectiveness in seeking out and correcting employee conduct but the primary responsibility to maintain order and impose discipline in a law enforcement agency must reside with the agency head. Proactive agency heads assess agency and personnel performance looking for strengths and frailties and indicators that a member(s) of their department may require additional support to meet the legal and ethical standards of the department.

Under any model, police must be candid and transparent in their communication and actions with community members as it relates to internal investigations and police conduct. If police are not trusted, unnecessarily limit disclose of information during the investigative process, or are not perceived as neutral investigators, the findings of their inquiry are less likely to be accepted as legitimate and the community will not be at ease.

This chapter explores the intra-department approach to professional standards. Implementing external processes to investigate police misconduct has its merits, but the nature of this book is prescriptive and designed to provide police departments and police managers with the tools to manage their departments effectively. Therefore, this discussion focuses on the policies and programs that reflect best practices and could be considered for almost universal implementation.

Some departments assign the internal investigative function to Internal Affairs or Professional Standards personnel. The commander of Internal Affairs or Professional Standards (if they investigate allegations of criminality or serious misconduct committed by a member of their department) should be a direct report to the agency head. The impact on the department and community from police officials who engage in criminality or serious misconduct is often devastating. Investigations into serious misconduct allegations or allegations of criminality should be limited to experienced competent investigators who have the authority, direction, and support of the agency head to follow the facts of the investigation wherever they lead. This is possible when the commander of these internal investigators reports directly to the agency head. Oftentimes the organizational chart of a law enforcement agency signals what the agency values or deems important by: who the function reports to, the rank of the person leading that function or the resources that are assigned. Bureau/division/units reporting directly to the agency head are usually deemed critical or sensitive to the agency. Functions deemed important to the agency that do not report to the agency head are often headed by a ranking member of the executive staff and/ or well-resourced and staffed.

From our perspective, the integrity function in a police department is best approached through a two-prong effort involving effective internal investigations into allegations of officer misconduct, and a robust risk management framework to address problematic conditions facing the department. Each area discussed below will have several action items that the reader could consider as they evaluate the operational performance of their department in this area.

Internal Investigations

Internal investigations are conducted when complaints ranging from minor misconduct to alleged criminality of members of the police agency are received. Because of the uniqueness of these complaints, consideration should be given to centralizing data collection and management.

Action Item One: Centrality of Data

For many reasons, one entity of the department should serve as the repository of all complaints alleging employee criminality or serious misconduct. One central repository, assessable by internal investigators, eliminates the need to query multiple databases to obtain an officer/civilian complaint history. To be clear, this database should not contain petty violations (i.e., improper uniform, extended meal period, etc.) where the conduct alleged is minor. Complaints of minor misconduct are best documented, investigated, and maintained at a level in the department not involved in day-to-day operations and sufficiently higher up in the organization to avoid undue influence. However, maintaining separate databases/records of complaints or criminality or serious misconduct spread across several divisions/bureaus hampers efficiency, can lead to an incomplete profile of an officer's complaint history, and likely frustrate investigative efforts. An investigator's skill, experience, training, resources, etc. required to complete an investigation into alleged criminality or serious misconduct differs vastly from that required for the investigator tasked with investigating allegations of minor misconduct. Therefore, assigning investigations of complaints of criminality or serious misconduct to a unit comprised of investigators specifically trained for this purpose makes sense. Assigning investigations of complaints of minor misconduct for completion at the division/bureau/command level also makes sense.

Action Item Two: "Direct-Report"

Internal investigations need to be managed by a "direct-report" to the chief. Allegations of serious misconduct or criminality are too critical and too sensitive to be dispersed throughout the department. These allegations have the potential to undermine public confidence in the department and those tasked with leading that department. In order to ensure the full cooperation of all members of the department, the authority and support of the agency head is required. The agency head can request, cajole and where necessary compel cooperation under the threat of discipline up to and including dismissal from the department. The agency head must receive timely updates on the progress of the investigation to ensure all reasonable steps are taken to determine the facts and reach investigative conclusions that are supported by the evidence.

Action-Item Three: Avoid Conflicts

There may be occasions where an allegation of serious misconduct or criminality must be assigned outside of the department for investigation. Clearly, if the initial allegation or during the investigation, evidence implicates the agency head, then that investigation cannot be conducted internally and must be turned over to an outside entity (with the requisite authority) to complete. Moreover, departments should defer undertaking investigations that present a conflict of interest or the appearance of a conflict/impropriety. Small departments have challenges conducting internal investigations that larger departments often do not. For example, surveillance by a small department's internal investigator (often one for the entire department) is impossible because everyone knows who that investigator is. Encountering or observing that investigator outside the normal course of department business may signal to the department employee that s/he is a potential target or person of interest in an internal investigation. Additionally, in departments where everyone knows everyone (and their families and friends, etc.) concerns of impartiality/neutrality exist or are perceived to exist. Some small departments may not have the capacity or competence to conduct complex investigations (i.e., financial transactions, interpreting digital evidence and other technology, etc.). In these circumstances, investigations (partially or in their entirety) should be assigned to another agency (i.e., local, county, state or federal) to conduct.

Action Item Four: Get Serious

Investigations of allegations of minor misconduct or minor policy violations, even if lodged with internal affairs, should be investigated within the accused/violator's chain of command. Only serious allegations of misconduct or criminality should be subjected to internal investigations. Isolating the investigation of serious misconduct away from other operational elements in the department and directly under the chief not only heightens the importance of these investigations but also preserves investigative efforts to be directed at these types of cases. Allegations or complaints of minor misconduct or minor rules violations, once documented by internal affairs, should be forwarded to the operational command of the subject officer or civilian member for investigation. This is referred to as "command-level investigations." The investigating officer should be at least one rank above that of the subject of the investigation. Command-level investigators to which these complaints are assigned should receive instruction/training on the fundamentals of internal investigations, interviewing techniques, case documentation, and preparation. The findings of these investigations should be reviewed through chain of command. These minor cases can be closed at the command level, reviewed by the bureau/division commander or forwarded to the chief (or designee) for review. Where the case is closed at the command or bureau/division level, a copy of the completed case file should be forwarded to Internal Affairs for archival purposes. Electronic case files are easily created, retrievable, reviewable, and stored.

Action Item Five: Trust But Verify

For quality assurance purposes, Internal Affairs personnel should randomly audit investigations completed and closed at the division/bureau/command level. Where deficiencies are found that could possibly change the outcome of a finding or penalty, that investigative file should be returned for additional investigative steps including appropriate corrective measures for the investigator and reviewers on the chain-of-command (i.e., training, discipline, etc.). Where the deficiency is unlikely to have changed the outcome of a finding or penalty, corrective measures are also appropriate but additional investigative measures are not required. Investigations initiated at the command level for minor misconduct (i.e., uniform violation, extended meal period, off-post, etc.) can and should be documented and closed at the unit/command level. A formal investigation as described below would not be required.

Action Item Six: Case Management

An electronic case management system with the functionality to document receipt of the allegation, create a case and track the assignment of the complaint to an investigator, document all investigative steps taken in that case to prove or disprove the allegation(s), document supervisory conferrals, supervisory reviews and guidance provided to the investigator while case is active and document the supervisory review process through the chain of command related to findings for each allegation and where appropriate, penalty recommendations. It is important that benchmarks for internal investigations be established so that the efficiency of investigators and the quality of the investigation, including supervisory oversight, can be assessed for each investigator and the unit overall.

Action Item Seven: Intake and Assignment

Filing a complaint against a member of the department should be no more difficult than filing a complaint for a crime. The same way departments welcome comments recognizing/complementing actions of its officers, the department should also welcome feedback of dissatisfaction with a service offered by the department or the performance of a member of the department. Members of the public should be able to file a complaint in person, over the phone, by letter, email or electronically via a portal featured on the department's website. Some departments will not investigate anonymous complaints or do so with less vigor. Also, some departments will not investigate complaints without the complainant signing the complaint form under an "advisement" of perjury. One of the hallmarks of a professional organization is its willingness to seek feedback, learn from it and where appropriate make adjustments in response to the information received. Perception matters. Creating what the public perceives to be hurdles in filing a complaint against an officer can result in the public believing that the department is not interested in hearing about the department's poor service or a problematic employee or that the department cannot be objective in investigating its officers. These perceptions, whether true or not, can have a chilling effect on complainants coming forward, particularly complainants with past criminal histories or who are known to the department in an unfavorable way. Moreover, these conditions needlessly impede the department's ability to acquire information about their employees, policies, practices, and processes of the department.

The intake process must be designed to obtain as much information as possible from the complainant, particularly when the complainant files the complaint by speaking with a member of the department (in-person or via phone). The intake of telephone complaints should always be on a recorded line so that the recording can be reviewed by investigators. This is a critical point in the process as some complainants may not be able to be contacted later, become uncooperative or withdraw their complaint. The individual receiving these complaints must take the approach that this may be the last time the department will be in contact with the complainant and attempt to obtain as much detailed information about the specifics of the allegation(s), the member(s) of the department involved, identify of witnesses, evidence like video/audio recordings they might possess (and attempt to secure that evidence) and obtain several ways to contact the complainant and witnesses, if any, like email, cell, residence and business phone numbers, home and business address, social media, etc.. The department must establish metrics to assess the efficiency and quality of the intake process. The thoroughness of the initial intake interview is critical. Metrics like the amount of time it takes: to document the complaint from the complainant, for Internal Affairs personnel to assess the seriousness of the alleged conduct (criminality, serious misconduct minor misconduct, etc.), and to assign the complaint for investigation are key efficiency indicators. Once the complaint is received by the investigating entity, a new set of metrics are necessary to assess the efficiency and quality of the investigative process and the review undertaken by supervisors tasked with approving the closing of the investigation or recommending additional investigative steps, if required. Important metrics in this process include the amount of time it takes the investigating entity to assign the case to an investigator, and for the investigator to contact the complainant to conduct a more thorough and detailed follow-up interview. Case assignment practices, in which cases are assigned to investigators on a rotational basis regardless of whether they are on extended leave (i.e., vacation, sickness, etc.), must be avoided. This practice unnecessarily delays the time in which the investigator makes initial contact with the complainant. Contacting a complainant two to three weeks after their complaint is filed is simply unacceptable and gives the impression the department cares little about following up on this complaint.

Action Item Eight: Electronic Cases

Once the complaint is assigned to an investigator, an electronic case folder should be created to document receipt of the complaint and all activities undertaken in the investigation to reach a determination concerning the alleged conduct. This includes directions received from the investigator's supervisors and other supervisory conferrals on the status/progress of the case.

Some departments use case checklists to ensure investigators complete basis investigative steps in each investigation. These checklists may identify records, documents, databases, persons, and other conferrals/sources that must be considered in each investigation. Some departments shun checklists out of concern that investigators will simply take the measures outlined on the checklist and little to nothing more. Investigations will often require investigators to take steps not contained on the checklist. Every reasonable measure that helps the investigator to reach a conclusion with respect to the alleged conduct must be undertaken. Departments that use checklists require a robust case management system and supervisory oversight to ensure investigators are not simply checking the boxes. With respect to checklists, whichever works best for the department is the way to go on case checklists. Several sample investigative checklist are available in the public domain, through membership in professional practice police organizations, and accreditation bodies.

Audios of recorded conversations and interviews with complainant(s)/witness(es) and respondents should be summarized. The audio itself and the summary thereof should be included in the electronic case folder. When possible, the investigator should attempt to interview the complainant and any witnesses in person and record these interviews. In-person interviews allow the investigator to observe the interviewee's behavior/demeanor and may provide insight when making an overall assessment of the person's credibility. Copies of all records, documents, videos, photographs, Body Worn Camera (BWC) videos, etc. (internal and external) should be summarized along with their significance and included in the case folder.

Periodic supervisory reviews of the case folder and conferral with the assigned investigator including directions/next investigative steps must be documented by the supervisor in the case folder. Supervisors must ensure that investigators are meeting department milestones/benchmarks with respect to the timeliness and thoroughness of internal investigations.

Where they are not, it is the supervisor's responsibility to provide the additional support needed to complete the investigation consistent with department benchmarks and quality standards. It is critical that supervisors not simply read the summaries included in the case but that they also listen to interviews in their entirety, and review videos completely to identify omissions or discrepancies/inconsistencies between the evidence contained in the case folder and the investigator's interpretation of said evidence. For example, during a case review, the supervisor noted that one complainant and no witnesses are listed in the electronic case folder. However, while the reviewing supervisor was listening to the investigator's audio recording of a telephone interview of the complainant, the supervisor heard the investigator ask the complainant a question about the encounter with the officer. The complainant is then heard on the audio recording asking another person with them the question posed by the investigator and that person provided a response. In the audio, the investigator failed to ask the complainant the identity of the person to whom the question was posed and whether that person was present during the encounter with the officer which led to the complainant filing the complaint. Here, had the supervisor not reviewed the audio recording of the interview, this witness would not have been identified or interviewed by the investigator. In this instance, the investigator should be directed to take steps to interview that person.

Action Item Nine: Closing

Departments may differ on how the investigator closes his/her investigation and submits the case file through the chain of command for review. There is a continuum of options in this regard. Some departments do not want the investigator to draw conclusions or make recommendations with respect to each allegation investigated or penalties if the allegation is substantiated. Instead, the investigator submits their findings on each allegation and as the case goes through the review process, a recommendation as to how each allegation should be closed (i.e., sustained, not sustained, unfounded, exonerated, etc.) is made. This recommendation may be offered anywhere between the first review through the final stage in the review process. The recommendation may or may not include a penalty recommendation with respect to sustained allegations. For departments that use a disciplinary matrix or equivalent, the prescribed penalty for violations of various department rules, regulations, or policies is established and can be modified considering the presence or absence of aggravating or mitigating factors. At the other end of the continuum, the investigator will make recommendations with respect to each allegation of misconduct and for those sustained, may provide a penalty recommendation. The final authority on disciplinary matters also varies. This authority may reside anywhere from the local or command level for minor misconduct through the agency head. Penalties imposed for sustained allegations of serious misconduct or criminality are likely decided by the agency head or a board that sits above the agency head that is tasked with, among other things, the resolution of personnel matters. Investigations of allegations of criminality are conducted in consultation with the prosecutor's office where it appears there is substance to the alleged criminality. In those instances where the prosecutor declines to bring criminal charges, the department may proceed administratively against the officer.

Action Item Ten: Penalty

Once a penalty is approved by the final authority, the implementation of the penalty should occur promptly, and consistent with the agency collective bargaining agreement (CBA).

Suspension or forfeiture of accumulated time must be deduced from the employees' leave balances/payroll records and documented accordingly.

Investigative Training

Like investigators of traditional crime, internal investigators require entry-level and in-service training, mentoring and appropriate supervision if they are to conduct thorough investigations. Internal Affairs investigators and investigators at the bureau/division level must receive training that prepares them for the cases they are assigned. This includes new assignment training upon initial assignment to this function, on-the-job training (OJT) alongside a seasoned internal investigator, as well as coaching, mentoring and appropriate supervision/oversight. In addition to in-service training required to maintain their sworn certifications, they must receive annual training that increases their knowledgebase and enhances their investigative abilities. Those assigned to an internal investigative function at the unit/command level also require investigative training as to the fundamentals of investigations but nothing near the level required for internal affairs investigators who conduct complex investigations.

Resources, including staffing and equipment, are essential to complete investigations. The staffing required depends on the unit's workload and the type of equipment required depends upon the type and complexity of investigations conducted. At times, some agencies may elect to "farm out" investigations or parts thereof where they lack personnel, equipment, experience, or the skillset to complete a particular investigation or aspect of an investigation. For example, in smaller agencies where the internal investigators are known to everyone, farming out the surveillance portions of the investigation or "actors" from another department may be used in integrity tests because the mere presence of a known internal investigator outside of the workplace may signal to the officer that s/he is the subject of an internal investigation. These investigations or portions thereof can be farmed out to the internal affairs/professional standards section of a local department, a county level law enforcement agency including the public integrity section of the office of the prosecutor, a state-level law enforcement agency, or depending on the severity of the allegations, a federal agency. In some instances, a private investigator can be used to conduct certain aspects of the investigation, like surveillance.

Conducting internal investigations, whether generated internally or by a community complaint, is an important and necessary function for a law enforcement agency. When internal investigations are conducted professionally, thoroughly and with as much transparency as permitted by law, agency policy and community needs, it demonstrates that an agency can police itself. This demonstrated ability helps create trust among agency consumers and stakeholders that their complaints will be investigated impartially, and the findings will be based on the facts of the investigation. While investigations of community complaints are reactive, police departments must also be proactive in recognizing emerging problematic conditions and/or employees before complaints of serious misconduct or criminality arise.

Assessment and Compliance – Identifying and Mitigating Risk

The "Professional Standards" function in any police department may also be tasked with auditing department operations and assessing key measures to determine whether its members are operating in compliance with the department's rules, regulations, orders, and policies. It is critical that departments have a system in place to regularly review those practice areas that are most challenging to law enforcement agencies and specifically the areas where the agency itself struggles. It is also important to develop assessment policies to ensure that the civil rights of all individuals in the community are protected.

Federal consent decrees and settlement agreements with state or local governments resulting from pattern and practice or similar inquiries are data rich in identifying areas where law enforcement agencies subject to those decrees/settlements have struggled and for which there were few or ineffective accountability/oversight systems in place to identify and correct deficient practices. Federal consent decrees regarding the police originated from the 1994 Crime Bill (H.R.3355 – Violent Crime Control and Law Enforcement Act, 1994). This law empowered the Department of Justice to conduct "pattern and practice" investigations into allegations of police abuse.

Since 1994, the Department of Justice has opened 25 investigations into law enforcement agencies, resulting in 19 agreements, including 14 consent decrees. These agreements bear an added expense to police and community budgets and a heavy-handed approach from the federal government imposing itself on local police departments (Johnson and Kennedy, 2023).

Policing, at its core, is the legal application of coercive force (Bittner, 1970). And police departments are made up of imperfect humans. The combination of these facts creates the conditions where police officers may violate peoples' rights and engage in misconduct. It is inevitable. Departments, therefore, must ensure that policies, programs, and strategies are in place to minimize misconduct by officers, mitigate the damage done because of this conduct, and prevent future misconduct from occurring.

The International Association of Chiefs of Police published an important handbook for police leaders to minimize instances of police misconduct. While the probability of ending up being investigated by the Department of Justice is remote, it is incumbent for all police departments to develop policies to address potential problems. IACP identified eight categories of misconduct that have led to pattern and practice investigations by the Department of Justice:

- Unlawful use of force
- Inadequate or absence of training on the use of force
- Racial Profiling
- Unlawful stops, frisks, and searches
- Police intimidation
- Harassment of civilians and retaliation for them reporting misconduct
- Inadequate supervision
- Failure to investigate allegations of officer misconduct. (IACP, 2006)

There are also policies and programs that police departments can implement to minimize the risk of officers engaging in misconduct. These initiatives must be managed effectively by the professional standards element of a police department, and reinforced continually through effective leadership and supervision. Accountability within the agency starts with the local commander, his/her command staff, and supervisors. A continuous process of review of key performance indicators must occur at the local level.

Risk Management = A.I.M. to Correct

We apply the acronym "AIM to Correct" to conceptualize the approach police departments should embrace with regards to risk management. "Analyze, Identify, Mitigate, and Correct" is the framework to minimize adverse risks in policing.

Analyze

A problem cannot be solved, and risks cannot be managed, unless there is empirical data that illustrates it. "If you can't measure it, you can't manage it"[1] is an oft-quoted management principle and in order to manage risk appropriately police departments must organize, track, and analyze the data that illustrates those risks. Now police departments are data warehouses and store a tremendous amount of information, therefore, it is necessary to isolate specific data that can alert police managers to potential problems. Departments should take heed of the direction of the IACP mentioned above and track the data associated with those problem areas, but there is more. Below is a list of data that professional police departments should be collecting, organizing, and analyzing to foster rigorous risk management.

Use of Force Incidents – The police are empowered to use force, including deadly force, to protect the public and themselves, make arrests, and prevent offenders from escaping custody. This is an awesome power and requires great responsibility to wield it properly. It is incumbent upon police departments, therefore, to ensure that the use of force by their officers is applied lawfully. This is likely the most critical piece of data that departments should collect, and many states have passed legislation requiring police departments to report uses of force. Deciding what kinds of force should be reported is a complicated matter. Obviously, firearms discharges would be something to track, but these are very rare events. Is yelling at a civilian force? Deploying a K9 dog? Brandishing a firearm? Perhaps the yardstick to measure whether or not force was used could be whether or not the police officer thought they were using force or where there could be a reason for a complaint by a member of the public that the actions were excessive force?

The NYPD established definitions of different levels of force and guidelines to report uses of force at these levels and their policy could serve as a model. According to the NYPD Patrol Guide, there are three levels of force. Level 1 force incidents include hand and foot strikes, forcible takedowns, use of OC spray, discharging a Taser, or using a restraining blanket. Level 2 force incidents include intentionally striking a person with a baton or other object, a canine bite, discharging a Taser in "drive stun" mode. And Level 3 force incidents are discharging a firearm or using any other deadly force that is capable of causing serious injury or death (NYPD, 2016).

This policy seems to be a good one to track the use of force by officers in a department.

"Trifecta" Arrests – A "trifecta" arrest is a charge made against a civilian for either obscene or offensive language, resisting arrest, and assaulting a police officer with no other underlying criminal conduct. These charges could imply an escalation of force or legal authority by the police officer as a punitive measure against an unruly or disrespectful member of the public. Departments would be well-served by tracking reports of these charges and scrutinizing the underlying encounters more carefully. They could signal an overly aggressive officer, or nothing, but tracking them would strengthen the risk analysis for a department. Also, command-level staff should proactively review arrests and summonses/citations (other than traffic enforcement related) by officers in which the complainant is the state (i.e., self-initiated enforcement in which there was no witness or complainant). Self-initiated enforcement and discretion exercised by officers must be guided by the commander and compliant with the law, department policies/procedures and community needs. Reviewing self-initiated enforcement activity, particularly offenses that do not advance public safety or goals collaboratively developed by the community and the department, can help identify miscommunication and/or misdirected community engagement practices with respect to that officer.

Vehicle Pursuits – car chases are perhaps the most dangerous tactics police employ. Speeding cars through a community pose a significant risk to the general public and can cause serious injury or death to the motorists, officers involved, and members of the public. Police departments should track these events very carefully. States, like Connecticut, require police departments to report the police pursuits (Connecticut General Statutes, 2023). Departments should define what is meant by a police pursuit and require officers to report these events.

Traffic Stop and Investigative (Terry) Stop Data – Officers should report on traffic stops and investigative stops and indicate the gender, race, age, and circumstances related to the stop. These data would be useful for departments understanding if officers are racially profiling members of the public. Terry stops should be documented on a department form/report and body worn camera (BWC) if implemented. The department form/report should contain a narrative section where the officer describes/explains the factors which created reasonable suspicion that the individual stopped was engaged, is engaged or was about to be engaged in criminality. This document should also contain a narrative section where the officer describes/explains the factors that created reasonable suspicion that the individual was armed and dangerous if the person was frisked and describe/explains the factors that created probable cause if the person was searched. This report and the associated body worn camera video should be reviewed by the officer's supervisor for accuracy between the written documents and the BWC video(s) capturing the Terry stop. Where the reviewing supervisor finds a deficiency, some measure (i.e., instructions, counseling, mentoring, training, discipline, etc.) must be taken to correct the deficiency and lessen the likelihood of a reoccurrence.

Similarly, traffic stops should be reported. Officers should make an account of why the motorist was stopped, the location and the outcome of that stop (warning, citation, arrest, search, etc.)

Off-Duty Conduct – Departments should monitor off-duty employment by their officers. Officers should be required to request permission to work off-duty beforehand and report the employer and nature of work to be performed. Officers should be prohibited from working at establishments where alcohol is served for on-premises consumption and generally be prohibited from working for employers that would bring disrepute to the department.

Civilian Complaints – Departments should accept, record, and track allegations of misconduct made by members of the public against members of the department. The National Association for Civilian Oversight of Law Enforcement provides several important elements of an appropriate policy for lodging complaints against police officers by member of the public. There should be a readily accessible form, a definition of what types of reportable allegations should be accepted for investigation and an easily understood process for making the complaint (National Association for Civilian Oversight of Law Enforcement, 2024).

Identification

The next step in the AIM to Correct framework is to identify problematic behavior. Processes need to be established for reviewing the data being collected by the department and identifying problematic officers, supervisors, units, or situations that pose an undue risk to the effectiveness of the department. Below are several recommendations that will improve a police department's ability to safeguard civil rights and minimize instances of police officer misconduct.

Routine self-inspections – Local commanders should have a proactive command-level inspection system that reviews regularly (i.e., monthly, quarterly, semi-annually, or annually) specific performance metrics to ensure their officers are following statutory and department rules regulations and policies and that when they do not, supervisors are identifying these deficiencies and taking corrective measures. The command-level review cannot end here. A member of the command staff should be tasked with reviewing a representative sample of these reports, along with the supervisor's findings and corrective measures when taken to evaluate the quality of the oversight provided by individual supervisors. Where there are deficiencies in the supervisory review, remedial measures (i.e., instructions, counseling, mentoring, training, discipline, etc.) with respect to that supervisor must be taken to correct that deficiency and lessen the likelihood of a reoccurrence.

The point here is that effective supervision and oversight must begin at the command level with the officer's immediate supervisor. The officer's immediate supervisor is best positioned to observe the officer in the field and on calls for service to evaluate their performance. Moreover, the immediate supervisor can evaluate officer performance when not on the scene by reviewing the officer's body-worn camera recording (if so equipped) to determine if that officer requires additional support from the department to improve their performance and ultimately the consumer's experience with the service provided by the department.

Body-Worn Camera Assessments – To ensure the accuracy of command-level proactive assessments, command staff or the Professional Standards personnel must have a system in place that regularly reviews a sample of BWC videos and the command-level review of those documents to assess how effective the command level accountability process identifies deficient practices and when they are identified, how they were addressed. Where there are deficiencies in the assessments conducted by the command staff member, or where the command staff failed to identify a deficiency, some measures should be taken with command staff to correct the deficiency and lessen the likelihood of a reoccurrence. This layered approach is one means to identify emerging or existing problematic issues/practices and correct them. When an agency fails to adequately police itself, authorities outside the agency with oversight responsibilities of that law enforcement agency must step in. When the issue comes to the attention of outside agencies to correct, it suggests systemic internal failures.

Early Intervention System – An Early Intervention System is designed to intervene at the earliest possible opportunity to support employee wellness and professional development. This is accomplished by identifying and mitigating factors reflected in poor employee performance, employee discipline, or negative interactions with the public.

Ideally, useful factors/indicators for analysis would be available with one database but rarely is that the case. Many departments have IT systems that were developed over time, for specific purposes, and are often stand-alone systems. Access to these systems is usually limited to those with a work-related need and these systems usually do not communicate/interface with other systems. As departments improve their IT infrastructure and systems, disparate databases should be consolidated or at least be able to communicate with one another. Professional Standards personnel must be able to draw from several data sources across the organization to identify personnel who are struggling and need support. Departments make a significant investment in terms of recruitment, training, equipment, supervision, and the financial compensation of employees. It just makes fiscal sense to support, remediate, and hopefully retain struggling employees before having problematic/troubling behavior manifest into terminable conduct. In many instances, termination is an avoidable outcome, and the agency can realize its return on its human capital.

Several data sources should be considered in assessing officer performance and identifying those who are struggling and require support. The department should establish thresholds for which an officer's overall performance will be assessed. For example, a specific number of community complaints, incidents of uses of force incidents, emergency excusals, command-level discipline, etc. within a specified timeframe. When an officer passes a threshold, a complete evaluation of the officer is warranted. The evaluation should determine whether the officer requires additional support from the department to improve performance and if so, what additional support is needed, who will ensure the officer receives the support s/he needs, and a follow-up assessment to determine if the corrective measures taken were effective or should be adjusted. At a minimum, departments should consider:

o Personnel records
  • Substandard overall performance evaluation or substandard ratings in specific areas/dimensions.
  • Excessive sick leave usage.
  • Exhausting annual leave or compensation time well before the end of the year.
  • Training deficiencies observed at in-service training courses and/or recertification requirements.
  • Whether member is approved to work in secondary employment.
  • Current assignment.
o Community Comments
  • Number of community complaints/pattern of behavior emerging among two or more complainants from two or more separate events.
o Discipline
  • Warnings, counseling, coaching for minor infractions.
  • Frequency of discipline.
o Enforcement History
  • Number of arrests (felonies, misdemeanors, violations).
  • Number of summonses (moving violations, personal summonses, parking violations).
  • Outcomes of suppression hearings where member's actions resulted in the suppression of evidence (physical or statements).
  • Number of occasions in which prosecutors decline to prosecute a case based on the actions of the officer.
  • Adverse credibility finding by the court (administrative or criminal) concerning an officer's testimony.
o Civil Judgement
  • Outcome of civil litigation against the officer including settlements.
  • Number of lawsuits filed against the officer based on the officer's actions/inactions regardless of the outcome.
o Number of instances officer employed force
  • Frequency and type of force as compared to peers.
o Vehicle accidents/pursuant
  • Number of vehicle accidents/pursuits in which officer was found at fault.

- Poor judgment exercised by officer in commencing pursuit or failing to terminate pursuit when threat to the public outweighs the need to arrest the motorist.
o Off-duty incidents
- Frequency and type of incidents the officer is involved in while off-duty.

The above metrics are not intended to be an exhaustive listing of factors an agency should review.

Property and Evidence – Storing and safeguarding property that comes into the possession of the department is a critical function. Similar to the self-inspection process identified above, departments should develop and implement periodic assessments of the property and evidence system. The International Association for Property and Evidence literally wrote the book on property and evidence management (Latta and Bowers, 2011). They recommend establishing routine and frequent audits of stored property and a robust system of managing property and evidence. The Professional Standards role of any police department should include the development and implementation of audits and assessments of this critical function.

The above systems and others are intended to identify issues/concerns while they are emerging and correctable. The purpose here is to identify issues/concerns and thus reduce the risk of substandard performance and the attendant liability to the department by proactively looking for emerging trends/patterns of behavior that forecast negative outcomes for the officer and/or the department.

Mitigation

Mitigation is the M in AIM to Correct and describes the most difficult yet most important part of the process. This is the need to act decisively and timely to mitigate the risk identified. Whether it is a problematic officer, unit, supervisor, or process, there must be accountability assigned to mitigate the problems. Bad news is not like fine wine, it doesn't get better with time, and problems identified in the risk management framework must be addressed as soon as practicable.

If an officer is experiencing problems, they should be put in the most favorable position not to do damage to themselves, the department or the community. If a unit is demonstrating problematic arrest practices or sustaining an inordinate number of civilian complaints, it must be curtailed immediately. If shortcomings in any processes are identified, they must be rectified immediately.

Best practices in this area suggest that the head of the professional standards function have the authority to act swiftly to mitigate the identified risks. Direct reporting to the chief of police ensures that the professional standards commander can easily and quickly notify the chief and act on her approval as soon as practicable.

Correction

Mitigate refers to the particular incident or officer at risk, and correction means the steps the department should take to address future risks of this nature. The following is a list of policy or programmatic steps that could be considered to hard-wire risk management practices into department operations.

Consider Accreditation – The Commission on the Accreditation of Law Enforcement Agencies (CALEA) is an organization that provides professional standards and recognition that participating departments show evidence of meeting those standards. Also, more than 30 states have developed police accreditation standards for departments in their specific states, with many programs being developed. Similarly, the Community-Oriented Policing Services office in the US Department of Justice (2023) has a law enforcement agency accreditation process. To obtain accreditation by the COPS office a department must work with a state accrediting agency or CALEA to adopt specific operating standards that are considered best practices in law enforcement. Accreditation can undoubtedly improve a department's policies and procedures and put them on solid footing to correct any risk-related conditions facing the department.

Training – Effective training is a central component of an effective risk management framework. Personnel involved in police training should occupy a key role alongside the police chief and professional standards commander in the risk management process. Through the analysis of data and identification of problems that pose a risk to the department, it is likely that corrections to these risks could be addressed by training. For example, if the analysis of Terry Stop data suggests that officers are stopping people on less than reasonable suspicion, there could be an opportunity to retrain incumbent officers, and strengthen this section of the entry-level curriculum for new officers, in order to address this issue. The potential list of training topics is extensive. The best approach, however, is to tailor the training to the identified problem. Providing training, just to say you are providing training is a waste of time. Instruction should be directed at correcting identified problems and risks.

Personnel Policies: Hiring and Promoting – Personnel policies with regards to hiring and promoting are also excellent places to correct risk management problems. Again, through effective data analysis and problem identification, patterns and trends can be identified that might be corrected by hiring and promoting different people. Many years ago, for example, police departments recognized that maturity and experience were key ingredients in effective police officers and their supervisors. Raising the hiring age, therefore, resulted in a more experienced and more mature officer. Requiring the officers spend a minimum number of years in rank likewise build in experience as a factor in making the next rank. Officers might need five years on the job before they can get promoted to sergeant, or sergeants might need three years as a sergeant before being promoted to lieutenant, etc.

Education could also provide a similar solution to address risk. Research has shown that education is related to better police performance and higher levels of education are associated with better communication skills, decision-making, report writing, and overall performance (Smith and Aamodt, 1997). Personnel policies that incentivize education for officers could be an effective way of correcting risk-related problems in departments.

Employee Assistance Programs – Developing robust employee assistance and employee wellness programs is undoubtedly an important component of a risk management framework. The President's Task Force on 21st Century Policing (2015) identified police employee well-being as one of the six pillars that organized their recommendations. Pillar Six was "Officer Safety and Wellness" and this recognized the need for police departments to develop programs to improve the well-being of their officers. The focus of the Task Force's work was around shift schedules and injuries, which are key elements in this area, but it can be expanded substantially to include all forms of well-being from physical fitness, to emotional and social health, financial security, and even contributing to charitable works in the community. The general approach here is that risks faced by the department could be identified by effective data analysis and identification, and then corrected by a holistic program to promote officer well-being. If officers are satisfied and content in their role, they will be less likely to create risk issues for the department. This is also a positive effort and does not necessarily imply negative sanctions or discipline. Well-being and fitness could be the cornerstone of a sound personnel management policy, which would then in turn minimize the risks the department might face by problematic officers or units.

Conclusion

This chapter explores the integrity function needed in every police department. Under the general description of professional standards, the chapter provides details on two distinct operations every police department must embrace: effective internal investigations and risk management and compliance. The chapter illustrates the many steps that need to be followed in order to conduct internal investigations. There are 10 essential elements to this important process and these steps need to be followed whether there is one person conducting the investigations or an entire bureau or division. In addition to these investigations, or dealing with allegations as they materialize, departments need to be proactive and seek to avoid misconduct from occurring in the first place. This is the area of risk management and compliance.

The chapter recommends that police departments embrace an "AIM to Correct" framework for risk management. This framework suggests Analyzing relevant data, Identifying problematic conditions, then Mitigating and Correcting them in the organization. There are several steps needed to enhance risk management and compliance, and put the department on sound footing to minimize misconduct or civil rights violations they might commit.

Note

1 Peter Drucker.

References

Bittner, E. (1970). *The functions of police in modern society*. Washington, DC: US National Institute of Mental Health.

Connecticut General Statutes. (2023). *Title 14 – Motor Vehicles. Use of the Highway by Vehicles. Gasoline, Chapter 248 – Vehicle Highway Use Section 14-283a. – Pursuits by Police Officers. State-Wide Policy*. Prohibitions. Reports.

Cornell Law School. (2022). *Castle Doctrine Defined. Legal Encyclopedia*. Legal Information Institute.

H.R.3355 – Violent Crime Control and Law Enforcement Act (1994).www.congress.gov/bill/103rd-congress/house-bill/3355/text

International Association of Chiefs of Police (2006). *Protecting Civil Rights: A Leadership Guide for State, Local, and Tribal Law Enforcement*. DOJ-Community Oriented Policing Services. www.theiacp.org/sites/default/files/all/p-r/PCR_LdrshpGde_Part1.pdf

Johnson, J., & Kennedy, S. (2023). *Police Reform by Decree: How DOJ Enacts Its Policing Agenda*. Law Enforcement Legal Defense Fund.

Latta, J., & Bowers, G. (2011). *Property and Evidence by the Book*. International Association for Property and Evidence, Inc.

Lindgren, J. (1981). Organizational and other constraints on controlling the use of deadly force by police. *The ANNALS of the American Academy of Political and Social Science*, 455(1), 110–119. https://doi.org/10.1177/000271628145500110?>

Manning, P. K. (1980). Violence and the police role. *The ANNALS of the American Academy of Political and Social Science*, 452(1), 135–144. https://doi.org/10.1177/000271628045200113?>

NYS Penal Law Article 35, Section 35.15, Sud 2.

NYPD. (2016). *Force Guidelines*. NYPD Patrol Guide Section 221-01. www.nyc.gov/html/ccrb/downloads/pdf/pg221-01-force-guidelines.pdf

President's Task Force on 21st Century Policing. (2015). Final Report of the President's Task Force on 21st Century Policing. Washington, DC: Office of Community Oriented Policing Services. https://cops.usdoj.gov/pdf/taskforce/taskforce_finalreport.pdf

Smith, S. M., & Aamodt, M. G. (1997). Relationship between education, experience, and police performance. *Journal of Police and Criminal Psychology*, 1(2), 7–14.

Terry v. Ohio 392 US 1 (1968).

US Department of Justice. (2023). *Police Reform and Accountability Accomplishments*. DOJ. Retrieved from www.justice.gov/opa/file/922461/dl#:~:text=Since%20the%20start%20of%20the,and%20one%20post%2Djudgment%20order

Chapter 6

Administration and Support

Introduction

This chapter will address two basic questions:1) how should modern American Police Departments be designed and structured?; and 2) how should they be managed and supported? Unfortunately, it is not possible to provide a simple answer to these questions as organizational structures will vary to a certain degree in all police departments, depending upon the precise mission of each organization. For example, the organizational chart of a large urban police department will vary considerably from that of a county sheriff's office (with responsibilities for prisoner detention and court security), or a campus police department of a regional college or university. Nevertheless, certain similarities exist in all departments, as first and foremost all police departments are primarily responsible for providing for the public's safety. Therefore, the patrol function is generally similar in structure in all police departments. But whether or not a particular department employs its own detectives or dispatchers, as opposed to relying upon county or state resources, will depend upon the department's size, its geographic area of responsibility, its mission, funding, etc. These are the factors that will dictate which specific units are created and where they are placed within the organizational chart.

Organizational Design and Structure

Police departments and sheriff's offices, like all organizations, "consist of a deliberate arrangement of people doing specific jobs following particular procedures in order to accomplish a set of goals determined by some authority" (O'Hara, 2005, p. 47). The basic structure and administrative practices of the American police department were established over 150 years ago. Traditionally, police departments have been characterized as "highly centralized, specialized, and formal organizations with tall hierarchies, large administrative units, and a diverse mix of occupational specialties" (Maguire et al., 2003, p. 251). The decision to have a hierarchical structure that centralizes power, authority and decision making at and near the top creates an organization that looks, reacts, and operates differently than one where authority and decision making is dispersed throughout the organization. In a "flatter" organization, managers closest to and executing the organization's operations are most knowledgeable of consumer/market conditions, and are generally empowered and encouraged to make decisions in response to changing conditions without first "running it up the chain of command" for permission. Not so under the traditional, hierarchical and paramilitary structure of many police departments.

DOI: 10.4324/9781003396437-6

From a command-and-control standpoint, the hierarchical and paramilitary structure of police departments ensured predictability, clear directives and close supervision, but left much to be desired with regard to leadership, creative thinking, problem-solving, responsiveness, and community engagement (Peak et al., 2010) During the 1980s and 1990s, police organizations in many countries "adopted different aspects of new Public Management (NPM) (which loosely can be defined as adopting a selection of private sector management tools) as the dominant approach to public administration so as to improve performance, efficiency and effectiveness" (Brunetto et al., 2020, p. 739) (citing Diefenbach, 2009, p. 893). Community policing emerged in the United States during this period, as an alternative approach to traditional policing, and represented a new operational paradigm.[1] As Stone and Travis (2011) explain:

> Implementing community policing is not a simple policy change that can be effected by issuing a directive through the normal channels. It is not a mere restructuring of the force to provide the same service more efficiently. Nor is it a cosmetic decoration, designed to impress the public and promote greater cooperation. For the police it is an entirely different way of life. It is a new way for police officers to see themselves and to understand their role in society. The task facing the police chief is nothing less than to change the fundamental culture of the organization.
>
> (p.4) (citing Sparrow, 1988, p. 2)

The *Final Report of the President's Taskforce on 21st Century Policing* (2015) included a recommendation (4.2) that "Community policing should be infused throughout the culture and organizational structure of all law enforcement agencies." (p.43) Community policing advocates and reformers "urged police executives to revamp their organizational structures and administrative practices in a number of ambitious ways; to de-specialize; to reduce the depth of their hierarchies, and to civilianize, replacing sworn officers with civilians in a variety of occupational specialties" (Maguire et al., 2003, p. 251).

Slowly, police organizations across the country recognized the need to create or re-align units and resources, out of necessity, in order to respond to new community demands.

While the traditional approach certainly still has value today, "such as [during] calls for service in times of emergency" (Ortmeier and Davis, 2012, p. 34), it is clear that policing entails more than enforcement of laws and emergency response. All departments now need the ability to actively engage and effectively serve the community. As a result, the organizational charts of American police departments continued to evolve.

Forward-thinking police departments began experimenting with new operational models. As the charts shifted, so did the roles and responsibilities of units and personnel operating with the various sub-systems within the departments. Gradually, American police departments began to adopt a *systems* approach which emphasized the "interdependence and interrelationship of each and every part of the whole" (Peak et al., 2010, p. 15).

Cordner and Scarborough (2007) provide perhaps the best articulation of how police departments operate and evolve as complex systems. They describe how the various units within a typical department continually rely upon one another:

> Police organizations consist of numerous involved, interdependent subsystems. The investigationsdivision, or subsystem, for example, depends on the recordsdivision for arrest records, the patrol division for back up, the intelligence division for information on organized crime, the laboratory for scientific investigative assistance, the property

unit for storage of evidence, the detention unit for the holding of prisoners, the maintenance division for servicing its vehicles, the communications division for radio contact,
the supply unit for weapons and ammunition, the training division to keep up with the
latest investigative techniques, the planning division to isolate high crime areas, and
the payroll unit to distribute paychecks. The work of the detectives who are assigned to
the investigations division is made much more difficult, and sometimes impossible, when
one or more of these other divisions perform poorly or works in a way that is incon-
sistent with the goals and objectives of the organization.

(p. 60)

As the open systems theoretical framework slowly began to take hold within the field of
policing, scholars and managers began to understand that "external variables or events play
a significant role in explaining what is happening within a [police department" (Allen and
Sawhney, 2015, p. 48) and therefore "focused on the interactions of the organizational sub-
systems and the interconnectivity of [police departments] with their environments" (Jones,
2008, p. 436). No longer could police departments or their respective units work, or even
be clearly understood, in isolation.

Police departments are expected and required to organize, staff and support all of their
operational and support units in order to accomplish their missions. They are now also
required to "make resource allocation decisions more transparent, to be able to evaluate
outputs and outcomes, and to be able to demonstrate that resources are being used to generate the best returns for specific communities and society as a whole" (den Heyer et al.,
2007, p. 196). Police chiefs must now align units, personnel, technology, and equipment
according to an "empirically validated need" (p. 196).

As discussed in Chapter 1, it is imperative for a chief to know what is happening within
his/her department. This means that it is not unfair to ask a chief:

"How are things going in the records unit?"
"Did they have a good May?"
"How would you know if they didn't?"
"What is considered to be baseline normal performance for that unit?
"What is their greatest operational challenge at the moment?"
"How large is that backlog of freedom of information requests (or subpoenas waiting to be
    processed)?"
"Do they have enough personnel to complete their work?"
"Why is the turnover rate so high in that unit?"

These would indeed be uncomfortable questions for many chiefs. Many would respond,
"*You will need to speak to the manager of that unit to get that information.*" But the
professional landscape for police managers has changed dramatically. These are now fair
questions that require clear answers. Modern policing has become committed to stricter
accountability, increased legitimacy, and continuous innovation. Stone and Travis (2011)
explain:

By a commitment to accountability we mean an acceptance of an obligation to account
for police actions, not only up the chain of command within police departments, but
also to civilian review boards, city councils and county commissioners, state legislatures,
inspectors general, government auditors, and courts. The obligation extends beyond these

government entities to citizens directly: to journalists and editorial boards, resident associations, chambers of commerce – the whole range of community-based organizations.

(p. 2)

To accomplish this, police chiefs must obviously ensure that necessary information flows upwards to command staff, in order to inform and support all management decisions, both tactical and strategic. Additionally, and this is perhaps the most difficult task, they must also ensure clear and open channels of internal communication and access to essential information *for all units and personnel*. Intra-department information silos can no longer be tolerated. They pose a significant liability and safety threat to the department, its employees, and the community. A well-organized police department must now encourage and support the managers of *all units* to seek and share necessary performance information in order to engage in the S.A.R.A. process of scanning, analysis, response, and assessment (Ortmeier and Davis, 2012). There must be open discourse (i.e., an active give-and-take) among managers, in a suitable forum (DeHaven-Smith and Jenne, 2006). We believe that the appropriate forum is monthly "Compstat-like" management meetings.

Cordner and Scarborough (2007) agree, observing that "to some extent, every manager in the police organization performs the six management functions of system building, planning, organizing, staffing, directing, and controlling," noting however that, "the relative importance of the function varies, depending on the manager's level in the police organization" (p.142). In other words, every unit's manager must be able to access and actively *use* necessary performance information. This means that the managers of the training unit, the property and evidence management unit, etc. must all use timely and accurate data to continually assess and then seek to improve their unit's performance. It entails assessing the "as is," identifying the "desired state" and performing "gap analysis" to move forward. Failure to do this results in stagnation and operational silos, where the poor performance of one particular unit can severely compromise overall organizational performance.

O'Hara (2005) notes:

Information is the lifeblood of organization. Information travels through the organization via the communication system. The organization is healthiest when the communication system is: robust – more rather than less information is transmitted; widespread – any unit that needs information gets it; and well-exercised – all parties, freely contribute, extract, and clarify information.

(p. 79)

Assessing the administrative and support capabilities of any police department therefore entails far more than simply determining whether necessary units are represented somewhere in the organizational chart.

Peak et al. (2010) suggest that organizational design must, at a minimum: 1) identify what jobs need to be done; 2) determine how to group jobs; 3) form grades of authority or supervision; and 4) equalize responsibility (p. 16). Virtually every police department has an organizational chart that accomplishes these things.

However, simply having the right units situated in the right position on the organizational chart is not, in and of itself, sufficient.

The key issue is whether or not these units are actually working in unison and helping to drive the performance of the department towards mission fulfillment. This is not simply a one-time question; this is actually an ongoing process of inquiry (i.e., SARA). This involves ongoing analysis of unit operations, as well as analysis of the department's internal communication and decision-making systems. DeHaven-Smith and Jenne (2006) call this process "inquirement." It entails continuously asking: "*What is happening?*"; "*When and where is it happening?*"; "*What is causing it?*"; "*How do we know/What are we missing?*"; "*What should we do?*"; "*How will we know if we've adequately addressed the issue?*"; and "*What should we do to prevent this from occurring again?*"

It is in fact the essence and art of modern police management.

Monthly "Compstat-like" management meetings (discussed at length in Chapter 11) are "a rich channel for effective communication of [even] non-routine and complicated messages" (Allen and Sawheny, 2015, p. 279), an effective tool and the obvious choice for ensuring robust and clear communications within the department. Managers from all operational and support units must be expected to attend and actively participate in these collaborative examinations of police operations. These meetings are obviously superior and far more useful than a series of emails, phone conversations, or memos. As Allen and Sawheny (2015) observe, "Face to face is the richest medium of communication because it allows direct experience of multiple information, cues, immediate feedback, and personal focus. Senders can provide instant clarification to any ambiguous information until a common understanding is reached" (p. 279). Teleconferencing is also useful, but should be avoided if the face-to-face option is available.

It is the responsibility of every chief to use these meetings to: 1) detect operational challenges and understand specific needs; and then to 2) provide the administrative support to those areas when needed. This not only applies to internal department operations, but to external ones as well. For example, it is possible that a particular police department's "Crime Prevention/Community Affairs" officer is simply not providing the level of services to the community that is now required. Perhaps that officer is overwhelmed, undertrained, or simply a bad fit for this position. It is the responsibility of the chief to figure this out. It is the chief 's responsibility to move resources and realign the entire organizational chart as necessary. The art of doing this on a continuous (i.e., month-to-month) basis is now simply understood as good management practices in our field.

We must be cautious, however, not to adopt an accusatory or punitive stance while placing these additional demands upon functional units and their managers. It is incumbent upon the department's chief to develop a culture of collaboration and continuous improvement. Rather than simply playing the blame game, police chiefs must set the tone by acknowledging that mistakes are expected and inevitably will occur in all operational areas. The key is to minimize them. As O'Hara (2005) notes, "well-designed and carefully implemented structures, policies and processes will produce errors as a matter of course in any organization" (p. 25). It should be the responsibility of every manager within the organization to identify operational problems within their areas of responsibility, to correct them, and to see that sufficient resources are devoted to the issue going forward, to ensure that similar problems do not re-occur.

Command staff are generally responsible for planning, budgeting and analysis but, in essence, all units within the department are responsible for these functions as well, with regard to their respective tasks. For example, a highly functioning training unit must plan its activities, budget for them, assesses the relative effectiveness of these operations, etc.

Much is now expected from managers assigned to all units.

But rather than feeling "put upon" by these expectations, it is likely that managers throughout the entire organization would embrace these responsibilities if they were adequately encouraged and properly supported. As Brunetto et al. (2020) found, "the engagement of police officers is arguably compromised by poor management. [However], if management practices, especially for police officers, ensure adequate support is provided for officers to do their jobs effectively, then ... possible consequences include higher ... engagement" (p. 755) Johnson (2015) agrees, finding that organizational commitment of employees is directly linked to perceived organizational support, and the degree of effective supervisor feedback that is provided.

These new demands for timely and accurate data have resulted in the development and implementation of new police technologies that have "had significant effects on the structures, practices, and culture of policing by shifting police organizations away from their traditional law enforcement function toward processing and sharing large amounts of information to help manage risk" (Willis et al., 2018, p. 483).

Organizational Structure and Design

When assessing the administrative and support capabilities of any department, a threshold question is: *What units are required and where should we place them?* (Perkins and Mijares, 2003).

Organizations place themselves at great risk if they fail to answer these questions properly:

> The legacies of the haphazard structuring of organizations include divided authority, inappropriate tasking, communications failures, questionable personnelselection, perverse incentive systems, and poorly designed processes. Alone or, just as likely, together, these *structural flaws can cause critical performance failures* in any organization.
>
> (O'Hara, 2005, p. 49)(emphasis supplied)

The key is, therefore, to avoid such *structural flaws* at all costs.

Since the inception of modern policing, units have been generally understood as being either "operational" in nature, or "support." This is equivalent to the military and corporate distinction between "line" and "staff" (Agsalud, 1972). All departments make this distinction in their organizational charts by creating separate bureaus or, in the case of smaller agencies, separate divisions. Patrol operations are obviously central to the police mission, thus patrol is always placed on the operational side of the chart. Which additional units are placed on the "operations" side of the house with patrol will vary however to a certain degree (Allen and Sawheny, 2015).

As O'Hara (2005) explains:

> The central mission of any organization, which is order maintenance and crime prevention for local law enforcement agencies, is carried out by the operating core which, for municipal police agencies, consists of units such as patrol and investigations and emergency services. Just about anything else layered onto an organization is in service to the operating core, or to the outside authorities, that chartered and continue to sanction the organization.
>
> (p. 47)

Cordner and Scarborough (2007) refer to an operations *subsystem* which exists within all police departments. They define it as follows:

Operations are activities that directly assist the public. The operations subsystem is the part of police work with which most people are familiar. Through the operations subsystem, police officers are deployed to take action, to fight crime, and to provide services to the public. ... The goals of the operations subsystem are identical to those of the entire police agency – primarily, maintaining order, and protecting life and property. All work in which operations personnel are involved is directed towards the accomplishment of these primary organizational goals. The tasks included within the operationssubsystem are aimed directly at achieving one over more of these goals and objectives. These tasks are patrol, traffic, criminal investigation, vice and drugs, organized crime, special operation crime prevention, juvenile services, community services, and school services.

(p. 68)

This suggests that police units should be grouped by function, either as *operations* or *administration/support*.

The exact list of operations units will vary, however, depending upon: a) the size; and 2) the unique history and operational philosophy of a particular department. For example, in many departments the operations designation is limited to patrol and other uniformed units such as traffic, special operations (i.e., SWAT), school resource officers (SROs) and K-9, whereas investigations are designated as support.

Size as a Determinant of Structure

Communities served by small departments may not need or want the expense of a full-service police department. Here the focus of the department may be providing a service (i.e., respond to medical calls, residence checks, crimes, etc.) and high visibility/deterrent patrols when not responding to calls for service. The municipality must determine if a full-service department makes financial sense. If quality safety services beyond those offered by the local department can be obtained elsewhere (i.e., an adjoining jurisdiction, county, or state) through mutual-aid agreements, memoranda of understanding or contracted cheaper than if the municipality provided those services itself, then it makes financial sense to obtain those additional services elsewhere.

Police officers in small departments are trained and expected to handle much of what they encounter during their patrol shifts. These officers do not have the luxury of simply responding to a call for service, completing an Incident Report and refering that report to an investigative or specialized unit or person within the department for follow-up. Those additional services may not be offered by their department. These officers perform as many functions as their training, experience, and capabilities permit before referring the incident/case for additional investigative steps or other measures.

As the department increases in size, organizations begin to specialize in one or more areas (i.e., traffic/criminal investigations, etc.) and provide competency/certification training to officers in the specialized areas created within that department. Small departments tend to be structured under a patrol or operations division with all but the chief (and one or two supervisors tasked with integrity or other critical issues working under the chief's office) not assigned to the patrol division. Patrol officers report to the patrol supervisor/first line supervisor who in turn reports either to the patrol division commander or to the chief/agency head. In departments using this structure, complex, time-consuming investigations and investigations of violent and other serious felony offenses are conducted by another department.

The patrol function is viewed as the backbone of the police organization. The core duties of police agencies are carried out through their patrol function. Departments that begin to specialize may create specialized functions within the patrol or operations division (i.e., traffic unit to investigate collision fatalities/serious injuries, etc.) or create a separate division to provide the specialized service(s) (i.e., investigations, community outreach, etc.). It is a common practice in smaller departments to reflect "divisions" or "units" on their organizational chart when the matter assigned to that division or unit is a function provided by a member(s) assigned to the patrol. For example, the organizational chart may reflect an applicant investigation/processing unit when in fact candidate screening is a function performed by a member assigned to the patrol division.

The size of the department is often the primary indicator and driver of whether its officers are generalists or specialists and the kinds of services it provides. The smaller the department, the more likely the police officers will be generalists and organized under one division. As the number of personnel in departments increases, specialization of functions is likely to occur. After patrol, an investigation division that conducts patrol follow-up and self-initiated criminal investigations is the next logical division created.

Operational Philosophy as a Determinant of Structure

The operational philosophy of a department may also influence how the organization organizes itself. Some approaches to policing require more personnel than others. How well or not an organization integrates and leverages technology to achieve organizational goals/objectives will affect the staffing levels required to implement the desired policing approach. Community policing, when implemented as the department's dominant operational philosophy, is personnel intensive. When the entire organization practices the principles of community policing, as opposed to having community policing responsibilities be assigned to one stand-alone unit, additional sworn and civilian personnel are needed. The task of building department capacity is given to sworn and civilian members of the department to create new or strengthen existing community ties that facilitate collaboration, build trust and the co-production of policies and practices are enormous.

Proactive, intelligence-led departments require sufficient staffing in the patrol division to allow patrol officers to both respond to calls for service (reactive) and address community concerns and the precursors to violence and other crime (proactive). This approach may require shifting personnel and other resources from other divisions into the patrol division. Here, the crime reduction approach is based on crime data and other intelligence, and direction/follow-up from supervisors to ensure officers address neighborhood conditions that are the precursors of crime and violence. Department leaders know that crime is concentrated by time, geography, and in persons. Deploying resources during the days, times, geographic areas (blocks and buildings on blocks), and focusing on specific conditions and persons (gang members, habitual offenders) that contribute to disorder or criminality is likely to provide a greater yield in terms of crime reduction than the random unfocused deployment of personnel and resources.

It is therefore difficult to state with certainty where certain units (such as detectives) will be placed on any particular organizational chart. What is far more important, however, is whether these units are working in unison for a common purpose.

Functionality and Need

Some police units clearly serve a support, rather than operational function. These would include:

- a training unit;
- a crime analysis unit;
- a recruitment unit;
- a crime scene/forensic tech unit;
- a communications/dispatch unit;
- a records unit;
- a property and evidence management unit; and
- a community affairs/engagement unit.

Obviously, each of these units perform a critically important function that supports police operations. However, some departments simply do not require their own communications unit, they can use the county's emergency communications system. Many others do not need to train and support a stand-alone SWAT unit, they can dedicate one or more officers to participate in a regional SWAT unit that will provide the same coverage. Few departments have their own K-9 units, narcotics unit or hostage negotiations team; they can quickly avail themselves of these services via a mutual aid agreement with a larger agency. There are certain economies of scale realized by regionalizing, rather than duplicating, certain police services.

The critical point here is that no department "outsources" patrol. Some support services can be outsourced, but they must be chosen very carefully.

We would suggest that any police department will, in the ordinary course of its business, find itself receiving, recording, and safeguarding property (such as vehicles, illegal narcotics, found property, firearms, etc.). In fact, they are legally bound to do so. Therefore, in addition to patrol officers, all police departments must have a designated property/evidence manager. In most departments, this is typically a detective, a sergeant, or even a non-sworn (i.e., civilian) member of the department, provided that person (perhaps a retiree from another law enforcement organization) is carefully vetted, selected, trained, and supervised.

All states and accrediting bodies require a department to have a designated training officer. In many smaller departments, this means there is no designated training *unit*, simply an individual who has been tasked with this function. It is possible for one person, in a relatively small department, to perform this role effectively. Unfortunately, the designated training officer is often an officer or perhaps a sergeant who is tasked with responsibility for the training of all department personnel *in addition to other duties*, such as patrol supervision. As a result, that "training officer" has little to no time to plan, develop, deliver and evaluate training and simply becomes the department's training "scheduler" or "coordinator." In other words, the training function is not being performed properly in that department. A civilian can schedule and record training received and ensure that all certificates are properly placed in the officers' training files. Who is preparing and delivering the in-service training? In a situation such as this, the department has not devoted sufficient resources to the training *function*. As a result, the training function is not being carried out in accordance with best practices. Hopefully this problem does not emerge during litigation after some tragedy has befallen the department, its officers, and the community.

We should note here that the artificial intelligence (AI) revolution that we are currently undergoing will no doubt prove beneficial to police training in some respects. However, face-to-face training delivered by trained professionals will always be required in the field of policing. Adequate resources and adequate time must be afforded to training officers in order to perform this function properly.

This concept of a sergeant wearing many hats makes sense, to a certain extent, as it is an economical use of resources. A patrol sergeant might have time available to also serve as the department's armorer, quartermaster or fleet manager, but training is a "mission-critical" function that must be performed at a sufficiently high level to ensure that a sufficient quantity and quality of training is delivered. The real question here is whether that sergeant has the time and resources to fulfill that responsibility.

We have now arrived at the key means of assessing a department's administrative and support capabilities. The two questions posed at the outset of this chapter – 1) *how should modern American Police Departments be designed and structured?*; and 2) *how should they be managed and supported?* – are too simplistic. They do not delve deeply enough. The real question is whether a particular department is effectively performing and supporting the essential *functions* of modern policing. These include training, recruitment, investigations, traffic control, crime analysis, etc. If they are not doing it themselves, have they effectively outsourced it? Is the county or regional fusion center providing the department with a sufficient quantity and quality of actionable intel products to properly support patrol and investigative functions? Is the detective who is designated as the department's "crime analyst," in addition to his/her other investigative responsibilities, properly trained and supported and using the right analytical tools to identify and track "hot" people and places within the community? (Bachner, 2013) Crime analysis is not merely an ancillary task; it is essential to modern policing. It is critically important for developing every department's capacity to learn and adapt. As Stone and Travis (2011) explain:

> There is a new way of learning within policing. The pace of innovation and knowledge development today is simply too fast for police organizations to rely on recruit training and occasional specialized courses. Rather, police departments need to become learning organizations of professionals. For example, analysts in police agencies should not only be studying crime patterns, but also analyzing what the police are doing about them and to what effect, informing the development of tailor-made strategies to deal with the underlying problems, and then sharing their analysis widely within the department, in forms that busy frontline officers and supervisors can easily digest, retain and apply.
>
> (p. 17)

The answers to these staffing and organizational design questions can only be found by performing a deep dive into the department's operations. There is no one-size-fits-all approach.

Simply examining an organizational chart, seeing where the pieces are placed and merely checking a box, is only a small part of accurately and honestly assessing a particular department's capabilities. This is why accrediting bodies perform site visits. This is why professional consulting firms are routinely engaged by municipalities to perform detailed studies of police operations and staffing, examine records, conduct focus groups, question stakeholders, etc.

Mintzberg (1989) suggests that, rather than adhering to some predetermined formal structure, or simply mimicking some other organization's design, any organization, including a police department, should allow organizational design to naturally configure itself into "internally consistent" groups as the units fall into natural clusters or configurations. Even if the placement of a particular unit is wrong, it can simply be adjusted. Nothing is set in stone. All organizations organize and reorganize themselves often to adjust to changing market conditions or to meet evolving customer needs. The key question here is whether a chief has the ability to identify a misaligned unit and the confidence to attempt a new organizational design.

There is no one organizational structure that works best. Agencies organize themselves in a manner that permits them to deliver public safety services in the most efficient and effective manner. Several models of organization are reflected in the approximately 18,000 law enforcement agencies throughout the United States. Nearly half of the police departments in the US have fewer than 10 sworn officers. Approximately 90% of US police departments have fewer than 50 sworn officers. Large police departments in the US are the anomaly. By far, public safety services are delivered by small departments. The size of the agency, abilities of its officers, and funding are among several factors that influence which services that organization can provide and how the agency organizes itself to best provide those services.

Should a particular department employ its own dispatchers? Who knows. One would need to perform a deeper dive (i.e., an economic and practical risk benefit analysis) into the internal and external environment of that agency to arrive at a reasonable conclusion. What we do know is that the communications/dispatch function must be performed by somebody. It is essential and it must be performed well. Communications should be considered yet another of the mission critical functions.

Throughout this text, we have identified and explored other mission critical functions. They include:

- recruitment;
- professional standards/internal affairs/auditing;
- training;
- property and evidence management;
- records/data management; and
- community engagement.

These are support functions that absolutely must be performed in every police department, and they must be performed well. We suggest that they be performed by members of the department. These functions should not be outsourced. Primary responsibility rests with members of the department.

Other support functions, such as crime scene response and investigation, or fleet management can and perhaps should be outsourced, in a particular case, depending upon the circumstances (e.g., perhaps the municipality's Highway Department can effectively perform the fleet management for the police department).

A Rapidly Changing Environment

It is generally understood that a department's command staff (i.e., chief, executive officer, captains) are responsible for the duties that are typically associated with management of any organization. They include:

- planning;
- budgeting;

- organizing;
- staffing/assigning;
- directing;
- developing;
- evaluating;
- controlling; and
- promotion/selection.

These are the duties and responsibilities identified in most police administration textbooks. Once again, however, we suggest that things are really not as simple as they might seem.

American policing now finds itself in the midst of what can honestly be considered its most turbulent period of the past century (perhaps ever). The "directing" and "controlling" of personnel referred to above becomes far more challenging during a period contending with: a nation-wide police (and civilian employee) recruitment crisis; the de-fund the police movement; foreign and domestic terror threats; decreasing tax base and funding ; the evolution of new types of cybercrime and new technologies; calls for civilian oversight and increased transparency; and a new generation of employees that place a priority upon their personal time off from work. A growing number of police departments are now also operating under consent decrees, as a result of civil rights litigation. In addition to contending with such pressing issues, police chiefs are also expected to inspire their personnel, to provide true leadership and to achieve tangible results.

There is indeed much for a modern police chief to contend with. It would appear that the stakes are now higher than they have ever been.

King (2009) suggests that police organizations experience distinct phases, from creation, to a period of growth, through declining periods and, ultimately, towards crisis. This is consistent with the concept or entropy which suggests that, over time, any system, including human organizations, moves towards a state of disorder and chaos. While this might be true, we do not believe that this is an irreversible process. It is the job of the police chief to ensure that internal order and stability is maintained, even in a turbulent environment. There is simply no choice when it comes to policing; failure is not an option.

So what is a chief to do?

Today, in the midst of an unprecedented hiring and recruitment crisis, it can no longer be argued that qualified personnel are any department's most valuable resource. We suggest, therefore, that all police chiefs focus primarily upon their department's greatest resource, their personnel. The *Final Report of the President's Taskforce on 21st Century Policing* (2015) recommended that every police department "should promote safety and wellness at every level of the organization." (Recommendation 6.2, page 112). This would include officer wellness programs, annual mental and physical health check-ups, and the development and implementation of early warning systems to detect problematic behaviors (Recommendation 6.1.3, page 111). Police chiefs are now required to manage personnel during a time of rapid transformation of business processes. Police chiefs must guide and direct officers while new duties and obligations are being developed, such as the duty to de-escalate use of force situations, and the duty to intervene in the face of another officer's malfeasance or nonfeasance of duty. In addition, police chiefs must embrace diversity and adequately address gender issues, fully leverage the use of civilian personnel,[2] create assignments and work schedules that result in optimal work–life balance, etc. Police chiefs are also responsible for creating and supporting an environment of continuous learning and improvement.

In many respects, these demands seem to be overwhelming. These functions must be performed continuously. The words "administer" and "support" are verbs. They describe ongoing actions and processes. They involve a continuous process of inquiry and response (DeHaven-Smith and Jenne, 2006). It is hard to envision one person performing all of these functions from month to month, as well as the other essential functions of a police chief, at a sufficiently high level for extended periods.

It is therefore critically important for every police department to have a well-trained, properly resourced, and motivated upper management team (i.e., command staff). In many police departments, the role of executive officer has already been transformed into a *de facto* position that more closely resembles that of chief information officer (CIO) (Bendig et al., 2023) or chief transformation officer (CTO) in a private corporation (Stackpole, 2023). They have been tasked with ensuring the smooth implementation of body-worn cameras (BWCs), or taking the lead on the department's outreach among minority communities, with an eye towards enhancing recruitment efforts and applicant yield from those communities. These are indeed tall tasks. To accomplish them, these police managers must be properly trained and prepared. Deputy chiefs, majors, and captains in every department should attend and successfully complete quality executive training courses (such as those offered by the FBI-LEEDA Command Leadership Institute and the FBI National Academy) in order to acquire these additional management skills.

Succession planning is quite difficult in American police departments. However, all police department should develop a program of preparing executive level personnel for higher office. As Ulrich et al. (1999) explain:

> Results based leaders have the responsibility to help other leaders achieve results, to establish a leadership "bench." Unless leaders build leaders, results will end when the leader who first achieved them moves on. Ultimately, the results-based leader succeeds because the next generation of leaders exceeds the results of the current generation.
>
> (p. 191)

This leads to a very provocative question; How long should a chief serve? This question is already answered in many jurisdictions. But the answer varies from jurisdiction to jurisdiction. As Allen and Sawheny (2015) explain, "police departments are municipal agencies that fall under the control of the mayor or city manager. The mayor influences the hiring or firing of the police, chief, and the activities of the department, directly and indirectly" (p. 321). As such, the chief's longevity is linked directly to City Hall and it is widely understood that the chief serves at the pleasure of the mayor and/or council. In other jurisdictions, such as the state of New York, the position of chief is a civil service rank rather than an appointed position. As such, the longevity of a New York police chief is far greater in New York than in many other states. Civil service laws ensure that New York chiefs remain in office for decades at a time. This obviously has both benefits and drawbacks for the community and the department. Continuity and expertise of a long-term chief can be offset by political involvement and professional "staleness." Sheriffs, by contrast, are publicly elected, serve predetermined terms in office and are therefore politically accountable for their actions and decisions (Baldi and LaFrance, 2012).

Some advocate for shorter terms of service for police chiefs, suggesting that the churning of the talent pool is actually healthy for American policing:

> Only in the last few decades has it become common for big city police chiefs to be recruited from outside of their departments and states, though even today most chiefs

have spent their entire careers in the departments they lead. That trend needs to deepen, and the profession needs to find ways to encourage greater movement from place to place and across state lines at every stage of police careers. The obstacles are substantial. Police pension rules can create powerful disincentives for officers to move. In some states, such as California, the pension system does not block movement within the state, but creates disincentives for wider moves. In Massachusetts, state laws and contracts, make it difficult for veteran officers and supervisors to move even within the state without loss in rank.

(Stone and Travis, 2011, p. 19)

Conclusion

The placement and alignment of units and personnel within a police force matters greatly. Form and structure relate directly to employee behaviors and performance.

The placement of a detective unit upon an organizational chart, or its physical proximity within the headquarters building to the patrol division, are less important questions than merely asking, *"Are the detectives working closely and effectively with patrol? How are they coordinating with the Narcotics Unit and our Crime Analyst?"*

Legacy structures should be presumed to be inadequate. Simply *"doing things the way we have always done them in the past"* is a recipe for disaster in the current environment.

The real question is *"How should the organization be designed today? To deal with these issues and challenges?"* As the foregoing discussion suggests, an incoming chief should focus upon function, rather than form, and look for proper alignment and coordination of effort. It is the chief who is best positioned to observe internal functions across the organization and to align resources in the most productive and cost-effective manner. Change must be made cautiously, which means that it must be evidence-based. We would suggest that the chief will receive all the evidence he/she requires by simply conducting monthly management meetings based upon timely and accurate performance data. These meetings represent the department's sense and respond capabilities to detect and respond to subtle changes in both the external and *internal* work environments. Misalignments will naturally emerge from the data, as will proper alignment and high performance.

A chief must be bold and confident enough to make necessary changes to organizational structure when necessary. This is truly what it means to properly manage and support the organization.

Notes

1 Ironically, this was actually the very model first proposed by the founder of "modern" policing, Sir Robert Peel.
2 Stone and Travis (2011) describe the ongoing process of "civilianization" within police departments, "to decrease costs, police departments will likely accelerate the shifting of work to non-sworn, and therefore less expensive, specialist personnel, especially in crime investigation units that are currently staffed, mostly with detectives. A range of new specialists, including civilian, crime, scene, technicians, data analysts and victim liaisons, might well replace half or more of today's detectives. A wide range of civilian roles could emerge, boosting the prominence of civilian police careers in much the same way that nurses and technicians have taken on many of the roles traditionally played by doctors within the medical profession." (p. 13)

References

Agsalud, J. C. (1972). Line-Staff Distinction and Its Relationship to the Patterns of Influence within the Management Organization, Dissertation, Wayne State University. www.proquest.com/openv iew/3d2f1f148d1aa784076abb2e4a9fb333/1?pq-origsite=gscholar&cbl=18750&diss=y

Allen, J. M., & Sawhney, R. (2015). *Administration and Management in Criminal Justice: A Service Quality Approach*. Sage.

Bachner, J. (2013). *Predictive Policing: Preventing Crime Data and Analytics, IBM Endowment for the Business of Government, Improving Performance Series*. www.businessofgovernment.org/sites/ default/files/Predictive%20Policing.pdf

Baldi, G., & LaFrance, C. (2012). Lessons from the United States sheriff on the electoral selection of police commissioners in England and Wales. *Policing*, 7(2), 146–155.

Bendig, D., Wagner, R. Piening, E. P., & Foege, J. N. (2023). Attention to digital innovation: Exploring the impact of the chief information officer in the top management team. *MIS Quarterly*, 47(4), 1487–1516.

Brunetto, Y, Farr-Wharton, B., Farr-Wharton, R., Shacklock, K., Azzopardi, J., Saccon, C., & Shriberg, A. (2020). Comparing the impact of management support on police officers' perceptions of discretionary power and engagement: Australia, USA and Malta. *The International Journal of Human Resource Management*, 31(6), 738–759.

Cordner, G., & Scarborough, K. E. (2007). *Police Administration*. Anderson Publishing.

DeHaven-Smith, L., & Jenne, K. C. (2006). Management by inquiry: A discursive accountability system for large organizations. *Public Administration Review*, 61(6), 693–708.

den Heyer, G., Mitchell, M., Ganesh, S., & Devery, C. (2007). An econometric method of allocating police resources. *International Journal of Police Science and Management*, 10(2), 192–213.

Diefenbach, T. (2009). New public management in public sector organizations: The dark side of managerialistic 'enlightenment'. *Public Administration*, 87, 892–909

Gregory, J. C. (2023). Leadership characteristics through the lens of translocational positionality framework: Trailblazing women in policing, *Sage Open*, 13(3). https://journals.sagepub.com/doi/ 10.1177/21582440231192136

Johnson, R. R. (2015). Organizational commitment. *Crime and Delinquency*, 61(9), 1155–1180.

Jones, M. (2008). A complexity science view of modern police administration. *Public Administration Quarterly*, 32(3), 433–457.

King, W. R. (2009). Toward a life course perspective of police organizations. *Journal of Research in Crime and Delinquency*, 46(2), 213–244.

Maguire, E. R., Shin, Y., Zhao, J., & Hassell, D. (2003) Structural change in large police agencies during the 1990s. *Policing: An International Journal of Police Strategies and Management*, 26(2), 251–275.

Mintzberg, H. (1989). The Structuring of Organizations. In Asch, D. and Bowman, C. (eds.). *Readings in Strategic Management*. Palgrave.

Office of Community Oriented Policing Services. (2015). *Final Report of the President's Taskforce on 21st Century Policing*. U.S. Department of Justice, Washington, DC.

O'Hara, P. (2005). *Why Law Enforcement Organizations Fail: Mapping the Organizational Fault Lines in Policing*. Carolina Academic Press.

Ortmeier, P. J., & Davis, J. J. (2012). *Police Administration: A Leadership Approach*. McGraw-Hill.

Peak, K. J., Gaines, L. K., & Glensor, R. W. (2010). *Police Supervision and Management: In an Era of Community Policing*. Prentice Hall.

Perkins, D. B., & Mijares, T. C. (2003). *Organization and structure of the crisis negotiation unit and related legal aspects. Journal of Police Crisis Negotiations*, 3(2), 73–77.

Sparrow, M. K. (1988). *Implementing Community Policing, Perspectives on Policing*. 9, Washington, DC, United States Department of Justice, Office of Justice Programs, November.

Stackpole, B. (2023, October 30). The rise of the chief transformation officer. CIO.com. Retrieved from www.cio.com/article/657416/the-rise-of-the-chief-transformation-officer.html

Stone, C., & Travis, J. (2011). *Towards a New Professionalism in Policing. New Perspectives in Policing.* Harvard Kennedy School, National Institute of Justice, Washington, DC, March. www.ojp.gov/pdffiles1/nij/232359.pdf

Ulrich, D., Zenger, J., & Smallwood, N. (1999). *Results-Based Leadership: How Leaders Build the Business and Improve the Bottom Line.* Harvard Business School Press.

Willis, J. J., Koper, C. S., & Lum, C. (2018). Technology use and constituting structures: Accounting for the consequence of information technology on police organizational change. *Policing and Society*, 30(5), 483–501.

Chapter 7

Critical Policy Assessment

Learning Objectives

Upon completion of this chapter, the reader will be able to:

- Understand the importance of developing policies and procedures in a police organization.
- Recognize the process by which a policy is created and implemented.
- Understand the common significant policy categories, such as dealing with the mentally ill, use of force, or racial profiling.
- Identify the structure and components of a comprehensive and detailed policy manual.

Introduction

Throughout history, humans have relied on rules and regulations. In the beginning, Adam and Eve received a verbal command from God not to eat from one tree in the Garden of Eden. Adam and Eve disobeyed the verbal command and changed the course of history. It was realized that humans need commands in writing, and God gave Moses a tablet of the ten commandments for humanity. These ten commandments guide humans on how we should live. Fast forward ahead and the world has now developed into 195 countries: 54 countries in Africa, 48 countries in Asia, 44 countries in Europe, 33 countries in Latin America and the Caribbean, 14 countries in Oceania, 2 in Northern America, and Vatican City and Palestine are recognized as independent nations (Britannica, n.d.). According to the U.S. Census Bureau on August 15, 2023, the U.S. population was 335,251,321 and the world population was 7,991,620,155. The estimated number of businesses in the world is approximately 334 million companies worldwide (Statista, 2022).

Moreover, the number of known and living languages worldwide is 7,168 (Appalachian State,, n.d.). Countries have rules and laws to control the behavior of their citizens. The multitude of businesses throughout the world also had to implement rules to enable organizations to forward their mission, streamline processes and procedures, provide for safety in the work environment, direct and control the employees, be accountable to governing boards, and be consistent in the delivery of services and products. The United States has international, federal, and state ordinances and rules for operating all businesses, communities, and individuals. Imagine no laws, rules, or regulations to manage the world's population and businesses. Chaos could not even describe how life would be on this planet.

DOI: 10.4324/9781003396437-7

Why Should Organizations Have Policies?

Organizations need policies and procedures to provide clear guidance as to what the organization expects from each employee. The organization can be public, private, significant, or minor, providing different services and products. Still, policies and procedures are part of the foundation for all organizations. Training and supervision are necessary for implementing policies and procedures and provide a framework for understanding and enforcing policies and procedures. Management philosophies and cultures are also part of an organization's framework.

There are approximately 18,000 law enforcement agencies in the United States, including federal, state, county, and local agencies. These law enforcement agencies are configured as small as one officer to agencies that have more than 30,000 police officers. According to the U.S. Department of Justice, Office of Justice Programs, and Bureau of Justice Statistics, "The most common type of agency is the small-town police department that employs ten or fewer officers. The decentralized, fragmented, and local nature of law enforcement in the United States makes it challenging to accurately count the number of agencies and officers" (U.S. Department of Justice, 2016, p. 1). Statista reports that in 2021, there were 660,288 full-time law enforcement officers in the United States. Statista defines law enforcement officers using the Federal Bureau of Investigation's definition as paid sworn officers with full arrest powers and carrying a firearm and badge. According to Statista (2023), data was tracked to enable the publishing of a graph to display the number of law enforcement officers in the United States from 2004 to 2021. As seen by examining the graph, there has been substantial variance in the number of law enforcement officers in the United States. In 2004, there were 675,734 full-time law enforcement officers; in 2008, the number of full-time law enforcement officers peaked at 708,569, followed by a continuous decrease, and in 2013, resulted in the lowest number of full-time law enforcement officers with 626,942. In 2014, the number of full-time law enforcement officers increased; in 2019, there were 697,195 full-time law enforcement officers. However, in 2020, the number of full-time law enforcement officers slightly decreased to 696,644, followed by a dramatic decrease to 660,228 full-time law enforcement officers in 2021 (Statista, 2023). When examining the number of full-time law enforcement officers regardless of year, it can be derived that policies are needed to ensure that officers understand the rules, laws, and guidelines for streamlining consistency in the application of laws or policies, internal processes, decision-making, and the successful operation of the agency. Table 7.1 presents an 18-year graph illustrating the fluctuations in full-time law enforcement officers.

The fluctuations in the number of full-time law enforcement officers can be attributed to many factors. Retirements, economics, social strife, the impact of COVID, police presented in a negative light by the media, critical incidents in communities involving the police and citizens, lack of community policing grants to fund additional positions, changing culture and values, and availability of other occupations offering better salaries, benefits, working conditions, remote offices, and flexible schedules. Newer generations prioritize time off as an essential benefit. Additionally, law enforcement is an exceedingly complex and stressful career for the officers and their family members. Each day, law enforcement officers and their families face the reality that officers may not return home to their families. According to the Officer Down Memorial Page, in 2021, there were 701 line-of-duty deaths. Covid played a significant role in the line-of-duty deaths. Table 7.2 lists the categories of causation and the number of deaths.

Table 7.1 Number of Full-time Law Enforcement Officers in the United States from 2004 to 2022

Year	Number of Full-time Law Enforcement Officers	Change in Number of Officers from Year to Year
2004	675,734	+/- 0
2005	673,146	-2,588
2006	683,396	+ 10,250
2007	699,850	+ 16,454
2008	708,569	+ 8,719
2009	706,886	-1,683
2010	705,009	-1,877
2011	698,460	-6,549
2012	670,439	-28,021
2013	626,942	-43,497
2014	627,949	+1,007
2015	635,781	+7,832
2016	652,936	+17,155
2017	670,279	+17,343
2018	686,665	+16,386
2019	697,195	+10,530
2020	696,644	-551
2021	660,288	-36,356
2022	708,001	+47,713

Source: Statista (2023).

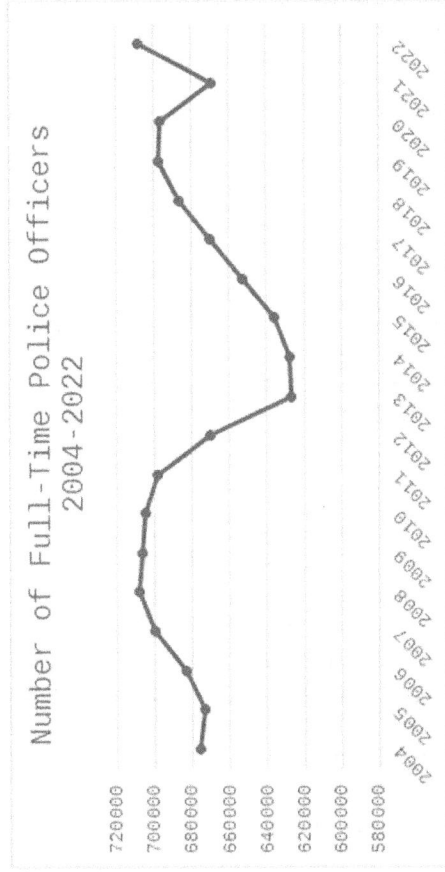

Number of Full-Time Police Officers 2004-2022

Table 7.2 Number of Line of Duty Deaths by Causation, 2022

Causation	Number of Deaths
9/11 Related Illness	24
Aircraft	6
Animal	2
Automobile Crash	33
COVID	83
Duty Related Illness	7
Fire	1
Gunfire	61
Gunfire (Inadvertent)	4
Heart Attacks	14
Heatstroke	2
Motorcycle Crash	3
Struck by Vehicle	5
Vehicle Pursuit	4
Vehicular Assault	14
Total	263

According to the Addiction Center, law enforcement officers are at a higher risk of suicide compared to other occupations, and in 2019, only 5% of current law enforcement agencies had suicide prevention programs for their employees (Addiction Center, n.d.). Law enforcement agencies have policies on how to handle mentally ill citizens. However, many agencies do not have policies for officers' mental health issues. We live in dynamic times, and keeping policies up to date to deal with critical incidents should be a priority for all law enforcement agencies. Law enforcement professionals deal with critical, complex, and diverse issues that demand up-to-date, clearly written, comprehensive policies and procedures for many internal and external processes and issues.

Law enforcement agencies must have clear policies and procedures to guide a workforce that deals with split-second decisions to have organizational alignment and effectiveness, clear guidance as to what the organization expects from each employee, consistency, transparency, and internal and external accountability with the public. Most importantly, policies and procedures, along with laws, ensure the law enforcement agency upholds the constitutional rights of citizens. Moreover, conversely, citizens also have the responsibility to uphold the law.

Definitions of Written Directives

Law enforcement agencies use a variety of written documents to guide and direct the performance and conduct of employees. Understanding the purpose of these written directives is essential for all law enforcement agencies. A written directive is a written document that guides the performance or conduct of employees. In law enforcement, policies, procedures, rules, regulations, general orders, special orders, standard operating procedures, personnel orders, post orders, memoranda, and employee handbooks fall under written directives. The terminology can sometimes be confusing; however, each has a purpose to direct and support the law enforcement agency. The International Association of Police Chiefs provides precise terminology to understand better the purpose of written directives (Orrick, n.d., p. 1).

- Standard – professional or legal guidelines or performance requirements that establish benchmarks for agencies to develop the organizational structure and measure its service delivery system.
- Policy – a course or line of action adopted and pursued by an agency that provides general guidance on the department's philosophy on identified issues.
- Procedure – a detailed description of how a policy is to be accomplished. It describes the steps to be taken, the frequency of the task, and the persons responsible for completing the tasks.
- General Orders – written directives related to policies, procedures, rules, and regulations involving multiple organizational units. General orders typically have a broad policy statement and policy implementation procedures.
- Standard Operating Procedure – a written directive is a detailed guideline for a specific agency activity.
- Special Orders – directives regulating one segment of the department or a statement of policy and procedure regarding a temporary circumstance or event.
- Personnel Orders – announcements of changes in personnel status, such as transfers or promotions.
- Rules and Regulations – procedures that apply each time a situation occurs with specific guidelines for staff to follow. Rules and regulations usually proscribe specific behavior that will result in employees being disciplined for failing to follow the guidelines provided.
- Post Orders – specific processes and duties to be performed at assigned locations or posts (i.e., front desk, security positions).
- Memoranda – directives developed by or at the direction of personnel with authority.
- Employee Handbook – manual provided by the governing authority that introduces employees to the organization, its benefits/compensation package, and an abbreviated listing of policies.

Law enforcement agencies require their members to know all the written directives the agency may invoke. Written directives have many common elements but may vary from one agency to another. The agency's Field Training Program plays a significant role in training law enforcement officers to understand the application of the written directives.

Most police television shows need to show the depth of the training police officers must complete. According to Police 1, the average length of a police academy is approximately 833 hours in the United States (Police1, 2021). Field Training Programs can vary from 14 weeks to 20 weeks. However, most police television shows have a theme of being in a state of constant action or tactical mode. The public is aware of the physical aspects of the job of a police officer, but only some know the knowledge requirements a police officer must learn. The cerebral part of the job is more intense than the physical aspects.

Sources for the Development of Policies

For policy development, the law enforcement agency must determine if they have internal resources to utilize to develop policies. For example, a sergeant or lieutenant with solid writing skills and diverse experience in the agency may be a good fit to tackle developing and updating policies. If the agency is starting at ground zero because the policies are too outdated or do not exist, the sergeant may want to identify subject-matter experts within the agency who have a solid working knowledge of procedures and utilize their knowledge to craft policies. This process takes time and internal resources, and the subject-matter experts likely also have their responsibilities in the agency. So, how does a law enforcement agency approach this daunting task? The sergeant might contact a similar-sized agency with strong written directives and utilize this resource to identify what parts of the policy can be utilized in the sergeant's agency. The sergeant would still need the subject-matter experts to provide their input on how to adapt the other agency's policies to fit the sergeant's department best. The sergeant is customizing the other agency's policy to fit the sergeant's agency. This approach is less time-consuming than starting at ground zero with policy development.

What are the Critical Policies for a Law Enforcement Agency?

There are critical policies such as Use of Force, Racial Profiling and Bias, Pursuits, and Active Shooter/Killer Shooter, to name a few. However, the critical aspect of policies is to develop policies for essential procedures that agency members must understand and be able to competently respond to and apply the appropriate actions according to policy. Most policy manuals are well over 250 pages, including small agencies of less than ten officers. A small department has similar tasks that large agencies also perform. This means a small department may have a policy manual with as many policies as a large agency of 500 or more sworn officers. Policies are also needed for civilian personnel, the tasks they handle, and the responsibilities they have. A comprehensive policy manual coupled with competent and engaging supervision will result in greater accountability for a law enforcement agency.

Most seasoned law enforcement professionals will have similar perspectives on the agency's critical policies. Various sources identify critical policies in policing. For example, when querying artificial intelligence through ChatGPT, the following policies are listed as standard critical policies for police departments.

- *Use of Force*: Guidelines for when and how police officers can use force in their interactions with individuals. This policy emphasizes the importance of using force only when necessary and in proportion to the threat faced by officers and others.
- *De-escalation*: Encourages officers to use communication and negotiation techniques to defuse potentially dangerous situations without force whenever possible.
- *Body Cameras*: Mandating the use of body-worn cameras by police to increase transparency and accountability during interaction with the public.
- *Racial Profiling and Bias*: Policies prohibiting racial profiling emphasize the fair and equitable treatment of all individuals regardless of race, ethnicity, or other characteristics.
- *Community Policing*: Fostering positive relationships between police officers and their communities, encouraging officers to engage with residents and collaborate on solving local issues.
- *Training and Continuing Education*: Regular and updated training for police officers to ensure they stay informed about the latest laws, best practices, and techniques for effective policing.
- *Transparency and Accountability*: Establishing mechanisms for civilian oversight and investigations of alleged police misconduct to build trust with the community.
- *Mental Health and Crisis Intervention*: Providing training for officers to handle situations involving individuals experiencing mental health crises with empathy and understanding.
- *Anti-Corruption Measures*: Policies and procedures to prevent and address corruption within the police department, ensuring officers act with integrity and uphold the law.
- *Use of Pursuit*: Guidelines for high-speed pursuits to minimize risks to public safety while apprehending suspects.

- *Data Collection and Analysis*: Utilizing data to identify patterns, track crime trends, and allocate resources effectively (Open AI, 2023).

Looking at another source, PowerDMS by NEOGOV, which has helped law enforcement agencies for decades create policies and provide police management software, believes numerous critical policies exist but identifies the following policies as some of the most critical in recent years. The corporation NEOGOV provides policy management software called PowerDMS, a secure, cloud-based repository to develop, review, approve, distribute, and track every policy. It ensures that there is only one published version of the policy. PowerDMS is utilized by a variety of institutions and not just law enforcement. According to the NEOGOV website, PowerDMS serves more than 5,500 public and private institutions, including law enforcement, healthcare, 9-1-1, fire/E.M.S., corrections, government, and corporations. The benefits of PowerDMS are that it can update policies four times faster compared to paper-based processes, clients save an average of 11,000 dollars in paper and printing, it promotes greater accountability, easy access to the policies 24/7, and contributes to building a culture of compliance (2020).

PowerDMS (2020) also explains what should be included in the policies listed below.

- *Law Enforcement Drone Policy* – The Federal Aviation Administration has established regulations for drones, as well as some states. A drone policy should address laws, regulations, procedures, and guidelines for keeping surveillance images and video footage.
- *Law Enforcement Social Media Policy* – The policy should include guidelines for both personal social media accounts and the law enforcement agency's account. Social media accounts should have guidelines for personal integrity and a code of conduct. The law enforcement agency's social media positions should reflect similar integrity, code of conduct, and who has the authority to post on the social media site.
- *Narcan/Naloxone Policy for Law Enforcement* – The policy needs to comply with state and local laws, provide a basic overview of drug abuse and addiction, recognizing the symptoms of an overdose, administration guidelines and dosage for Narcan, understanding the process an individual experiences after an overdose, stabilization for the individual, and follow-up considerations such as emergency medical services and addiction referral and recovery programs.
- *Law Enforcement Body Camera Policy* – A policy needs to outline when to turn on the body camera, limitations of recording victims, witnesses, and other private situations, length of archives for the video, whether officers can view the video before writing a report, and to whom and under what circumstances the videos can be released.
- *Policing the Mentally Ill Policy* – One of the most challenging issues in law enforcement is policing the mentally ill. Training must go together with the policy. Training can include crisis intervention, de-escalation, and partnerships with the local mental health community. The policy should include signs of mental illness and best practices for policing the mentally ill.
- *Law Enforcement Use-of-Force Policy* – Use-of-force incidents are high liability areas for law enforcement. Thousands of lawsuits are filed each year against law enforcement agencies. A Use-of-Force Policy should state levels of force, define each in detail, identify weapons use and de-escalation tactics, and provide an understanding of appropriate and inappropriate uses of force.
- *Understanding the National Consensus Policy on Use of Force* – In 2017 and revised in 2020, the Fraternal Order of Police, the Federal Law Enforcement Officers Association,

the International Association of Chiefs of Police, the Hispanic American Police Command Officers Association, Association of State Criminal Investigative Agencies, Commission on Accreditation for Law Enforcement Agencies, International Association of Directors of Law Enforcement Standards and Training, National Association of Police Organizations, National Association of Women Law Enforcement Executives, National Organization of Black Law Enforcement Executive, and National Tactical Officers Association published the *National Consensus Discussion Paper on Use of Force* to guide law enforcement agencies to improve use-of-force policies. The publication is comprehensive and detailed on the issue of use-of-force, de-escalation, less-lethal force, and justifications for lethal force. It is an excellent resource for strengthening use-of-force policies.

- *Communicable Disease Policy in Law Enforcement* – A Communicable Disease Policy should have input in development from local hospitals, E.M.T.s, and researchers. Information from the C.D.C., OSHA, and NIOSH can also serve as resources to enable law enforcement officers to know how to deal with individuals who might have been exposed to a communicable disease. COVID-19 propelled the Communicable Disease Policy to the top of policy considerations in law enforcement agencies.

- *Law Enforcement Active Shooter Response Policy* – The policy should be written so that an officer, unit, or entire department has a step-by-step in chronological order of what response should be taken from when 911 receives the call through the after-action debriefing stage. The response philosophy to an active shooter has radically changed since the Columbine shooting on April 20, 1999. The policy should also contain but not be limited to situation assessment, individual officer intervention, response team, rescue task forces, unified command, community notification, debriefing, and training. Perhaps the most essential part of the debriefing is to identify strengths and weaknesses in response, tactical acumen, and the need for additional training. This can only occur if the law enforcement agency conducts tabletop exercises and frequent active shooter training in various environments. Why should this be a critical policy? According to PowerDMS by NEOGOV, reports that just within three years, in 2021, there were 327 mass shootings by the end of June 2021, with 360 people killed and 1,343 people wounded. In 2020, there were 615 mass shootings, with 521 killed and 2,541 wounded, which is incredibly high considering the pandemic. In 2019, there were 441 mass shootings, with 475 killed.

- *Law Enforcement Pursuit Policy* – Today, more law enforcement agencies limit high-speed pursuits unless the suspect has committed a violent crime. Pursuits are a risk to law enforcement officers even when justified. Many high-speed pursuits can be determined as unjustified and may result in accidents, injuries, death, and lawsuits. Most unmarked vehicles without special equipment are prohibited from conducting pursuits. PowerDMS (2020) notes that the International Association of Chiefs of Police (IACP) "recommends that vehicular pursuits should only be initiated only when the officer has a reasonable belief that the suspect, if allowed to flee, would present a danger to human life or cause serious injury" (International Association of Chiefs of Police 2023). Many departments have pursuit policies, but some do not, or they have not kept their policy current. Law enforcement agencies must have a robust vehicle pursuit policy to protect the citizens and the law enforcement agencies.

- *Law Enforcement Racial Profiling Policy* – This is also referred to as bias-based policing. This policy sets the standard for what is expected from law enforcement officers and the department when dealing with individuals of a different race, religion, nationality, or sexual orientation. Race, color, ethnicity, religious beliefs, sexual orientation, or national origin cannot influence enforcement action. The policy needs to cover in detail the protection of these different categorizations to ensure the enforcement does not consider these categories as reasons for selective enforcement. Police standards should be impartial and fair, and training should enforce the policy and the intent of the policy.

- *Law Enforcement Take Home Car Policy* – Law enforcement agencies that have take-home vehicles need a policy that determines the parameters for utilizing the take-home vehicle, responsibilities of operations, maintenance, cleaning, dress codes, who can ride in the vehicle, insurance responsibilities, and are there any financial stipulations for driving the take-home car into another city or county where the officer may reside.

In comparing Artificial Intelligence ChatGBT policies to PowerDMS, they differ in some of the policies they present as critical. These policies are only the tip of the iceberg regarding what policies law enforcement agencies need. Law enforcement agencies need policy manuals that are comprehensive, clearly written, easy to interpret, and provide staff with detailed guidance for all aspects of an agency's operations. Developing policies requires the agency's members to be actively involved in developing and updating the policies. Laws change, accreditation standards change, and the agency's philosophy may change regarding some issues. Accreditation standards can help an agency develop policies that reflect best practices in law enforcement.

There are other professional resources to assist with policy development and maintenance. For example, Lexipol provides police departments with comprehensive state-of-the-art policies that have been researched and created by subject-matter experts and vetted by attorneys. According to Lexipol (n.d.), more than 2 million first responders and local government officials utilize Lexipol policies, accreditation services, training, grant assistance, and wellness support. Furthermore, more than 5,400 public safety agencies and municipalities utilize Lexipol policy services, 30 percent of the 18,000 law enforcement agencies. Lexipol has legal and research policy teams that review new legislation, statutes, and case law on the state and federal levels, which may have the ability to impact policy content. Lexipol utilizes a five-step process for the development and update of policies. Listed below is the five-step process:

1. Lexipol's legal team and policy content experts monitor numerous sources of information to identify new standards, legislation, court decisions, and regulations at the state and federal levels.
2. Lexipol authors the recommended changes and delivers them to the client through an online platform with email notification.
3. Lexipol's online platform shows the client the changes in mark-up form, with the updated language side-by-side with the previous version—so the client knows instantly what is changing.
4. The client will also receive release notes explaining the changes and their reasons.
5. The client can accept, reject, or customize each policy update using the local legal and community review process. Then, it is just a few more clicks to issue the updated policy to department personnel. (Lexipol, n.d.)

Lexipol also provides additional services to help police departments train on the policies, web-based platforms, and mobile apps that enable officers to access their department policies 24/7 and document storage.

Another resource for model policies is the International Association of Police Chiefs (IACP) Law Enforcement Policy Center. The International Association of Police Chief Law Enforcement Policy Center provides four resources for police departments: model policies, considerations, concepts, issues, and what IACP refers to as "need to know." The model policies are structured in one format, but the Law Enforcement agency can customize the policy for their agency. The law enforcement agency provides concrete guidance and directives describing actions, tasks, and procedures for specific functions and operations. IACP model policies enable a law enforcement agency to customize the policy due to the agencies' expectations and capabilities. IACP provides background information on the policy for law enforcement agencies to consider and summarizes the critical points of the policy in a one-page brief.

The International Association of Police Chiefs Policy Center, Lexipol, NEOGOV PowerDMS, and ChatGPT are presented in the chapter as resources for developing critical policies and creating and maintaining policies. Why are policies so critical for law enforcement agencies? With 18,000 law enforcement agencies in the United States and approximately 660,228 full-time law enforcement officers in 2021, policies provide the pathway for law enforcement officers to handle incidents and reduce the possibility of litigation consistently.

What Policies are Presented in a Comprehensive Policy Manual?

Some law enforcement agencies post their policies on the Internet to provide transparency for the public. The Atlanta Police Department has accreditation by the State of Georgia and national accreditation CALEA. The Atlanta Police Department's comprehensive policies cover many potential issues and situations. The policies have an effective date and a review date to enable the Atlanta Police Department to keep its policies current. Listed below is the table of contents for the policies. A table of contents should appear in all policy manuals.

The Atlanta Police Department is a model for all departments to emulate for providing public policy transparency. The policies are posted on the Internet and are easy to locate. Additionally, click on a particular policy on the Internet, and the entire policy is visible to the public.

The Atlanta Police Department also provides a table with a brief description of the intent of each of these policies. This summation of each policy assists agency members in finding the policy that they need guidance for their responses to issues and incidents. Table 7.3 presents the titles of each policy. Listing policies gives the public easy access to locating the policy they seek to review. The policy manual can be retrieved from https://public.power dms.com/APD13/list.

References

Addiction Center. (n.d.). *Police Are at Higher Risk for Suicide than Any Profession*. Addiction Center. Retrieved July 1, 2023, from (www.odmp.org/search/year?year=2021)

Appalachian State (n.d.). *Ethnologue: Languages of the World*. APP State University Libraries. Retrieved July 5, 2023, from https://library.appstate.edu/find-resources/databases/ethnologue-languages-world

Atlanta Police Department. (n.d.). *Atlanta Police Department Policies*. Retrieved August 1, 2023, from https://public.powerdms.com/APD13/list

Table 7.3 Atlanta Police Department Policy Manual

- 2022 Annual UOF Analysis Report
- APD.SOP..2140 Employee Referral Incentive Program
- APD.SOP.1010 – Mission and Organization of the Department
- APD.SOP.1020 – Oath of Office and Law Enforcement Code of Ethics
- APD.SOP.1030 – Written Directive System
- APD.SOP.1031 – Forms Management
- APD.SOP.1050 – Records Management and Retention
- APD.SOP.1060 – Public Affairs
- APD.SOP.1061 – Open Records Unit
- APD.SOP.1070 – Coordination with Outside Agencies
- APD.SOP.1080 – Internal Communication
- APD.SOP.1090 – Inspections
- APD.SOP.1100 – Requests for Legal or Ethics Opinions
- APD.SOP.2010 – Work Rules
- APD.SOP.2011 – General Conduct
- APD.SOP.2020 – Disciplinary Process
- APD.SOP.2021 – Workplace Safety
- APD.SOP.2022 – Early Intervention and Early Warning System
- APD.SOP.2024 – Random Drug Screening
- APD.SOP.2025 – Peer Support Program
- APD.SOP.2030 – Awards
- APD.SOP.2040 – Grievance Procedure
- APD.SOP.2050 – Timekeeping
- APD.SOP.2051 – Long Term Military Deployment and Reintegration
- APD.SOP.2052 – Overtime Accountability And Tracking
- APD.SOP.2060 – Extra Jobs
- APD.SOP.2070 – Recruitment and Hiring Process
- APD.SOP.2071 – Filling Full-time Civilian Vacancies
- APD.SOP.2080 – Training
- APD.SOP.2081 – Training Reimbursement and Collection Procedure
- APD.SOP.2082 – Protocol for Outside Agencies Training
- APD.SOP.2083 – Citizens Police Academy Alumni Association
- APD.SOP.2084 – Georgia P.O.S.T Recertification
- APD.SOP.2085 – Atlanta Police Leadership Institute
- APD.SOP.2086 – Firearms Training Unit
- APD.SOP.2090 – Performance Evaluations
- APD.SOP.2100 – Appointment to Investigator or Senior Police officer
- APD.SOP.2101 – Specialized and Temporary Assignments
- APD.SOP.2110 – Duties of Senior Police Officers
- APD.SOP.2120 – Employee Transfers
- APD.SOP.2130 – Dress Code
- APD.SOP.2131 – Collection of Department Equipment
- APD.SOP.2150 – Injury on Duty
- APD.SOP.2160 – Employee Assistance
- APD.SOP.2170 – Honor Guard
- APD.SOP.2180 – Utilization of Civilian Personnel
- APD.SOP.2181 – Workload Analysis and Personnel Allocation
- APD.SOP.2190 – Atlanta Retired Police Reserve
- APD.SOP.2191 – Retired Officer Firearms Qualification Program
- APD.SOP.2200 – APD Junior Police Cadet Program
- APD.SOP.2300 – Department Cooperation with the Atlanta Citizen Review Board (ACRB)
- APD.SOP.3010 – Use of Force
- APD.SOP.3011 – Critical Incident Review Team
- APD.SOP.3020 – Search and Seizure
- APD.SOP.3030 – Arrest Procedures
- APD.SOP.3031 – Repeat Offender

(Continued)

Table 7.3 Atlanta Police Department Policy Manual (Continued)

- APD.SOP.3032 – Felons in Possession of Firearms
- APD.SOP.3033 – Use of Temporary Detention Cells
- APD.SOP.3040 – Weapons
- APD.SOP.3041 – Investigating Police Discharges Towards Animals
- APD.SOP.3042 – Conducted Energy Weapon
- APD.SOP.3043 – Animal Cruelty Enforcement & Prevention Squad
- APD.SOP.3050 – Pursuit Policy
- APD.SOP.3060 – Reports and Report Writing
- APD.SOP.3061 – Methods of Clearing a Crime
- APD.SOP.3062 – In-Vehicle Computers
- APD.SOP.3063 – Accounting for Field Reports
- APD.SOP.3064 – Online Reporting System
- APD.SOP.3065 – Field Interviews
- APD.SOP.3066 – Bias Crime Data Reporting
- APD.SOP.3067 – Gang Data Reporting
- APD.SOP.3068 – Vehicle Storage for Investigative Purposes
- APD.SOP.3070 – Roll Call
- APD.SOP.3080 – General Procedures
- APD.SOP.3081 – Crime Scene Investigation
- APD.SOP.3082 – Responding to Persons Experiencing a Mental Health Crisis
- APD.SOP.3083 – Family Violence
- APD.SOP.3084 – Disabled Persons
- APD.SOP.3085 – Missing Persons
- APD.SOP.3086 – Project Lifesaver Atlanta
- APD.SOP.3087 – Civilian Passengers in Police Vehicles
- APD.SOP.3088 – Signals and Codes
- APD.SOP.3089 – Supervisor Notification
- APD.SOP.3090 – Continuity Books
- APD.SOP.3100 – Victim Witness Assistance
- APD.SOP.3110 – GCIC and NCIC Information
- APD.SOP.3120 – Computer Voice Stress Analyzer
- APD.SOP.3130 – Radio Operation/Usage
- APD.SOP.3131 – Mobile Video and Audio Recording
- APD.SOP.3132 – Real Time Crime Center
- APD.SOP.3133 – Body Worn Cameras
- APD.SOP.3140 – Night Commander
- APD.SOP.3150 – Vehicle Management
- APD.SOP.3151 – Use of Marked Take-Home Vehicles
- APD.SOP.3152 – Employee Involved Motor Vehicle Collision Investigations
- APD.SOP.3160 – Court Responsibilities
- APD.SOP.3161 – Delivering Reports and Citations to Municipal Court
- APD.SOP.3170 – Citation Book Accountability
- APD.SOP.3180 – Critical Incidents
- APD.SOP.3181 – Emergency Operations Plan
- APD.SOP.3182 – Bomb Squads and Explosive Detection Unit
- APD.SOP.3184 – Threat Level Advisories and Responses
- APD.SOP.3185 – Active Attack
- APD.SOP.3186 – Strategic Response Unit
- APD.SOP.3190 – Juvenile Procedures
- APD.SOP.3191 – Truant Children
- APD.SOP.3192 – Police Athletic League
- APD.SOP.3200 – Criminal Justice and Social Services Diversion Programs
- APD.SOP.3220 – Atlanta Streetcar System
- APD.SOP.4010 – Traffic
- APD.SOP.4020 – Zone Discretionary Units
- APD.SOP.4030 – Citizen Advisory Councils
- APD.SOP.4040 – Special Operations Section
- APD.SOP.4041 – Aviation Unit

Table 7.3 Atlanta Police Department Policy Manual (Continued)

- APD.SOP.4042 – Hostage Negotiators
- APD.SOP.4043 – Special Weapons and Tactics (SWAT)
- APD.SOP.4044 – Tactical Field Operator
- APD.SOP.4045 – Unmanned Aircraft Systems
- APD.SOP.4070 – Bicycle Patrol
- APD.SOP.4080 – Mounted Patrol
- APD.SOP.4090 – Airport Section
- APD.SOP.5010 – Criminal Investigations Division
- APD.SOP.5011 – Major Crimes Response Unit
- APD.SOP.5040 – Homicide Unit
- APD.SOP.5050 – Cyber Crimes
- APD.SOP.5060 – Fugitive Operations
- APD.SOP.5070 – Gangs and Special Investigations Unit
- APD.SOP.5080 – Asset Forfeiture Squad
- APD.SOP.5100 – Pawn Desk
- APD.SOP.5130 – License and Permits Unit
- APD.SOP.5140 – Airport Drug Interdiction Unit
- APD.SOP.5141 – Narcotics & Tracking Canines (K-9)
- APD.SOP.5142 – Violent Crime Interdiction Section
- APD.SOP.5190 – Guidelines for Participating in Investigative Task Forces
- APD.SOP.5193 – License Plate Recognition System
- APD.SOP.5210 – Special Victims Unit
- APD.SOP.5220 – Fraud Investigations
- APD.SOP.6010 – Communications
- APD.SOP.6011 – Smartphone Procedures
- APD.SOP.6020 – Central Records
- APD.SOP.6030 – Property and Evidence Control
- APD.SOP.6032 – Donate Horses and Dogs
- APD.SOP.6033 – Logistical Support Unit
- APD.SOP.6040 – Identification Unit
- APD.SOP.6045 – Criminal Laboratory
- APD.SOP.6050 – Department Employees' Duties with Regards to Information Technology
- APD.SOP.6060 – Fiscal Management Unit
- APD.SOP.6061 – Reporting Revenue
- APD.SOP.6070 – Grants Management
- APD.SOP.6080 – Personnel Files and Orders
- APD.SOP.6100 – Planning, Research, and Accreditation Unit
- APD.SOP.6101 – Atlanta Police Historical Society
- APD.SOP.6110 – Chaplaincy Corp
- APD.SOP.6120 – Tactical Crime Analysis Unit
- APD.SOP.6141 – Mobile Community Outreach Police Station
- APD.SOP.6142 – Crime Stoppers Greater Atlanta
- APD.SOP.6143 – Limited English Proficiency
- APD.SOP.6150 – The Atlanta Police Club
- APD.SOP.6160 – Drug Testing and Destruction
- APD.SOP.6161 – Administration of Naloxone Nasal Spray (Narcan)
- APD.SOP.6170 – Lesbian, Gay, Bisexual, Transgender, and Queer (LGBTQ) Liaison Unit
- APD.SOP.6180 – Transgender Interactions
- APD.SOP.7010 – Community Services Division
- APD.SOP.7030 – Community Oriented Policing Section (COPS)
- APD.SOP.7032 – Crime Prevention Unit
- APD.SOP.7035 – Path Force Unit
- APD.SOP.7036 – APD Explorer Program
- APD.SOP.7037 – Homeless Outreach Proactive Enforcement (HOPE) Team
- APD.SOP.7050 – Code Enforcement
- Carbyne Introductory Video
- Change of Command Bridging Document
- Policy Manual Table of Content

Powered by https://public.powerdms.com/APD13/list

Braga, A., MacDonald, J., & McCabe, J. (2020). Body-worn cameras, lawful police stops, and NYPD officer compliance: A cluster randomized controlled trial. Technical report, working paper, Retrieved September 29, 2023, from http://nypdmonitor.org/wp-content/uploads/2020/12/12th-Report.pdf.

Commission on Accreditation for Law Enforcement Agencies (2023). *Law Enforcement - Standards Titles*. CALEA. Retrieved August 1, 2023, from www.calea.org/node/11406

Encyclopedia Britannica. (n.d.). *How many countries are there in the world? Encyclopedia Britannica*. Retrieved July 24, 2023, from www.britannica.com/story/how-many-countries-are-there-in-the-world

F.B.I. Bureau of Justice Statistics (2023). *U.S. Law Enforcement Officers 2021*. Statista Research Department. Retrieved July 29, 2023, from www.theiacp.org/sites/default/files/2018-08/BP-PolicyProcedures.pdf

International Association of Chiefs of Police (2023). *IACP Law Enforcement Policy Center Vehicular Pursuit Model Policy*. Texas Police Chiefs. Retrieved July 28, 2023, from www.texaspolicechiefs.org/plugins/show_image.php?id=1308

International Association of Chiefs of Police. (n.d.). *IACP Law Enforcement Policy Center*. International Association of Police Chiefs Policy Center. Retrieved July 7, 2023, from www.theiacp.org/policycenter

Lexipol. (n.d.). *Policy Management and Updating Processes*. Retrieved July 25, 2023, from www.lexipol.com\

NeoGov. (2023). *Policy Management Software*. PowerDMS. Retrieved July 28, 2023, from (www.powerdms.com/policy-management-software

Officer Down Memorial. (n.d.). *Line of Duty Deaths*. Officer Down Memorial Page. Retrieved July 1, 2023, from (www.odmp.org/search/year?year=2021)

Office of Justice Programs (2023). *National Sources of Law Enforcement Employment Data*. Office of Justice Programs. Retrieved July 24, 2023, from https://bjs.ojp.gov/content/pub/pdf/nsleed.pdf

Open AI. (2023). *Critical Police Policies*. Retrieved July 28, 2023, from https://chat.openai.com/c/5c32e248-4e48-43a2-a670-e3e8994a8459.

Orrick, W. (n.d.). *Best Practices Guide: Developing a Police Department Policy-Procedure Manual*. International Association of Chiefs of Police. Retrieved July 24, 2023, from www.theiacp.org/sites/default/files/2018-08/BP-PolicyProcedures.pdf

Police1 (2021). *What to Expect from Police Academy Training*. Police1 by Lexipol. Retrieved July 15, 2023, from www.police1.com/how-to-become-a-police-officer/articles/what-to-expect-from-police-academy-training-TphD8qpkqgg68nYc/

Power DMS. (December 22, 2020). *12 Crucial Law Enforcement Policies*. Law Enforcement Policy Management. Retrieved July 1, 2023, from www.powerdms.com/policy-learning-center/12-crucial-law-enforcement-policies

Statista (2022). *Estimated Number of Countries Worldwide from 2000 to 2021*. Retrieved July 15, 2023, from www.statista.com/statistics/1260686/global-companies/#:~:text=There%20were%20estimated%20to%20be,were%20around%20328%20million%20companies.%20

Statista. (2023). *Number of Full-Time Law Enforcement Officers in the United States from 2004 to 2021*. Statista. Retrieved July 7, 2023, from www.statista.com/statistics/191694/number-of-law-enforcement-officers-in-the-us/

U.S. Census. (2023). *U.S. and World Clock*. U.S. Census Bureau. Retrieved August 15, 2023, from www.Censusgov/popclock?>

U.S. Department of Justice (2016). *National Sources of Law Enforcement Employment Data*. 1–17. U.S. Department of Justice, Office of Justice Programs, Bureau of Statistics. https://bjs.ojp.gov/content/pub/pdf/nsleed.pdf

U.S. Department of Justice. (2020). *Hearing Thirteen, Accreditation and Standards*. U.S. Department of Justice, President's Commission on Law Enforcement, and the Administration of Justice. Retrieved August 1, 2023, from www.justice.gov/archives/ag/page/file/1319441/download

Chapter 8

Assessing Recruitment and Retention Capabilities

Part I. Overview and Scope of the Problem

American policing has evolved dramatically during the past several decades. As a result, the demands placed upon police professionals have increased greatly. New personal skill sets are required for performing more specialized and complex police work. To face new challenges such as terrorism, untreated mental illness, substance abuse, and homelessness, police officers "must be skilled communicators, who can analyze and solve problems related to personal crises, using evolving technology, and in partnership with diverse groups of people" (Rhodes and Tyler, 2019, p. 492) (citations omitted).

In many respects, this is a very tall order for police recruiters. Finding such talented and skilled applicants would be a difficult task, even in a stable and robust hiring market. Unfortunately, the current labor market for American policing is anything but stable or robust. Indeed, it is quite the opposite.

The severity of the police recruitment situation is accurately captured in the title of a 2019 report from the Police Executive Research Forum (PERF); "*The Workforce Crisis, And What Police Agencies Are Doing About It*" (PERF, 2019) . This crisis has existed for many years and now affects every region of the United States.

Departments throughout the country are now losing seasoned officers faster than they can hire new ones (Lentz, 2022; PERF Survey, 2022). A recent nationwide survey conducted by the Police Executive Research Forum (PERF) revealed three separate problems: 1) fewer people are applying to become officers; 2) more officers are leaving their departments – and, in many cases, leaving the policing profession – well before they reach retirement age; and 3) a growing number of current officers are becoming eligible for retirement (PERF, 2019).

Police managers and recruiters are now scrambling to react and adjust, asking the very same question, "Why is this happening?" As with most vexing problems, the current hiring and recruitment crisis has many causes:

1) Periodic fluctuations in the national birth rate have a direct impact upon the number of young men and women in a population twenty years later. Enrollment management professionals at colleges and universities are aware of the "baby booms" and "baby busts" that periodically occur and spend a considerable amount of time and resources monitoring regional census data to identify and understand developing trends. The current recruitment crisis coincides with a dramatic demographic shift, known as a "baby bust" (see, Carey, 2022). These fluctuations in population are cyclical and, in some respects, quite predictable (Marcus, 2021). What is unusual about the 2022-24situation, is that this baby bust coincides with a prolonged period of anti-police sentiment.

DOI: 10.4324/9781003396437-8

2) The "defund the police movement" has unfortunately resulted in a pervasive negative sentiment among young people that makes them far less interested in the police profession. Both officers and police applicants cite low morale, low pay, diminishing respect for the police, and increased scrutiny as the major factors driving them away from the job (Westervelt, 2021). The 2014 shooting of Michael Brown in Ferguson, MO, and the ensuing nation-wide public unrest was "an environmental jolt to law enforcement," as it disrupted the normal functioning of many American police departments and placed them into a state of crisis (Rhodes and Tyler, 2019, p. 493). The killing of George Floyd in Minneapolis in 2020 and the ensuing protests and public disorder further damaged the image of the police and marked a tidal shift in attitude that placed many police departments directly at odds with the communities they serve.

   Negative views towards the police are now contributing to a sharp decline in police applicants (Rhodes and Tyler, 2019, p. 493). Nation-wide surveys have also identified a significant "racial confidence gap," whereby "blacks are about half as likely to have a positive view of the job police are doing" (Pew Research Center, 2016). This severely hampers every department's effort to diversify its workforce.

3) As the American economy improves, "debt-laden college graduates are choosing substantially higher-salary jobs over low-paid 'public interest' jobs out of college" (Rhodes and Tyler, 2019, p. 494). There are now more options available and much competition for well-educated young talent (PERF, 2019). Police departments find themselves at a competitive disadvantage. Economics and basic labor market dynamics likely explain much as to why young people are less attracted to the police profession. Simply put, they have better options.

4) Millennials and members of Gen Z have psychological, intellectual, and behavioral characteristics and motivations that are vastly different from past generations of police applicants (Williams and Sondhi, 2022; Schuck, 2021; Cox, 2012). As Smith (2016) explains, "Those professionals who 'live to work' are largely gone, having effectively been replaced by a generation of people who 'work to live.'" Financial incentives that have succeeded in the past (in terms of attracting and retaining a qualified workforce) are less likely to appeal to young individuals who value their time off far more than any financial incentives.

   Indeed, the characteristics of Millennials and Gen Z likely vary from one another to a considerable extent. It also goes without saying that the personal and psychological characteristics of both vary greatly from their Baby Boomer predecessors. While a sufficient supply of Baby Boomers was attracted to the profession in the past, "the often-rigid, quasi-military organizational structure of most police agencies does not align with the preferences of many of today's job applicants" (PERF, 2019, p. 7). One exasperated chief stated, "I have to go out to these kids when recruiting and tell then they have to work holidays, they can't see their family, you may get shot – How do you sell this job?" (Wimbley, 2021, p. 1).

   Interestingly, federal law enforcement agencies are now also experiencing greater recruitment challenges. For example, "the FBI's application pool has been shrinking. According to the *Wall Street Journal*, applications for the position of Special Agent dropped from 68,500 in 2009 to 11,500 in 2018" (p. 32). The military is struggling similarly for recruits. These generational differences in attitude must be fully understood and recruitment adjustments must be made, as necessary.

5) The core risks that are inherent to the police profession, such as being physically injured or killed in the line of duty, are understood, and accepted by most police applicants.

These risks are always present. There are, however, several additional risks that have developed in recent years that are now making the police profession far less appealing.

Negative views towards the police and declining public support since the death of George Floyd certainly make the job more difficult for current police officers and reduce morale. These factors reduce quality of work life and could negatively impact officer wellness. However, they might not, in and of themselves, force individuals to leave policing, or never consider the profession it in the first place. New pressures, responsibilities, and risks have developed because of the paradigm shift from "warrior" to "guardian," as suggested by the *President's Task Force on 21st Century Policing* (2015). Simply put, the job has clearly become more difficult. Perhaps more importantly, greater levels of managerial, public, and legal scrutiny have developed in connection with the evolution of new legal concepts such as:

- de-escalation of deadly physical force;
- liability for "officer-created" jeopardy;
- the duty to intervene (when faced with significant mal-feasance or non-feasance of duty by a fellow officer); and
- the erosion of qualified immunity for police officers.

These new pressures amount to new and additional personal risks for police officers. When combined with a fear of lack of support by supervisors, this naturally prompts officers to question, "Is it worth it?" (Ali, 2017, p. 1).

Former NYPD Chief Charles Campisi accurately describes the situation:

It's different [today]. There are too many cell phone cameras, too many surveillance cameras, too many police brutality lawyers, too many reporters looking for a police brutality story, too much department supervision – not to mention the many [internal affairs] investigators standing by to pursue cops who intentionally cross the line.

(Campisi, 2017, p. 164)

Police officers, like most individuals, are rational actors. They weigh risks versus rewards when considering their employment choices. It is a rather simple calculus; when the risks substantially outweigh the rewards, it is generally time to find new employment. The chart in Figure 8.1 is instructive.

Police officers, like most rational actors, will therefore seek employment opportunities in quadrant 4 and flee from those in quadrant 1.

Many frustrated police recruiters understand this well and echo the refrain "Nobody wants this job anymore!" These factors, combined with what has now been officially

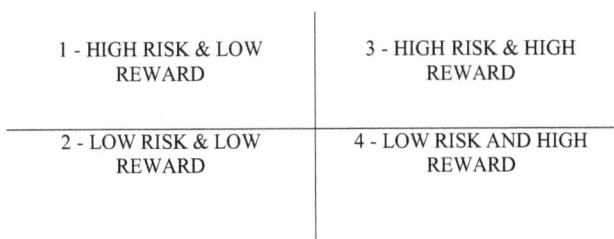

1 - HIGH RISK & LOW REWARD	3 - HIGH RISK & HIGH REWARD
2 - LOW RISK & LOW REWARD	4 - LOW RISK AND HIGH REWARD

Figure 8.1 Employment Decision Making.

recognized nationwide as "the Great Resign" and the unprecedented rate of Baby Boom retirements, result in a demand for personnel that greatly outstrips supply (Felton, 2022). Traditional recruitment practices, which for many police departments were minimal, are now having little effect. Departments that once had hundreds of applicants per open police position are now receiving mere handfuls of applications. Many departments have now switched to "open" or "rolling" application periods, with little to show for it.

Not only is the aggregate number of interested applicants dropping, so is the percentage of viable (i.e., qualified) candidates within that population. "Among individuals who do apply to police departments, practitioners argue that fewer are eligible for police work" (Rhodes and Tyler, 2019, p. 493). For example, "rising obesity rates in the United States, may mean fewer young adults are able to pass physical fitness standards for policing" (Rhodes and Tyler 2019, p. 494). During the COVID pandemic, it was not uncommon for many departments to completely suspend their recruitment efforts. They now find it particularly challenging to "ramp up" their recruitment efforts in the current environment. When they do, they find fewer interested and viable candidates.

There are other troubling dynamics at play. "While numbers of recruits have been flagging, police departments have simultaneously faced shortages of workers, due to budget, cuts, retirement, military deployment, and increased turnover among younger workers" (Rhodes and Tyler, 2019, p. 497). Recruitment cannot therefore be fully understood or addressed without considering retention. These two issues, recruitment, and retention are inextricably linked and we simply will not find an adequate solution for one without addressing the other. As Jolicoeur and Grant (2017) explain:

> Retaining qualified applicants after their initial hire has become an increasingly critical task for law enforcement agencies. Unfortunately, many agencies tend to focus more effort on recruiting qualified applicants than they do on retaining those officers they have already hired. This is unfortunate, given the in ordinately high recruiting and training costs that are inherent in in the policing field, when compared to other professions. Given that it is much less expensive and less difficult to retain an existing employee than it is to hire a new one, retention efforts have taken on increased significance in the law enforcement field. Retention efforts appear to offer a vehicle that can help alleviate much of the ongoing expense and uncertainty that is an inherent part of the law enforcement recruitment process.
>
> (p. 342)

Poor retention has a corrosive effect upon a police department. "Not only is it costly to replace veteran officers with new recruits, but significant attrition can cause staffing shortages, increase reassignment of officers to different units (limiting police knowledge of their beats and making community partnerships more difficult to maintain), lower employee morale, and create a leadership vacuum" (Rhodes and Tyler, 2019, p. 504). From an operational standpoint, this dynamic severely hampers and disrupts virtually all police functions (e.g., training, investigations, community outreach efforts) and poses a significant liability and public safety threat to the community. Understaffing due to increased turnover and a dearth of qualified replacements "has the potential to overshadow nearly all other considerations" (Smith, 2016, p. 1).

As Minneapolis Police Chief Medaria Arradondo told his city council, reduced staffing was "making his department 'one-dimensional,' with officers mostly responding to 911 calls and not having time to do proactive policing" (PERF Survey, 2021, p. 1).

Some unfortunate departments have reduced services entirely (Ahmed and Salter, 2023; Clark, 2023).

As a result, American police departments are now struggling to contend with an unprecedented hiring crisis. This crisis has unfortunately existed for several years (Kaste, 2018; Jackman, 2018; Smith, 2016). For example, a national survey conducted during 2017 by the Center for State and Local Government Excellence found that "governments [were] having more trouble hiring police than any other category of personnel" (Maciag, 2018, p. 1). Similar results were obtained in the 2018 survey. New strategies, including relaxation of hiring standards are being used across the nation. Unfortunately, the lowering of standards represents a very real liability and public safety risk to any department that might consider it.

On May 31, 2018, a Town Hall meeting was convened by the Police Executive Research Forum (PERF) entitled *"The Changing Dynamics of Policing in the Police Workforce,"* to address "the challenges that law enforcement agencies are facing in recruiting new officers" (PERF, 2018). In September 2019, PERF published a report entitled, *The Workforce Crisis, and What Police Agencies are Doing About It.* The report concluded that, "Most law enforcement agencies are sensing a crisis in their ability to recruit new officers and to hold onto the ones they have" and that there are simply "fewer young people today who have any interest in policing" (p. 5).

Other troubling information was obtained:

> The policing profession is facing a workforce crisis. Fewer people are applying, and more people are leaving the profession, often after only a few years on the job. The workforce crisis is affecting law enforcement agencies of all sizes and types. There are ominous signs that the workforce crisis in policing may be getting worse.
>
> (p. 7)

During "normal" times, there has always been a natural flow of officers moving among police departments, as they seek better compensation packages and working conditions, or simply changing jobs for personal reasons. For example, the city of Baltimore "often loses officers to neighboring agencies that offer comparable pay and less stressful work experience, because suburban areas typically have lower crime rates" (p. 32). Officers in other major cities, such as New York and Chicago, similarly seek better opportunities in the suburbs. This natural movement has intensified with the current crisis. Police departments of every size are now actively competing against one another for viable candidates by attempting to lure early and mid-career police officers away from their current employers.

The phenomenon of "poaching officers" through lateral transfer further complicates recruitment and retention efforts. Poaching agencies aggressively advertise their compensation and benefits package to police officers employed by other departments. For example, the state of Florida recently commenced a "law enforcement, relocation initiative to lure police officers living outside Florida" (Snelling, 2023, p. 1). Through this program, Florida was able to entice police officers, many of whom were previously working in New York, Texas, Pennsylvania, and California to accept police officer positions in the state of Florida. This $13 million program provided $5,000 signing bonuses to officers agreeing to transfer to Florida. Many other states have taken similar steps. Some departments openly focus their advertising on personnel from other agencies, or more secretly have their members make subtle overtures to colleagues from other departments who might be attracted to switch departments for the right price. Some enterprising chiefs actively target police departments with low pay and low morale. As the Chief of the Aurora, CO Police Department stated, "It is a cutthroat environment right now among police chiefs to recruit talent, and we all desperately need it" (Marcius, 2022). These are indeed unprecedented times.

As a result, every police department in the country now needs a sophisticated response, one that is likely to produce a sufficient flow of candidates to offset attrition. Specifically, every department in the United States now needs to strategically address the following four challenges:

- The Overall Drop in Interest in the Police Profession.
- The Unacceptably High Voluntary Drop off/out Rate During the Recruitment and Hiring Process.
- Voluntary Quits During the First Few Years of Law Enforcement Employment.
- Retaining Early and Mid-Career Officers in a Highly-Competitive Market.

The real question is, what is your human resources (HR) department doing about all of this? Are they suggesting one-time hiring bonuses? If so, is that a viable long-term solution?

Unfortunately, many police departments that do recognize the severity of the current recruitment and retention crisis have been completely frustrated by their municipality's HR department. It is not uncommon for an HR department to follow the very same process and strategy for the recruitment and on-boarding of police officers as they do for new hires in the highway department. This is done supposedly for the purpose of uniformity of process across city/county departments. While legal requirements certainly do need to be met, the time has now come for HR departments to recognize the extent of the police crisis and divest some control of the police recruitment and hiring process.

It is imperative that HR professionals work collaboratively with members of the police department to revise and adapt internal processes to be more active in maintaining constant communication with applicants and shepherding them through the entire process. HR departments likely do not have the time or resources to make such frequent contact with police applicants, but police departments do. Forward-thinking police departments have sought and received permission to do such things as:

Have several uniform and non-sworn members of the department personally contact applicants via telephone and email for periodic "check-in" conversations and reminders for upcoming dates, such as a medical examination or a meeting with an investigator (Note: These communications are not only important for maintaining the applicant's interest in the department, but also as a means of communicating the culture of the department while also affording additional opportunities to informally assess the applicant's communication and inter-personal skills);

Offering ride-alongs (with a patrol supervisor or FTO) for applicants new to the profession (Once again, this is an effective way to highlight the distinctiveness of the agency and to informally assess the applicant);

Offering an on-site training course for applicants prior to the scheduled physical agility test. Many departments have the facilities and certified trainers who can effectively deliver such training; and

Introducing new recruitment incentives such as: assistance with childcare; relocation assistance; housing assistance; and student loan forgiveness.

(p. 33)

All these methods serve to develop and maintain applicant interest, develop rapport, and forge a personal connection with the department and the community it serves. Police departments that expend such efforts distinguish themselves from the competition and appear to yield better results than those departments that rely upon legacy practices and procedures.

Specific responses must also be developed to enhance retention. There is much work to be done. Some particularly advanced mid-sized and large police departments are now requesting that HR professionals be imbedded within the police department, so that they can work more actively and more effectively address police issues. Police departments typically represent a major part of any municipality's budget and therefore routinely generate a good deal of work for the HR department, in terms of sick leave, disability leave, retirements, etc. It is likely that there is sufficient routine work of this type that, when combined with the need for new thinking and the development of new hiring and selection practices, would justify having a full-time HR professional imbedded within the police department. It is analogous to a police department that is required to submit a series of individual work orders to the IT department, and having each request addressed by a different IT professional. When a competent IT professional is assigned and housed within the department, efficiencies are realized in terms of responsiveness, understanding, continuity of service, and effectiveness.

Other departments, such as the Davenport (IA) Police Department, have simply requested that a talented and motivated member of the municipality's HR department be assigned as liaison to the department. This is often sufficient, if that individual is qualified and able to devote the necessary time and effort to fully address the department's needs.

And yet, despite all this turmoil, many police and HR departments have not only failed to adapt their recruitment processes and resources during the past twenty years, but many have also utterly failed to review them even critically.

There is an immediate need for new ideas, new insights, and approaches. Many departments are just now learning that they need to actively monitor their "yield rate," like the college admissions and enrollment process. They need to determine what percentage of individuals who have been offered a position by the department enroll in the police academy and, ultimately, get hired? They should also monitor the percentage of applicants who move successfully through each successive phase of the screening process up to the ultimate date of appointment as a police officer. For example, all departments should be generating data to answer the following:

"What percentage of individuals who registered for the entrance exam actually took it, passed it?"

"What percentage of individuals who passed the written exam passed the criminal background investigation?"

"What percentage of individuals called in for the psychological examination, passed it?"

"What is the department's retention rate for police academy recruits?"

"What is the current and historic retention rate for officers over the first five years of their careers?," etc.

Once these questions are answered, they must be actively monitored for trends. As PERF suggests, "To stay ahead of current and future changes, agencies need to monitor workforce trends, collect and analyze data on their staffing needs, and adjust their recruiting and retention strategies accordingly" (2019, p. 12). This takes time and effort, but it is necessary.

Data such as this is crucial to fully understand the dynamics within the workforce. For many departments, the numbers are not promising.

Part II. Assessing a Department's Recruitment and Retention Capabilities (and Possible Solutions Going Forward)

Challenging times call for innovative responses. Unfortunately, "American law enforcement recruitment, and hiring efforts have remained largely the same for the last several decades, because agencies traditionally had more than enough applicants to fill all of their available positions" (Jolicoeur and Grant, 2017, p. 343). Those days are now gone, perhaps forever (Brown, 2022). Traditional approaches to recruitment and retention need to be abandoned as they "are insufficient to meet the need for officers who possess the skills and temperament needed for modern policing" (PERF, 2019, p. 14).

During such a crisis, it is especially important to be able to accurately assess a particular department's recruitment and retention processes and capabilities. Any deficiencies or vulnerabilities must be quickly detected and addressed, for a department to survive and to advance in a strategic manner.

Therefore, what every American police department now needs is "an immediate, contemporary, and relevant recruitment plan to begin addressing a critical deficit in entry-level law enforcement (and, ultimately, a plan that will strengthen succession planning)" (Smith, 2016, p. 1). They must all begin to create and employ a sophisticated and effective recruitment and retention strategy that has a reach throughout the state, and beyond. Police departments will only remain competitive if they understand and fully utilize best practices in recruitment and retention (Hoisington, 2018).

Departments can longer simply defer to their HR department to design and control the recruitment and hiring process. The tail can no longer wag the dog. Police officer candidates must be recruited in a different way than one would recruit a member of a highway department. Processes, materials, and specific strategies must be tailor-made for policing.

To this end, all American police departments must have a formal, multi-year recruitment plan with specific strategies and means of assessment. They must work closely with HR professionals to design, implement, and evaluate this plan. Ideally, this recruitment plan would be incorporated into a department-wide multi-year strategic plan. Indeed, it is very likely that recruitment and retention is now the number one priority (i.e., top strategic objective) of most American police departments.

Almost every police department in the nation must fully staff and support the position of "recruitment and retention officer." In a department with more than 40 uniformed personnel, this would likely be a full-time position, due to the extraordinary recruitment challenges currently being experienced. This should not be considered as simply an ancillary administrative position. The individual selected must be a uniformed officer whose personal and professional demeanor demonstrate the characteristics and culture of the department. Much like a field training officer (FTO), this officer should possess exceptional communication skills and serve as a role model for the department. This individual must be able to positively reflect the brand, image, and culture of the department, while effectively engaging with all applicants and probationary officers.

Specific strategies could include the following:

Clarify and Streamline the Hiring Process as Much as Possible

Departments must work closely with the town's human resources office to streamline the application, screening, and selection process as much as possible. Generic HR systems and processes that are used for all municipal employees must be modified and adapted for police purposes. Every effort must be made to reduce time delays and increase response times, while still properly investigating and vetting candidates. The department's policies and procedures for recruitment and selection of personnel must be clear, comprehensive, and consistent with best practices in American policing.

Most American police employers have adjusted, such as shifting to a continuous filing and testing period, but these steps alone are unlikely to produce the needed supply of police officers. Linos and Riesch (2020) have closely studied the benefits of reducing the administrative burden during police recruitment:

> Switching to a simpler, standardized form is associated with less candidate drop off. Expedited testing is positively associated with how long a candidate remains in the process. Defaulting to an online process and simplifying instructions for candidates further increases the likelihood that candidates will comply. These efforts seem to equally impact candidates from diverse, racial and gender backgrounds.
>
> (p. 100)

They continue:
We find that reducing administrative hurdles can have significant impact on drop-off rates, even in a high stakes environment such as hiring. Form standardization early in the process resulted in applicants completing nearly one more step in the recruitment process. Expedited testing is associated with applicants remaining for an additional two steps in the process. Simple, *behaviorally informed nudges* to complete a key stage in the process, increased overall compliance by 8%, with a 60% increase in compliance within two weeks (p. 93) (emphasis supplied)

Increase the Quantity and Quality of Communication with Applicants

The "behaviorally informed nudges" referred to above, can take many forms. One thing is certain though, that police applicants today must be contacted frequently and effectively throughout the entire process, by means of texts, emails, phone calls, or personal visits. Frequent applicant contact is an essential recruitment technique, as many departments typically lose a significant portion of applicants as they proceed through the qualification process. Quickly inviting an applicant in for an initial interview is critically important. Many police departments and municipalities have traditionally defused responsibility for recruitment widely, thereby causing unnecessary delay in the process. Allowing an applicant to linger for an extended period greatly increases the risk that the applicant will decline any offer of employment and simply look elsewhere. Applicants today have many employment choices and police departments actively compete with one another to attract and secure the most qualified applicants.

In past years, police recruiters were loath to send a reminder to an applicant that his/her physical agility test was coming up next week. The prevailing attitude was, "if they need to be reminded about something this important, our department doesn't need them." That attitude must change because the attitudes of young people have now changed. Such communication is appreciated and, in many ways, expected by these young applicants who are new to the profession. This applicant pool consists of a population of young people who are likely to require far more contact from police recruiters. The quantity and quality of applicant contact matters greatly. Departments that fail to contact an applicant for months at a time will inevitably lose that person to another agency. It is analogous to vessels in a commercial fishing fleet competing with one another in fishing grounds that have been severely over-fished. Other departments will take viable applicants from you with no compunction, as they would naturally expect you to do the same to them.

This ongoing dialog with applicants is an excellent opportunity to convey and highlight the department's philosophy and culture. Linos and Riesch (2020) explain,

> "We know that job seekers look for information about the organization through its personnel practices. When surveyed, job seekers suggest that the candidate's experience affects the overall perception of the employer or organization. Interactions with recruiters may signal to candidates how they might be treated by the organization. Thus, the recruiting experience itself provides signals to candidates about what it would be like to work for the employer."
>
> (p. 94)

If a department expects to aggressively compete in such a turbulent employment market, these changes must be made. It is in every respect a complete paradigm shifts for recruiters. The sellers' market that has existed for decades has now clearly shifted to a buyers' market. Police recruiters must now actively partner with HR professionals to "reduce friction costs" and increase the likelihood that applicants comply with, and ultimately complete, the application and hiring process.

Focus Upon Branding and Messaging

All police departments must now fully understand and give great attention to their messaging and branding (McLean, 2023). The content of recruitment materials clearly matters since, "the ways departments characterize the organization and job in recruitment materials may influence perceptions of general job attractiveness, job intentions, job fit, and organizational fit" (Aiello, 2022, p. 459). In particular, "recruitment videos are an excellent source of capturing visible themes that may represent or signal the values of the recruiting organization to potential recruits" (Koslicki, 2021, p. 705). Visual imagery can be "particularly persuasive in this regard, given the unique influence that they can have on the attitudes, motivations and actions of prospective applicants" (Jolicoeur and Grant, 2017, p. 343). Recruitment materials, particularly promotional videos, must be aligned with preferred vocational skills, such as community engagement and problem-solving. Departments should not unintentionally reinforce the "societal myth that modern policing consists primarily of enforcement activities undertaken by officers acting as crime fighters" (Jolicoeur and Grant, 2017, p. 350).

Police recruitment materials must absolutely avoid any depiction of military equipment or firearms training. Departments have been roundly criticized for "hyper-militarized" recruitment materials (see, e.g., Krauss and Harlow, 2023). In their place, it is preferable to include materials that better reflect a department's community policing and public engagement activities. It is suggested that:

> There may be a need to rebrand departmental recruitment identities, to provide those seeking employment with a more realistic and meaningful depiction of the duties associated with the profession. This is an essentially especially important consideration, if the desire among police agencies and administrators is to define policing along professional, as opposed to purely occupational lines.
>
> (Jolicoeur and Grant, 2017, p. 340)

Ensuring an accurate representation of professional duties in recruitment materials is an important factor in ensuring that law-enforcement agencies are better able to recruit those best suited for the field, and to then retain those individuals for a longer duration after their initial employment. Not only can an unrealistic perception of police duties exacerbate problems with recruitment and retention, but it can also contribute to an employee base, which values enforcement duties at the expense of other important policing duties that have a direct impact on the efficacy of the larger police function in contemporary American society (p. 351).

Gendered messages can also unintentionally complicate the recruitment of female candidates (Aiello, 2022). Merely stating physical requirements of the job does not appear to limit the pool of female candidates, however. It appears that a truthful and upfront description of the physical demands associated with the job can improve the quality of the applicant pool (Aiello, 2022).

Honesty is in fact an extremely important factor in all aspects of the recruitment process. Findings from several research studies suggest that "the inclusion of realistic depictions of both the duties performed in a position, and the compensation and benefits associated with that position have been found to reduce turnover and improve workplace satisfaction" (Jolicoeur and Grant, 2017, p. 342). As Skaggs et al. (2022) explain, "individuals have preconceived expectations about police work, leadership, and departmental goals and policies, which, when not met, result in voluntary resignation. In contrast, when these expectations are met, turnover rates within the agency are reduced" (p. 464).

Use Existing Social Networks

It is now very clear to even the casual observer that police recruiting must be "more purposeful and targeted in its approach" (COPS OFFICE, 2022, p. 2). Departments must now "creatively, target women and minorities through informal networks (e.g., local churches and businesses)" (Rhodes and Tyler, 2019, p. 495). Recruitment officers cannot do this alone. They should reach out to uniformed and non-sworn members of their departments to assist with identifying potential candidates who they know as members of community groups, fraternal organizations, a local gym, etc. (Stubbs, 2023). Some departments have now begun offering current employees a "finders' fee" for identifying viable individuals who are ultimately hired by the department.

Relax Non-Essential Entry Requirements

To increase the pool of viable candidates, many departments have critically examined their hiring criteria with an eye towards distinguishing those essential (and therefore non-negotiable) criteria, such as significant criminal history or prolonged and current drug use, from a criterion that might not provide any indication of one's inability to adequately perform the job (Jenkins, 2021).

Since it is now a fact that "fewer people want to apply because of changing career-lifestyle preferences" and "fewer people are qualified to meet the rigid standards of becoming a police officer," many departments have relaxed their requirements regarding such things as: pre-employment physical agility tests; history of minor drug use; personal debt; obesity; tattoos and facial hair; and even minor criminal history (COPS Office, 2022, p. 3). American policing has now:

[Witnessed] a relaxation of standards with respect to the prior illegal possession of drugs, while other data reveal[s] that young adult up to age 23, now have a 41% likelihood of having a criminal prior criminal non-traffic arrest. In the case of some minority groups, that statistic can rise to as high as 60%. Recruiters, background investigators, and the law enforcement managers, who make the hiring decisions need to take note of this inescapable fact and consider how it might affect their recruiting and employment practices.

(Smith, 2016, p. 1)

Some researchers suggest that departments and their HR colleagues spend more time and effort to identify sought-after traits, such as integrity, honesty, compassion and empathy, and shift towards a "screen-in" rather than a "screen-out" selection process (e.g., Terpstra et al., 2022).

Signing Bonuses

Major cities, such as Indianapolis are now seeking to attract applicants by increasing starting salaries for police officers (16%) and offering significant signing bonuses ($10,000) (Cheang, 2023). These efforts are no doubt necessary, but perhaps they are not enough.

Signing bonuses might appear to be a "quick fix," but they are likely not a long-term solution. Lump sum payments dissipate quickly and such payments are typically not pensionable. They represent a stopgap measure that might benefit a municipality or county only until such time as a neighboring community "ups the ante" by offering even more of a financial incentive (Smith, 2022). In a highly competitive market, it will be difficult to retain qualified personnel. This is yet another example of how the issues of recruitment and retention are inextricably linked.

In recent years many municipalities moved away from offering traditional defined benefits pension plans to their police officers. These plans guarantee a certain amount of income based upon salary, years of service and age. In their place, they now offer defined contribution plans, such as 401K plans. Since traditional "vesting" requirements do not apply, officers with these plans are more easily able to transfer these funds out of state. We are therefore seeing a greater amount of mobility as mid-career officers seek and obtain other employment opportunities and move out of state. Research suggests that "millennials are now far less likely to stay until retirement. Research as far back as 2009 suggests that only 50% of adult workers at the time had been at their jobs for more than five years, and adult workers will quite likely have 10 to 14 jobs by their late 30s. As veteran officers retire at younger ages, and younger officers, move between agencies or careers, a critical employee gap seems likely" (Smith, 2016, p. 23).

This geographic shift of police personnel across various regions of the country will likely continue as more agencies move towards 401K retirement plans and actively compete for personnel. Such a shift will hurt many departments not simply due to lower staffing, but also due to the loss of tacit knowledge and skills, institutional memory, and a viable cohort of field and in-service training staff.

Signing bonuses and a departmental strategy of active "poaching" will likely prove to be temporary solutions. In such a dynamic labor market, as the competition increases, a desirable and successful department can rapidly turn into an undesirable and struggling one. Once again, we see the extremely close connection between recruitment and retention.

Flex Time

All departments must now seriously consider offering "more flexible scheduling to support a desirable work-life balance, including time for family responsibilities" (PERF, 2019, p. 10). When designing compensation and benefits packages, the offering of additional paid time off (PTO) should be strongly considered. It is likely that this benefit will be more attractive to younger applicants and junior officers than additional pay.

Departments should also afford officers the option of either receiving additional salary for accrued overtime or receiving "comp time" in terms of additional days off. This allows officers to choose either cash or additional time off, as their personal circumstances require. If a collective bargaining agreement needs to be adjusted, so be it. Time off is now considered to be a very valuable commodity.

Finally, departments should consider allowing their officers to perform "mutuals" with their colleagues. That is, they should be allowed to swap a particular patrol shift with a fellow officer, provided sufficient notice is given and approval received from patrol supervisors. This allows an officer to have a particular day off from work (for a wedding, family commitment, etc.) without expending a vacation day. This provides an additional degree of flexibility that would likely enhance work–life balance for many.

Retention Bonuses

Many departments are now considering and/or offering financial incentives to officers who remain on the job (i.e., "stay bonuses"). These payments are no-doubt helpful in terms of boosting retention, but they are unlikely to be a long-term solution. As with hiring bonuses, if these payments are not considered "pensionable," departments will likely find themselves in a bidding war of sorts with competing agencies that offer higher amounts.

A more permanent solution would be to work with the municipality and labor unions (if applicable) to simply structure salary and pay grades in such a way as to provide meaningful financial incentives for officers of every rank to remain with the department through the normal pension vesting period.

The key point is that every community must now continue to monitor the regional market for police officers. They must actively review and match salary and benefits packages currently offered by other departments in the region or risk losing the officers they already have. In many respects, a police department will either be aware of, and responsive to regional market forces, or become victimized by them.

Increase the Use of Ride-Alongs and "Sit-Alongs" for Applicants Who Are New to the Profession

As mentioned previously, individuals new to the profession should have ample opportunities to see the department that they have applied to "from the inside." Recruiting officers should offer opportunities for job shadowing or ride-alongs with officers and encourage applicants to visit the department to personally observe operations and to interact with police personnel. This provides useful information and experiences, while affording the department additional opportunities to observe the applicant.

Efforts such as these will reduce the likelihood that the applicant will be surprised by the nature of the work and demands of the job once they have been hired and trained. Every effort should be made to introduce the candidate as early as possible. There is nothing more demoralizing to a department than to select, hire, and train a qualified officer, only to lose them one or two years later when the officer states, "The job just isn't what I thought it would be."

Fully Leverage Volunteer, Cadet, Police Explorer, and Internship Programs

Many departments have experienced recruitment success with robust Explorer and Cadet programs. The purpose and underlying philosophy behind such programs are "to encourage interest in policing at a younger age" (PERF, 2019, p. 14). They are also useful in terms of supervising, guiding, and monitoring youth during a period when they are likely to engage in activities that would, ultimately, disqualify them for law enforcement employment.

Perhaps if police officers would assume and embrace the roles of mentors and educators, a long-term solution could be found.

As Smith (2016) explains:

> It would appear that "growing their own" may be the only realistic and productive, long-term solution to recruitment needs. It has been argued that the failure of public safety agencies to intervene in the lives of young people likely means that their own personal choices may place them on an irrevocable path of an eligibility by the time they reach adulthood. The job of the modern public safety officer is more than just responding to calls for service – there is an urgent need for officers to function as recruiters, mentors, and role models, despite the negative press that appears almost daily in the media. (p. 24)

A robust police recruitment program leverages existing programs to engage young people, such a Police Explorer program or innovative "youth camps" or "youth academies." School resource officers (SROs) who are so inclined could be trained and supported to "stand in front of the classroom and deliver "street law" classes to the youth of this [country] to prepare them for encounters with the police by explaining constitutional protections as well as expectations for personal conduct." (O'Connell, 2015)

In 2009, California POST partnered with local schooldistricts, and colleges to develop a *Career Pipeline* program for middle-school students which consists of after-school meetings and programs, career day presentations, teambuilding, and character and leadership training, similar in nature to components of the DARE program. It is still too early to accurately measure the program's long-term impact in terms of increased yield of viable recruits (California POST, 2014). It is quite possible that the drop-out rate of fifth and sixth graders will ultimately prove to be higher than that of high schoolers (as these younger children will need to be engaged for a longer period and might lose interest over time). Nevertheless, exposure to such a positive program for any period should increase the future employability of the students. Programs such as these also provide a valuable means of partnership and connection with communities, and the young people who are the potential police applicants of tomorrow. They could prove to be the long-term solution that many departments are seeking.

Every department should develop and/or strengthen relationships with local colleges and universities that offer degrees (associates, bachelors, and masters) in criminal justice and public administration. They should reach out to full-time faculty in criminal justice programs throughout the region, particularly full-time professors with prior law-enforcement experience. In addition to simply attending job fairs on campus and handing out pamphlets, uniformed members of the department should request the opportunity to meet with and present to criminal justice club members. Departments should develop their own college intern program (or partner with other nearby departments). Such efforts were perhaps not necessary several years ago but, considering the current reality, every effort should be made to make meaningful connections with young persons interested in the field and to distinguish departments in the minds of these potential applicants.

Leverage Information Obtained from Exit Interviews

Most police departments follow a procedure for conducting "exit interviews" for officers who voluntarily separate from the department (i.e., resignations). Unfortunately, these are typically pro forma meetings that are conducted in a perfunctory manner, without any real depth of communication or interaction between the participants. Typically, the one-page form is completed by a supervisor in a matter of minutes and the narrative section of the report that calls for "reason(s) for leaving the job" (if indeed there is such a narrative section) is filled in with "Better job opportunity." This is no longer acceptable.

Exit interviews represent an excellent opportunity to obtain a treasure trove of information (indeed, intel) for police departments in terms of : how are they are losing employees? Why are they losing employees? What type of employees are leaving? etc.

Much has been learned by departments that seek these answers. "Enhanced pay, improved benefits, merit-based promotion systems, increased job, flexibility, greater recognition of employee, achievement, opportunities for promotion and personal fulfillment and more equitable supervisory practices have all been cited as important factors in retaining existing employees, and minimizing the frequency with which officers leave the policing profession" (Jolicoeur and Grant, 2017, p. 342).

Sadly, most police and municipal HR departments are not capturing this information and are, quite literally, asleep at the wheel. An imbedded police HR professional can, however, capture and use this information. Indeed, this should be a major function for this person. Once captured, that information must be analyzed and any discernable patterns or commonalities of experience can then be reported back to the police administrators and, ultimately, used to inform future practices and strategies. Those departments that choose to do this will certainly obtain a competitive advantage in the police employee marketplace.

Individuals who voluntarily drop out of the testing and hiring process are similarly an extremely valuable source of actionable information. We need to capture as much data as we can. We are not speaking here of individuals who fail to pass a physical agility or psychological test, or background investigation, but an otherwise qualified candidate who simply chooses not to move forward in the process.

Departments must dive deeply into the thoughts, feelings, and perceptions of those who start the process, yet voluntarily drop out of the hiring process. Applicants who have moved far along in the process are particularly useful. If you ask them what occurred, in terms of their changing life circumstances or why they simply changed their minds, they are very likely to tell you. Exit interviews such as these are therefore a valuable component of a highly-effective recruitment program. As Linos and Riesch, 2020) note

When asked directly, candidates who voluntarily dropped out [of the hiring process] cited the lack of clarity in the application process, the absence of support from personnel, and the length of the application process as the most prominent factors in their decision making.

(p. 92) (citation omitted)

In essence, these individuals are telling us what we must do in the future to secure viable candidates.

Boost Retention Through Career Planning, Mentorship, and Officer Wellness Programs

Once a qualified police applicant is hired, trained, and assigned to patrol, the natural expectation of a police department is that the officer will continue to work until retirement. High numbers of "voluntary quits" suggest organization ineffectiveness. Every effort should be made to reduce this number as much as possible.

The PERF study (2019) concluded that, "the majority of voluntary resignations are occurring within the first 5 years that officers are on the force" (p. 8). This is, therefore, the period when retention efforts must be concentrated. But what exactly should be done?

We believe that all police departments should partner with their HR colleagues to develop the means of assessing what their officers want in their careers and "explore ways to broaden officers' experiences and career planning" (PERF, 2019, p. 15). Career planning can manage expectations and provide incentives for remaining in the job. Many departments miss the opportunity to do so, by failing to perform meaningful annual performance reviews. Meaningful feedback is required during annual performance reviews, as well as an opportunity for officers to communicate their interests and desires for additional specialized training and new opportunities (Gul and O'Connell, 2013).

In many ways, training and career development with real opportunities are the key to high retention rates. As PERF explains:

> One way to increase retention is to offer professional development opportunities, especially opportunities to gain experience in other areas within an agency. For example, the Phoenix Police Department supports this type of growth by encouraging employees to work in a different assignment for up to 80 hours annually. Opportunities like this can help officers feel valued and see themselves staying with the department long term.
>
> (PERF, 2019, p. 15)

Mentoring is rapidly becoming another strategy "that can help with [police] recruitment and retention, as well as aid with building diversity within leadership roles" (Ennis and Craven 2023, p. 26). Many departments are now developing and implementing a formal process of pairing senior officers (mentors) with newly-hired officers (mentees) as a means of facilitating the transfer of tacit knowledge and skills, while providing personal support and guidance to mentees. This is over and above existing field and in-service training programs. Such programs can demonstrate an organization's commitment to staff development and foster a culture of collaboration and support. In many ways, these programs might be exactly what the new generation of officers are seeking.

Much thought and planning are required. Crucial questions include, "How do we select, train and support mentors?" "How do we match mentors with mentees? and, "How do we fund the program?" It is best to move slowly and cautiously so as not to design a program that is likely to fail. A badly designed program can in many ways do more harm than good.

As these programs proliferate, state and federal funding will likely become available. Departments currently operating under a mandate for greater diversity should be particularly interested, as such programs have been "found to be the most impactful activity for increasing diversity and inclusion at work, compared to diversity training, and a variety of other initiatives" (p. 26).

Tuition Assistance

During the 1970s, the federal government sponsored a national tuition assistance program for police officers known as the Law Enforcement Assistance Program (LEAP). The program included financial grants and loans made to "qualified full-time employees of publicly-funded law enforcement and criminal justice agencies" (Bennett & Marshall, 1979, p. 148). This program was quite popular and was widely used by police officers across the United States. In fact, the LEAP program was in many ways responsible for the initial development and rapid growth of stand-alone Criminal Justice departments in colleges and universities across the country.

While there are still federal and state funding sources available for police officers seeking to advance themselves through higher education, we believe that more needs to be done. Tuition assistance and re-imbursement are a very real incentive for many individuals to initially seek employment with and/or remain with a particular law enforcement agency. It is likely that legislatures will revive these programs in the future, to attract more people to the profession.

In the interim, there is nothing preventing a particular municipality from offering its own financial incentives, in terms of tuition reimbursement payments, grants, or loans (perhaps interest free) to active-duty police officers. Doing so would enhance the compensation package offered to officers and entice them to remain with that department through degree completion, while building capacity (in terms of a highly-skilled workforce) within the department. Granted, once a degree is completed, an officer becomes more marketable to other agencies (and a ripe candidate for poaching). Nevertheless, there is always another degree to achieve, or certificate to be obtained. If there is a real incentive and support (in terms of scheduling) for officers to continue their educations, it is likely that this process can continue during many years of service.

More Global Solutions

If the current police hiring crisis continues or worsens, as many predict it will, it is likely that more global solutions will need to be considered. Departments and municipalities can only do so much. State legislators will be required to take action. To this end, we believe that all states (i.e., their executive and legislative branches) should now consider other creative financial incentives that would attract prospective candidates such as: 1) student debt forgiveness (for individuals who attended state universities); and 2) state and/or local tax relief, such as a waiver of state income tax or property tax for active-duty police officers. Any state that enacts such legislation is likely to have a considerable advantage in attracting officers.

Fully Staff and Support a Robust Field Training Program

Field training represents a critical time in an officer's career. During this period, probationary officers observe their trainers as they operate in the field, interact with citizens and co-workers. These junior officers are greatly impressionable at this point in their career and they model the style of their trainers. For this reason, the role of field training officer (FTO) is certainly one of the most critical positions within a department during a recruitment and retention crisis. As O'Connell and Straub (2007) explain:

> The role of field training officer (FTO) is of critical importance. All too frequently, police organizations fail to understand the impact that FTOs have on the professional development of newly assigned officers. FTOs must be properly selected, trained, supervised, and supported. Ideally, FTOs are professionals who demonstrate a level of professionalism and commitment that distinguish them from their peers. Although FTO's need not have advanced degrees of formal education (such as a master's degree), additional education can be helpful. Most importantly, the ideal FTO should demonstrate a heightened degree of personal integrity and practical reasoning and decision-making skills. FTOs must lead by example, but should also be able to communicate clearly, so that trainees can benefit as much as possible from their expertise.
>
> (O'Connell and Straub, 2007, p. 65)

An excellent FTO will boost retention. An ineffective one will reduce the likelihood that officers in training will remain committed to their department. Unfortunately, chronic understaffing often results in the backfilling of patrol positions and a drain on field training programs:

> As a result of retention issues, new recruits, after completion of academy training, are placed with inexperienced FTO's who feel disgruntled over salary and lack of support. The discontent is inevitably passed on to the new recruits through poor, inadequate training, producing an inexperienced, poorly trained officer. If these factors are not addressed by the department, the cycle will undoubtedly continue to deteriorate over time.
>
> (Skaggs et al., 2022, p. 473)

Every effort should therefore be made to fully staff field training programs with superior officers, even if this means pulling investigators and supervisors who previously served as FTOs from other positions.

Consider "Over-Hiring"

In recent years, the authors have observed several departments and municipalities that are now considering the "over-hiring" of personnel, in terms of securing qualified candidates *prior* to an anticipated vacancy. Some have done so. This is done in recognition of the fact that: a) the market for police officers has become far more competitive and challenging; b) it takes many months to fully train and prepare an officer who can fill an open position; and c) a qualified candidate is too valuable to lose.

Those departments that are fortunate enough to have an abundance of fully-qualified applicants are now choosing to secure them as soon as they can. A candidate is hired and placed in a recruit training program some time *before* the vacancy has occurred, knowing that the position will in fact be open once the recruit's training is completed. This is a luxury that unfortunately very few departments can afford. Most departments will experience the personnel shortage first, then simply make do with schedule adjustments and ordered overtime until the position can be posted; the testing can begin; qualified candidates can be identified; training can begin; and training is completed. This reactive approach serves to magnify staffing challenges by increasing workload among the remaining staff and can lead to low morale and a high level of burnout. It is obviously far less desirable, from a resource and officer wellness standpoint.

Many rapidly growing communities that have the resources and ability to attract qualified applicants chose to build capacity now, rather than wait until significant operational deficiencies manifest themselves.

References

Ahmed, T., & Salter, J. (September 5, 2023). *Some Small Towns in America are Disbanding Police Forces, Citing Hiring Woes.* APNews.com. https://apnews.com/article/police-departments-hiring-disbanding-defunding-minnesota-6bc707834152806264dce7bfa80d9b29

Aiello, M. (2022). Procedural justice and demographic diversity: A quasi-experimental study of police recruitment. *Police Quarterly*, 25(3), 387–411.

Ali, S. S. (March 18, 2017). *Police Shortage Hits Cities and Small Towns across the Country.* NBCnewscom. www.nbcnews.com/news/us-news/police-shortage-hits-cities-small-towns-across-country-n734721

Bennett, R. R. & I. H. Marshall. (1979). Criminal justice education in the United States: A profile. *Journal of Criminal Justice*, 7(2), 147–172.

Brown, T. (2022). A qualitative evaluation of changes to police recruitment. *Dissertation Abstracts International Section A: Humanities and Social Sciences*, 83(9-A), pp. 25–29.

California Commission on Peace Officer Standards and Training. (2014). *Program Guide Building a Public Safety Career Pipeline, Update 2014, Addressing Today's Law Enforcement Recruitment Challenge.* https://post.ca.gov/

Campisi, C. (2017). *Blue on Blue: An Insider's Story of Good Cops Catching Bad Cops.* Scribner.

Carey, K. (November 21, 2022). *The Incredible Shrinking Future of College: The Population of College-Age Americans is About to Crash. It will Change Higher Education Forever.* Vox. www.vox.com/the-highlight/23428166/college-enrollment-population-education-crash

Cheang, K. L. (October 19, 2023). *Indy Budget Emphasizes Public Safety: $1.4B Total Boosts Police Recruitment, Retention.* Indianapolis Star, A1.

Clark, J. (August 15, 2023). *Entire Police Department Resigns in Minnesota City, Leaves Mayor 'Blindsided': 'Zero Applicants.* Fox News. www.foxnews.com/media/entire-police-department-resigns-minnesota-town-leaves-mayor-blindsided-zero-applicants

COPS Office: United States Department of Justice. (2022). *Reframing the Police Staffing Challenge: Strategies for Meeting Workload Demand,* 15(1), *January.*

Cox, G. M. (2012). Crisis in police recruitment: Public service motivation and changes in generational preferences. *Dissertation Abstracts International Section A: Humanities and Social Sciences*, 73(5A).

Ennis, A., & Craven, K. (August 26, 2023). *Mentoring Models for Recruitment, Retention and Diversity.* Police Chief Magazine. www.policechiefmagazine.org/mentoring-models-for-recruitment-retention-and-diversity/

Felton, J. (December 2, 2022). *Pittsburgh Needs to Step Up Police Recruitment Efforts, Officials Say.* Pittsburgh Tribune Review. https://triblive.com/local/pittsburgh-needs-to-step-up-police-recruitment-efforts-officials-say/

Gul, S. K., & O'Connell, P. (2013). *Police Performance Appraisals: A Comparative Perspective.* CRC Press.

Hoisington, E. (2018). Police recruitment best practices to ensure a competent, skilled workforce. *Dissertation Abstracts International Section A: Humanities and Social Sciences*, 79(9-A).

Jackman, T. (December 4, 2018). *Who Wants to be a Police Officer? Job Applications Plummet at Most U.S. Departments.* The Washington Post. www.washingtonpost.com/crime-law/2018/12/04/who-wants-be-police-officer-job-applications-plummet-most-us-departments/

Jenkins, C. (2021). Effective police recruitment: Professional misconduct risk Regression analysis for law enforcement officers. *Dissertation Abstracts International Section B: The Sciences and Engineering*, 82(8-B).

Jolicoeur, J. & Grant, E. (2017). Form seeking function: An exploratory content analysis evaluation of the imagery contained in law enforcement agency police officer recruitment brochures. *Police Journal*, 91(4), 339–355.

Kaste, M. (2018). Shortage of officers fuels police recruiting crisis. *National Public Radio: Morning Edition*, December 11.

Koslocki, W. (2018). Advertising underlying assumptions: A quantitative content analysis of militarized and community-oriented artifacts in police recruitment videos. *Dissertation Abstracts International Section A: Humanities and Social Sciences*, 79 (11-AE).

Koslicki, W. (2021). Recruiting warriors or guardians? A content analysis of police recruitment videos. *Policing and Society*, 31(6), 702–720.

Krauss, L., & Harlow, T. (January 9, 2023). *Brooklyn Center Police Recruitment Video Draws Backlash*. Star Tribune. www.startribune.com/brooklyn-center-police-recruitment-video-draws-backlash/600242030/

Lentz, B. (2022). The national crisis of police recruitment and retention. *Dissertation Abstracts International Section B: The Sciences and Engineering*, 83(8-B).

Linos, E., & Riesch, N. (January/February 2020). Thick red tape and the thin blue line: A field study on reducing administrative burden in police recruitment. *Public Administration Review*, 80(1), 92–103.

Maciag, M. (March 2018). *With Fewer Police Applicants, Departments Engage in Bidding Wars*. Governing.com. www.governing.com/archive/gov-hiring-police-officers.html

Marcius, C. (December 9, 2022). *NYPD Officers Leave in Droves for Better Pay in Smaller Towns*. The New York Times. www.nytimes.com/2022/12/09/nyregion/new-york-police-department-attrition.html

Marcus, J. (May 22, 2021). *Declining Birthrate Means Hard Times Ahead for Colleges*. The Washington Post. www.washingtonpost.com/local/education/college-enrollment-birthrate-decline/2021/05/21/52d7e5a6-ba47-11eb-a5fe-bb49dc89a248_story.html

McLean, K., Cherry, T. & Alpert, G. (2023). Recruiting for change: Shifting focus to address a workforce crisis. *Police Practice and Research*, 24(4), 446–460.

O'Connell, P. (2015). *Testimony Before the New York State Senate, Hearings of the Committee on Crime Victims, Crime and Corrections, February 4*.

O'Connell, P., & Straub, F. (2007). *Performance-Based Management for Police Organizations*. Waveland.

Office of Justice Programs. (2015). Final Report of the *President's Task Force on 21st Century Policing. Washington, DC, United States Department of Justice*.

Pew Research Center. (September 12, 2016). *The Racial Confidence Gap in Police Performance*. Survey of U.S. Adults, www.pewresearch.org/social-trends/2016/09/29/the-racial-confidence-gap-in-police-performance/

Police Executive Research Forum. (2018). Police leaders discuss challenges in recruiting at PERF town hall meeting in Nashville. *Subject to Debate: A Newsletter of the Police Executive Research Forum*, 32(1), 1.

Police Executive Research Forum. (September, 2019). *The Workforce Crisis, and What Police Agencies Are Doing about It*. www.policeforum.org/assets/WorkforceCrisis.pdfhttps://www.policeforum.org/assets/WorkforceCrisis.pdf

Police Executive Research Forum. (June 11, 2021). *Survey on Police Workforce Trends*. Workforce Survey. www.policeforum.org/workforcesurveyjune2021

Police Executive Research Forum. (March 2022). *PERF Survey Shows Steady Staffing Decrease over Past Two Years*. Policeforum.org. www.policeforum.org/workforcemarch2022

Police Executive Research Forum. (April 1, 2023). *New PERF Survey Shows Police Agencies Are Losing Officers Faster than They Can Hire New Ones*. Workforce Survey. www.policeforum.org/staffing2023

Rhodes, T., & Tyler, D. (2019). Is it cool to be a cop?: Exploring the differential impact of Ferguson on police applicants. *Policing*, 15(1), 492–507.

Schuck, A. (2021). Motivations for a career in policing: Social group differences and occupational satisfaction. *Police Practice and Research*, 22(5), 1507–1523.

Skaggs, S., Harris. C., & Montgomery, L. (2022). Impact of police-community relations: Recruitment and retention concerns of local police agencies. *Policing: A Journal of Policy and Practice*, 16(3), 462–475.

Smith, S. (June 2016). *A Crisis Facing Law Enforcement: Recruiting in the 21st Century*. Police Chief. www.policechiefmagazine.org/a-crisis-facing-law-enforcement-recruiting-in-the-21st-century/

Smith, M. (December 25, 2022). *As Applications Fall, Police Departments Lure Recruits with Bonuses and Attention*. The New York Times. www.nytimes.com/2022/12/25/us/police-officer-recruits.html

Snelling, D. (June 1, 2023). DeSantis' police recruitment plan hired some with a criminal past. *South Florida Times*, 33(22), 1A–2A.

Stubbs, G. (2023). Embeddedness within police recruitment: How social networks and relationships influence the hiring of new recruits. *Dissertation Abstracts International Section B: The Sciences and Engineering*, 84(9-B).

Terpstra, B., White, M., & Fradella, H. (2022). Finding good cops: The foundations of a screen-in (not out) hiring process for police. *Policing*, 45(4), 676–692.

Westervelt, E. (June 24, 2021). *Cops Say Low Morale and Department Scrutiny Are Driving Them Away from the Job*. NPR: Criminal Justice Collaborative. www.npr.org/2021/06/24/1009578809/cops-say-low-morale-and-department-scrutiny-are-driving-them-away-from-the-job

Williams, E., & Sondhi, A. (2022). A narrative review of the literature on the recruitment of younger police officers, in age and in service: What are the implications for the police service in England and Wales?. *Policing: A Journal of Policy and Practice*, 16(4), 241–246.

Wimbley, L. (October 2, 2021). *How Do You Sell This Job?': Police Recruitment Declines Across Pittsburgh and Allegheny, While Some Departments Flourish*. Pittsburgh Post–Gazette. www.post-gazette.com/news/2021/10/02/How-do-you-sell-this-job-Police-recruitment-across-Pittsburgh-and-Allegheny-declines-while-some-departments-flourish/stories/202108080028

Chapter 9

The Assessment of Police Training Systems

Introduction

In many respects, the assessment of police training systems is a rather straightforward matter. All that is required is to identify whether a particular department has the tools necessary for information delivery. This would include the appropriate staffing, budget, facilities, equipment, programs, curriculum, and lessons for the delivery of field training; in-service training; and management training/executive development. Police Officer Standards and Training (POST) and accreditation bodies are very adept at this means of evaluating a particular department's training capabilities by merely identifying the necessary capabilities; in essence, by simply checking off the boxes.

The problem is, this approach is based on a rather simplistic view of training. Perhaps too simplistic. Is training merely the delivery of information, or is it something more? Think about this. How should we really *assess* police training? Should we simply document what was taught, what was delivered, or said? Do we evaluate the effectiveness of a piano teacher or a horse-back riding instructor merely by the total number of lessons or students taught, or by the way that the students can play or ride?

It is simply not sufficient to merely count the number of lessons or instruction hours. That just indicates what was delivered or said, or how much was said. The real question here, as you would no doubt agree, is *"What was actually learned?"* Has this new knowledge led in any way to the acquisition of new skills and behaviors? Are the students processing the information in a way that leads to practical application, demonstrated skills, and desired behaviors? Has the student in fact mastered, internalized, and used the material?

How would you know? For too long police departments have neglected the assessment of training *impact*. Far too much emphasis has been placed upon the mere verification of process or effort, the documentation of training activities such as the number of courses taught, total number of training hours, and personnel trained, with little to no emphasis placed upon training impact. Satisfaction surveys are not sufficient. We need to look for the desired changes in behaviors, however subtle they might be. Beyond merely verifying that an effort has been made, we need to evaluate actual training impact.

The real question to ask any police department is, "Are your officers doing what they were trained to do, what is required of them?" Another way to state this is, "How does your training program contribute to mission accomplishment and the meeting of organizational goals?"

This is the only way to truly assess training. It is analogous to how we properly evaluate patrol operations. We do not merely measure and report the total number of calls responded to and response times (i.e., effort). We now want to know whether the police response made

DOI: 10.4324/9781003396437-9

any difference (impact). Are crime rates increasing or dropping in these response areas? Are the needs of community members being met? In other words, we need to see actual results.

Training For Results

Results can be seen, but only if one knows where (and how) to look. First, let's consider firearms training. The assessment process in this area is a rather straightforward matter. Simply document that an appropriate effort was made to instruct (i.e., appropriate trainer, appropriate lesson, equipment, etc.) then record the student's actual performance (shooting score). This approach is appropriate for a para-military organization like a modern police department to use when instructing civilians with no prior knowledge or skills regarding firearms to load, clean, and shoot a handgun. This is training at its best and is often expertly delivered. But there is more that needs to be considered here.

What is the real purpose of this training, to simply prepare employees for an upcoming shooting competition at a firearms range, or to prepare them for potentially deadly street encounters? The answer is obvious. This is why police firearms training has evolved over time into using more practical/tactical training methods such as tactical villages, low lighting exercises, and state-of-the-art immersive judgmental use of force training systems, like the VirTra 300.

De-escalation training is now perhaps the most important topic in police use of force training. Is it enough to simply show that all your officers have "undergone" the state-mandated training? What does this mean? Did they simply receive instruction in a classroom or online, and then complete some type of culminating performance assessment? How are they going to react in the field? Did the training "work" (in terms of producing any of the desired effects)? How long do the training effects last (if at all)? Do we have any means of knowing any of this?

It is no longer sufficient to merely show that all police officers have received the requisite training in de-escalation. Show me the data regarding that department's use of force reports, line of duty injuries, and civilian complaints. These are the issues that relate directly to actual performance in the field. Are firearms discharges down in this department and is Taser usage up? How many "near misses" have occurred? Are line of duty injuries up? Is anyone asking these questions? This is where behavioral changes of the students, if any, can be detected and evaluated. It is all in the data.

Many departments have this ability and do *use* such data to evaluate training impact. Many more simply do not and cannot. They have limited staffing and a very antiquated approach to police training.

Do you agree that it is important to know whether your department's training regarding community outreach/relations has been effective, that community members are actively engaged with the police, rather than simply attesting that an attempt has been made to deliver it? To establish proof of effectiveness, just look for effects (i.e., impact). Once again, show me the data, such as:

- the quantity and quality of community programs engaged in with the business community, homeowners' associations, advocacy groups, houses of worship, etc.;
- the number and membership of neighborhood watch groups;
- the number of attendees at sponsored events;
- the number of residential and commercial security surveys performed;
- the number of graduates from the department's Citizens' Police Academy program;

- social media efforts including the number of hits and followers on social media home pages; and
- commendations from the community, positive stories in the media, etc.

If one really knows where to look, you will find ample evidence of training impact (for better or worse) in any police organization. This is how a police department can move beyond the assessment of training *efforts* and begin the assessment of actual learning. Let's call this Assessment 2.0.

This however requires a "systems thinking" approach and perspective (Senge, 1990). Although developed decades ago, this is still a relatively new approach in our field that views police departments as complex systems, rather than a mere amalgamation of stand-alone functions. Simply stated, police departments are relatively complex systems and everything is related. For example, the implementation of body-worn cameras (BWCs) has been found to have a significant impact upon criminal investigations, prosecutions, police misconduct, etc. (Petersen, 2022). No single police function exists in a vacuum.

Training is most certainly not a stand-alone function. It needs to be understood and examined in the context of its relationship(s) with other essential functions (such as risk management, community relations, performance evaluations, etc.).

Now for the bad news, many police departments in the United States are simply unable to do any of this. They have absolutely no means of developing and delivering in-service training lessons or in-house continuing education programs for their police officers and supervisors because they have never been properly staffed for this function. Sure, they comply with state mandates regarding certification maintenance, but only by relying upon off-site or online courses, or "canned" lessons to their officers (obtained from other departments), often delivered by uninspired and minimally qualified training personnel. No one person within the department develops an integrated multi-year training plan (which includes distinct learning objectives for all units and personnel) and curriculum. No one person attends management meetings and views ongoing operations of the department through the lens of training. Rather, the supervisor who heads the "administrative services division" (which typically includes the training unit) represents training at these meetings, as well as all the other administrative and support functions under his/her command.

Training opportunities are thereby missed. They would not be missed if a qualified training sergeant (who is properly trained and supported) were actively involved in these management meetings. For example: A skilled training sergeant participating in a monthly management meeting learns about a recent motor vehicle accident with a department vehicle. The sergeant notes, *"That's the third one of those we've had since the beginning of the year, and it is not limited just to officers undergoing field training. I think all personnel could use a refresher on operating department vehicles on icy roads."* This provides the organization with a necessary sense and respond capability, with regard to safety, risk management and organizational learning.

More on organizational learning in a moment. Traditionally, police training in America has been delivered in a disjointed, rather haphazard manner. Stand-alone modules of instruction are often delivered randomly, based largely upon an officer's work schedule, with no thought whatsoever given to curriculum design, an over-arching departmental training plan, the officer's actual training needs, or the possible interactive effects among lessons. But lessons can no longer be delivered or understood as discrete topics. For example, when we send officers for "active shooter" training, we need to review and reinforce the lesson regarding taking proper cover, or when we teach officers how to perform felony car stops, we need to review and reinforce other lessons such as how to deal with emotionally disturbed persons, the law of search and seizure, or off-duty confrontations between police officers (in uniform and plainclothes). Lessons cannot be delivered randomly. Considerable thought must be given to the conceptual linkages between lessons and their specific learning objectives, as well as the order in which they are delivered. Everything is connected.

Lessons need to integrate and build upon the content and associated skills of prior lessons. This affords officers additional time to acquire, reflect upon, and demonstrate all necessary skills, as well as an extended period within which to access an officer's progress. Training must be interactive, scenario-based, dynamic and, above all, realistic. Officers undergoing training should actively participate in debriefs and critiques provided afterward.

Unfortunately, some departments do not offer any on-site instruction at all. The assigned "training officer" in many departments is nothing more than a training "coordinator" who ensures that all certifications are maintained, that the mandated minimum number of training hours are met, and that training certificates are properly deposited and maintained in the officers' official files. No real learning or advanced skill development takes place as officers in these departments receive no training other than those lessons required for mandatory re-certifications in such areas as firearms or emergency vehicle operation (EVOC) that are required by the state. They simply "check the box" when it comes to training. All that check signifies is that an attempt has been made.

External assessors simply look to see if there is: 1) a designated training officer (i.e., a training coordinator); 2) adequate training facilities; 3) certified instructors for each type of lesson; 4) a training "plan" (simply a calendar used for scheduling); 5) written lesson plans (that may or may not contain clear learning objectives and means of assessment); and 6) secured training records indicating that all personnel meet minimum state in-service standards. If a particular department meets these minimal criteria, they are thought to be "proficient" in terms of training capacity, despite the fact that no real learning is occurring and the officers themselves feel severely undertrained.

Even more troubling is the fact that many departments have grown accustomed to this situation and this approach to training delivery and are content to simply attempt delivery (i.e., try to teach a particular practice or concept), then they hold officers strictly, and personally, accountable for any poor performance or non-compliance. In other words, the department essentially takes the position, "*We trained you on this and our job is now done. Now it's your problem. If you fail to perform as directed, you will suffer the consequences.*" This is unfair and it is particularly troubling when it comes to use of force training and integrity management/ethics training.

This is obviously an unacceptable situation. It is not merely a missed learning opportunity. From a risk management standpoint, it is a tragedy and a lawsuit waiting to happen. Our officers, departments, and communities deserve better.

Even departments that have a sufficient training infrastructure and the capability to develop and deliver their own lessons (that is, primarily with their own personnel) simply deliver them without any real assessment of impact. We would suggest that many American police departments today suffer from an acute organizational learning disability that greatly compromises their ability to prepare and guide their personnel in such a way as to fulfill their organizational mission. Some outspoken critics suggest that police training methodologies "have stagnated over the last fifty years" (Sheehan, 2023, p. 75).

It all seems to stem from a fundamental misunderstanding of the human learning process. It seems obvious that many departments need a new approach, a complete paradigm shift. They no longer have the luxury of conducting business as usual. They need to abandon those mental models associated with traditional hierarchical and para-military police training delivery and move towards a more effective means to educate and evaluate their personnel for context, not merely content. In many respects, they need to learn from other institutions that effectively train and *educate* their personnel.

Training vs. Education

The training vs. education dichotomy has been discussed and debated among academics and professionals for many years. It is now time for police professionals and the wider community to realize that there is a subtle, but very real difference, between these two terms. *Training* is the approach traditionally used and relied upon by American police departments. Training is indeed the most effective means of transmitting basic information to large groups of individuals in an efficient manner. Once again, the best illustration of this would be firearms training delivered to new recruits. A one-directional flow of information with an assessment (or not) at the end.

However, police departments across this country have been fooling themselves into thinking that ethics, or the topic of police–community relations, are appropriate subjects for training. We have scratched our heads for decades wondering why some police officers who had received the mandatory instruction on ethics have nevertheless engaged in unethical and unlawful conduct. One reason the bulk of ethics training that has been delivered to police officers across the country has been ineffective, is because it was delivered as *training*, typically in a perfunctory manner, with a "thou shall not" tone that was intended simply to scare officers straight and to get the departments on the sheet in terms of saying that all officers are now deemed ethical, because they have attended the mandatory 90-minute training session and passed a multiple-choice test on the topic. In essence, the department has done its job and completely fulfilled all its obligations by transmitting this material. Any subsequent malfeasance or nonfeasance of duty is entirely the officer's fault and he/she will suffer the consequences.

Far too much emphasis was based upon the material and the efficiency of the delivery method, with little to no concern for the needs of the learner. We have also failed to appreciate how dynamic changes in the American policing landscape (e.g., the death of George Floyd and the De-Fund the Police movement) have impacted police training needs (Police Executive Research Forum, 2022).

Is this really the best that we can do for our officers and the communities they serve? Ethics, as you no doubt can see, is a topic for *education*. It requires a deep conceptual understanding. We need to engage a person's higher level thought processes, if we are ever to expect to make them agree to explore their core personal beliefs, to internalize their learning, and to conform their personal behaviors while serving the needs of their communities. We need to explore actual case studies, where police officers made the wrong choices, and to challenge ourselves to learn how such mistakes can be made or, more importantly, avoided. We can no longer deliver "stale" content with few links to actual practice through outdated delivery systems (Moll, 2016).

Education is based upon a bi-directional flow of communication and an opportunity for inquiry and exploration (see McDermott and Hulse, 2016).

Ethics is just one example. We can also add integrity, community policing, fair and impartial policing, procedural justice, and other key components of contemporary policing to the list of needed *educational programs*. As entirely new concepts, obligations and duties continue to evolve, such as the "duty to intervene" when observing the misconduct of fellow officers, sufficient time must be devoted to carefully crafting learning goals, case studies, interactive debriefs and assessments that have meaning.

It therefore seems fair to question our entire approach to continuing professional training for police professionals (Davenport & Prusak, 1998). Staleness of content and poor linkages to actual high-risk practices can no longer be tolerated (Moll, 2016).

It seems that we have tried to force too much material into the narrow framework of traditional police training mechanisms that were originally designed along tight command and control functions. Critics are now challenging "traditional pedagogical techniques and primary teaching methods [as being] inadequate for producing critical thinkers, necessary for community-oriented policing" (Dwyer and Laufersweiler-Dwyer, 2004, p. 18). Luckily, other approaches are available.

Pedagogical techniques are now yielding to a new approach to adult learning (called "andragogy"), particularly around in-service training. This model is based upon six basic principles:

1) Adults take interest and invest time and effort in topics they know have applicability for them.
2) Adults are responsible for their actions and deciding their own direction and they want to be treated accordingly, which is contradictory to being dependent [i.e., merely being told what to do].
3) Adults have experience bases instructors should tap, and they can contribute to problem solving and aiding peers.
4) Adults are ready to learn knowledge, and skills that will help them in the real world.
5) Adults center their learning on life issues and problems rather than on isolated subject matter.
6) Adults are motivated more effectively by internal factors, such as job satisfaction, self-esteem, and quality of life. (Dwyer and Laufersweiler-Dwyer, 2004, p. 19)

Police departments must ensure that these principles are fully considered when developing and delivering all in-service (and many recruit) lessons (Police Executive Research Forum, 2022). This has developed into an international movement (e.g., Thompson and Payne, 2019). What is now required, is to allow officers to participate more fully in the process. For example, utilizing this new conceptual framework, some departments have begun addressing the use of force by attempting to develop an officer's social interaction skills. Early research results suggest that this is an effective approach (Sherman et al., 2020).

As Dwyer and Laufersweiler-Dwer (2004) explain:

The adult learning model constitutes **active learning** for students by instructors aiding their education, rather than lecturing them. This model uses problem-based methods and scenarios with students working through issues, the same way they will in the real world – by their own means. Learners develop critical thinking skills and replace memorization with knowledge of resources where to find answers based on the latest data and how to implement what they discover. Subject matter experts provide feedback to students, who present required material after finding answers on their own.

(p. 22)

Here is a major point: assessment is about quality control and seeking an answer to the basic question "Are our efforts having any impact?" It is not limited to the act of merely documenting that an effort was made. Assessment is not something that is done at the conclusion of a process. It must be done throughout the entire process. It is like the art of sailing.

A sailor constantly assesses while steering a sailboat, considering wind direction and speed, currents, etc. The sailor knows the final desired destination but needs to make assessments (and adjustments) throughout the entire journey. This is called the process of sailing. It is a skill that not everyone possesses. It must be learned and mastered.

The type of assessment that we have been discussing in this text is a similar process. It is a continuous process, not a one-time culminating event like doing your taxes at the end of the year. The art of properly assessing training (or any other police operations for that matter) is similarly not a skill that everyone naturally possesses. It also must be learned and mastered.

Culminating assessments, such as a ten-question quiz at the conclusion of a lesson, are clearly insufficient. There are many ongoing assessment techniques available in academia that can easily be incorporated into recruit and in-service police training, such as periodic quizzes or "muddiest point" exercises, where the student is asked to identify the portion of the curriculum or lesson that is personally most difficult to grasp. Adjustments are made accordingly and "on the fly" (see, e.g., Enos, 2023). This is the most effective way to ensure that the material meets the training needs of the audience.

Police departments (more specifically police training officers) need to apply the "SARA" method, which they are no doubt quite familiar with, to the training function. This would entail:

1) *Scanning*:
   - identify a recurring operational problem (such as several department-involved auto crashes);
   - confirm that the problem exists;
   - gather data;
   - develop a broad goal (such as reduction in the number of crashes).
2) *Analysis*:
   - understand the events that precede or accompany the problem and conditions that give rise to the problem (icy weather);
   - determine frequency and how long this problem has been occurring (look back at data from winter months in prior years);
   - narrow the scope of the problem (no need to be concerned during summer months).
3) *Response*:
   - brainstorm intervention(s) (enhanced/supplemental driver training under icy conditions);
   - choose from among alternative solutions;
   - outline response plan (who, what, when, and where will training be delivered);
   - state specific goals for response plan (all uniformed members of the department trained within # months);
   - identify relevant data to be collected during response for evaluation purposes (daily observation reports of all officers undergoing training, prepared by instructors);
   - initiate training.
4) *Assessment*:
   - determine whether goals were met (have the number of weather-related crashes been reduced?);

- identify any new strategies to augment original plan (perhaps the training should be directed primarily towards officers with less than three years on the job);
- engage in ongoing assessment to ensure continued effectiveness.
  (https://copstrainingportal.org/project/problem-oriented-policing-the-sara-model/)

Once again, ongoing evaluation and adjustment is the key. Every police department must master the skill of "learning while doing" (Davenport, 2006).

Police departments must become less reliant on "canned" lessons and more aware of the actual training needs of their personnel. They must look for deficiencies, look for performance gaps, and implement necessary corrective actions.

The awareness, analysis, and understanding of one's own thinking and learning processes is known as *metacognition*. This is a process that rarely, if ever, occurs in many American police departments. The problem is, the dynamics and daily challenges of policing are now evolving at such a rapid rate, that this skill of reflecting on learning is now absolutely required. We would suggest that most police departments in the United States now need to take the time to "learn how to learn."

Organizational Learning

There is an old saying, "If you're not moving forward, you are moving backward." This is particularly true regarding organizational learning. Organizations either acquire and use timely and accurate information to enhance performance, or they stagnate and fall behind. This is particularly true of police organizations.

Garvin et al. (2008) describe three essential factors that are necessary for organizational learning:

1) A supportive learning environment
2) Concrete learning processes and practices; and
3) Leadership behavior that provides reinforcement.

Without an open mindset, the right data, and a genuine sense of creative tension among the workforce, police organizations run the risk of "falling asleep at the wheel" (in an operational sense) and being victimized by a stale operational plan in a turbulent work environment. Fortunately, there are steps that can be taken to avoid this fate.

Police departments differ greatly in their ability to manage knowledge and improve operations via multiple evaluative feedback loops. In other words, some continually learn and improve, while others do not. What's the difference? Is it merely strong leadership that provides some departments with an advantage, or is it perhaps something more?

We believe that subtle but essential modifications to the organizational architecture of any police department (in terms of its internal management, data, and training systems) can build capacity and develop an effective "sense and respond" capability that allows it to use information to full advantage. In other words, any police department can learn how to learn.

All police managers must recognize and fully understand the subtle, but nevertheless important, distinction between *adaptive* and *generative* learning.

Adaptive learning entails merely reacting or adapting to environmental changes. For example, a department's crime analyst might notice a pattern of disturbance calls that have occurred in a certain neighborhood. The department then initiates some directed patrols to those areas. If the problem reemerges later, a similar response will be made.

Generative learning is different. It entails "creativity and innovation, going beyond, just adapting to change to being ahead of, and anticipating change" (Luthans, 2011, p. 59). To do this, the organization must examine its assumptions and modify underlying norms, policies, and objectives as necessary (Li, 2016). Using the above example, perhaps the chief or a representative should meet and engage with residents and business owners in the area, to explore the root causes of these calls and determine what steps could be taken to reduce the likelihood of such incidents. Perhaps the chief should have scheduled these meetings before the disturbances ever occurred, maybe once the plans for commercial or residential development in that area were approved.

Luthans (2011) explains that generative learning entails mastering both the art and practice of "double-loop" learning. He explains the difference between "single-loop" and "double-loop" learning as follows:

Single-loop learning involves improving the organization's capacity to achieve known objectives. It is associated with routine and behavioral learning. Under single-loop, the organization is learning without significant change in its basic assumptions.

Double-loop learning reevaluates the nature of the organization's objectives and the values and beliefs surrounding them. This type of learning involves changing the organization's culture. Importantly, double-loop consists of the organization's learning how to learn. (p. 59)

Single-loop, or adaptive learning is "learning that fits prior experiences and existing values, which enables the learner to respond in an automatic way. Double-loop learning, or generative learning [citation omitted] is learning that does not fit the learner's prior experiences, and it requires learners to change their mental schema in a fundamental way" (Li, 2016, p. 2). Generative learning is particularly difficult to accomplish in hierarchical, para-military organizations such as police departments, which have rigid rank structures and operate on a presumption that "the highest-ranking person is the most intelligent" and invariably has all the answers. This is indeed foolhardy.

Simply stated, the boss, in any human organization, never wants to appear stupid or ill-informed, particularly to subordinates. However, as Chawla and Renesch (1995) note,

Learning involves risk: looking dumb, feeling frustrated, losing time, wasting money, appearing stupid, and so on. The universal risk reward ratio applies to learning: the higher the risk, the greater the reward, and vice versa. Without risk taking, any learning is probably of minimal value.

(p. 118)

Police managers must not only accept but embrace this risk, by admitting that they do not personally have all the answers. They must adopt an open mindset (Dweck, 2006), admit to not having all the answers, and engage all available resources within the organization to make the most informed decisions possible.

Police departments must therefore devote sufficient resources to build "double-loop" or generative learning capacity. In most departments this would entail: 1) a designated training officer (not simply a scheduler or "coordinator;" one who is properly trained, certified, and supported); 2) a crime and traffic analyst; and 3) regularly-scheduled management meetings that serve as a performance review and problem-solving forum. Smaller departments that do not have sufficient personnel must nevertheless find a way to effectively perform these functions, or risk having an inaccurate picture of their internal and external work environments.

Proper staffing and support of a designated training officer or unit is therefore essential to create an effective learning environment, for all personnel, and for the organization itself (Chawla and Renesch, 1995). Corrective actions also call for an alteration to organizational structure and the belief systems of those operating within it (Stewart, 2001).

What To Look for When Assessing Police Training Systems

The foregoing discussion provides a theoretical framework for a "macro" analysis of any given police department's training capabilities. The critical question for any assessor to ask is, "*Does this organization have the ability to effectively transmit necessary lessons and information to its personnel in order to guide and assess them in the accomplishment of the organization's mission?*" Or is training simply an ancillary function that is being performed in a vacuum, with no real linkages to or coordination with the department's strategic direction or any of its other internal operating, communication, or information systems?

As is often the case, big questions such as these can only be answered when several more specific questions have been answered (i.e., micro analysis). For this reason, we offer the following as a quick guide to identifying evidence, or as accrediting bodies say "proofs," of necessary training capabilities and characteristics of an effective police training program. We believe that this is what assessors should look for.

It is not an exhaustive list, but it is certainly helpful and instructive:

- All departments must have a designated training officer who is properly trained, certified, and supported.
- All departments must develop and follow a multi-year training plan with specific learning objectives for personnel assigned to all units (both sworn and nonsworn). A simple training calendar, which merely lists course offerings and scheduled dates, is not sufficient. Curriculum must be thoughtfully planned, delivered, integrated, and evaluated. This training plan should be incorporated into the department's overall multiyear strategic plan.
- The department should form a standing training committee to meet regularly to consider the training needs of the department and set the agenda and training goals for the entire department. The training committee should be representative of all operational units and should solicit ideas, identify operational problems and training opportunities, formulate specific training plans, and evaluate and periodically report on the success of training received by members of the department.
- Departments obviously must comply with all state-mandated, recruit, field training and in-service (continuing) training requirements. For example, failure to provide required annual training to personnel assigned as detectives or supervisors will unnecessarily subject the department and its personnel to liability and/or create a threat to public safety.
- All departments must have an adequate training budget relative to their size and scope of operations.
- All police departments must have access to appropriate training facilities, such as classrooms, firearms, and emergency vehicle (EVOC) driving ranges, a gym or multipurpose room for PT training, etc.
- Departments should utilize state-of-the-art equipment (of their own or belonging to another agency) for judgmental use of force training.

- Active shooter exercises should be regularly scheduled at various locations throughout the community. Ideally, these exercises should be conducted at schools or large businesses, preferably while the facilities are occupied. Emphasis should be placed upon interoperability, inter-agency coordination and cooperation among first responders.
- All personnel performing the investigative function should be required to attend and successfully complete a basic investigations course prior to beginning their assignment.
- All personnel appointed to the rank of sergeant must be required to attend and successfully complete a basic management course, with specific learning objectives and methods of assessment.
- Individuals who are promoted beyond the rank of sergeant should be required to attend and successfully complete additional management or executive development courses (such as those offered by LEEDA).
- All newly promoted sergeants should be required to undergo and successfully complete a supervisors' field training program. The program should be well-structured and include specific learning objectives and methods of assessment (such as daily observation reports [DORs]).
- Lesson plans must be developed and utilized for all lessons delivered "in-house" (i.e., within the department), including those delivered by instructors from outside of the department, such as local prosecutors or community advocates. Lesson plans must be numbered (preferably as page 1 of 5, 2 of 5, etc., for chain of custody purposes) and be securely and properly maintained.
- All individuals performing the functions of detective should attend and successfully complete a basic investigations course.
- Procedures for authorizing and attending offsite training must be clearly outlined. All training records must be properly secured and maintained.
- All departments should utilize and take full advantage of rollcall or "turnout" briefings at the commencement of patrol shifts by delivering, reinforcing, and documenting important training, updates, and refreshers. When conducted properly, this training can be quite interactive and can provide the department's leadership with information and timely feedback from line officers that it might not otherwise have access to.

Some Additional Thoughts

Civilians should be used to supplement police actors during scenario-based training exercises. Arguably, a diverse cohort of civilian actors are more likely to mimic the behaviors of the individuals that our officers are likely to encounter on the streets. Some police executives might argue that such partnerships unnecessarily disclose police tactics to the public. But a simple internet search will disclose that many police tactics are already in the public domain. Moreover, training staff will ultimately determine what lessons are appropriate for civilian participation. The key is to re-frame police training, to make it more *transparent* and *inclusive*.

Taking this notion one step further, we believe that all training academies throughout the United States and most of our larger police departments should have curriculum advisory committees, made up of civilian educators, clergy, and community leaders who can serve an advisory function when developing and delivering police training. This would do much to provide transparency, build trust, forge the bonds necessary for true community policing, and hopefully avoid many of the problems that we are now experiencing.

Several years ago, the Westchester County (NY) Police Academy developed a program whereby local criminal justice professors, with prior police experience in addition to having advanced/terminal degrees, were invited to serve as "visiting professors" to the County Academy, to review curriculum, and to teach recruits, as well as experienced officers and their supervisors via in-service training. Participants report that it was a learning experience for all involved and led to a new level of transparency that can only improve the overall quality of policing. Creative collaborations of this type should be replicated throughout the United States.

We should also examine the notions of: 1) developing the next generation of citizens' police academies (making them more substantive and inclusive); and 2) encouraging properly trained police officers currently serving as *school resource officers* to deliver classroom instruction via "street law" classes to the youth to prepare them for potential encounters with the police by explaining constitutional protections as well as expectations for personal conduct and safety.

We must make every effort to improve the overall quality of police training and *education* in the United States. There are indeed costs associated with this, but the costs of inaction are far greater. The most important and serious cost is the loss of legitimacy and an erosion of credibility and respect for the important government institution our police officers represent. From a risk management and community relations standpoint, it is the only logical way forward.

References

Chawla, S. & Renesch, J. (1995). *Learning Organizations: Developing Cultures for Tomorrow's Workplace*. Productivity Press.

Davenport, R. (2006). Future of the profession: For workplace learning and performance professionals, the pace picks up, and the stakes get raised. *Training and Development*, January, 41–43.

Davenport, T., & Prusak, L. (1998). *Working Knowledge: How Organizations Manage What They Know*. Harvard Business School Press.

Dweck, C. (2006). *Mindset: The New Psychology of Success*. Random House.

Dwyer, R. G., & Laufersweiler-Dwyer, D. (2004). A need for change: A call for action in community-oriented police training. *FBI Law Enforcement Bulletin*, 73(11), 18–24.

Enos, K. (2023). The use of academic assessments in police training. *IADLEST Standards and Training Director Magazine*, 35(3), 86–89.

Garvin, D. Edmondson, A., & Gino, F. (2008). Is yours a learning organization?. *Harvard Business Review*, 86(3). 109–116.

Li, C. (2016). From adaptive to generative learning in small and medium enterprises: A network perspective. *Journal of Global Entrepreneurship*, 6(1), 1–12.

Luthans, F. (2011). *Organizational Behavior: An Evidence-Based Approach*, 12 ed. McGraw-Hill.

McDermott, P., & Hulse, D. (2016). Learning the art of active listening and responding: An ethical imperative for police training. *Police Chief*, 1, 26–31.

Moll, M. (2016). How far have we come? The state of police ethics training in police academies in the United States. *Dissertation Abstracts International Section A: Humanities and Social Sciences*.

Petersen, K. (2022). Looking at the big picture: Using systems theory to understand the impact of body-worn cameras on police accountability. *Critical Criminology*, 30(4), 861–878.

Police Executive Research Forum. (November 2022). Transforming police recruit training: Forty guiding principles. *Critical Issues in Policing Series*. www.policeforum.org/assets/TransformingRecruitTraining.pdf

Senge, P. (1990). *The Fifth Discipline: The Art and Practice of the Learning Organization*. Doubleday/Currency.

Sheehan, G. (2023). Our officer training programs haven't evolved to meet today's Policing needs: How do we change that? *IADLEST Standards and Training Director Magazine*, June, 75–77.

Sherman, L., Wolfe, S., Rojek, J., McClean, K., & Alpert, J. (2020). Social interaction training to reduce police use of force. *Annals of the American Academy of Political and Social Sciences*, 687(1),124–145.

Stewart, T. (2001). *The Wealth of Knowledge: Intellectual Capital and the Twenty-First Century Organization*. Doubleday/Currency.

Thompson, J., & Payne, B. (2019). Towards professionalism and police legitimacy?: An examination of the education and training reforms of the police in the Republic of Ireland. *Education Sciences*, 9(241), 1–23.

Chapter 10

Community Engagement

Introduction

Protests, at times violent, following the May 25, 2020 murder of George Floyd by a Minneapolis police officer and several deaths of individuals resulting from encounters with police fueled a movement to change the way the police operate. There were calls to defund the police (headcount/operational budgets) and remove certain responsibilities from law enforcement officers (i.e., mental health calls, homeless individuals, enforcement of minor traffic violations, etc.) and assign these responsibilities to mental health and other professionals believed better prepared to resolve these matters. This movement also called for increased police transparency and accountability for their actions and a demand for a policing style more responsive to the community.

Police-community relations have suffered in many communities due to police use of excessive force and the gap/disconnect between police and the communities they serve has increased. Attempts to reduce police headcounts and operational budgets continue in some parts of the United States (despite an uptick in crime) and there are local legislative efforts to increase police transparency and accountability. Interest in policing as a profession and its related academic disciplines of study are waning. College enrollments in Criminal Justice and related majors has shown a drastic reduction in recent years, and recruitment and retention of law enforcement officers are increasingly difficult (PERF, 2023). There is also the trail of missed opportunities when sometimes programs start with vigor but lose momentum leaving behind unfinished projects and disillusion (Cheng, 2019).

The dynamic political and social environment and shifting public sentiment concerning police policies and practices present an excellent opportunity to explore the process by which the police deal with the communities they serve. A single chapter is insufficient to discuss the complex, interdisciplinary, and intersectional issues associated with police–community relations as they relate to police policies and practices in the communities they serve. Much more than a chapter is needed to provide a full discussion of these issues. There are numerous books and scholarly articles that explore police–community relations, customer satisfaction, customer engagement practices, etc. at a granular level. While that type of examination is better suited for the study of policing in a democratic society, this text is intended as an awareness guide for city/town managers and police leaders .

At their core, businesses and commercial enterprises exist to make money from the products or services that they provide. Those who use and consume those products or services create revenue and potential revenue for these businesses. How well a business meets its customers' needs and how it can grow its customer base is important to its success. As such,

DOI: 10.4324/9781003396437-10

the way in which businesses engage their customers and grow its customer base is a dominant theme and unifying thread interwoven throughout the entire business enterprise. The business of policing and public safety and the police organizations that deliver these services are not profit centers. They spend much more money than they generate. That said, police agencies must operate efficiently (financially) and effectively (quality of outcomes of services delivered). Like businesses and other commercial enterprises, the needs, and desires of consumers of public safety services must be an organizational priority. Policy making and operational decision-making must be informed by and tailored to meet the varied needs of the communities and consumers it serves. The initial question for the police agency is who are its consumers and what are their needs? The first question is simple: anyone present within the geographical jurisdiction of the police agency is a potential consumer of their services. However, not everyone within their geographical jurisdiction will consume their services. The second question, what do these consumers need from the police agency. Concerns among those who live, work, recreation, or visit within a department's jurisdiction can vary from person to person, block to block, neighborhood to neighborhood, and community to community. The metrics used internally by police leaders to assess organizational performance do not always align with the metrics used by consumers to determine how well or not that agency is meeting their needs.

Before delving into the discussion of police operational performance when it comes to community engagement, it is important to identify what we mean by the phrase "community engagement." What is the community? What does it mean to engage? We purposively choose the term engagement to describe the level of association among police departments and their respective communities. Government officials in the public safety space (City Managers, Police Chiefs etc.) undoubtedly recognize that there are degrees of association that various members of the community exhibit with their local police department. We also intentionally use the word "engage" to signal that police departments should have a more intense and more deliberate association with the community and not just be "involved." According to the Merriam-Websters Dictionary "involvement" denotes recurring participation and interest in certain things, whereas "engagement" denotes attraction and interlocking with another person. For example, when we ask another person to wed, and they agree, we call that an "engagement" which implies a more intense, more serious, and long-term relationship. Involvement implies participation with the community in certain processes and events and a more superficial form of relationship. Therefore, involvement implies "doing to" and engagement involves "doing with" and implies a shared and continuous responsibility for operational performance. We argue here that police departments must engage with their communities and develop a strategic approach to improve operational performance. In other words, we recommend that police departments take the view that they must be fully engaged with the communities they serve, develop the plans and programs, and commit the resources, to support this engagement. This is more than "being involved" in community relations or public relations campaigns; more than simply hosting "coffee with a cop" events or proclaiming your department does "Community Policing" by having Bicycle Patrols. We envision a more robust and comprehensive approach to providing police service that involves the spectrum of communities served by police departments.

So, what do we mean by the term "community"? For the purposes of this discussion, we envision communities to exist across two dimensions: internal and external communities. In addition, each dimension can be described by two categories: transactional communities and stakeholders. Figure 10.1 illustrates these dimensions.

COMMUNITY DIMENSIONS		COMMUNITY TYPE	
		TRANSACATIONAL	STAKEHOLDER
LOCUS	INTERNAL	Officers	Employee Groups, Units
	EXTERNAL	"Customers" 911 Callers	Community Groups

Figure 10.1 Community Dimensions.

External Communities

An external community is defined as people or groups outside the police organization. This is the common understanding of the definition of "community" when it comes to policing. It's the people, groups, organizations, etc. that deal with the police on a regular basis. However, discussions about the police and communities are often limited to communities that exist "outside" of the department, in other words, groups or people that are not police employees, groups, or police officers.

Internal Community

We are making the argument that consideration must be given to the needs of internal communities. These are the groups or people that work in police organizations that require the same attention and strategic approach to manage and engage.

Transactional Community

There are "transactional" members of both communities. Members of the external transactional community are people or groups that, from time to time, request police services. This could be 911 callers, victims, witnesses, visitors to the police facility, etc. They engage the police in a transactional way: request services and move on.

From an internal perspective, this community is the actual members of the police organization. Although this book has several chapters on understanding police operational performance from a management perspective, this approach is different. Police and governmental managers responsible for the operations of police departments must also view their employees in the context of them being a transactional community that needs identification and attention.

In the private sector, the external transactional community would be considered a customer. The private sector is very deliberate and thoughtful in determining who its customers are (and could/should be) and how best to meet the needs of current and potential consumers. The success of the business depends upon it. Companies go to great lengths and expense to identify their customer base and potential customers (to grow that customer base). Competition among providers of similar products or services can be intense as they pursue the same consumer pool. The US constitution and Declaration of Independence make clear the responsibility for the health, safety, and welfare of a nation's people rests solidly with the government. The "take care" clause and similar language found in the federal and many state constitutions task the Executive branch of government to enforce laws, etc., to accomplish among other things public safety. Municipal/local, county/equivalent, and state entities are the government providers of public safety services. They are the emergency first responders to incidents within their geographical areas. Most often, federal agencies are secondary responders.

Unlike the private sector, public sector agencies face limited competition from peer public sector agencies. The government (i.e., municipal, county, state or federal) in a sense maintains a near monopoly on providing public safety services. The private sector does not and cannot offer the equivalent services in terms of quality and quantity (i.e., cannot leverage the coercive powers of the state in a similar manner as a government itself etc.) to be considered a meaningful alternative to the public sector provider.

Police departments should consider every member of the transactional community it serves as a potential consumerstomer. While every person within the jurisdiction of a police agency is a consumer, not all consumers use public safety services and of those that do, not all consume them equally.

It is a simple process for police agencies to determine who is using their services. Computer-Aided-Dispatch (CAD) data, Incident Reports, Vehicle Crash Reports, Juvenile Reports, Arrest Reports, and other data collected during the normal course of business help identify the department's actual consumers. How they are treated is very important and police departments should consider the police–community transaction as an opportunity to improve their performance. In other words, while they may be transactional in nature, short-term and incident driven, there is a potential to influence their attitudes and opinions about the police and engaging them from this perspective is an important strategic approach that needs to be embraced.

The private sector has also recognized the need to engage their employees and ensure they are satisfied in their roles. There is a recognition that even though customers are the ones generating business, they wouldn't do it as readily if it weren't for the employees. Companies that put their employees' welfare first, and their customers second enjoy enormous success (Burkus, 2016; Platner, 2020). In any service industry, investing in the employee is an avenue to provide excellent customer service. Policing is a service industry, and employees represent the largest investment most police departments make, yet little attention is paid to their well-being. The *President's Task Force on 21st Century Policing* recognized this and challenged police departments across the country to examine and improve officer well-being. We submit here, that as an internal transactional community, police department employee well-being should be subject to a strategic management approach to improve operations similar to the other dimensions of community engagement.

Stakeholders

"Stakeholders" are people or groups in the community that could potentially have a sustained and long-term relationship with the department. Community groups, block associations, elected officials, civic, religious, or business organizations, local schools, etc. would be considered stakeholders. These groups are organized for a specific purpose, generally have a leadership and organizational structure, meet regularly, and depending on their mission, require services from the police. Some groups exert greater influence than others: the Mayor or the City Council obviously is a more prominent stakeholder than a local block association, but all stakeholders require deliberate attention to foster long-term relationships. All stakeholders matter.

There are several ways to organize those who have used, are currently using, may use, or have a vested interest in the services offered by public safety service providers. Public safety consumers/stakeholders can occupy one or more categories. When useful, public safety consumers can be categorized geographically, by demographics, affiliation, interests, goals, etc. Each category contains numerous subcategories, and their interests range from the simple to the complex and at times compete with one another. However, knowing your customers does not necessarily inform you of their varying needs. All consumers and stakeholders are important to the agency. Their strengths, weaknesses and interests vary, and departments must take this into account when developing messaging strategies and engagement decisions/practices. For example, elected officials are representatives of the geographical area from which they were elected. Elected officials have a platform that comes with their office, can exercise great influence among their votes/supporters and may even exercise direct oversight over agencies, their personnel, or their budget. Elected officials can be very helpful in acting as a conduit to obtain from and disseminate information to constituents, particularly in times of a police-involved incident, crisis, or unrest. Engaging elected officials must be regular, purposeful, and strategic. This includes regular updates on public safety or other agency matters. The mode of communication will often depend on the information being conveyed. Routine, non-controversial matters could be the subject of an email blast. As the volatility, significance, or importance of the matter increases, a more personal mode of communication must be considered (i.e., an email or text message may not be read immediately, etc.). Elected officials should be apprised of or briefed about important matters before the information is disclosed to the public at large or media. You want to avoid having an elected official being contacted on an important or emerging public safety matter by a constituent or media outlet without that elected official having been apprised of or briefed by your agency on the matter. When elected officials are knowledgeable on matters, they are better positioned to speak with authority about a matter based on facts and not rumor or speculation. Moreover, elected officials can address immediately and dispel false or misinformation and become a trusted source of information that is influential in the community. It goes without saying that the agency's response to elected officials' inquiries must be timely, and comprehensive. Good practice requires police leaders to tell elected officials what they know (within the bounds of the law and that which will not unnecessarily impede an ongoing criminal investigation), what they don't know and what their next steps will be.

While there is little need for police agencies to undertake efforts like the private sector to identify its consumers/stakeholders, it must however invest resources to ascertain the current and future needs of its consumers. Data from the local planning office, Census Bureau, schools, etc. can be helpful in terms of projecting population growth, demographic shifts, economic development, socioeconomic shifts, etc. These indicators can inform decision making in terms of positioning your department today for the emerging needs of tomorrow. A simple way to determine the current and future needs of your customers is to ask your customers. Surveys are informative in terms of customer satisfaction, perceptions, needs, and how to align the services offered with customer needs.

Organizational Identity

How a department sees itself (organizational identity) and embraces that identity shapes how it engages its customers, which services it offers, and how they are delivered. Police agencies have a dominant organizational identity. This identity changes over time, through evolution or in response to a crisis or event.

Warrior v. Guardian. "Warrior" or "Guardian" mindsets are displayed in some law enforcement agencies (Rahr and Rice, 2015). The warrior mindset or mentality is believed to be an outgrowth of officer safety concerns. At times, the police officer's work environment is violent and unpredictable. This violence is more often perpetrated on members of the community by other members of the community but on occasion, that violence is perpetrated on police officers by members of the community.

Police officers must be prepared to face each situation they may encounter during their shifts, and this is often accomplished through training, tactics, policies, and practices. However, an outsized focus on the dangers and unpredictability of policing and the need to take precautions can lead to an officer survival mentality. The on-boarding process, police academy training, field training, and agency policies and practices, socialize new employees to the organization and its culture. If a theme of violence, danger, and unpredictability is woven into the fabric of the organization, its customer engagement practices will reflect it.

A warrior mindset has an excessive concern for officer safety, which is not supported by statistics (BLS, 2023). This hypersensitivity to danger, violence, and unpredictability in their work environment is reflected in their appearance, equipment/tools, and the tactics used by patrol officers in routine police–community encounters. In these departments, it is not unusual to see patrol officers wearing battle-dress-uniforms (BDUs), tactical body armor worn on the exterior of the uniform shirt, and patrol vehicles equipped with patrol rifles. These officers may not be part of the department/regional Special Weapons and Tactics Team (SWAT), Special Response Team (SRT), or the equivalent name for the cadre of specially trained officers who are called upon in high risk/dangerous situations.

The visual militarized appearance of police officers on routine patrol can be intimidating, unsettling, off-putting, or alienate segments of the department's communities. The Guardian mindset differs appreciably from the Warrior mindset. While not projecting a Warrior appearance, guardian departments are fully capable and prepared "for the fight" when that becomes necessary. The guardian approach lies in cooperation, collaboration, communication, and viewing consumers as essential partners in the production and delivery of public safety services. The tools of the Guardian include de-escalation, employment of procedural justice, community building, etc. (Rahr and Rice, 2015). What is interesting about organizational identity is that it is difficult to reflect externally that which is not practiced internally. Notwithstanding an agency's slogan, motto, mantra, etc., it cannot cloak its true identity for an extended period.

There are scores of videos on YouTube[1] depicting the first day of the police academy training experience for recruits. Some videos depict police instructors behaving like military drill instructors. There is lots of yelling proximate to the faces of the recruits, and direction to perform pushups, jumping jacks or other calisthenics for recruits who did not know or could not recite specific trivial information. For academies that continue that model throughout the training cycle, what they unwittingly teach their recruits is how to exercise their power and authority over someone. In most police–community encounters, there is an asymmetrical relationship where the officer occupies a higher position over the community member. This is often the case due to the inherent powers of the state that the police officer brings to every police–community encounter. Given the model used by some police academies for recruit training school, there is little wonder why some recruits, upon graduation from the police academy, exercise their power and authority over community members consistent with the model practiced during their entry-level training. The values or principles of the department which state that members of the public will be treated with dignity and respect, are inapposite with this training model. If the department fails to treat its members with dignity and respect, why should one expect members of that department to treat the customers they serve with dignity and respect?

We are the Police – Not report Takers. This is a NYPD operating principle. For over 30 years, performance-based management models (notably COMPSTAT or a variation thereof) used across US law enforcement agencies focus on how well the agency is at reducing reported crime. Operational commanders are expected to have intimate knowledge of the crime in their communities, and the factors driving those crimes. This myoptic focus on crime reduction, particularly violent crime reduction, played a large role in how commanders were viewed by the senior command staff. Promotions or more desirable assignments are usually linked to some degree to the commander's success in reducing reported crime. While communities benefitted from the success of this singular focus on crime reduction, some people within these communities suffered due to how these reductions in reported crime were achieved (PERF, 2013)

It is said that today's solutions create tomorrow's problems. Arguably, some of the crime reduction practices of public safety agencies (i.e., overuse of Terry stops, etc.) worsened and to a degree alienated some segments of communities it served. These public safety practices resulted in calls of over-policing with community members citing the number of officers assigned to specific communities and the hyper proactive focus of quality-of-life and other enforcement activities (Floyd et al v. City of New York, 2013).

Some police departments, in pursuit of their crime reduction goals, lost sight of the fact that how you reduce reported crime or disorder matters. The singular focus on crime reduction by some public safety providers did not always align with the overall interests of the communities served. Given the mandate and near monopoly the government retains as the primary provider of public safety services, communities have few options over the provider of these services. Whether services are provided at the municipal, county, town or state level, a government entity will always be the primary public safety service provider.

The peaceful enjoyment of one's home and community should be non-negotiable. While the quality of life in one's community is clearly impacted by violence and other crime, it is also affected by minor offenses or public disorder. Police services providers must be mindful and responsive to the needs of the various communities it serves. For example, calls for service for quality-of-life offenses (i.e., noise, animal nuisance, parking, disorderly persons, etc.) receive a lower response priority than calls for violent crimes or crimes in progress. Moreover, department staffing levels may exacerbate response time to low priority calls (PERF, 2023). Reporters of quality-of-life offenses are sufficiently annoyed that they call the police. However, the length of time it may take for the authorities to arrive to address quality-of-life conditions may suggest that the caller's concerns is not important or that they do not matter much to the authorities. In any event, the consumer of these public safety services is left dissatisfied and without meaningful alternatives. Public safety organizations should take note of the private sector's efforts to provide or enhance the "customer experience" as it relates to the consumption of its services.

Strategic Alignment

The initial question for the agency is what is the primary purpose, goal, or desired outcome for engaging communities they serve? In short, what does the organization seek to achieve through this process? This question is important as it will determine whether community engagement is essential to obtaining agency goals. If it isn't, then the need for community engagement becomes less compelling. If community engagement is deemed essential to achieving agency goals, then those goals will influence greatly the community engagement strategy that is developed to obtain the stated goals. If the main purpose of community engagement is crime reduction, then a community engagement strategy may include the adoption of a collaborative approach to public safety such as community/neighborhood-oriented policing. The core components of these forms of policing are community partnership and problem solving. These two components are used in combination to a greater or lesser degree, specific to the needs of the individual community in the strategies developed to address crime and the perception of crime or disorder. The Department of Justice's (DOJ) Office of Community Oriented Policing Services (COPS Office) provides technical assistance and some financial support for departments in developing or expanding their collaborative policing initiatives or programs. This partnering and problem-solving approach to policing can improve communication, cooperation, community organization, and help police solve more crimes. A cohesive organized community can also help deter criminality. The research, however, is mixed on the effectiveness of community policing and/or neighborhood policing regarding crime reduction (Beck et al., 2022).

It is possible that the specific community policing or neighborhood policing model employed by the agency may not serve or poorly serves the specific needs, interests, or challenges faced by the community. It is equally possible that the metrics used to measure the success of the program should be revised. Police departments typically amass large amounts of quantitative data. They look at outputs (i.e., UCR data, arrets, summons, community contacts, etc.) to help draw conclusions about the effectiveness of initiatives. Measuring the outcomes of those efforts is equally important. If increased enforcement (produces greater outputs) has not abated or eliminated the issue (outcome), then how can those efforts be viewed as a success? It is possible that less enforcement and greater referrals/treatment may have a greater impact on the issue of community concern. In short, there should be a qualitative component to the assessment metric. If the primary purpose of community engagement is to improve overall communication and build stronger relationships among the police and the communities it serves, then that goal should drive the selection of the engagement model or strategy employed.

Having regular and substantive dialogue during day-to-day public safety operations can have ancillary benefits. The first time a police commander communicates with a community leader should not be during a crisis. It is during an evolving crisis event when the personal relationship between the police official and the stakeholder can facilitate the resolution of the incident. Police officials and community leaders can leverage a relationship built on trust, mutual respect, and transparency to share and disseminate timely and accurate information to the public regarding an ongoing event. The police official and their community partners can serve as the source of information and the repository of information collected among the parties. In any event, the information, good or bad, is shared among and disclosed by trusted and respected officials. Trust and respect of the individuals addressing the crisis and transparency of the process used to resolve it can increase confidence and acceptance in the outcome of the incident. The success of community engagement strategies employed depends on its stated goals for the engagement and the methods used to measure how well or not the agency achieved those goals. What is consumer engagement? "In the broadest sense, engagement is a form of participation, a way of involving (or sometimes, re-involving) citizens in the processes of governance" (Stewart, 2018, p. 3). "In communities around the country, law enforcement agencies are recognizing that an agency that is highly attuned to the needs of a community can serve it better than one that sees the community as the 'other,' or even as the entity 'served'" (U.S. DOJ Office of Community Oriented Policing Services, 2021 p. 9).

Community engagement can be thought of as a partnership with the community in which community members are active collaborators and co-producers of public safety (U.S. DOJ Office of Community Oriented Policing Services, 2021). Community engagement includes substantive communication among the police department and the communities it serves to identify common issues of concern, the priority in which to address these common interests, and the preferred strategy or approach the police and community should take to resolve them.

Community engagement models are varied. Stewart (2018) offers a useful continuum model to conceptualize engagement with the substantiveness of the engagement increasing as you move across the continuum. This is a good explanatory model to discuss various forms of engagement. However, Stewart cautions that it is nearly impossible to analyze engagement in this clear-cut fashion. The several points along the continuum may shift or blend elements of two or more points over the course of the engagement process. This model starts with the least substantive and interactive form of engagement, information consultation. Through consultation, a proposed policy change is provided to community members/stakeholders and feedback on said policy change is sought. This is characterized by one way communication and the feedback sought is community/stakeholder reaction to a policy that was developed without their input or prior consultation.

The next point is deliberation. Through deliberation, the agency attempts to learn from the community/stakeholders through structured conversations. Deliberation seeks to identify community/stakeholder preferences as it relates to the creation/modification of policies and practices. Next point is partnerships. Through partnerships, the agency contracts with non-government organizations to perform functions such as service delivery or the co-production of policy resources. It is not unusual for law enforcement agencies to contract for counseling services for trauma survivors or interpretation services for languages not spoken by members of their department with organizations that are better suited to perform those functions. The next point is participatory governance. Through participatory governance, community members/stakeholders are directly involved in policy making. The last point on the continuum is delegation. Through delegation, non-governmental entities are given full authority to make key decisions. This is a useful model to conceptualize engagement.

Regardless of what model is used and to what degree police agencies collaborate with the communities they serve, regular, timely, and substantive communication, based upon available facts, among police and community members is foundational. Pal et al. (2023) assert that strong communication helps develop trust, legitimacy, and transparency among law enforcement agencies and the communities they serve. Good communication helps connect law enforcement with the communities and stakeholders they serve. Regular, timely, honest, and plain communication helps to demonstrate an agency's commitment to transparency with communities/stakeholders.

The days when law enforcement agencies controlled the information about incidents and parsed it out on their terms and at their convenience are long gone. Even then, when law enforcement agencies did not "feed the beast" and provide news organizations with sufficient information to report on an incident, the news organization would often confer with some talking head (former law enforcement official or informal expert) who would, without more information about the incident than was publicly available, speculate on what was happening and offer opinions based on conjecture. Even then, police agencies may have controlled the information but did not control the narrative. Today, nearly every smartphone has photo and video recording capabilities. Everyone with a smartphone is potentially an "incident reporter." Some community members record events as they are unfolding. Traditional news organizations are no longer the primary source of information. Social media platforms provide average people the ability to go "live from the scene" or post videos along with their commentary in near real time of the evolving incident. In the moment, no one or entity fact checks or challenge the accuracy of the information provided by the on-scene community reporter. This reporting does not undergo rigorous vetting of information and sources common in responsible journalism prior to its release. As such, the events and commentary describing events may be biased, inaccurate or completely wrong. The ability of nearly anyone to access social media platforms and disseminate information broadly challenges responsible news organizations' efforts for exclusive reporting or first to report "breaking news." On occasion, traditional news organizations opted for speed to get information out over the accuracy or completeness of information being released. Once information is released by other than the law enforcement agency, the police no longer control the narrative and oftentimes finds itself wasting time and resources (while managing the crisis at hand) attempting to correct inaccuracies contained in initial reports. This highlights the need for a law enforcement agency and/or the municipality to have a communications strategy to disseminate information quickly and accurately. The preference is to be the source for the information and thus lessen the likelihood of having to react to rumor and false information released by others purporting to be facts. Law enforcement organizations must work toward becoming or remaining a trusted source for information. Thus, law enforcement agencies must communicate all information legally permissible, as quickly as practicable (Pal et al., 2023).

"Bad news isn't wine. It doesn't improve with time"[2] and this is surely the case when it comes to critical police incidents and police-involved shootings. Police departments should be mindful to release what they can as soon as they can and open up a channel of communication with community stakeholders so they can be kept updated on information as it becomes available.

Communication

If open and honest communication are essential for productive collaborative police–community partnerships, then withholding or hiding information just doesn't make sense. Solutions are possible when the stakeholders fully understand the issues and reach consensus on identifying the problem. Intentionally or negligently suppressing, withholding, or simply failing to disclose information is a losing community engagement strategy. It erodes trust and confidence as a partner. Moreover, the information sought to be withheld eventually becomes public. Criminal justice practitioners have seen time and again that the cover-up of an incident or suppression of information can be as bad or worse (politically and criminally) than the incident itself. When the information becomes public, and it will, in addition to the issues presented by the information itself, the agency will have to address why the information was not released or worse, was suppressed. For example, the Chicago Police Department's dashboard camera video that captured the October 20, 2014, shooting of Laquan McDonald was not released to the public for 13 months and then only after a judge ordered its release (Lah, 2015). The rationale offered for not releasing the video was based on a concern that its release might hamper the FBI and US Attorney's investigation into the shooting. However, many have speculated that the video may have resulted in the mayor losing an already close April 2015 re-election bid and thus was not released voluntarily. Whatever the reason for the delay in releasing the video, the delay itself became a major issue and remained an issue for the mayor during his second term.

Development of inter- and intra-communication methods should be a collaborative effort between the political subdivision of government that appoints/supervises the agency head, or if elected, the agency head in consultation with their communications team (i.e., public information officer, etc.). A single medium for all internal and external communication is ill-advised and ineffective. Effective and persuasive communicators know not only their audiences but also how those audiences prefer to be engaged and consume their information.

The President's Task Force Report on 21st Century Policing (Office of Community Oriented Policing Services, 2015) recommendations were centered around six topic areas or pillars. Two of the six (33%) focused on the relationships or engagement among police and the communities they serve. Pillar #1, Build Trust and Legitimacy, and Pillar #4, Community Policing and Crime Reduction, focus on how police and communities interact with one another. The task force recommended community engagement, and for that matter internal engagement within police agencies, be based upon the four principles of procedural justice: treating people with dignity and respect, giving individuals "voice" during encounters, being neutral and transparent in decision making and conveying trustworthy motives (Office of Community Oriented Policing Services, 2015). The task force report provided recommendations along with action items for each of the six pillars to assist law enforcement agencies in developing their professional practice in these areas.

Each police–community interaction should be viewed as an opportunity to establish, reinforce, or improve relationships among police and the various communities that are serve. Engagement opportunities should be sought out and leveraged fully at all points of contact (virtual and in-person) in which members of the police organization, both sworn and unsworn, interact with the public or consumers of public safety services. The conventional thinking is to leverage community engagement opportunities during informal encounters where officers aren't expected to apply their authority in a manner with adverse consequences for the community member. While that makes sense, community engagement opportunities must also be sought on occasions where the interests of the police and the communities are not aligned. Not all enforcement situations end with an individual being arrested, receiving a summons or some other "negative" outcome. So, these situations are ripe community engagement opportunities. Even situations where a negative outcome is unavoidable presents opportunities for community engagement. The way the officer handles the situation and how he treats the parties go a long way in shaping the perceptions of the individuals directly involved and witnessing the situation. Leveraging these community engagement opportunities requires training and practice. Police officers must receive training, direction, coaching, and be empowered to seek out community engagement opportunities when exercising their broad discretionary powers. Understanding the needs, goals, and practices of stakeholder groups as they relate to public safety issues is helpful in learning how to communicate with these groups. Relationships based on mutual trust and transparency can help create stakeholders who can deliver the agency's message within the stakeholder group more effectively than the agency itself.

Community Engagement Strategies

People committed to police community engagement strategies need to consider this topic from an internal/external and transactional/stakeholder perspectives. The following is a brief discussion on various tactics that can be used to improve operational performance in this area. The various approaches mentioned here need to be used in context with the department's organizational identity, strategic goals, and communications approach discussed above. The tactics provided below are not "quick fixes" or "one-shot deal" but should be viewed as potential elements to a comprehensive community engagement strategy for the entire department.

Internal-Transactional

As discussed above, employee well-being is essential for effective performance and should be viewed as one of the main elements of a department's community engagement strategy. If you were to ask the ordinary officer assigned to patrol in most police departments in the U.S. "how is morale?", you will get the response: "Morale has never been worse that it is today." Ironically, even within the current "national police crisis" related to a widespread perceived lack of trust and support for the police, the issue of police morale is always thought to be low. The issue of low morale within police departments is a timeless tradition that is a function of the nature of the work, the subculture of the profession, and the style of management employed by police departments. However, officers on patrol are the department's single greatest resource. Personnel expenses are likely to be in excess of 85% of any police budget, and with more than 60% of the entire sworn complement of officers assigned to patrol, this results in approximately 50% of an entire police department's budget dedicated to officers on patrol. Considering the investment communities make in patrol operations, it is incumbent upon police and town managers to ensure that these officers are performing well, properly trained and supervised, properly equipped, and physically, mentally, and emotionally fit. Unfortunately, this is not always the case, and officers undoubtedly report the perception of being the forgotten group in the department. The patronizing expression "backbone of policing," which is meant to describe the importance of patrol operations, pays lip-service to the reality of patrol. It is a difficult job, performed at all hours of the day and night, on weekends and holidays, with dangerous and sometimes fatal outcomes. Regular assessment of the individuals assigned to this important function is paramount.

According to the National Law Enforcement Officers Memorial Fund, line-of-duty deaths were down 64% in 2022, from 623 in 2021 to 224 in 2022. Sixty-three of these 224 line-of-duty deaths were firearms-related, 46 were traffic-related, and strikingly, in 2022, there were also 228 suicides among law enforcement officers, which was 33% increase from 2018 when there were 172 suicides. Seventy-eight percent more officers died by suicide than they did during all other line-of-duty incidents. It appears that officers are about five times more likely to die from their own firearms than from a firearm related incident from another person. To understand and address this alarming trend, PERF published a Critical Issues in Policing Series "An Occupational Risk: What Every Police Department Should Do to Prevent Suicide among Its Officers" in October of 2019. The causes and solutions to this epidemic are well beyond the scope of this section. However, while suicide and line-of-duty death are the ultimate price paid by police officers, departments can take meaningful and concrete measures to improve the overall mental health of officers, particularly officers assigned to patrol. These measures will not only improve officer well-being but will likely improve the quality of service they will provide the community (PERF, 2019).

Workplace stress is causing harm to officers and communities. Stress is crippling the law enforcement profession. The psychological stress that comes with police work puts officers at significantly higher risk for long-term physical and mental health than the general population. Officers are four times more likely to suffer sleep deprivation, have the poorest cardiovascular health than any occupation, with 40% obesity rates, and nearly double the rate of depression compared to the general population. In fact, police officers live 10 years less than the average person does in the U.S. Stress is literally killing the law enforcement profession. In addition, nowhere is this more acute than for officers on patrol.

For officers this stress can come in many forms, from traumatic events experienced over a career to the "toxic" work environment that officers experience every day. In his seminal study of the police in the U.S., Wilson (1968) referred to the "dirty work" done by cops every day. They experience daily micro-traumas of victimization, injury, accidents, mental illness. This "dirty work" shapes the subculture of the profession and contributes to a hardened demeanor and a cynical outlook on the world. If not managed properly, these micro-traumas can lead to negative personal outcomes in the form of mental and physical illness, as well as the negative work-related outcomes in the form of inappropriate use of force, civilian complaints, discourtesy, and shoddy service.

Police departments are not going to be able to change the nature of police work. Police officers will always be called to emergency situations and must deal with trauma daily. However, the way a department manages the stress associated with this trauma can mitigate it and promote a healthy lifestyle. The adaptive strategies that a department engages in can make a difference. From a patrol perspective, those strategies should focus on communication, work–life balance, and assessment.

Communication – It might seem obvious that an open line of communication between the command staff and officers on patrol is essential. However, organizational communications with patrol are often dysfunctional. Most departments thrive on the "rumor mill" and officers working nights and weekends without direct contact with the administration rely on these types of informal communications systems to stay informed. Being "out of the loop" can be stressful and exacerbate an already stressful job. Not knowing about policy or personnel changes, or disciplinary decisions, or training opportunities, is a source of great frustration for officers on patrol. Not only do officers on patrol get excluded from the decision-making process, but a perception of unfairness creeps into these processes. Untethered from the conventional day-to-day management processes also aggravates the sense of social isolation experienced by officers on patrol. More, and accurate, information needs to be communicated and police managers should consider several mechanisms to facilitate this process.

Social Media – departments must leverage social media to keep officers informed and involved in department affairs. Anyone with a smartphone and an internet connection can check on their local happenings. We can access real-time information about world events from the palms of our hands. We have never had the ability to be so connected with the free flow of information. If the digital age can keep us informed and up-to-date with world events, departments should use this technology to keep officers informed about department events. Moreover, officers should not be viewed as mere passive recipients of information from the department, but active participants that should be engaged in policy development and a myriad of other issues that face police departments. Global emails to all officers are not an effective way of communicating with personnel. There are numerous ways that two-way flow of information can be facilitated, and departments need to explore these media to promote organizational effectiveness and officer well-being.

Group meetings and interpersonal contact – When patrol officers think about the command staff in police departments several disparaging concepts come to mind:

"The 2nd Floor Boys" (ranking officers sequestered in their offices on the second floor of headquarters)

"Carpet Land" (executive offices are carpeted while all others are not)

"Cowboy Typist" (cop that dresses the part but sits at a desk all day)

"Stealth Chief" (the boss that is never seen on patrol)

These expressions illustrate the perception that police management is disconnected from the actual work done by patrol. Patrol operations cannot be led or managed from an office during business hours. Communications with officers need to be as personal as possible. In large organizations, this presents challenges. It would be impossible for the Police Commissioner in the NYPD, for example, to foster interpersonal communications with 50,000 employees, or the approximately 20,000 officers on patrol. This challenge is less in a department of 25 employees, but nonetheless, a system of personal communication needs to be established to personalize the message and the messenger. Police managers, especially those responsible for patrol operations, need to manage and lead from the street and not the office. Officers need to be communicated with in person to the greatest extent possible, and forums need to be established where interpersonal communications can be established. Monthly shift meetings, periodic focus groups, department-wide "town hall" meetings should all be considered to improve communications. Employees should be encouraged to participate, minutes should be taken, and decisions should be clearly articulated and communicated to the officers.

24x7 executive patrol coverage – Ask the average officer "how often do you see the chief?" and the likely answer will be "Never." The Chief and the command staff need to be visible on patrol. Do the chief and command staff wear a uniform? Do they work nights, weekends, and holidays? The answer to all these questions should be a resounding YES. Some mechanism, no matter how big or small the department, should be created to ensure a regular and frequent presence of the chief and command staff in patrol operations. Their presence is critical to ensure that patrol operations are carried out efficiently and effectively, as well as creating an open and direct line of communications between the rank-and-file patrol officers and the command staff.

Promote Work–Life Balance – Police departments should take an active interest in promoting a healthy work–life balance. This is meant to include all aspects of health: physical, mental, emotional. The nature and quality of the type of program implemented is as important as including officers in its design. Officers should be encouraged to develop programs that promote nutritional health and recuperative sleep. Does the department's shift schedule include ample time off, and ample time between shifts? Are officers required to work excessive overtime, or secondary employment jobs? Do these interfere with their ability to eat right and get enough sleep?

Does the department promote physical health for the officers on patrol? Is there time allocated before, during, or after work to engage in physical fitness. Many departments prohibit officers from working out during their shift. Perhaps this is for good reason, but is there a way to accommodate fitness during the shift to promote health? In addition, what about emotional fitness? Are officers encouraged to foster a stable network of friends and family that can support them as a buffer to stress? Social connectedness has been shown to be a greater predictor of longevity than any other single lifestyle factor. What does your department do to promote officer sociability? Social connectedness can also promote positive police–community relations. Developing programs that allow officers to volunteer or otherwise connect with the community they serve can promote officer mental health and community relationships. When the community sees the police in a positive light this adds to their legitimacy and will foster relationships that are more positive. Every police department needs to develop and implement a health and wellness plan for officers on patrol (and all police officers regardless of assignment). This plan should be created with the active participation of patrol officers and medical and psychological professionals and updated regularly to support the officer's well-being.

Assessing Officer Well-Being – It's one thing to promote officer well-being, it's another thing altogether to measure and track that well-being. The overall effectiveness of an employee wellness plan is a function of the department's ability to assess the outcome of that plan. Quantitative and qualitative measures need to be identified by the department to track employee well-being. It is incumbent upon police managers to make this a central part of their mission. To accomplish this goal a combination of direct and indirect measures should be considered.

Indirect Measures – These types of measures are typically included in a department's Early Intervention System (EIS). An EIS is a personnel management tool designed to identify and mitigate performance and behavior-related issues that are interfering with organizational goals and officer well-being. EISs are repositories of data on a wide array of performance indicators, such as uses of force, resisting arrest charges, civilian complaints, absence and lateness records, sick-time usage, line-of-duty injuries, motor vehicle accidents, poor performance ratings, and so on. These data points act as a "dashboard" of indicators that could signal performance or behavioral problems. In November 2018, The National Policing Institute published a report on the "Best Practices in Early Intervention System Implementation and Use." This report discusses the use of these indicators and stresses the role of managers and supervisors in the process. There are no "perfect" EIS, but the ones that are most successful employ an integrated approach that makes EIS a part of an overall performance management system along with appropriate strategies to assist officers in need.

Police departments need to implement EIS as an indirect measure of officer well-being. CALEA accreditation standards require this type of system, and EIS is considered an integral part of effective personnel management. Does your department have an EIS? Is it used effectively? Do the officers believe the system to be credible and helpful or punitive and disciplinary in nature? Creating an indirect measure of employee well-being is not just good management, it is essential.

Direct Measures – These types of measures involve data that is collected directly from the officer. These measures can be both quantitative and qualitative. The most valid way to assess an officer's well-being is to ask directly. Employee surveys can provide a valid and quantitative measure of well-being. Anonymous surveys, however, will not isolate officers in distress, therefore, caution must be exercised using them. This methodology is rarely used in police management, but departments that use survey instruments find opportunities to improve the overall work–life in the organization. The worst thing a police manager can do though is to ask for officers' feedback, and then do nothing with it. Departments that use surveys to assess officer well-being must be prepared to act on the information collection. Not responding to the officers' feedback reinforces the cynical outlook already fostered by the work.

Qualitative direct measures would be in the form of actual interviews, conversations, observations, or focus group meetings with officers on patrol. This approach goes together with the recommendation to be more visibly present with the officers on patrol. Ride along in their patrol cars, back them up on emergency assignments, and speak to them before and after roll call or when they are booking prisoners. There is no good or bad time to "check-in" with officers to find out how they are doing. The more police managers engage in this approach, the more open officers will become. Doing perfunctory or one-off interactions will not solicit the same level of information nor communicate the care and concern that this approach can create. It is not uncommon for police managers to meet individually with every member of their department periodically. Similarly, frequent, and regular focus groups with rank-and-file officers facilitated properly can generate an enormous amount of information about the needs and attitudes of the officers.

Again, the exact approach is less important than engaging this method in the first place. Each police department and police manager will gravitate towards his or her preferred method. Implement the key take-away that some method of direct measurement of officer well-being, both quantitative and qualitative, is needed. The data collected through these methodologies can then be combined with the indirect measure to understand the individual and collective well-being of officers in the department. Armed with this information, plans can be developed and implemented along the lines of the ones discussed above to improve officer well-being.

There is no greater resource in any police department than the officers. That resource needs to be protected, cultivated, and managed for improved performance in the form or of officer well-being, police–community relations, and effective crime reduction, traffic safety, and disorder control. Every police department needs a well-articulated plan in this area to improve organizational communications and promote a healthy and positive work–life balance. In addition, these areas need to be measured and tracked regularly through an integrated mix of indirect and direct measures. The foundation of a successful plan rests on an active and engaged command staff and first-line supervisors. Creating a visible and open cadre of managers and supervisors is essential to the overall success of this plan.

Internal Stakeholder

Labor Management – The topic of police labor management relations is a complex one. It is estimated that approximately 80% of police officers in the United States are represented by a Union, Police Officer Association, or employee group (DeLord and York, 2017). Dealing with difficult personnel matters and collective bargaining agreements requires great skill and often occupies a great deal of time from all parties involved. This chapter does not intend to delve into the specific structures of these complex problems; however, there must be a recognition on the part of the department itself that internal stakeholders are an important part of the "community" that needs to be engaged. Again, there needs to be a positive and long-term relationship between the police department and the internal stakeholder communities to benefit the overall success of the entire organization. Without this balanced approach, a strategy of community engagement would not be accomplished.

The approach recommended to effectively engage internal stakeholders is similar to the approach recommended for external stakeholders and rests on three straightforward principles: recognition, communication, and results.

Recognition – In areas of the U.S., police unions have legal standing to represent the employment interests of their members. They are legally recognized and must be engaged on a wide variety of matters that impact police officers employment. Clearly, the legal designation provides for a formal recognition of them as police officer representatives. Regardless of whether or not an employee group benefits from official legal status, police departments must "recognize" the groups and leadership of those groups that intend to represent the employees of the organization. This transcends collective bargaining and legal representation during internal investigations. This approach requires that employee groups receive the recognition they deserve as interested stakeholders in the well-being of the people they represent.

In many respects, when police officers are formally represented by a Union or POA the recognition of the groups is simple. The group exists and there is a formal relationship between it and the department. However, there are other departments that do not have such formally recognized groups and it is incumbent on the department to create an environment where stakeholder groups are formed. The main goal of these groups (formal or informal) is to promote the well-being of the officers in the department. Organizing and engaging police officers to commit to the betterment of their work conditions is a critical component of any police department's mission.

Communication – It's not enough just to ensure that employee groups are recognized. Police departments must develop a robust means of communication between the parties. Research has shown that better internal communication is key to improving police officer morale (Police1, 2022). The foundation of internal stakeholder communications rests on a strategic approach that is grounded in trust and openness. This approach is deeper and more involved than simply holding periodic meetings or managing disputes or contract negotiations. The implication here is that an effective communications strategy creates relationships committed to inform a community of advocates. The police chief or the command staff alone cannot foster the well-being of officers in the department. They need a team of people and groups committed to the same goal. This will promote well-being, safety, and undoubtedly provide better services to the community (Pal et al., 2023). Open and regular communication with internal stakeholders is essential and police departments must explore all avenues in this regard. Text chains, social media, periodic meetings, direct face-to-face meetings, etc. can all be used to communicate with internal department stakeholders. There is no preferred way except to ensure that communication is part of a strategic plan to keep people and groups informed about the issues they care about most.

Results – Nothing succeeds like success[3] and winning cures all problems.[4] The purpose of achieving results as a part of internal stakeholder engagement is the essence of this approach. Groups organize for a reason; police departments included. Police officers, and their efforts, are the primary tool that police departments have to achieve their goals. Providing those individuals with the things they think they need to accomplish their personal goals is the most effective method of achieving the department's goals. In other words, their success as individuals promotes the overall success of the department.

Employee groups are involved with the individual needs of their members, therefore, promoting the success of the employee group and providing what it wants promotes the overall success of the department. This indirectly impacts the department's "bottom-line." Again, the philosophy here is that a satisfied police officer will provide better service to the community and that internal stakeholders are an instrumental part of that satisfaction. Attending to the needs of the group and helping work towards positive results promotes officer, group, and department success. Oftentimes police managers view employee groups as adversaries. Perhaps, in certain respects they could be, but an effective community engagement strategy suggests that these groups be viewed as partners in the production of police officer well-being.

External – Transactional

External transactional communities are perhaps the least understood and most overlooked when it comes to the topic of community engagement. In some sense, the identification of them as a "community" would be considered controversial and misguided. They are the customers of policing services and the ones that occupy the most frequent and regular interactions with the police in any community. Engaging them as a community is admittedly a challenge, but a challenge that must be embraced.

The often quoted mantra of "protect and serve" as the mission of the police can be thought of the general framework for dealing with the external-transactional community. But what does it mean to "protect and serve?" Couper (2015) suggests that local police can be rated by examining the leadership, organization, and policy characteristic of the department. Although his approach has value understanding the organization of the department, it is only an indirect way of assessing the day-to-day interactions police officers have with members of the public. These day-to-day interactions have powerful potential to influence public opinion about the police and happen to be the interactions police departments have the most control over. We suggest that police departments should engage in a rigorous process of assessing these interactions and using them as the foundation of a broader community engagement strategy.

Interactions with the public, whether it is during a call-for-service through 911, a traffic stop, or a visit to the police facility, should be as professional and productive as possible. In other words, people that interact with the police should have their problems solved (to the extent they can be solved by the police), in a fair, timely manner. At the core of the police role, however, is the use of force, either implied or actual; therefore, routine encounters with the police are often tense, coercive, and result in the negative application of the law. It is difficult indeed to produce "satisfied customers" when you are involved in interactions of this type.

In order to engage external transactional communities effectively, the police need to be viewed as legitimate. The police must enjoy the public's trust and be supported in the overall belief that they have the authority to enforce the law they are empowered to enforce. This concept is known as procedural justice (Tyler, 1990; 2003), and there is a substantial body of evidence that suggests that the more legitimate the public views the police, the more likely they will be to obey the law (Bowers and Robinson, 2012). Above all things, police departments should develop policies and training programs that foster procedural justice to build and maintain the public trust.

A full discussion of procedural justice is well beyond the scope of this chapter but the approach rests on developing the dynamics between the police and the public where members of the public believe they are being treated fairly, believe that the officer is being transparent with her actions, understand they have an opportunity to have their voice heard, and believe that the officer is being impartial with her decisions (Community Oriented Policing Services, 2015a). These principles of fairness, voice, transparency, and impartiality that we recommend for dealing with internal interactions inside a police department should be embraced when dealing with members of the community. How then can a police department ensure that its officers are engaging in the transactional external community with procedural justice and providing excellent services? We recommend several tools that should be leveraged to this extent. We also recommend that these tools not be leveraged to discipline or penalize officer misconduct but to promote the positive interactions officers have with the public every day.

Body-Worn Cameras (BWC) Assessment – The police use of BWCs in the U.S. has grown dramatically over the last decade. In 2020, almost 80% of all police officers in the U.S. were equipped with BWCs compared to only 32% in 2013. And in larger departments with 250 or more officers almost all of them have BWCs (Reaves, 2015; Goodison and Brooks, 2023).

In general, the research on police BWCs has been mixed. BWCs have been shown to reduce complaints against the police by the public (Lum et al., 2019), some studies shown a reduction in the use force (Braga et al., 2018), and others that show possible effects with regards to civilian injuries, and police enforcement (White et al., 2018). The impact of police use of BWCs on community relations, however, is not clear. Many studies have shown that there is no relationship between the police wearing BWCs and the person's perception of the police (Braga et al., 2023), the lawfulness of the encounter between the police and the public (Braga et al., 2022), and there is little research on whether or not the BWC has any impact on the quality of the police–civilian encounter from a customer service perspective. Nonetheless, BWCs provide police managers and supervisors with a window into everyday interactions with the public.

This technology should be leveraged by police departments to assess the quality of these interactions. Good "customer service" and procedurally just interactions should be recognized and celebrated. Policies and processes should be identified where supervisors, or independent reviewers, sample and review BWC recordings of police–civilian encounters and evaluate them on such qualities as:

- Was the officer respectful?
- Did the officer address the problem?
- Did the officer explain how to solve the problem if it couldn't be handled immediately?
- Did the officer show concern for the person's problem?
- Did the officer listen and provide the person with an opportunity to speak their mind?
- Did the officer respond and handle the incident in a timely manner?
- Did the person appear satisfied with the officer and the way the encounter was handled?

These dimensions and others could be assessed by reviewers and used to evaluate individual officer and department-wide performance when it comes to customer service. Police officers do excellent work every day and they are rarely given credit for it. Using BWCs and systematically categorizing interactions with the public will give police departments data to promote the good works officers do, and perhaps identify any problems that are occurring during these day-to-day interactions.

Satisfaction Survey – The use of community satisfaction surveys regarding the police has a long tradition in the U.S. and abroad (Miller and Davis, 2008). The Commission for Accreditation for Law Enforcement Agencies (CALEA) requires that police departments accredited by them must undergo regular and periodic surveys of the public (CALEA, 2023). These surveys, however, explore attitudes and perceptions about the department in general, which is a good thing, but police departments should also consider understanding the dynamics of individual police–civilian encounters, including "involuntary contacts" such as encounters where civilians are arrested, issued citations, or stopped.

To understand the quality of police–civilian interactions, even ones where the civilian is arrested, cited, or stopped, police departments should explore opportunities to conduct regular and periodic surveys. Using civilian contact data already possessed by departments from arrest reports, tickets, complaint reports, etc., police departments could reach out to these individuals to assess the quality of the interactions they had with their officers. Undoubtedly, developing rigorous sampling methods and validated survey instruments to measure "customer" satisfaction are beyond the skill-set of most police managers. However, those skills do exist in the community and police departments should seek out individuals and groups that would be willing and able to assist them (McCabe, 2010). The Appendix in this chapter presents survey instruments that have been used to assess customer satisfaction of police services.

Again, the data obtained by these surveys should be used to promote positive police–civilian interaction, of which there will be many. Using the data to discipline or sanction officer could have a negative impact and undermine the overall value of this method from a strategic standpoint.

Customer Service Orientation at Department Facilities – Entering a police facility, to report an incident or visit a member of the department, can be an intimidating experience for members of the public not accustomed to them. To say the least, the typical public area of a police facility is generally not public-friendly and might feature various security measures such as bullet-resistant glass, intercoms, and locked doors. Security is important at police facilities and this is not intended to suggest that police departments reduce their security profile to promote community satisfaction; however, there could be measures taken to soften the environment and not blast the message "you are not wanted here" to members of the community that enter.

This element of community engagement, ironically, requires the help of the community. By partnering with local community groups, police departments could collaboratively explore the elements of the police facility that work and create this customer service orientation. The department-community team would be tasked with evaluating the current space and determine what things are needed. They might consider space issues, services needed, public access times/days, technology cost, etc. The goal would be to create a public-access space at the police facility, with the community in mind, driven by community input.

User-Friendly Website – In the current social media age, having a user-friendly website is as critical as any other asset a police department uses. The first thing a member of the public will do when they want to learn about their local police department is to search for them on the internet. With this in mind, police department websites should be viewed as tools that help bridge the gap between the department and the community. They can be passive, where content exists for the visitor to explore, or active where visitors can conduct "business" with the department as if they were actually visiting, such as file a report, request permits, etc. or perhaps offer recruiting information for prospective officers.

At a minimum, police websites should have the following features:

- Responsive layouts (highlighting the department and its mission and goals).
- User-friendly navigation (adapting to different screen sizes).
- Engaging content (safety tips, updated stories, crime and traffic initiatives).
- Integration of Services (crime maps, incident reporting).
- Accessible (every member of the community).
- Secure (compliant with cybersecurity standards).
- Community Focused (interactive features: events, forum, calendars).

Here again, the community should be involved with the design and development of the site and the site should be periodically tested to ensure all the features are functional and up to date. Having a "Message from the Chief" from three chiefs prior is not the public message a department wants to send.

Public Relations – Public relations for the police are the various things done by the department to shape perceptions and influence the attitudes of the public about the police in their community. Most people have little or no contact with their local police so direct interactions have a limited effect on the attitudes of an entire community. Therefore, it is incumbent upon police managers to engage in a robust public relations effort. But why? When assessing the operational performance of a police department in this area you should look for three critical processes:

1. Traditional media – if your department is big enough, or you are lucky enough, a professional Public/Press Information Officer (PIO) is critical in this area. A PIO can develop and maintain positive relationships with the traditional mainstream media and act as their point of contact in the department. The PIO can provide a consistent message and manage all external communications. If there is no PIO, the Chief or a high ranking member of the department with good communications skills should act in this capacity. There is no specific way to deal with the traditional media, but the department should consider policies related to who in the department is authorized to speak to the media, what information will be released and in what form, and who gets access to certain incidents (IACP, 2019a)

2. Social Media – social media is a powerful tool and a very quick way of disseminating information. Police departments must be aware that there are many potential uses of social media for both community engagement and investigations. In addition, police departments must develop policies and procedures for the use of social media by their employees (IACP, 2019b). Chapter 4 mentions the use of social media for criminal investigations, and for community engagement there are three general areas where social media is essential:

   a. Outreach and Information – unlike traditional media where the department responds to news stories published by others, social media gives departments the opportunity to "push" messages to the public. Crime prevention tips, seeking tips about unsolved crimes, missing persons, positive police-civilian encounters can be distributed. Social media could also be a two-way tool to promote trust and community building.

   b. Notifications – social media can be used to provide the community with information regarding ongoing events, road closures, emergencies, parades, etc. that might impact normal life. Departments can deliver accurate and timely information about ongoing police incidents without having to go through the traditional media and hope they will publicize it.

   c. Recruitment – social media can give departments a tool to attract potential candidates. Content for Instagram, blogs, Twitter, TikTok, etc. can be developed and managed to recruit police officers.

3. Internal Management – Regardless of whether your department has a PIO or the chief is the department spokesperson, it is critical that one individual in the department be responsible for managing these processes. This includes dealing with the traditional media, developing and implementing a robust social media presence, and equally important, monitoring the social media of members of the department.

Police employees obviously enjoy the right to freedom of expression and nothing here is intended to inhibit that freedom. However, police officers have an important role in our society and their use of social media can reflect badly on their department if they make racist or controversial posts. Officers also need to be mindful of divulging law enforcement sensitive information or make posts that contradict the policies of their departments. Therefore, it is critical that departments develop policies that regulate official and personal use of social media. A sample police for social media from the IACP is included in the Appendix of this chapter.

External – Stakeholders

The last part of this section deals with what would typically be referred to as Police–Community Relations. This is the process of engaging with stakeholders that are external to the police department. The reality is that there is not just one external community stakeholder that the police need to engage. If it were only that simple. The U.S. is a diverse country and the individual cities and towns often reflect this diversity. There are numerous countries of origin, languages, religions, customs, social classes, political views, etc. that police departments need to engage and provide service. The first step in developing an external stakeholder community engagement strategy is to collect data on those many communities.

Community Data – In order to understand the community, police departments must collect and manage information about the various communities they serve. Below is a list of items that should be tracked regularly.

o   Demographics (age, race, gender, income, occupations, etc.)
o   Community groups (leaders, members, meetings, special events)
o   Elected officials (federal, state, local, community-based)

Armed with a census of the various groups and group leaders, police departments can then begin to develop a comprehensive strategy to engage these groups, make them advocates of public safety for their constituents. No two police departments are the same, and no two communities are the same. They consist of different people and preferences. However, below are some elements that should be considered when developing a comprehensive community engagement strategy involving external stakeholders.

Citizens Police Academy (CPA) – This is a program designed to educate residents and local citizens on the various aspects of law enforcement. It is for those interested in learning more about how the departments operate. The idea started in the U.K. and was first implemented in Orlando, FL in 1985. Typically, the goals of the Citizens Police Academy is to expose community members to police training, the environments of police work, and to open up lines of communication with the community. The NYPD, for example, designed a six-week community training program that provides members of the community with a background and deeper understanding of NYPD policies and activities, as well as the structure and limit of police power. Programs can be tailored to fit the needs of the department and community. There is no one size fits all. However, CPA programs require a substantial amount of time from the participants and reach only a small segment of the community (PERF, 2000; NYPD, 2024).

People's Police Academy – An interesting twist on the Citizens Police Academy concept is the People's Police Academy. This program developed by Reverend Que English in the Bronx, NY is designed to orient newly assigned police officers to the various cultures, values, residents, and stakeholders in the community they are serving. It was designed to create a platform that brings all members of the community together to co-create public safety, build trust and cohesion and commit to better understand the role that each of us plays in supporting safe, healthy communities (Medgar Evers College, 2024). www.mec. cuny.edu/centers/dubois-bunche-center-for-public-policy/peoples-police-academy/

Community Ambassadors – These individuals are representatives of the community and the police department that are tasked with keeping each other up-to-date about incidents and events important to one another. As the term implies, the ambassador is a representative or promoter of a particular constituency. For an effective community engagement strategy, police departments should consider identifying "ambassadors" both inside and outside the department.

Community Notification Protocol – It should be department policy to keep community leaders and organizations informed of local conditions, activities, and events of mutual concern to the communities. Departments should take responsibility for notifying community leaders directly and personally (not through general social media outreach) about unusual events, newsworthy, or sensitive incidents that have the potential for concern or unrest, and about the intended police response to these incidents. Community leaders should include, but not limited to, local elected officials, community board chairpersons, community council members, civic, religious, educational, business, and tenant leaders, also representatives from any notable governmental agencies operating within the confines of the precinct. A current list of these key community members should be maintained and used to inform local community members about incidents as they unfold.

Department Liaisons – This is the "ambassador" concept, but in the opposite direction. In this approach, every identified community stakeholder should be aligned with a specific member of the department that they can contact for assistance. Department representatives should be at a sufficiently high level in the department where they will be accessible readily, and able to provide an organizational response. For example, a local high school principal might be assigned to the day-shift lieutenant. Any questions or concerns about the department or its operations could be specifically directed to this lieutenant. If the lieutenant did not know or was not responsible for the area being inquired about, it would be their job to find the information and communicate it back to the principal. In addition, it would be incumbent upon this lieutenant to regularly interact with the principal to ensure the policing needs of that school were being met. Perhaps this would involve supervision of the School Resources Officers, a sporting event needing security, safety lectures, or whatever the school needed. The liaison would be the first point of contact and they would be responsible for maintaining an open line of communication.

Police Clergy Council – Local clergy leaders are respected and trusted leaders in the community. Police departments should leverage faith leaders to ensure police services are being delivered to the community. The Houston, TX police department, for example, has a robust program involving local clergy, called the "Police and Clergy Alliance (PACA)." PACA, allows local clergy volunteers, in partnership with the HPD, to provide valuable services and resources in areas such as responding to call-out situations where they can offer support to HPD employees, victims and their families, participate in ride-alongs to personally experience what police officers are faced with on a daily basis, go into apartment complexes and schools to mentor at-risk students or those who need additional guidance in their lives, assist with disaster relief efforts, and other significant incidents.

Police departments should look to the model created by the HPD to develop relationships with the local clergy and create an entity that can work alongside the police to accomplish their goals.

Community Sentiment Meter – This is similar to the "customer" satisfaction surveys discussed earlier in the chapter, except this approach involves survey of the same people or community leaders. Instead of a cross-sectional assessment of services, this sentiment meter would provide an on-going longitudinal assessment of community stakeholder satisfaction. Each month community leaders, and persons from identified community stakeholder groups could be surveyed using a short questionnaire to determine satisfaction level. The results would be useful to a department keeping a pulse on community satisfaction and a gauge to evaluate policies and programs being implemented in the community.

Community-Based Initiatives – The community-based initiatives (CBI) represent the various programs that departments have implemented to engage their communities. There is no empirical research that shows the effectiveness of one program or another. However, they are presented here as a catalogue of sorts detailing the various CBIs that have been facilitated by local police departments (Moore, 2023). They should be considered as part of an overall community engagement strategy, but not necessarily the only components of that strategy.

- Coffee with a Cop
- Shop with a Cop
- Prescription Drug Takeback
- Positive "Tickets" redeemable for discounts at local retail shops
- Coat Drive
- MADD
- SADD
- Holiday Safety (Halloween, Christmas, etc.)
- Youth Sports (Police Athletic League)
- Food Drives
- Police Chief for a Day contest
- Community Safety Training (Active Shooter Awareness)
- Senior Citizen Outreach

All of the above are popular programs in local police departments and should be considered by others as part of an overall engagement strategy.

Conclusion

Community engagement is essential to the successful operations of a police department. Crime reduction, traffic safety, and disorder control must be approached with an active and engaged commitment of the community. This chapter conceptualizes communities across two main dimensions: internal and external, and views these communities from two different perspectives: transactional and stakeholder. To understand a department's operational performance in this area it must be evaluated across these dimensions/perspective. Department leadership should be held accountable for developing a plan to improve community satisfaction with the department and develop programs and policies that reach community members in each of the four community types. Success in this area is as important, if not more important, than effective crime reduction, patrol operations, or investigations.

It is the essence of what the police do and should be embraced by all members of a police department.

Notes

1 www.youtube.com/watch?v=ZJGirITl6sE
2 Attributed to Colin Powell, former US Secretary of State, Army General and Chairman of the Joint Chiefs of Staff.
3 Alexander Dumas.
4 Kevin Harwick.

References

Beck, B., Antonelli, J., & Pineros, G. (2022). Effects of New York City's neighborhood policing policy. *Police Quarterly*, 25(1), 470–496.

Bowers, J., & Robinson, P. H. (2012). Perceptions of fairness and justice: The shared aims and occasional conflicts of legitimacy and moral credibility. *Wake Forest Law Review*, 47(2), 211–284.

Braga, A. A., MacDonald, J. M., & Barao, L.M. (2023) Do body-worn cameras improve community perceptions of the police? Results from a controlled experimental evaluation. *Journal of Experimental Criminology*, 19, 279–310 (2023). https://doi.org/10.1007/s11292-021-09476-9

Braga A. A, Macdonald J. M, &McCabe, J. (2022). Body-worn cameras, lawful police stops, and NYPD officer compliance: A cluster randomized controlled trial. *Criminology*, 60, 124–158. https://doi.org/10.1111/1745-9125.12293

Braga, A. A., Sousa, W., Coldren, J. R., Jr., & Rodriguez, D. (2018). The effects of body-worn cameras on police activity and police-citizen encounters: A randomized controlled trial. *Journal of Criminal Law and Criminology*, 108(3), 511–538.

Bureau of Labor Statistics. (2023). *National Census of Fatal Occupational Injuries in 2022*. US Department of Labor.

Burkus, D. (2016). *Under New Management: The unexpected truths about leading great organizations*. Hughton Mifflin Harcourt Books

Cheng, T. (2019). Influence without input: The silence and scripts of police community relations. *Social Problems*, 67(1), 171–189.

Commission on Accreditation for Law Enforcement Agencies. (2023). *Standard 45.2.2. Citizens Survey*. CALEA.

Community Oriented Policing Services. (2015a). Organizational change through decision making and policy: A new procedural justice course for managers and supervisors. *Community Policing Dispatch*, 8(4), April 2015. https://cops.usdoj.gov/html/dispatch/04-2015/a_new_procedural_justice_course.asp#:~:text=Procedural%20justice%20speaks%20to%20four,being%20impartial%20in%20decision%20making

Community Oriented Policing Services. (2015b). Ready, set, engage! Ideas and options for community engagement and partnership building. *Community Policing Dispatch*, 8(6), June 2015. https://cops.usdoj.gov/html/dispatch/06-2015/community_engagement_and_partnership_building.asp

Couper, D. (2015). *How to Rate Your Local Police: A User Guide for Civic, Governmental, and Police Leaders*. Create Space Publishing.

DeLord, R., & York, R. (2017). *Law Enforcement, Police Unions and the Future: Educating Police Management and Unions about the Challenges Ahead*. Charles C. Thomas Publisher, Ltd.

Floyd, et al. v. City of New York, et al., 959 F. Supp. 2d 540 (S.D.N.Y. 2013).

Goodison, S. E., & Brooks, C. (2023). *Local Police Departments, 2020: Equipment and Technology*. Bureau of Justice Assistance.

International Association of Chiefs of Police. (2019a). *Media Relations*. IACP. www.theiacp.org/sites/default/files/2024-03/Media%20Relations%20-%202019.08_0.pdf

International Association of Chiefs of Police. (2019,). *Social Media*. IACP. www.theiacp.org/sites/defa ult/files/2019-05/Social%20Media%20Paper%20-%202019.pdf

Lah, K. (2015). *Laquan McDonald Shooting: Why Did It Take 13 Months to Release the Video*. CNN, Dec. 2 2015.www.cnn.com/2015/12/01/us/chicago-police-shooting-explainer/index.html

Lum, C., Stoltz, M., Koper, C. S., & Scherer, J. A. (2019). The research on body-worn cameras: What we know, what we need to know. *Criminology & Public Policy*, 18(1), 93–118.

McCabe, J. (2010). Assessing citizen satisfaction with voluntary and involuntary police encounters in the Norwalk, CT Police Department. *Journal of Criminal Justice Research and Consulting*, 1(2), 1–37.

Medgar Evers College, "People's Police Academy." www.mec.cuny.edu/centers/dubois-bunche-center-for-public-policy/peoples-police-academy, accessed September 22, 2024.

Miller, J., & Davis, R. C. (2008). Unpacking public attitudes to the police: contrasting perceptions of misconduct with traditional measures of satisfaction. *International Journal of Police Science & Management*, 10(1), 9–22. https://doi.org/10.1350/ijps.2008.10.1.9

Moore, M. (2023). *Taking a Back to Basics Approach to Community Engagement*. *Police1*. Lexipol Media Group.

National Law Enforcement Officers Memorial Fund (2023). *Annual Report 2022*. NLEOMF.

New York City Police Department. (2024). *Citizens Police Academy*. Website retrieved, April 16, 2024. www.nyc.gov/site/nypd/bureaus/administrative/training-citizens-police-academy.page

Office of Community Oriented Policing Services. (2015). *The President's Task Force on 21st Century Policing Implementation Guide: Moving from Recommendations to Action*. Office of Community Oriented Policing Services.

Pal, J., Khadijah, C., Kowalczyk, E.., & Townsend, C. (2023). *Strategic Communications for Law Enforcement*. DOJ, Office of Community Oriented Policing Services.

Platner, O. (2020). "Customers first, employees second," is Jack Ma serious? *LinkedIn Magazine:*www.linkedin.com/pulse/customers-first-employees-second-jack-ma-serious-ofir-platner/

Police 1 (2022). What Cops Want in 2022 *Digital Edition, Police1*. , February 28, 2022. www. police1.com/   police-products/body-cameras/articles/digital-editionwhat-cops-want-in-2022-CkFK0jUZrpFOUjeR.

Police Executive Research Forum. (2000). *Citizens Police Academy: Success through Community Partnerships*. PERF.

Police Executive Research Forum. (2013). *Compstat: Its Origins, Evolution, and Future in Law Enforcement*. PERF.

Police Executive Research Forum. (2019). *An Occupational Risk: What Every Police Department Should Do to Prevent Suicide among Its Officers*. PERF.

Police Executive Research Forum. (2023). *Survey of Police Agency Staffing*. PERF.

Rahr, S., & Rice, S. K. (2015). From warriors to guardians: Recommitting American police culture to democratic ideals. *New Perspectives in Policing Bulletin*. US Department of Justice, National Institute of Justice.

Reaves, B. A. (2015). *Local Police Departments, 2013: Equipment and Technology*. Bureau of Justice Assistance.

Stewart, J. (2018). *The Dilemmas of Engagement: The Role of Consultation in Governance*. Australian National University Press

Tyler, T.R. (1990). *Why People Obey the Law*. Yale University Press.

Tyler, T. R. (2003). Procedural Justice, Legitimacy, and the Effective Rule of Law. *Crime and Justice*, 30, 283–357. www.jstor.org/stable/1147701

White, M. D., Gaub, J. E., & Todak, N. (2018). Exploring the potential for body-worn cameras to reduce violence in police–citizen encounters. *Policing: A Journal of Policy and Practice*, 12(1), 66–76

Wilson, J. Q. (1968). *Varieties of Police Behavior*. Harvard University Press.

Appendix

Survey Illustration

The Heartland Police Department is reaching out to members of the community who have had a recent encounter with the police. The Heartland Police Department wants to find out if people are satisfied with the way the encounter was handled. This short survey will take about 5 minutes to complete, and your answers will help the police to do a better job of serving the community. This information you give will be used for statistical purposes only, and your identity will not be associated with your answers. Please read the following questions carefully and base your responses on the recent encounter that you had with the member(s) of the Heartland Police Department:

1. How professionally would you say the officer treated you? Would you say that you were treated...

   • Very professionally
   • Somewhat professionally
   • Not at all professionally

2. How respectfully would you say that you were treated by the officer(s)...

   • Very respectfully
   • Somewhat respectfully
   • Not at all respectfully

3. How well did the officer(s) explain where you could get help for problems you might have had as a result of the incident? Would you say the officer(s) explained this...

   • Very clearly
   • Somewhat clearly
   • Not at all clearly

4. How knowledgeable was the officer(s) in dealing with the problem you were experiencing? Would you say the officer(s) was...

   • Very knowledgeable
   • Somewhat knowledgeable
   • Not at all knowledgeable

5. How interested was the officer(s) in your problem? Would you say the officer(s) was...

   • Very interested
   • Somewhat interested
   • Not interested at all

6. How promptly did the police respond to your situation? Would you say they responded....

   • Very promptly
   • Somewhat promptly
   • Not at all promptly

7. Overall, how satisfied are you with how the officer(s) handled your situation...

   - Very satisfied
   - Fairly satisfied
   - Not at all satisfied

Now, we would like you to think about the Heartland Police Department in general and give us your opinions about how well the department is doing its job....

8. Considering the recent encounter you had with the member(s) of the Heartland Police Department, how would you say that encounter affected your satisfaction with the department? As a result of the encounter, would you say you feel...

   - More satisfied
   - No change in satisfaction
   - Less satisfied

9. In terms of overall performance, would you say the Heartland Police Department is doing...

   - A good job
   - An adequate job
   - A poor job
   - I'm not sure

10. In terms of fighting crime, would you say the Heartland Police Department is doing...

    - A good job
    - An adequate job
    - A poor job
    - I'm not sure

11. In terms of traffic safety, would you say the Heartland Police Department is doing...

    - A good job
    - An adequate job
    - A poor job
    - I'm not sure

12. In terms of drug enforcement, would you say the Heartland Police Department is doing...

    - A good job
    - An adequate job
    - A poor job
    - I'm not sure

13. In terms of crime prevention and community service, would you say the Heartland Police Department is doing...

    - A good job
    - An adequate job
    - A poor job
    - I'm not sure

14. In terms of dealing with the citizens in a fair and courteous manner, would you say the Heartland Police Department is doing...

   - A good job
   - An adequate job
   - A poor job
   - I'm not sure

15. How concerned are you about safety and security in your community?

   - Very concerned
   - Somewhat concerned
   - Not concerned
   - I'm not sure

16. Are there any ways that the officer(s) could have handled your situation better?

   _____
   _____
   _____

17. Is there anything you can suggest that the Heartland Police Department can do to better meet neighborhood needs?

   _____
   _____
   _____

The remaining questions will help us better understand the people the Heartland Police Department is serving. If you are uncomfortable answering these questions you may refuse to do so. Keep in mind that your responses will be kept strictly confidential.

18. Which of the following categories best describes your racial or ethnic heritage?

   - White
   - Black
   - Hispanic
   - Asian or Pacific Islander
   - Other: specify _____

19. What is your age? _____

20. Please indicate you gender:

   - Male
   - Female

21. What is your income level?

   - Less than $25,000
   - $25,000–$50,000
   - $50,001–$100,000
   - $100,001–$150,000
   - More than $150,000

22. What is your education level?

- Less than High School
- High School Graduate
- Some College
- College Graduate
- Graduate Study

23. On what media source do you use most regularly to formulate your opinions about the police?

- Personal Observation
- Newspaper
- Television
- Internet
- Radio
- Other

Thank you for your time. Your responses will be combined with the responses of many others to develop a measure of how the Heartland Police Department is dealing with citizens. The department will use this measure to help the way it interacts with the public and improve essential services. Thank you!

Sample Social Media Policy

Policy

The Heartland Police Department endorses the secure use of social media to enhance communication, collaboration, information exchange and effectiveness of investigations. The Department further recognizes that social media tools play a role in the personal and professional lives of the employees of the Department.

Department employees must be credible, unbiased and impartial enough that they can credibly testify in courts of law. Indeed, an officer or employee's credibility and impartiality is essential to his/her ability to perform his/her sworn or assigned duties. The compelling governmental purpose of this policy is to preserve and protect that essential integrity and the faith and trust of the citizens of Heartland. This policy is unconcerned with content of an employee's social media communications so long as Departmental operations, confidentialities and functions are not adversely impacted, and so long as employees can participate credibly as witnesses in courts of law and in sworn hearings. Employees are advised and cautioned that the indiscreet use of social media, including personal use, may have a negative impact on their career, professional wellbeing and credibility in court.

Purpose

To establish the Department's position on the utility, management, administration, and oversight of social media. This policy is not meant to address one particular form of social media, rather social media in general, to allow for new tools and future technologies.

Definitions

1. Avatar: An image or username that represents a person or group online within forums and social networks.
2. Blog: A self-published diary or commentary on a particular topic that may allow visitors to post responses, reactions, or comments. The term "blog" is short for Web Log.
3. Chat: Interaction on a social media platform with a number of people, adding text items one after another into the same space occurring in real time.
4. Content: Any text, picture, video or other meaningful material located on the internet.
5. Forum: Also known as a message board, a forum is an online discussion site.
6. Instant Messaging: Instant messaging (IM) is a form of real-time direct text-based communication between two or more people.
7. Page: With regard to social media, the term "page" is used to define the specific portion of a social media website where content is displayed and managed by an individual or individuals with administrative rights.
8. Post: Content an individual shares with a social media site or the act of publishing content on a site.
9. Profile: Information that a user provides about him/herself on a social networking site.
10. Social Media: Internet-based resources that integrate user-generated content and user participation, including but not limited to: social networking sites (Facebook, MySpace), micro-blogging sites (Twitter), photo and video-sharing sites (YouTube, Flickr), wikis (Wikipedia), and blogs and news sites.
11. Social Networks: Online platforms where users can create profiles, share information and socialize with others using a range of technologies.
12. Speech: Expression or communication of thoughts or opinions including, but not limited to: spoken words, writing, expressive conduct, symbolism, photographs and video.

Procedure

1. Social Media Uses

   A. Social media is a valuable investigative tool when seeking evidence or information about:

      1) missing persons;
      2) wanted persons;
      3) gang participation;
      4) crimes perpetrated online, and;
      5) photos or videos of a crime posted by a participant or observer.

   B. Social media can be used for community outreach and engagement by:

      1) providing crime prevention tips;
      2) offering online-reporting opportunities;
      3) sharing crime maps and data, and;
      4) soliciting tips about unsolved crimes.

C. Social media can be used to make time-sensitive notifications related to:

1) road closures;
2) special events;
3) weather emergencies;
4) missing or endangered persons.

D. Social media can be used when conducting background investigations as follows:

1) The department has an interest to include Internet-based content that is publicly accessible when conducting background investigation of job candidates;
2) Searches should be conducted by a non-decision maker. Information pertaining to protected classes shall be filtered out prior to sharing any information found online with decision makers;
3) Persons authorized to search Internet-based content should be deemed as holding a sensitive position;
4) Vetting techniques shall be applied uniformly to all candidates; and,
5) Every effort must be made to validate Internet-based information considered during the hiring process.

E. Social media may be used in other areas, but not limited to:

1) recruiting;
2) advertising employment opportunities;
3) publicizing volunteer positions; and
4) offering training opportunities.

2. Department Sanctioned Presence on social media.

A. Where possible, each Department created social media page shall include an introductory statement clearly specifying the purpose and scope of the agency's presence on the website.
B. Where possible, the page(s) should link to the Department's official website.
C. Department-related social media sites or pages shall be approved by the Chief, or designee. Social media pages shall be administered by the Support Services Section/Crime Prevention Sergeant. Any changes or suggestions to the social media sites shall be routed through the Support Services Section/Crime Prevention Sergeant.
D. Where possible, social media pages shall clearly indicate they are maintained by the Department and have Department contact information prominently displayed.
E. Social media content shall adhere to applicable laws, regulations, and policies, including all information technology, records management, Department, and City policies. Content is subject to public open records laws. Relevant records retention schedules apply to social media content. Content must be managed, stored, and retrieved to comply with open records laws and e-discovery laws and policies.
F. Where possible, social media pages should display or link to the City of Heartland webpage and to the City of Heartland "Report a Concern" form in order for viewers to leave comments or concerns.
G. Where possible, social media pages should state that the opinions expressed by visitors to the page(s) do not reflect the opinions of the department. Pages shall clearly indicate that the posted comments will be monitored and that the department reserves the right to remove obscenities, off-topic comments, and personal

attacks. Pages shall clearly indicate that the content posted or submitted for posting is subject to public disclosure.

3. Department Sanctioned Use – Department personnel representing the Department via social media outlets shall:

   A. Conduct themselves at all times as representatives of the Department and adhere to all Department standards of conduct.
   B. Identify themselves as a member of the Department unless conducting an investigation under Section 4 of this order.
   C. Not make statements about the guilt or innocence of any suspect or arrestee, or comments concerning pending prosecutions, nor post, transmit, or otherwise disseminate confidential information.
   D. Not conduct political activities or private business.
   E. Observe and abide by all copyright, trademark, and service mark restrictions in posting materials to electronic media.

4. Investigative Uses

   A. The Heartland Police Department recognizes the value of social media with regard to investigative lead development, suspect identification, covert operations and case development. Members of the Department requiring access to various social media sites as part of their official duties must request approval through their chain of command to their respective Division Deputy Chief.
   B. An officer desiring to pursue investigative information through the interactive use of social media (as opposed to merely browsing or researching) is required to notify his/her direct supervisor of the intention and the expected benefits of pursuing the lead through social media resources before utilizing social media.
   C. Official Department information may only be disseminated by the Public Information Officer, Chief of Police, or designee.

5. Personal Use – Department personnel shall abide by the following precautions and prohibitions when using social media:

   A. Department personnel are free to express themselves as private citizens on social media sites to the degree that their speech does not impair working relationships of the Department for which loyalty and confidentiality are important, impede the performance of duties, or negatively impact the public perception of the Department.
   B. As public employees, Department personnel are cautioned that speech, on or off-duty, made pursuant to their official duties is not protected under the First Amendment and may form the basis for discipline if deemed detrimental to the Department. Department personnel should assume their speech and related activity on social media sites reflects upon their office and this Department. Any speech involving themselves or other department personnel reflecting behavior that would reasonably be considered reckless or irresponsible is prohibited.
   C. Per General Order 2601.1.A.24: "Employees shall treat official business of the department as confidential. Information regarding official business shall be disseminated only to those for whom it is intended and in accordance with established departmental procedures." Department personnel shall not post, transmit, or otherwise disseminate any information to which they have access as a result of their employment without written permission from the Chief, or designee. This includes, but is not limited to the following:

1) Photographs, videos or other depictions (avatar) of Department marked or unmarked police vehicles or other markings identifying the Department.
2) Photographs, videos or other depictions of the inside of police buildings.
3) Photographs, videos or other depictions of crime or accident scenes.
4) Photographs, videos or other depictions of Departmental training, activities or work-related assignments.
5) Information concerning crimes, accidents or violations of ordinances.
6) Photographs, videos or other depictions of Department computers, servers, switchboards, phones, MDCs, or radios.

D. Department personnel may not display logos, uniforms, badges or similar identifying items on personal web pages. This does not include the display of such items when associated with a public service type event or in memory of a fallen officer. If an employee is unsure whether the display of such items is acceptable, approval shall be obtained from the Chief of Police or designee.

E. When using social media, Department personnel should be mindful that their speech and posted information becomes part of the worldwide electronic domain indefinitely, even when original postings are deleted by the poster. Caution should be used in the type of information published on social media venues so as not to unduly jeopardize the safety and security of the employee, the employee's family or that of fellow employees within the Department. Consent must be obtained from any affected employee before posting any information, to include photos and video regarding that employee. Officers who are, or who may reasonably be expected to work in undercover operations, shall not post any form of visual or personal information. Adherence to the Department's Code of Conduct, Ethics and Sexual Harassment Policy are required in the personal use of social media.

F. Department personnel should be aware that speech containing obscene or sexually explicit language, images, or acts and statements that ridicule, malign, disparage, or otherwise express bias against any race, religion, sexual orientation, or protected class of individuals is prohibited and may provide grounds for undermining or impeaching an officer's testimony in criminal proceedings.

G. Department personnel may not divulge information gained because of their authority; make any statements, speeches, endorsements, or publish materials that could reasonably be considered to represent the views of the Department without express authorization.

H. Department personnel should be aware that they may be subject to civil litigation for the following:

1) Publishing or posting false information that harms the reputation of another person, group, or organization;
2) Publishing or posting private facts and personal information about someone without their permission, which has not been previously revealed to the public, is not of legitimate public concern, and would be offensive to a reasonable person.
3) Using someone else's name, likeness, or other personal attributes without that person's permission for an exploitative purpose.
4) Publishing the creative work of another, trademarks, or certain confidential business information without the permission of the owner.

I. Department personnel should expect any information created, transmitted, downloaded, exchanged, or discussed in a public online forum may be accessed by the Department at any time.

J. Department personnel should be aware that privacy and security settings found on social media sites are constantly changing; therefore, employees should never assume that personal information posted on such sites is, or will remain, protected.

K. Any employee becoming aware of, or having knowledge of, a posting on any website, webpage or social media tool in violation of these provisions, is required to notify a supervisor immediately.

L. Engaging in any of the prohibited behaviors may provide grounds for impeaching an officer's testimony in a criminal or civil proceeding. As such, employees subject to any judicial sanctions as a result of behavior associated with social media are also subject to discipline by the Department.

M. Violations of this directive on Social Media may subject employees to discipline up to and including termination.

Chapter 11

Assessing, Understanding, and Managing Organizational Culture

Highly Resistant Organizational Cultures

It is widely accepted that the unique mission and paramilitary nature of police organizations has led to the development of a distinct, complex, and particularly strong organizational culture (see Wincelowicz, 2004, Paoline, 2001; Crank, 1997). The values and practices associated with this police culture greatly affect employee and organizational performance. It is virtually impossible to obtain an accurate assessment of any police organization without fully understanding its culture. Simply reviewing data regarding police–citizen encounters such as the number of investigative stops, uses of force, or civilian complaints, will only provide a partial understanding of that department without a qualitative assessment of how the officers view, understand and carry out their roles and responsibilities vis-à-vis the public.

The term organizational culture is generally defined as:

A pattern of basic assumptions – invented, discovered, or developed by a given group as it learns to cope with its problems of external adaptation and internal integration – that has worked well enough to be considered valuable and, therefore, to be taught to new members is the correct way to perceive, think, and feel in relation to those problems.

(Luthans, 2005, p. 122)

Organizational cultures are generally characterized by: 1) observed behavioral regularities; 2) norms (i.e., standards of behavior); 3) dominant values; 4) philosophy; 5) rules; and 6) organizational climate (Luthans, 2005). They tend to be stable and resistant to change. Culture is learned, both formally and informally, through a complex system of human interaction, whereby meaning is derived from shared understandings (Langan-Fox and Tan, 1997). As Reuss-Ianni (1993) notes:

It does not happen in the police academy, and one cannot learn it from books or criminal justice courses. A cop learns it from his [or her] own street experience, as an apprentice to officers already on the job and from contact with a peer structure of working cops in a precinct. The lessons are constantly reinforced by the "war stories" and experiences of other officers and through the traditions of police practice which developed in these networks. As the officer is socialized into the precinct social structure and into one of its subunits, the job comes to be governed by a series of conventions or mutual understandings among the officers.

(p. 67)

DOI: 10.4324/9781003396437-11

However, "a common misconception is that an organization has a uniform culture ... There can be a dominant culture as well as subcultures throughout a typical organization" (Luthans, 2005, p. 124) Often, multiple cultures develop and vie for dominance at any time. Their existence and impact will positively or negatively affect organizational performance (Strati, 1998)

Harry Levinson (1994) developed a list of psychological "truths" about organizations that are quite helpful in understanding how and why cultures develop and persist over time. He notes that:

1) All organizations recapitulate the family structure and the behavioral practices of the culture in which they are embedded.
2) All animals and human beings differentiate themselves into ingroups and outgroups and develop what might be called in the ingroup narcissism, the "we-they" phenomenon.
3) All organizations, by definition, being made up of people, are living organisms. They have developmental histories and evolve adaptive patterns that deal with different levels of complexity.
4) All living organisms experience continuous change, both within themselves and in their environments.
5) All groups follow a leader. Different groups at different times in their life experience require different styles of leadership, but the founding leaders' policies, practices, and organizational structure frequently endure (p. 429).

Reuss-Ianni (1993) identified a dichotomy of culture that was specific to police organizations in *Two Cultures of Policing: Street Cops and Management Cops*. As the title suggests, she identified the emergence and functioning of two competing, and sometimes conflicting, cultures within police departments. She contended that competition (and sometimes open antagonism) between "street cops" and their "bosses" was at the heart of the organizational dilemma of modern urban policing. This dichotomy is certainly not limited to police organizations. Many other public service organizations experience this general split between practitioners and supervisors. Indeed, even in the private sector, one can normally identify distinct subcultures based on one's overall level of motivation to conform to established rules and to achieve organizational (as opposed to personal) goals (see, e.g., Lipman-Blumen and Leavitt, 1999). Her findings were consistent with the work of Edgar Schen (1997) who identified disabling learning dysfunctions that often exist in organizations due to the existence of multiple subcultures (such as the *operator* culture and the *executive* culture).

These cultural problems must be understood and addressed before any significant steps for performance improvement can be undertaken. Perhaps more importantly, if any efforts are undertaken to move police personnel from a "warrior" to a "guardian" mindset, a department's organizational culture must be acknowledged, understood, and managed.

Organizational Culture Influences the Transfer and Use of Information within Police Organizations

An organization's culture is its personality and *modus operandi*.

Berthon et al. (2001) explain that, "Within organizations, individual managers are transient, yet artifacts, organizational processes, schemata, values, and assumptions endure and operate as a type of supra-individual memory that preserves learning" (Berthon et al.,

2001, p. 136). These enduring patterns of values and assumptions are often unconscious and unrecognized. They can be identified, however, when we examine what information the organization views as valuable. Culture influences the way in which information is obtained, interpreted, and communicated within the organization.

Organizational culture therefore has a direct impact upon the way in which an organization learns. It has been found to influence "managers' processing of information and wider sense making and ultimately affect business performance" (Berthon et al., 2001, p. 136) (citations omitted). Organizational cultures vary in intensity (or perhaps density) and once established, are often very difficult to change (Langan-Fox and Tan, 1997).

Various subcultures coexist with the apparently predominant one. In such circumstances, the "culture" that is openly acknowledged serves as a façade, masking the work of groups of individuals who tacitly shape understanding and practice within the organization. These groups can be identified through the methods or organizational ethnography. A newer and perhaps more fruitful approach draws upon the methods associated with social network analysis. Social networks are certainly not a new phenomenon, they have existed within organizations for centuries. What is new is the effort by scholars and practitioners to identify and leverage otherwise invisible networks to open lines of communication and to enhance organizational performance (see Cross and Thomas, 2009).

Unfortunately, "as organizations age and grow in size, their repertoire of cognitive schema becomes more developed, and they become more passive in their information search" (Berthon et al., 2001, p. 138) (citations omitted). Large, well-established organizations become complacent and less inclined to react to and use information or novel ideas that challenge accumulated institutional memory. They "question, test, and probe their environment less and come to rely more and more on their accumulated experiences. The environment thus comes to appear less uncertain and more structured" (p. 140). Upper-level managers can quickly become careerists, individuals who are less concerned about organizational performance than they are about personal success and the management of their own careers. Taken to its logical extreme, complacent top-level managers might be inclined to ask, "*Why look for trouble? We might find it!*"

But public service organizations do need to look for trouble, so that they can avoid it. Think of a pilot viewing a Doppler radar screen in order to understand the path of an approaching storm. Police organizations are no different. They need to be agile and responsive, to derive new responses to changing environmental stimuli. They must avoid intellectual laziness and self-confidence. This calls for creative thinking, open communication, coordination and decisive action.

Everyone understands that organizational structure has a lot to do with performance – it can facilitate or hinder operations. For example, if a police department does not have a designated crime analyst on the organizational chart, there is great likelihood that the department is not approaching its work in an analytical and strategic manner. If that position does not exist, it is likely that certain detectives or patrol supervisors are individually performing crime analysis on an *ad hoc* basis; but that a comprehensive survey of hot spots and "hot people" is not being performed. More importantly, information will not be widely shared, due to organizational structure. Isolated pockets of analytics – information silos – can guide and inform individuals as they approach their work, but this is insufficient to guide the entire organization and to formulate enterprise-wide solutions. Staffing and organizational structure really matter.

But what if the organizational structure is correct and positions are properly staffed, but we simply have the wrong people in the wrong positions? Consider a department that assigns a newly promoted Sgt. to serve as the department's training supervisor; even though this individual has virtually no background in this area, no training and, perhaps most importantly, no interest or desire. What does that mean for the department?

Unfortunately, it likely means that individual and organizational learning will simply not be a priority for this department. It means that the field training officer (FTO) program will not receive the attention and support that is required to produce and properly prepare the next generation of professionals. The training supervisor is more likely going to serve merely as a training coordinator – signing off on training requests and placing certificates of completion in officers' personnel folders after they have attended off-site courses.

Consider also what will occur if this individual stays in this position for several years, only to hand it off to another newly appointed sergeant who similarly has no interest in the position. What if this continues for three, five, or seven years? What does this mean for the department? What effect does it have upon the department's culture? What will its officers think? What about morale?

Merely creating and filling the position of "training supervisor," or school resource officer (SRO), is not enough. We need to know how well suited these officers are for these important positions and how well trained and supported they are. If a department has a negative culture that does not value or understand the importance of these functions, it will assign personnel to them blindly (perhaps solely based on seniority), then suffer poor performance, bad morale, and a stagnant organizational culture that will persist for many years.

The Shift Towards a "Performance Culture" in American Policing

For approximately 150 years, American policing primarily had a retrospective or reactive orientation. The primary task of the police was to respond promptly to calls for service. This, however, proved to be quite ineffective in terms of reducing overall crime rates. The theory was to respond as quickly as possible and simply hope for the best.

In 1973 the field of American policing was quite surprised with the results of the Kansas City preventive patrol study (Pate et al., 1975). This experiment was designed to prove that the overall number of police officers assigned to a locale would relate directly to the rate of reported crime in that area. Upon reviewing the results however, both researchers and police professionals were shocked to find that the overall number of police officers assigned to preventive or random patrol had little to no effect upon the rate of reported crime. This result was astounding. It was always assumed that the police could deter crime by their mere presence. Clearly, this was not the case.

Many suggested that the study proved that the police simply make no difference at all; crime rates fluctuate due to the economy, demographics, politics, or similar matters well beyond the control of the police. All the police could be expected to do was respond promptly to calls for service. It did not appear that the police could dramatically impact crime rates. This was an unfortunate and incorrect conclusion. The Kansas City study examined "preventive" or random patrol, it did not evaluate other methods, such as undercover police operations. Nevertheless, the study resulted in a pervasive feeling that the police had less impact on crime than was originally believed.

Things changed in 1994 when William Bratton arrived at the NYPD. Bratton quickly made it known that a laissez-faire attitude towards crime rates would simply not be tolerated. Bratton insisted that the police mattered a great deal, and they could dramatically reduce the overall rate of reported crime in any community in the United States. In February

1994, Bratton developed what has come to be known as the Compstat model of police management, and American policing has not been the same since.

Bratton developed a form of performance-based management that centered upon regularly conducted management meetings attended by representatives from all operational units. Unlike traditional command staff meetings, Compstat meetings brought together units from the *entire organizational chart*. Essentially, Compstat meetings involved the entire organization meeting in one locale and thinking out loud, strategizing, to collectively problem solve and address the pressing issues of the day. Much has been written about Compstat and many scholars and practitioners agree that it represents a watershed moment in the history of American policing.

The Advent of Compstat

In 1994, the New York City Police Department ("NYPD") developed a management system that rapidly spread throughout policing in America and abroad, and "revolutionized crime fighting" (Serpas and Morley, 2008, p. 60) (see also, Mazerolle et al., 2007; Burnett, 2007).

Its effectiveness in reducing crime is well documented (but see Rosenfeld et al., 2005 who suggest that reductions in crime rate might be attributable to factors other than Compstat). It is an evidenced-based methodology for utilizing timely and accurate information to support tactical and strategic decisions. Compstat was designed as a mechanism to help the organization learn from its errors and ensure accountability. It involves "accumulating and applying knowledge of what is working and not working in different situations and contexts" (Hall and Jennings, 2008, p. 695).

Compstat represents a dramatic departure from traditional police management techniques. It entails a rigorous search for timely and accurate data and the use of such information in an interactive and collaborative forum known as the Compstat meeting. These regularly scheduled meetings take place at a central location and are chaired by the highest echelon within the organization. The most distinctive aspect of these meetings is the fact that the entire organizational chart is present and participates. That is, not only field commands but support services and specialty units attend and render their expertise and opinions.

This is a new cognitive and behavioral model that actively challenges the assertion that "bureaucracies are impersonal, technocratic machines that are incapable of wisdom" (Rooney and McKenna, 2008, p. 709). It is an evidence-based process that relies upon rigorous evaluation of accurate and timely data. But the purpose is to transform raw information into wisdom that can be acted upon. It ensures "that the best available evidence is considered in any decision to implement a program designed to prevent crime" (Welsh and Farrington, 2005, p. 338). Having the organizational chart present in one room can also serve as a protection against organizational myopia. That is, to avoid the tendency to focus on the issues at hand and to "ignore the long run" (Levinthal and March, 1993, p. 101).

Compstat is particularly effective at identifying and building upon successful practices. It also moves the point of decision making lower on the organizational chart, closer to field level, "where the decision process is less formal, where problems arise unexpectedly [and] where key choice points are embedded in the everyday flow of workplace activity" (Chapman, 2006, p. 1404). Generally speaking, it is wise to seek to resolve all problems at the lowest possible level. This utilizes local knowledge, coordination, and innovation. It also "acknowledges the sensory and visceral as important components of decision making and judgment" (Rooney and McKenna, 2008, p. 715). When raw data is interpreted in this manner it can provide true meaning and actionable knowledge.

Until recently, such evidence-based decision-making was rare in public service as

It is costly in both time and resources for governments to seek information pertaining to a particular program or practice, and policy makers rarely can await 'systemic evidentiary support' before acting. Governments are faced with short decision contexts and settings of incomplete information.

(Hall and Jennings, 2008, p. 696)

Sherman (1998) offers it, however, as an entirely new paradigm for policing. He identifies it as a particularly effective means of providing "systematic feedback to provide continuous quality improvement" (p. 6).

Since its inception within the NYPD in 1994, Compstat has rapidly spread to police departments across the United States and has transcended the field of policing. Perhaps the best example of Compstat's true potential as a public service management model exists in Baltimore, MD, where the model was adapted as CitiStat. CitiStat is a particularly effective program that was used to manage virtually all city services, such as police, fire, housing, public works, and transportation (Behn, 2005). In essence, the stat process combines the IT and decision-making resources of various agencies into one seamless network.

"It's All About the Meetings"

The Compstat model therefore allows the organization (or a group of organizations) to gather necessary information and leverage knowledge to increase organizational effectiveness, in terms of desired outputs and outcomes. It entails a relatively straightforward technology, so it is certainly not distinctive from an IT perspective (O'Connell and Straub, 2007). By far the most unique aspect of Compstat is the Compstat meeting. Rather than being a simple "staff meeting," a Compstat meeting is a dynamic interactive forum where *all levels of administration* regularly attend and participate in the decision-making process. It provides an ability to create, share and apply knowledge across organizational boundaries (Wenger et al., 2002). Weisburd et al. (2003) describe it as a system for strategic problem-solving based on management techniques and data analysis e customized into a single program for police organizations. They identify six management principles as the core of Compstat's design:

1) Clarify the agency's mission by focusing on its basic values and embodying them in tangible objectives.
2) Give priority to operational objectives over administrative ones.
3) Simplify managerial accountability for achieving those objectives.
4) Become more adept at scanning the organization's environment to identify problems early and to develop strategies to respond (data driven).
5) Increase organizational flexibility to implement the most promising strategies.
6) Learn about what works and what does not by following through with empirical assessment of what happened (p. 423).

It is imperative that all levels and branches of the organization have representation at these meetings and that the participants communicate freely and honestly. In essence, these discussions represent the organization talking aloud, listening to itself, and challenging all administrative levels to arrive at the best possible course of action. Any shared understandings that are held among senior staff members are challenged by field level managers who provide their views of the current organizational landscape.

Sociologists and psychologists agree that it is beneficial for a family to share at least one meal together each week. If this is not done, we are told that a host of problems can result. From a management standpoint, it will be virtually impossible to keep track of all the activities and plans of each family member without such a face-to-face get together. E-mail correspondence or texting only goes so far. Regularly scheduled in-person meetings are needed just to ensure that everyone "is on the same page."

Compstat meetings are akin to the family dinner table. They serve the same general purpose; a "check-in" designed to determine what is going on and how everyone is doing. Consider the following scenario: Mom and dad are seated around the dinner table with their three children, as the conversation naturally drifts towards the topic of what is going on in everyone's lives. The father might question the teenage son, "how was school today? How did you do on that math test?" The son's response might be, "how did you know I had a math test today?" The father responds, "today is Tuesday, isn't it, last week you told us that you had a big math test coming up. How did you do on it?" The son replies, "okay I guess." "You guess?" says Dad, "You're not sure? Did you study for the exam? How much effort did you put into studying for it?" At this point, the other two children are preparing their responses for a similar exchange. Immediately, everyone at the table understands that they are responsible for their activities. This is also an excellent opportunity to provide guidance, to re-enforce positive behaviors and demonstrate what poor performance looks like. A great deal of learning occurs as well.

Compstat meetings substantially alter the normal systems of discourse in a police department and increase organizational effectiveness by fostering what Rooney and McKenna (2008) call "wisdom management." (See also Argyris, 1994.) Personnel situated at field level can directly communicate with the highest level of administration, literally the chief or commissioner. This amounts to somewhat of a leap of faith on the part of top-level management who never wish to seem vulnerable or indecisive. Many no doubt initially fear the loss of control that comes about from opening the process up for discussion. It is therefore interesting that Compstat developed within the rigid rank structure of the NYPD. Perhaps its founders felt more secure in their professional status dictated by civil service rank structure.

Although Compstat has dramatically changed the NYPD and many other adopting departments, the paramilitary hierarchy remains intact. It is still up to senior-level management to select a solution, implement and evaluate it. The organization has certainly not morphed into a democracy. As O'Connell and Straub (2007) note, at the end of the day, the boss is still the boss, and the final call will always be made by the highest ranking official in the room. What differs is simply the extent of, and attitude towards, open and honest exchange during the process of fact finding and analysis.

Bureaucracies are typically quite adept at "managing" internal information, but often struggle in their efforts to obtain and use information from the external work environment. They frequently do not obtain a clear picture of the current organizational landscape and all its attendant opportunities and challenges. As Macdonald (1995) explains:

As an information organism, an information system, the firm is capable of managing its own information quite superbly. This efficiency in handling the familiar contrasts with the difficulty encountered in dealing with unfamiliar information, the sort important for change and more likely to be found outside the firm than within. Indeed, it is perhaps because the firm is geared to dealing so efficiently with its own information that it can be so clumsy with external information. The information which the firm requires to function is led along established channels within the firm to where it will be used. Established systems determine what information will flow along which channels. Such channels and systems cope best with codified and explicit information, and less formal systems have often developed to deal with tacit and uncodified information, and with information that is embodied in goods or people.

(p. 560)

Compstat meetings were designed as a mechanism of "forced" or "structured" reflection. They capture and use tacit information, institutional knowledge, and otherwise unspoken opinions held in the minds of participants. Compstat meetings draw upon the experiences of its people who are on-the-ground, people who, traditionally, never had a voice or direct access to the policy makers at the apex of the organization. Best practices and promising practices can be quickly identified and relayed throughout the organization. Compstat therefore also serves a powerful training function.

Compstat meetings lead to a degree of spontaneity and clarity that is quite unprecedented in hierarchical public service organizations. Compstat is the venue and mechanism for ongoing operational assessment.

Typically, the established rank structure stifles true open exchanges between senior administrators and their subordinates. After all, the people at the top have all the answers, don't they? What is truly unique about both Compstat and CitiStat is that top-level administrators reach beyond their inner circles (of senior staff) and really do want to hear what their subordinates think, what they see and what they do. These experiences from the field are typically clouded by internal politics and agendas, as well as sheer vertical distance within the organizational architecture. Holgersson et al. (2008) agree, noting that "an employee's perspective is caused by the position he or she has in the organization. *Higher rank officers have a totally different reality* compared with police officers at the street level" (p. 79) (emphasis supplied). They continue:

A common argument from high-ranking officers, especially among those who have once been patrol officers, is not only that they understand the street-level perspective, but that they have more knowledge than patrol officers. Often high-ranking officers believe that personnel with the street-level perspective do not fully understand phenomena in the organization. We would point to an old and well-worn problem: information is filtered on its way up in an organization. Thus, there is a great risk that decision-makers at a high level in the organization are not as well informed as they believe themselves to be.

(p. 80) (citations omitted)

The Compstat model is premised on the fact that people at the top need to hear from front line personnel, even if only to confirm the accuracy of their personal world view. It recognizes the very real need for diverse perspectives, critical discussion, self-reflection, and candor. Wide-open seeking of options and alternatives avoids selective bias, incomplete survey of options and risks, repression, and denial, and virtually every negative practice associated with groupthink. It corrects the "insufficient dialogue" that occurs in most organizations (Holgersson et al., 2008, p. 86). This radically alters the responsibilities of all members of the organization and how knowledge is obtained and used within the organization.

An even more powerful benefit is the fact that Compstat emphasizes mission focus. It demonstrates how the organization can pool its resources to collectively address current opportunities, threats, and challenges. It conveys a clear message to people situated in the lower ranks of the organization that they too have a stake in the organization's business and that their ideas and opinions have value (Ellis and Norman, 1999). This sense of trust and ownership is consistent with the general notion of the "wisdom of crowds" (Surowiecki, 2004; Fleenor, 2006).

Using the dichotomy of "street cops" versus "management cops" suggested by Reuss-Ianni (1993), the Compstat model serves to open a direct channel of communication and knowledge transfer between these two distinct sub-cultures. (See also, Holgersson et al., 2008.) More often than not, senior administrators do obtain a differing perspective that can prove to be very useful as they "steer the ship" along its strategic and tactical course.

If an organization does not script or stage its meetings, these sessions should be quite open-ended and creative. It is that degree of spontaneity and creativity that enables the organization to draw from the collective expertise of the workforce as the organization engages the inevitable uncertainties that have become a part of public service.

The adage "ask a silly question…" apparently applies. If a senior-level administrator asks the opinion or judgment of a subordinate, and if it is the job of that subordinate to respond, that administrator must be prepared for an honest response. As these meetings become incorporated into the organization's management system, its employees will become more comfortable and forthcoming and less inclined to engage in the type of self-censorship that frustrates honest exchange.

Lave and Wenger (1991) were among the first to suggest that:

> Learning is situated within a process of engagement in a "community of practice" and these are everywhere. A [community of practice] is a set of people who "share a concern, a set of problems, or a passion about a topic, who deepen their knowledge and expertise in this area by interacting on an on-going basis."
>
> (Rooney and McKenna, 2008, p. 713) (citations omitted)

A well-functioning Compstat meeting should therefore be understood as a community of practice. The meeting is an open communicative process whereby participants generally share a sense of "mutual engagement, shared repertoire, and joint enterprise" as they share knowledge, and develop and maintain long-term organizational memory (p. 713). Once the Compstat process becomes institutionalized, it quickly becomes internalized in the actions and attitudes of participants.

It represents quite a departure from typical interactions and decision patterns present in most public service organizations. Insightful, open-minded, and curious managers can be utilized to combat highly normative institutional behavior and the "natural tendency for organizational actors to be unconsciously corralled into acting 'appropriately' in routinized processes" (p. 714). It fosters true dialogue.

Dialogue is understood as "the process of discovering the meaning moving through a group of people. [It] is mutual inquiry, which is different from discussion whose root is the same as percussion and concussion. [I]t is uncovering the group mind" (Smith, 1998, p. 119). Authentic dialogue typically entails such techniques as deep listening, assumption identification, and suspension of judgment (Smith, 1998, p. 120). Deeper discussion can reveal that public service employees often operate out of personal motivations, rather than "a general altruistic motivation to serve the interests of a community of people, a state, a nation, or humankind" (Rainey and Steinbauer, 1999, p. 17).

Dialogue of this type rarely extends vertically across the administrative strata of bureaucracies.

Dehaven-Smith and Jenne (2006) have provided the most thoughtful and revealing analysis of the discursive dimension of Compstat. Applying Habermas's theory of communicative action (2001), they explain that communication is far more than the simple transfer of information. They identify Compstat as an example of "inquirement," or "management by inquiry," a process that "takes advantage of universal communicative norms" to foster genuine dialogue across organizational boundaries (p. 64). They explain that this is rarely the case in public administration:

> Today, most management systems used in American government rely more on material sanctions and incentives than on discursive communication to manage street-level administrative behavior. Although discursive processes are often employed by upper management when formulating agency objectives and strategies, they are generally considered to be incapable, by themselves, of directing administrative down through the ranks. If structured discourse is used at all for administrative personnel beneath the upper echelon, it is typically a pseudo democratic effort to foster buy-in and defuse employee dissatisfaction, not a genuine dialogue across administrative levels to set and adjust the course of administrative action.
>
> (p. 65)

They note the "surprising efficacy" of Compstat's structured discursive management processes in evaluating and directing the behavior of individuals throughout the entire organization (p. 68). Compstat's effectiveness, they believe, is attributable to its ability to foster social cooperation by asking employees to respond discursively and publicly to questions regarding how best to "assess units and personnel, allocate resources and set agency priorities" (p. 69). They believe that people within organizations generally do wish to provide their opinions, the reasons for their actions, and to stand behind what they say publicly:

> Administrative agreements reached in *inquirement* processes take on the character of vows. In part, this is because they are expressed publicly ... As Participants reveal their motives, expectations, and reasoning, and as they discursively adjust their intentions and beliefs, they are constructing their own identities as responsible professionals. To subsequently ignore agreements reached in this way is psychologically painful because it violates the individual's personhood.
>
> (p.69)

Management by inquiry is "implicitly based on the belief that motives and actions are shaped primarily by interpersonal communications and agreements. Compstat [is] designed to intensify the normal sense of obligation that human beings feel about keeping their word. The format of the discursive sessions, the physical layout of the rooms in which [it is] held, the composition of the audiences, and other features of the interrogative meetings magnify the public character of management decisions" (p. 70).

We must therefore closely examine and effectively use "the social structures and processes required to foster wisdom in organizations" (Rooney and McKenna, 2008, p. 712). Managers must understand that organizational decisions are influenced by social relationships, structures, and interactions. Such an understanding will help us determine how to foster "wise practice" (Rooney and McKenna, 2008, p. 712). on those rare occasions when the department is "hitting on all cylinders" and enjoying optimal performance, every effort should be made to maintain this pace and to continue to build upon this success. Such periods afford an excellent opportunity to learn from and explain why things are working smoothly at present; to explain and understand this success. Thus, the work is never complete. There is always much to do, even in a high-performing Police Department.

To develop an effective system of management by inquiry an organization must identify a devoted community of practice to serve as stewards and to move the model forward. This view is echoed by Willis et al. (2007) who suggest that "perhaps the limitations of Compstat's implementation [in some organizations] derive from failures of these particular organizations to execute Compstat properly" (p. 189). See also Vito et al., (2004) whose study found that, "When an individual found something wrong with any part of Compstat elements, it was not that something was wrong, but simply that the initiative could not be implemented in his or her department" (p. 194). Compstat clearly cannot be effectively implemented unless the host organization has properly prepared itself and its people.

For such a system to succeed, it must be a continuous process of collective problem-solving that ultimately becomes a mindset. Managers must always be able to evaluate where the organization is and how it has got to this point. Managers need to ask, what do we know? And what are we missing here?

In many ways Compstat re-defined the way that daily operations were performed through codifying reflection back into the decision-making process. Through a structured and facilitated dialogue, departments openly question what is happening, why it is happening, current assumptions and then change course as appropriate. This organizational self- awareness and reflection time is a radical departure from the behavior of so many organizations that are often biased towards action for action's sake. Collective wisdom cannot be properly harnessed unless thought and reflection time is scheduled and codified into the habits of routine so that knowledge can inform decisions around the re-deployment of scarce resources to meet threats.

Unfortunately, there are still many American police departments that do not fully understand the value of a Compstat-like internal performance measurement (PM) system. It is not unusual for a small to midsized American police department to schedule "command staff meetings" or "supervisors' meetings" on a quarterly basis. This is simply insufficient. The failure to have monthly meetings means that the uppermost management levels of the department simply do not know what is taking place at field level. Police chiefs are often quick to state that they are "aware of everything that is going on within their agency." But this is rarely the case. Most times, a police chief has a skewed or partial view of reality due to the lack of meaningful conversations with the men and women performing the work in the field.

In its most effective form, Compstat allows managers at the very top of their organization to have an open dialogue and obtain an intimate understanding of conditions in the field. The most essential feature of Compstat entails field commanders having direct communications with the highest levels of the organization concerning short-term tactical and long-term strategic decision-making. Compstat dramatically alters the flow of communication and decision-making in departments that have adopted it. Field commanders are afforded greater authority to make tactical decisions as they see fit. In exchange, they are held accountable for reducing crime rates and enhancing the overall level of organizational efficiency. This is the quid pro quo; a chief will relinquish a certain amount of authority and provide a field commander with additional resources, in exchange for better performance.

Compstat has been adopted with great success in many jurisdictions. Unfortunately, it has also been adopted by many jurisdictions that simply have not understood its basic philosophy and methods (Willis et al., 2004). Compstat will never succeed unless the organizational culture has been modified and prepared to accept it. Those departments that simply mimic its processes are not surprisingly doomed to failure. To succeed, departments must have regularly scheduled management meetings. Ideally, this would entail monthly management meetings. All personnel at or above the rank of Sgt. must attend these meetings, if nothing else, simply to be present, to hear the issues that are being addressed, and to be able to relay that information to the rank and file. Departments that do not meet regularly rarely have success. The most successful American police departments invariably have regularly scheduled management meetings where the issues of the day are collectively addressed, discussed, and considered, and resolved in in intelligent and collaborative fashion. This approach varies widely from the traditional hierarchical, bureaucratic approach that American police departments have historically followed.

Today, police managers must be collaborators, team builders and facilitators. The wise police manager listens more than he/she speaks and knows what they do not know. Knowledge is indeed power and the more information that a manager has, the better prepared he/she will be to address the issues of the day. Knowledge management and transfer is the key, and a wise police manager now understands that "no one of us is as smart as all of us." Management models such as Compstat take that philosophy and enable managers to reap the benefits of literally hundreds of years of experience represented by those attending monthly management meetings. The old days of the highest-ranking officer being the smartest person in the room are long gone. Police managers today utilize a more collaborative approach to management and problem solving. American policing is far "smarter" than it was years ago.

To succeed in today's environment, police managers must have an unshakable belief in continuous improvement. This attitude must be shared throughout the department. This is perhaps not as difficult as it seems. Police chiefs have a tremendous capacity for shaping the attitudes of personnel throughout their entire department. They can impact culture. Granted, rank conveys authority, but a chief's actions and demonstration of character can have a far longer lasting impact upon a department's culture than a mere order or command. Chiefs need to sincerely want to find and fix operational problems. This attitude can be contagious. A clear message from above of the need for, and value of, "continuous performance improvement" combined with sincere efforts, is all that is required.

Even if the organization is performing at peak performance levels, a great deal of work will be required to maintain that pace. Police organizations must become learning organizations. They not only need to progressively get smarter and smarter, but they also need to learn how to learn. A new culture of learning and collaboration is required of any department that is looking to improve its overall levels of performance.

Medical Grand Rounds and "Evidence-Based" Practice

The practice known as medical "grand rounds" is analogous in many ways to a Compstat meeting (in its purest form) and certainly bears discussion.

Grand rounds occur when medical professionals regularly meet to engage in open discussions regarding patient care and hospital operations. For centuries, physicians have engaged in group consultations to discuss patient care. In this way, a cardiologist can avail him or herself of the expertise of a neurologist, or a practitioner of virtually any other recognized field of medical specialization. Physicians routinized these consultations into regular meetings that occur today, in one form or another, in virtually all healthcare facilities.

Multi-disciplinary grand rounds of this type serve both as a traditional educational format and as a means of bringing an organization's (i.e., hospital's) collective resources to bear on clinical issues and individual patients' care (Derenzo et al., 2006). Its ultimate purpose is to improve the overall quality of decisions and their outcomes. Past cases are reviewed, and "real-time" decisions are made concerning the clinical care of current patients. While opinions are openly solicited, there is an underlying assumption that they must all be evidence-based. It would obviously be foolhardy to disregard clear evidence. Grand rounds have proven to be a very powerful tool for reacting to and learning from errors, complications, and unanticipated outcomes (Kravet et al., 2006).

Why is it that doctors naturally speak freely to one another about their work and seek opinions from their peers? Perhaps it is because each member of the group is a licensed physician and is therefore recognized to be a professional. Can the same be said of individuals working in large public service organizations?

The most provocative aspect of this medical model is that the concept of grand rounds has been expanded in many institutions to include the participation of *all* medical or healthcare professionals. Hospitals typically host multi-disciplinary grand round sessions that include the participation of the nursing, facilities, housekeeping, and food service departments to assess "total patient care." This is a rather holistic view that recognizes the need for effective collaboration amongst different types of professionals, but most importantly recognizes that the best person to address a nursing issue is often a nurse. All departments within the organization are presumed to conduct themselves as "professionals" within their area(s) of expertise and to assist in the core mission of the institution, quality patient care.

Akin to the Compstat model, medical professionals force reflection and think time into their schedules. Haphazard bias towards action can have catastrophic consequences for patient lives and the organization's reputation.

While all physicians working in a hospital certainly need not attend these sessions, some representatives will. All other divisions will similarly send representatives who are prepared and willing to represent their colleagues' views and opinions. Multi-disciplinary grand rounds are far more effective than a flurry of personal memos or e-mails passing from the chief surgeon, through channels to the director of nursing concerning an equipment problem in the operating room (no doubt a time-consuming process). This issue can be more effectively addressed at a group meeting where decision makers can hear from the people who purchase, maintain, and regularly use this equipment and utilize their input as a basis for a more thoughtful response.

Again, this process does not alter the existing power structure within the organization. The person with decision-making authority will, at the conclusion of discussions, still have the authority and responsibility to make the decision. It will simply be a more informed one. There is no loss of power within the organization. Power is not transferred, knowledge is.

Top-level management must be represented at these meetings, for them to proceed in an orderly fashion. Hofmann (1993) also emphasizes the symbolic significance of having top-level executives participate in these exercises. It demonstrates the importance of the undertaking and conveys a pervasive sense of mutual respect for individuals with diverse talents and responsibilities.

However, the quest for supportive evidence can obviously be taken to an extreme. Rigorous experimental evidence is certainly not required for everyday, more mundane decisions. Some decisions obviously have more significant consequences than others.

Hall and Jennings (2008) have developed a model that suggests that high-risk decisions require more rigorous evidence in the planning and implementation stage. Conversely, they suggest that "Where risk is low, the level of evidence required to adopt a practice should not be prohibitively high. Thus, normative, and practice-based findings are probably adequate for most low-risk settings" (p. 701).

There is obviously a very fine line here. To avoid satisficing, organizations will seek additional evidence. Over time, too many metrics and data points can drown out clarity as information overload simply buries key insights. The goal is to draw the distinction between data and meaning. Too much data can obscure meaning. T Perhaps organizations should not always seek "best" practices, but rather "strateg[ies] that [are] superior when directly compared to all other strategies and interventions." This requires a qualitative judgment that a course is supported by data and the collective judgment of the organization.

The "Red Team" Approach

Decision teams have a tendency of only seeing data that supports their beliefs. The use of the "Red Team" structure has traditionally been used in military war gaming scenarios. The concept has also been applied outside of the military context, to address private security issues, such as attempts to breach highly secured facilities (Adcox and Engells, 2007). The main purpose is the activation of a "counterfactual mindset" (Kray and Galinsky, 2003). (But see, Moon et al., 2003, who question the assertion that promoting divergent views in groups is always beneficial.)

Red Team group dynamics entails the designation of a team of experts who can openly challenge and attack current assumptions, policies, and practices. Thus, the Red Team concept has applicability to any group decision making. Under this construct, group members are, on a macro level, formed to challenge their cultural values and norms, rational method of thinking and world views. This concept is designed to offset the so-called "mirror image" type of thinking evident in either an organizational structure or individual.

Red Teams are ideally composed of members from different echelons, organizations, or individual backgrounds (which can include socio-economic or cultural). They are generally directed to "get outside traditional ways of thinking" (Craig, 2007, p. 57). This technique goes one step beyond self-criticism. It entails the designation of a team of experts to openly challenge (i.e., attack) current assumptions, policies, and practices.

The decision-making is taken away from the traditional collective "group think" management structure. At its elemental level, discussions are dynamic and adversarial – challenging standard precepts and thereby expanding decision making options. To work effectively, the Red Team "thinks" as an adversary would, by considering the range of outcomes based on unique assumptions that an adversary would use. It is analogous to a "white hat" hacker being hired to attack a company's data systems. Much useful information can be learned.

Red Team assessments can be made at either a strategic or tactical level and often are a departure point from traditional linkage analyses. T All analysis has biases, but the Red Team concept tries to mitigate these biases. This is not an easy task for "it remains very difficult to get beyond the typical interaction and decision patterns in our organizations (Smith 1998, p 119). In essence the Red Team "de biases" thinking by actively seeking "disconfirmatory" information (Kray and Galinsky, 2003).

Red Team members must have a detailed knowledge and understanding of the adversary's operational environment in order to function effectively. An effective Red Team membership therefore must be composed of individuals with a wide range of expertise – often this is what sets the Red Team apart from normal decision-making groups.

In this manner, the Red Team can "role play" how an adversary would act based on in-depth knowledge of influence factors. To operate effectively, it is essential that members of the group be intimately familiar with the target, or if possible, have similar ethnic or neighborhood background and character or life experiences. At a minimum, members of the Red Team must have extensively operated in a similar environment as the adversary.

The Red Team concept is only as good as decision makers are willing to consider data presented. This type of discussion must not denigrate into unbounded wild ideas, for there must be a minimum criterion to consider acceptable ranges of actions. The boundaries placed on consideration of alternative courses of action is the most challenging aspect of running a Red Team, as the process must be an open and iterative process.

T. At its best, the Red Team challenges underlying assumptions by analyzing problem sets from the perspective of an adversary's preferences – it extends the range of decision outcomes available. Red Team assessments do not always lead to consensus or uncover all ranges of options, but can lead to a critical review of potential courses of action that were previously dismissed or unanticipated. In this manner effective policy, resource, technical or operational decisions can then be structured.

Clearly, the average American police department is simply not large enough to establish a red team practice within its performance measurement (PM) system. But every American police department can in fact learn much from this practice. It is the concept of the red team, its underlying philosophy (that none of us is as smart as all of us) that holds the potential for increasing operational efficiency and avoiding unnecessary risk in police operations. While risk can never be totally eliminated from policing, it can certainly be managed and minimized. The open and honest exchange of opinions within a Compstat meeting can achieve the same result. By asking subordinates to critically review a department's plans while they are still in the development stage, many needless mistakes can be avoided at a time when corrective action can be taken.

It is important for an organization to have mechanisms designed to actively seek "disconfirmatory" information (Kray and Galinsky, 2003) and provide an opportunity for opposition to build up (Schwartz, 1994). Perhaps this could occur more frequently if there were a "loosening of the reins" of leadership. This is certainly not to suggest a total or permanent divestment of power and authority. It is simply an occasional technique that can be signify an openness to new ideas and the ability to "get beyond the typical interaction and decision patterns in our organizations" (Smith, 1998, p. 119).

Peter Senge (1994) describes the need for creative tension within organizations:

> Imagine a rubber band, stretched between your vision and current reality. When stretched, the rubber band creates tension, representing the tension between vision and current reality. What does tension seek? Resolution or release. There are only 2 possible ways for the tension to resolve itself: whole reality toward the vision or pull the vision toward reality. Which occurs will depend on whether we hold steady to the vision.
>
> (p. 150)

Every police department needs to have a vision and a framework for decision-making. *Ad hoc* decisions are generally not effective ones. They are certainly not long-term solutions to problems. Police managers must reject the simplistic problem-response approach to management. This is akin to playing the carnival game of "*Whack-A-Mole*." While this

approach moves the organization forward by solving problems as they arise, it stifles learning and true improvement. A better and more thoughtful process would yield better results.

Managers need to always know where the organization is now (in terms of operational
performance) and what the options are. It is always best to perform environmental scanning
of this type prior to developing or implementing any plans. As Luthans point s out, many
organizations have unfortunately grown accustomed to an approach that more resembles
"ready, fire aim." Important decisions and actions often take place in police departments
without sufficient consideration. In a misguided attempt to resolve matters quickly, police
managers often act first and then worry about providing justification (if it is even necessary at all) afterwards. Clearly, this is not a recipe for success. Managers must understand
that not every issue that initially gets labeled as an "emergency" is one. There is usually
enough time to assess and consider before acting; take advantage of this opportunity. Albert
Einstein once said, "It is much more important to get a good grasp of the problem than to
get an answer."

Police managers must listen to diverse voices and should do so frequently. Ideally, these
discussions will take place at Compstat meetings. Police managers must mediate those
diverse voices by having a moral compass, a set of convictions or personal beliefs that are
consistent with the organization's goals.

Police managers must have humility and the confidence to give voice to dissent at some
point during the management process. There is much useful information that can be
accessed. There is always much to be learned. Feedback is in fact a gift. A large ego on the
command staff can be quite an impediment to progress. In most police departments, egos
must be contended with as much as the rigid rank structure. Both can be fatal to learning.

Remember: Police chiefs can accomplish great things if they don't care who gets the
credit.

Bosses need to be transparent and honest with one another, regardless of rank. Thus, captains and sergeants, lieutenants and the deputy chief should all be communicating openly
and honestly during Compstat-like command staff meetings. This is often difficult, but it
certainly is possible. The key is for the chief to set an example. It starts at the top. If not:

> If the team leader is reluctant to acknowledge his or her mistakes or fails to admit to a
> weakness that is evident to everyone else, there is little hope that other members of the
> team are going to take that step themselves. In fact, it probably wouldn't be advisable for
> them to do so because there is a good chance that their vulnerability would be neither
> encouraged nor rewarded. The only way for the leader of a team to create a safe envir-
> onment for his team members to vulnerable Is by stepping up and doing something that
> feels unsafe and uncomfortable first. By getting naked before anyone else, by taking the
> risk of making himself honorable with no guarantee that other members of the team will
> respond in kind, a leader demonstrates an extraordinary level of selflessness and dedi-
> cation to the team. And that gives him the right, and the confidence, to ask others to do
> the same. When team members trust one another, when they know that everyone on the
> team is capable of admitting when they don't have the right answer, and when they are
> willing to acknowledge when someone else's idea is better than theirs, the fear of conflict
> and the discomfort it entails is greatly diminished. When there is trust, conflict becomes
> nothing but the pursuit of truth, an attempt to find the best possible answer. It is not only
> okay but desirable. Conflict without trust, however, is politics, an attempt to manipulate
> others in order to win an argument regardless of the truth.
>
> (Lencioni, 2012, p. 35–38)

American policing is certainly not a democracy; nor is it a free for all. We want and need to encourage input and buy-in from all supervisors, but not all opinions, once they are stated, deserve equal time. All of them must be supported by evidence or they deserve to be rejected.

Police managers must clearly communicate expectations. For this reason, all police departments must have clear and comprehensive job descriptions for every sworn and unsworn employee of the department. Employees should not have to guess as to what exactly is expected of them. Supervisors need to review and discuss these expectations with subordinates regularly, during annual performance evaluations and at the end of each month as unit performance is evaluated.

Uniformed members of the service at or above the rank of sergeant should be understood as members of a leadership team. Senior command staff typically consists of higher ranks, but all sergeants and above should understand their roles as managers and leaders. Unfortunately, supervisors who are assigned to distinct units typically focus their attention upon their little corner of the world and fail to see the big picture. Their roles and function within the department might resemble a "working group," but these individuals are certainly not acting as a true team. As Lencioni (2012) explains:

> A good way to understand the working group is to think of it like a golf team, where players go off and play on their own and then get together and add up their scores at the end of the day a real team is more like a basketball team, one that plays together simultaneously, in an interactive, mutually dependent, and often interchangeable way. Most working groups reflexively call themselves teams because that is the word society uses to describe any group of people who are affiliated in their work. Becoming a real team requires an intentional decision on the part of its members. I like to say that teamwork is not a virtue. It is a choice – and a strategic one.
>
> (p. 21)

Real team members "go to meetings to help their team members solve problems even when those problems have nothing to do with their [individual units or area(s) of responsibility]." (p. 25)

The following section describes the "best practices" of any Compstat – like performance management system – one that utilizes interactive meetings as an essential component. It contains various recommendations for establishing and maintaining a culture of performance in any police department. It also suggests how to obtain the maximum benefit from this form of management system. These best practices were initially derived by O'Connell and Straub (2007) from observations of large police departments, such as New York, Baltimore, and St. Louis. Since then, they have been observed in scores of small and midsize police departments across the United States:

Regarding Implementation

- For any performance-based management system to function properly, top level management must express and reaffirm its dissatisfaction with the status quo. Performance-based management is based on ongoing organizational learning and continuous improvement; it adheres to the idea of "better" rather than "best practices."

- To achieve success, traditional bureaucratic management models should be replaced with more intelligent. The CompStat philosophy is based on a presumption that field commanders are best suited to make field decisions. Even in a relatively small police department, a patrol supervisor who was at the scene is typically in a better position to analyze and determine an appropriate course of action. Field commanders must receive adequate resources, personnel, decision-making freedom, and support from the uppermost levels of the organization. In return, upper management can expect a higher degree of personal accountability from commanders. There is a clear quid pro quo here. While some aspects of reported crime rates are clearly beyond the field commanders' control, what is under their control is the commitment to use best efforts to reduce crime. Some percentage of violent crime is unavoidable and unpredictable, since it is spontaneous (such as a stabbing in a nightclub); however, diligent, and effective policing techniques can reduce the likelihood of tragic occurrences (such as aggressive enforcement of alcohol beverage control laws, local noise ordinances, etc.).
- Performance-based management systems should monitor more than the organization's relative success at achieving such short-range goals (i.e., a "snapshot" or "dipstick" measure of current performance). They should be used to set and to monitor short, medium, and long-range goals.
- Performance-based management systems help the organization "identify emerging conditions, problems, needs and issues [and to] view them as change opportunities" (Downes, 1998, p. 657)
- To ensure success, there must be a modern organizational and information technology (IT) infrastructure in place. GIS capabilities might not be necessary if analysis is not going to be based on geographic comparisons (modern spreadsheet capabilities might be sufficient to produce descriptive statistics, graphs, etc.).
- There must be an auditing and inspections unit to ensure the timeliness and accuracy of the data used. Sometimes, data is simply too old to be useful. Some data do not have "the currency program managers usually need to react" (Hatry et al., 2003, p. 13)
- The process should always be understood as evolutionary, not stagnant; it must be modified and perfected constantly. There is always room for improvement in seeking better practices.
- The performance-based management system must be the prevailing management philosophy throughout the entire organizational chart. To maximize effectiveness, it must be pervasive – not limited to disciplinary or auditing functions, nor to one unit or section. It requires a buy-in by all members of the organization.
- Selection of performance indicators must be a collaborative and fluid process focused on what is important to the organization at this time. Managers should consider the existence of multiple plausible measures to capture each concept (Nicholson-Crotty et al., 2006)
- When selecting indicators, it is important to address core business practices. Identify the organization's most important functions and focus on those 1sts. The list of performance indicators can always be expanded and refined later. It was only after the New York City department of correction was able to control inmate violence (one of the first things measured by its performance-based management system, known as TEAMS), that they were able to address other issues (such as tracking and addressing in many complaints and grievances, or producing inmates for court appearances in a

timely fashion, etc.). Since virtually nothing could be accomplished until the organization provided a safe and secure environment for both staff and inmates, it was important to address violence (a "reactive" process) before more constructive (proactive) measures could be taken.

- The following is a list of performance indicators that are commonly monitored in sophisticated police departments:

  o The total number of training hours performed, and the type and total number of personnel trained.

  o The type and number of use-of-force reports prepared, personnel involved, time and place of occurrence, and general description of circumstances.

  o The geographic location (i.e., zone) and time of all arrests.

  o The geographic location and time of citations issued.

  o The type and number of civilian and internal complaints (and dispositions).

  o The type, number, location, and time of civilian vehicle accidents.

  o The type, number, location, and time of department vehicle accidents, both "at fault" and "no fault" accidents.

  o The type, number, location, and nature of all firearm discharges.

  o The results of systematic and random audits and inspections of all police operations (i.e., calls for service response and dispositions, property receipt and safeguarding, etc.).

  o The type, location, and number of any Terry stops (i.e., investigatory stops of suspects, otherwise known as stop, question, and frisks, or field investigations) performed, as well as a description of all individuals involved, and a description of all actions taken. Data obtained in connection with these stops should be analyzed and actively tracked. This means that it is imperative that officers record all such investigative encounters in the department's RMS. It is important for the department to know: 1) how many stops are being made, 2) by whom, 3) who is being stopped, 4) where, 5) when, and 6) for what reason(s). Note: Information of this type is recommended by the *Final Report of the President's Task Force on 21st Century Policing.*

- The purpose and practices of a performance-based management system should be incorporated into the training curricula for all personnel, from the initial hiring through in-service training for all personnel.

- Whenever a performance-based management system is adopted, the organization must afford its managers ample opportunity to adjust to the new management system and to alter their practices accordingly. This involves training and emphasis on the transition process. Too rapid a shift in organizational philosophy and management approach could do more harm than good, particularly in a struggling organization.

- Implementation is only the "tip of the iceberg." A considerable amount of time and energy must be expended to ensure that the mechanism survives. Short-term success is encouraging and not sufficient. Continual cooperative effort and commitment are mandatory ingredients for further success.

- To ensure the long-term viability of a performance-based management process, agencies must utilize enough motivated and creative administrators who are both students of, and be levers in, the process. High level personnel changeovers and provide opportunities for creativity and innovation if there is also continuity and strong leadership.

Regarding the Meetings

- The entire organizational chart must be represented at all meetings. Participants should include all supervisors at or above the rank of Sgt. representing all operational units within the department.
- In large police departments (e.g., a major city or large Sheriff's Department) there should be a dais made up of senior command staff. The dais must include one or more "operational" people with extensive field experience in the respect of those in the field. Less experienced commanders can be stonewalled or more easily misled. You must know the job to monitor the work properly and to move the organization forward.
- There must be a competent and creative chief inquisitor, a top-level administrator who leads the discussions at all meetings. This will usually be a member of the senior command staff. Another method of enabling participation is to "deconstruct" meetings by letting subordinates (captains or lieutenants) determine the agenda and run the meeting (in its entirety or only a designated portion) in the presence of leadership. For this method to be effective, leaders must overcome the temptation to take charge. This concept does not prevent participation by leadership, but rather enables subordinates to engage directly in leading discussions that should present effective options to decision makers.

  This structure has multiple benefits. It obviously serves a symbolic purpose, demonstrating a degree of trust and authentic openness to new ideas, methods, and approaches. Perhaps some group members will be more inclined to participate when speaking with managers who are situated more closely on the organizational chart. Also, leaders can gauge the effectiveness of subordinate's leadership and presentation styles, and subordinates can have direct impact on the decision process. Most likely a more lively and wide-ranging discussion will ensue. In this manner, subordinates are made "stakeholders" in the overall process.

- Meetings should be held at headquarters away from many of the distractions in the field. This serves a symbolic purpose and draws on additional resources (personnel, equipment) that are rarely available in the field.
- There must be an authentic and spontaneous dialogue during meetings – a lively discussion, not in the Inquisition. Like the Socratic method of inquiry used in most US law schools, it involves point, counterpoint, and thoughtful responses to questions. It should not, however, resemble a deposition, where the respondent is interrogated. It is an art, a skill developed over time.
- The meetings are not disciplinary tools – there is always a need to address successes as well as failures. A negative connotation for these meetings is bad for morale and will severely limit their utility.
- In large departments, all presentations should include a profile of the department/unit presenting, as well as its highest-ranking administrator. This would include date of appointment, geographic areas of responsibility, personnel and resources under command, a photograph, etc. This alleviates the need to have introductions, which take time and detract from the overall quality of presentations (this would obviously not be necessary in small departments or agencies).
- Meetings must be scheduled early in the workday, preferably 7 AM, so that participants will not be distracted by other issues and matters.
- A review of patrol operations, detective investigations/ case updates, narcotics enforcement, community policing efforts, traffic analysis and enforcement operations, training

updates, community outreach/crime prevention efforts should always be included on the agenda and should generally be presented in the same order at every meeting.

Not every problem deserves the same amount of attention. A certain amount of triage is required. It is important for leadership to decide which set of problems are least problematic. These can be delegated or put off until another day. Others require immediate solutions. Knowing the difference makes all the difference when it comes to good management.

- All meetings should be recorded. It is always preferable to send presenters back to their commands and units with either a tape or a stenographic record/minute of what exactly was said during the meeting. This is necessary for follow-up purposes and for critiques of one's own performance.
- Non-presenting units or agencies should send a representative to attend meetings if it is anticipated that the agenda will include issues pertinent to them. Ultimately, meetings should all be available online and be interactive (e.g., Zoom or Skype) so that the entire organization (and perhaps select outside agencies and officials) can observe and participate.
- Someone on the dais must be chiefly responsible for recognizing instances of micro-management; detailed discussions that are not pertinent to the entire organization which should be discussed by the interested parties later.
- Participants must always be on the lookout for collaboration opportunities with outside agencies.
- A businesslike atmosphere should be maintained, always characterized by mutual respect. Top level management must constantly be alert for personal attacks or unwarranted criticisms. One person at a time should have the floor.
- Meetings must be scheduled frequently, based on the needs of the specific organization. The process is the equivalent of the organization checking its own pulse; better health depends on proper monitoring. If departments and subunits are obtaining useful information and redirection, they will look forward to these meetings.
- Positive comments must be communicated with the same level of sincerity and concern as criticisms. It is important not only to praise the presenter(s), but also the individuals performing the work within the agency as well.
- Top level administrators should be aware not to get bogged down in retrospective analysis. They should look back only as far as necessary to explain what's going on now and what can be expected in the future. Too much attention on the past prevents progress.
- Discussions about poor performance typically led to training opportunities, and learning takes place in both directions. Presenters should describe their standard operating procedures – how they do things. Top administrators generally know and understand the ends (organizational goals) but not always the means (how things get done in the field). This process provides a perfect opportunity for bridging the knowledge gap between management and the rank and file.
- Preparation is the key. All data and information must be shared well in advance of the meetings. An agenda should be prepared and distributed to all participants several days prior to the meeting. Comments from top administrators should be relayed to field units prior to the scheduled meetings. This does not mean everything is scripted but major issues should be communicated so that participants can reflect on potential questions and formulate thoughtful responses.

- Field units should engage in many meetings to prepare for the larger, more comprehensive meetings. They should meet well in advance of the larger meeting to address anticipated areas of inquiry.
- It is very important to have a recap, "what we have learned today," at the conclusion of each meeting and to clearly articulate and record who is going to be following up with whom.
- Questioners should always be on the lookout for training opportunities to identify potential topics for additional in-service training. Indeed, the director of training, or his/her representative should also be in attendance and should be primarily charged with doing this as well. If a mistake is made by one manager or officer, it is often likely that others will make the same mistake. Negative trends can be stopped sooner if the process includes constant monitoring of areas needing additional training.

Regarding the Flow of Information and Ideas

- Meetings are the organizational equivalent of thinking out loud: weighing options for addressing information obtained from the internal and external work environments; reflecting; brainstorming; attempting to select the most rational and effective course of action; and drawing on all organizational resources, including the practices and opinions of key personnel.
- The flow of information must be in two directions. There must be an active dialogue. All parties actively teach and learn.
- This process relies primarily on the information that is compiled in the ordinary course of business, but it also draws on tacit knowledge in the organization – information that is possessed in the field and is more associated with personal skills (Cook and Brown, 1999).
- Interactive discussions like these "generate new knowledge and new ways of knowing" (Cook and Brown, 1999, p. 381)
- Presenters should be dissuaded from responding with statements such as, "where working on that," or "we will take that under advisement." Such platitudes stifle the dialogue and are nonproductive. Officials should keep the momentum moving in a positive direction: "please get back to us with an action plan that outlines the steps you will be taking to correct this situation." Follow-up questions are important to encourage more dialogue.
- Top level administrators should use questions like: how did this happen? Why did this happen?; What is causing it to happen?; When did this happen and how long has it been like this?; and What can we do to change (or sustain) this?
- An effort should be made to develop the public speaking and critical thinking skills of individuals who will be expected to be present at meetings. This can be done by creating an executive development program or by engaging outside consultants to develop necessary skills for managers and administrators. The NYPD introduced a Compstat college, where newly promoted managers are introduced to the process through practice meetings; the New York City Department of Corrections calls a similar program of its own the "leadership Institute."
- In addition to executive development courses, a system of personal (one on one) mentoring could be valuable. Newly promoted managers could and should learn from the experiences of more senior personnel.

- The performance management process is a philosophy as well as a mechanism or technique. For some, it is an entirely new way of thinking and approaching one's work. Agency goals and methods must be internalized by managers; they must believe in the utility of their department's performance management system and should begin to incorporate it into their day-to-day decisions and actions.

Regarding the Collection, Analysis, and Dissemination of Data

- The key issue is the timeliness and accuracy of the data (i.e., how quickly does the information come to the research unit from the field?). If the accuracy is questionable or if the information is stale, it gives presenters "wiggle room" to explain away poor performance. For example, "those numbers are not up to date, we are actually doing much better than that today!" or "We have already corrected that condition." Stale data will slow and entirely undermine the process.
- To be truly meaningful, all data must be reviewed by senior management – both positive and negative performance information. They should not view performance indicators in a vacuum. They must always have a "global" or "systems" (Senge) perspective to truly understand the overall health and performance of the entire organization.
- Managers should be vigilant to avoid pitfalls associated with the "paradox of data overload" (Kamarck, 2005, p. 9) in many instances, so much information is made available that it makes analysis and effective use virtually impossible.
- Managers who are being reviewed should be geographically and/or temporally accountable. That is, they should have a proprietary interest, or a specific responsibility for the work being performed in a particular area or during a particular shift, by a specific group of people. They need to have a "stake" in the work being performed if they are to be held accountable.
- Accountability only goes so far. There will always be instances where a crime wave occurs spontaneously despite the best efforts of the police all where a school district's test scores drop precipitously from the rapid influx of non-English speaking immigrants. Events are explainable and understandable if we see them in context and use the information provided to us by statistics. Statisticians referred to these situations as outliers. There will always be "unusual" situations that fall on the extreme ends of the bell curve. The key is to understand the uniqueness of situations and to learn from them. We need to create and use institutional memory to provide contexts for all events.
- It is important to identify equivalent units to have effective comparisons, so that comparisons are considered "apples to apples."
- All performance measures must be meaningful and must address the core mission and basic goals of the organization. Don't measure what does not matter.
- Performance measures must be relevant – they must be meaningful and of real use to the organization. Managers must resist the tendency to measure the measurable – "focusing on what's easily measured leads to 'looking good without being good'" (Senge, 1994, p. 304)
- Performance indicators must continually be reviewed and revised. It is imperative that the entire organization understand the meaning of each of the indicators and that they use a common definition. There must be a common understanding. Perhaps the number of recorded public "complaints" are, on further reflection and analysis, requests for information.

- Numbers do not have any meaning unto themselves, they must be interpreted. Police managers must familiarize themselves with the concept of bounded rationality (Jones, 2003), whereby decision-makers tend not to fully explore all possible options and explanations.
- Managers must recognize that they will never have all the information regarding any upcoming decision. The key question to ask is whether you have all the information you need.
- Police managers should also be aware of the phenomenon known as confirmation bias. This occurs "when people observe more, give extra emphasis to, or intentionally look for evidence that would validate their existing beliefs and expectations and are likely to excuse or completely ignore evidence that could reject their beliefs" (Byrd, 2006, p. 511)
- When measuring an agency's efficiency, a key question is "efficient for whom?" Administrators must always understand the needs of their end users and stakeholders (i.e., the public, business owners, homeowners, advocates for the homeless, senior citizens, etc.). And efficiently performing public service organization can nonetheless be "inefficient" if it fails to meet the goals and expectations of the public, or a major subset thereof.
- Positive trends or increases in productivity must be sustained and thoroughly examined. There is much to be learned here. Focus must be placed on sustaining positive trends, not just identifying, and eliminating negative ones.
- Top level managers or individuals on their staff must have a working knowledge of statistics. They should know how to use and interpret comparative statistics; they should also understand the phenomenon of regression towards the mean. "Bottoming out" is a natural phenomenon. It is likely that a skilled crime analyst can be utilized to provide additional support in this regard.
- A fundamental knowledge of statistics includes familiarity with the term's correlation and causation and the distinction between the two.
- Managers should be aware that "even when a program is doing what it showed, there may be a long-time lag between program activities and observable impacts" (Gilmour, 2006, p. 28)
- Management must understand that statistics can always be interpreted in several ways; however, they must always be intelligently interpreted. This applies to all types of performance measurement systems, not just police management systems. For example, if sanitation trucks are completing their routes more quickly, one would assume that to be a good thing. But perhaps not. Maybe they are coming into soon by not making all their pickups. Sometimes quality is far better than quantity; it depends on what you are measuring. Managers need to look at the big picture rather than a single performance category. They need to use the entire constellation of performance measures for the entire agency. That is where the true story is. Police managers can, for example, compare the relative performance of officers assigned to patrol, investigative units, community affairs, etc.
- Managers must always be aware of similarities and distinctions between units. Returning to waste disposal and analogy, perhaps one garbage route in a downtown area is inherently more difficult and slow work than many others. Just like police patrol sectors or commands in different neighborhoods, each has a different top biography, traffic flow, population density, etc. Managers obviously need to know their agency, the nature of the work, and their people. Once appropriate baselines are established (means, medians, and

modes) for each unit, they will have a proper frame of reference. Then they will be able to judge the overall and relative performance of different units.

- Managers need to establish "reasonable" (obtainable and sustainable) baselines for each unit and supervisor. Geography remains the same, it is therefore considered in the establishment of baselines. It is unreasonable to assume that baselines will be identical for all units, although one could expect them to be substantially similar if their overall mission and operations are similar.

- The increases or reductions indicated in performance measures should never be viewed as absolutes but rather as a basis for intelligent inquiry and discussion. Without meaningful dialogue among decision-makers and rank and file, top level managers run the risk of relying exclusively on data reflected in performance indicators and it might only obtain a partial view of organizational performance (Buckmaster, 2000).

- Data must be delved into and truly analyzed. There should be a constant search for statistically significant variations and possible correlations.

- It appears that there is a generic "fistful response" used by presenters during these meetings to deflect criticism: "I'm aware of that [condition or deficiency] I don't have the resources available to address that, I have more important issues to address." Such a response could stifle further discussion. In effect, it insulates the party from further criticism and justifies deficiencies in performance. Budgetary constraints should be no surprise to either party. If a particular corrective measure cannot be undertaken for fiscal reasons, it should be discussed in detail, either during the meeting or later with interested parties in attendance.

- Every effort should be made to ensure that a form of tunnel vision does not develop, whereby managers become overly "stat conscious" and work exclusively on crimes and matters included as performance indicators. "Constantly holding district commanders accountable for the same crimes at CompStat [meetings] may lead to potentially useful crime related information being overlooked." (Willis et al., 2004, p. 34)

- Other agencies, such as probation and parole departments and offices of the prosecuting attorney should participate in the process. For a variety of reasons, other agencies might not be able to send a representative to participate in the meetings. If this is the case, the police agency should ensure that relevant information that was addressed at these meetings is forwarded to the necessary parties, either through one-on-one meetings or via an ongoing transfer of analyzed data.

- Some recapitulation of periodic meetings should be made available to the public, preferably via the department's website.

- Although meetings should not generally be open to the public due to the sensitive nature of many of the data and discussions concerning criminal activity and ongoing police investigations, select members of the community might be periodically invited to attend and participate. Their observation of the proceedings will strengthen police community relations [akin to the benefits of a citizens police Academy] and their insights could be used to provide the police with community members' perspectives and concerns. The importance of public involvement cannot be overstated. As Mark Moore and Anthony Braga (2004) suggest, the important question that lies at the core of developing any adequate measure of police performance is for citizens and their elected representatives to decide what it is that they as a political community value in the activities and operations of a public police department (p. 4, see also Collier, 2001).

- A performance management system will ultimately fail unless it is utilized for true organizational brainstorming. The system must be used to identify organizational strengths, weaknesses, opportunities, and threats (both internal and external to the organization). It should be used not only to identify and close performance gaps but also to ensure that they stay closed.
- Performance indicators must have the ability to detail and measurable evidence necessary to demonstrate that an intervention has achieved desired results. For that reason, each performance indicator should be tied logically and expressly to the stated strategic goals of the department. These, in turn, should be directly linked to the overriding organizational mission (as expressed in the agency's mission statement); there should be no guesswork involved. All employees should understand the importance of these indicators and why they need to be tracked continually.
- Practitioners must understand that progress might be made in a certain performance category even though the performance measurement system does not yet detect any significant improvement. This occurs due to the phenomenon known as non-linearity:

There is probably a dynamic of change that we all misunderstand. We must recognize that all of us have a predisposition to linear thinking (A leads to B, B leads to C, etc.) when in fact an awful lot of change comes from situations where things get worse before they get better. It's similar to the case of non-linear thermodynamics, where we talk about the system having to become more and more in this equilibrium, or disharmony, in order to move to a new state of order.

(Fulmer and Keys, 1998, p. 37)

- Brainstorming and innovative problem-solving techniques should be employed by all participants. Managers should be free to "think outside the box" and suggest innovative solutions to pressing problems. The key is to engage these individuals. Pascale and Sternin (2005) stressed the need for identifying "positive deviance." That is, individuals who are "on the periphery of their organizations ... Who are far removed from the orthodoxies of mainstream change endeavors. These innovators uncommon practices and behaviors enable them to find better solutions to problems than others in their [organizations]" (p. 72) police managers and become hesitant to concern themselves with the issues that arise outside of their geographic area of responsibility (Willis, Mastrofski, and Weisburd, 2003). They might also refrain from rendering opinions for fear of testing their colleagues in a bad light, particularly during meetings. These problems can and will undoubtedly occur unless the tone is set from above. The performance management model will only succeed with a full and open exchange of information. This involves not only timely and accurate crime data but also the collective wisdom of all participants. While it is no doubt difficult to establish this type of atmosphere, it can be accomplished if the top levels of management encourage it. Each department or agency had must continually reinforce the need for open channels of communication. Opinions should be solicited and freely offered. As problems occur, the overriding question should be, "why is this happening Western Mark" the manager with geographic responsibility for that area will obviously be in an ideal position to understand the who, what, when, and where of the incident, but not necessarily the why.

In many instances, scores, if not hundreds of years of policing experience are assembled in one meeting room. It would be foolhardy to neglect to tap into this extensive, specialized knowledge base. Some problems will continue to exist, but many can be solved by using the collective wisdom of all participants. When any proposed course of action is suggested, an essential feature should be the cost-benefit analysis. As a manager proposes a certain tactic or response, others should be encouraged to voice their opinions regarding possible ramifications and to identify all relevant pros and cons. For example, a tactic proposed by a field commander might prompt a response from a legal, budgetary, or collective-bargaining perspective.

- During meetings, some individual or unit needs to be charged with identifying and discussing the relative costs and benefits of all proposed action plans, versus ignoring those needs and tasks. In a financial sense, this function is generally referred to as "cost consequences analysis" and seeks to determine "prospective return on investment estimates for potential solutions" (Leigh, 2004, p. 625). Discussions that are entirely theoretical or utopian in nature will only generate unfeasible or impractical solutions that will serve no real purpose for the organization. Someone should always be asking the following questions: can we do it? Is it practical? How much will it cost? And how will it affect our other plans and operations? And often more important and provocative question is, "how much will it cost us to ignore it?"

- The crime analysis unit (or some equivalent) should regularly interact with field managers and should be fully integrated into the agency's ongoing management operations. Unfortunately, this is often not the case (see Willis, Mastrofski, Weisburd, and Greenspan, 2003). What is desired is a state of synchrony, where managers from all units work as a team (Kamarck, 2005).

- Whenever the performance management system is used to spearhead or direct any specific initiative, operation, or program, there should be consensus among all stakeholders concerning the following: 1) the activities that constitute the program; 2) the intended the effects of the program; 3) the order in which effects are expected to occur; 4) the activities that are expected to produce the effects; and 5) the effects that will be used to determine the success of the program (Chapel, 2004, p. 642)

References

Adcox, W. H., & Engells, T. E. (2007). The red team: An innovative quality control practice in facility security. *The Police Chief*, 74(7), 54.

Argyris, C. (1994). Good communication that blocks learning. *Harvard Business Review*, 72(4), 77–86.

Behn, R. D. (2005). The core drivers of Citistat: It's not just about the meetings and the maps. *International Public Management Journal*, 8(3), 295–319.

Berthon, P., Leyland, F. P., & Ewing, M. T. (2001). Corollaries of the collective: The influence of organizational culture and memory development on perceived decision-making context. *Journal of the Academy of Marketing Science*, 29(2), 135–150.

Buckmaster, N. (2000). The performance measurement panacea. *Accounting Forum*, 24(3), 264–277.

Burnett, E. (2007). Crime analysis reporting and mapping for small agencies: a low-cost and simplified approach. *FBI Law Enforcement Bulletin*, 76(10), 15–22.

Byrd, J. S. (2006). Confirmation bias, ethics, and mistakes in forensics. *Journal of Forensic Identification*, 56(4), 511–526.

Chapel, T. (2004). Constructing and using logic models in program evaluation. In Roberts, A. R. and Yeager, R. (eds.). *Evidence-Based Practice Manual: Research and Outcome Measures in Health and Human Services*. 636–647. Oxford University Press.

Chapman, J. (2006). Anxiety and defective decision making: An elaboration of the groupthink model. *Management Decision*, 44(10), 1391–1404.

Collier, P. M. (2001). Police performance measurement and human rights. *Public Money and Management*, 21(3), 35–39.

Cook, S. D., & Brown, J. S. (1999). Bridging epistimologies: The generative dance between organizational knowledge and organizational knowing. *Organization Science*, 10(4), 381–400.

Craig, S. (2007). Reflections from a red team leader. *Military Review*, 87(2), 57–61.

Crank, J. P. (1997). *Understanding Police Culture*. Anderson.

Cross, R., & Thomas, R. J. (2009). *Driving Results Through Social Networks: How Top Organizations Leverage Networks for Performance and Growth*. John Wiley and Sons.

Dehaven-Smith, L., & Jenne II, K. C. (2006). Management by inquiry: A discursive accountability system for large organizations. *Public Administration Review*, 66(1), 64–75.

Derenzo, E. G., Vinicky, J., Redman, B., & Lynch, J. J. (2006). Rounding: A model for consultation and training whose time has come. *Cambridge Quarterly of Healthcare Ethics*, 15(2), 207–216.

Downes, B. T. (1998). Recent literature on leading and managing change in public service organizations. *Social Science Journal*, 35(4), 657–673.

Ellis, C. M., & Norman, E. M. (1999). Real change in real time. *Management Review*, 88(2), 33–39.

Fulmer, R. M., & Keys, J. B. (1998). A conversation with Peter Senge: New developments in organizational learning. *Organizational Dynamics*, 27(2), 33–42.

Gilmour, J. B. (2006). Implementing OMB's program assessment rating tool (PART): Meeting the challenges of integrating budget and performance. IBM Center for the Business of Government. https://upload.powertrain.com/plcdev/uploaded_files/Gilmour0806.pdf

Hall, J. L., & Jennings, E. T., Jr. (2008). Taking chances: Evaluating risk as a guide to better use of best practices. *Public Administration Review*, 68(4), 695–708.

Hatry, H. P., Morley, E., Rossman, S. B., & Wholey, J. S. (2003). How federal programs use outcome information: Opportunities for federal managers. IBM Endowment for the business of Government. www.businessofgovernment.org/report/how-federal-programs-use-outcome-information-opportunities-federal-managers

Hofmann, P. A. (1993). Critical path method: An important tool for coordinating clinical care. *Journal on Quality Improvement*, 19(7), 235–246.

Holgersson, S., Gottschalk, P., & Dean, G. (2008). Knowledge management in law enforcement: Knowledge views for patrolling police officers. *International Journal of Police Science and Management*, 10(1), 76–88.

Jones, B. D. (2003). Bounded rationality and political science: Lessons from public administration. *Journal of Public Administration Research and Theory*, 13(4), 395–412.

Kamarck, E. C. (2005). *Transforming the Intelligence Community: Improving the Collection and Management of Information*. IBM Center for the Business of Government. www.belfercenter.org/sites/default/files/legacy/files/kamarckfin.pdf

Kravet, S. J., Howell, E., & Wright, S. M. (2006). Innovations in education: Morbidity and mortality conference, grand rounds, and the ACGME's core competencies. *Journal of General Internal Medicine*, 21(11), 1192+.

Kray, L. J., & Galinsky, A. D. (2003). The debiasing effect of counterfactual mind-sets: increasing the search for disconfirmatory information in group decisions. *Organizational Behavior and Human Decision Processes*, 91(1), 69.

Langan-Fox, J., & Tan, P. (1997). Images of a culture in transition: Personal constructs of organizational stability and change. *Journal of Occupational and Organizational Psychology*, 70(3), 273–294.

Lave, J., & Wenger, E. (1991). *Situated Learning: Legitimate Peripheral Participation*. University Press.

Leigh, D. (2004). Needs assessments: A step by step approach. In Roberts, A. R. and Yeager, R. (eds.). *Evidence-Based Practice Manual: Research and Outcome Measures in Health and Human Services*. 622–627. Oxford University Press.

Lencioni, P. (2012). *The Advantage: Why Organizational Health Trumps Everything Else in Business*. Jossey-Bass.

Levinson, H. (1994). Why the behemoths fell: Psychological roots of corporate failure. *American Psychologist*, 49(5), 428–436.

Levinthal, D. A., & March, J. G. (1993). The myopia of learning. *Strategic Management Journal*, 14(1), 95–112.

Lipman-Blumen, J., & Leavitt, H. J. (1999). *Hot Groups: Seeding Them, Feeding Them and Using Them to Ignite Your Organization*. Oxford University Press.

Luthans, F. (2005). *Organizational Behavior*. McGraw-Hill Irwin.

MacDonald, S. (1995). Learning to change: An information perspective on learning in the organization. *Organization Science*, 6(5), 557–568.

Mazerolle, L. Rombouts, S. & McBroom, J. (2007). The impact of COMPSTAT on reported crime in Queensland. *Policing*, 30(2), 237–256.

Moon, H., Conlon, D. E., Humphrey, S. E., & Quigley, N. (2003). Group decision process and incrementalism in organizational decisions. *Organizational Behavior and Human Decision Processes*, 92(1), 67.

Moore, M. H., & Braga, A. (2004). Police performance measurement: A normative framework. *Criminal Justice Ethics*, 23(1), 3–19.

Nicholson-Crotty, S., Theobald, N. A., & Nicholson-Crotty, J. (2006). Disparate measures: Public managers and performance-measurement strategies. *Public Administration Review*, 66(1), 101–113.

O'Connell, P. E., & Straub, F. (2007). *Performance-Based Management for Police Organizations*. Waveland.

Office of Community Oriented Policing Services. (2015). *The President's Task Force on 21st Century Policing Implementation Guide: Moving from Recommendations to Action*. https://portal.cops.usdoj.gov/resourcecenter/RIC/Publications/cops-p341-pub.pdf

Paoline, E. A. (2001). *Re-Thinking Police Culture: Officers' Occupational Attitudes*. LFB Publishing.

Pascale, R. & Sternin, J. (2005). Your company's secret change agents. *Harvard Business Review*, 83(5), 72–81.

Pate, T., Kelling, G., & Brown, C. (1975). A response to "What happened to patrol operations in Kansas City?. *Journal of Criminal Justice*, 3(4), 299–320.

Rainey, H. G., & Steinbauer, P. (1999). Galloping elephants: Developing elements of a theory of effective government organizations. *Journal of Public Administration Research and Theory*, 9(1), 1–30.

Reuss-Ianni, E. (1993). *Two Cultures of Policing: Street Cops and Management Cops*. Transaction Books.

Rooney, D., & McKenna, B. (2008). Wisdom in public administration: Looking for a sociology of wise practice. *Public Administration Review*, 68(4), 709–721.

Rosenfeld, R., Fornango, R., & Baumer, E. (2005). Did ceasefire, Compstat and exile reduce homicide?. *Criminology and Public Policy*, 4(3), 419–450.

Schen, E. H. (1997). *Organizational culture and leadership*. San Francisco: Jossey-Bass.

Schwartz, A. E. (1994). Group decision-making. *The CPA Journal*. www.nysscpa.org/cpajournal/old/15703015.htm.

Senge, P. M. (1994). *The Fifth Discipline: The Art and Practice of the Learning Organization*. Doubleday.

Serpas, R. W., & Morley, M. (2008). The next step in accountability: 'Compstating' the Compstat data. *The Police Chief*. www.policechiefmagazine.org/the-next-step-in-accountability-driven-leadership/

Sherman, L. W. (1998). *Evidence-Based Policing. Police Foundation, Ideas in American Policing*. www.policinginstitute.org/wp-content/uploads/2015/06/Sherman-1998-Evidence-Based-Policing.pdf

Smith, J. (1998). An on-going learning Dialogue: An experiential model in progress. *Empowerment in Organizations*, 6(4), 119.

Strati, A. (1998). Organizational symbolism as a social construction: A perspective from the sociology of knowledge. *Human Relations*, 51(11), 1379–1408.

Surowiecki, J. (2004). *The Wisdom of Crowds*. Random House.

Vito, G. F., Walsh, W. F., & Kunselman, J. (2004). Compstat: The manager's perspective. *International Journal of Police Science and Management*, 7(3), 187–196.

Weisburd, D., Mastrofski, S. D., Greenspan, R., & Willis, J. J. (2003). The growth of Compstat in American policing. *Police Foundation Reports*. www.policinginstitute.org/publication/the-growth-of-compstat-in-american-policing/

Weisburd, D., Mastrofski, S. D., McNally, A. M., Greenspan, R., & Willis J. J. (2003). Reforming to preserve: Compstat and strategic problem solving in American policing. *Criminology and Public Policy*, 2(3), 421–456.

Welsh, B. C., & Farrington, D. P. (2005). Evidence-based crime prevention: Conclusions and directions for a safer society. *Canadian Journal of Criminology and Criminal Justice*, 4(2), 337–353.

Wenger, E., McDermott, R., & Snyder, W. M. (2002). *Cultivating Communities of Practice: A Guide to Managing Knowledge*. Harvard Business School Press.

Willis, J. J., Mastrofski, S. D., & Weisburd, D. (2004). COMPSTAT and bureaucracy: A case study of challenges and opportunities for change. *Justice Quarterly*, 21(3), 463–488.

Willis, J. J., Mastrofski, S. D., & Weisburd, D. (2003). Compstat in practice: An in-depth analysis of three cities. Washington, DC: The Police Foundation. www.policinginstitute.org/wp-content/uploads/2015/06/Willis-et-al.-2004-Compstat-in-Practice.pdf

Willis, J. J., Mastrofski, S. D. & Weisburd, D. (2007). Making sense of Compstat: A theory-based analysis of organizational change in three police departments. *Law and Society Review*, 41(1), 1.

Willis, J. J., Weisburd, D. & Greenspan, R. (2003). Compstat and organizational change in the Lowell Police Department. Washington, DC: The Police Foundation. www.policinginstitute.org/publication/compstat-and-organizational-change-in-the-lowell-police-department/

Wincelowicz, V. C. (2004). *The Police Culture and the Marginally Performing Employee*. Edwin Mellon Press.

Chapter 12

Strategic Management and Planning

Setting and Assessing a Department's Strategic Direction

There is an old adage, "if you're not moving forward, you are going backwards." We believe that this certainly holds true in the field of policing.

Like all organizations, police departments need to have an effective plan of action. They need to explain, in advance, the direction in which they intend to move, what their destination is, and how they intend to get there.

Unfortunately, strategic planning is not taught in the police Academy. Additionally, most basic management courses (i.e., those that are presented to first-line supervisors) typically do not address the subject either. It is only in upper-level executive development courses, or perhaps in college-level or graduate coursework that police managers will first be formally introduced to the topic of strategic planning. Fear not. The art and practice of strategic planning is relatively straightforward. Many police leaders have already engaged in one form of strategic planning or another (see, e.g., Kurz, 2000). This text should do much to provide a more useful outline of the practice and instill confidence as police managers attempt to formulate a formal multiyear plan of action for their departments.

For decades, it appeared that American police departments were immune or excused from engaging in the practice of strategic planning. That seemed to be something that only corporations did. As hierarchical and paramilitary bureaucracies, police departments generally fear change and were consequently wedded to the status quo. Unlike business corporations which have a distinct "bottom line," police departments were viewed as a monopoly that simply performed the same functions year after year, with little to no foresight or interest in changing environmental conditions. But conditions do change, particularly in the field of policing. As Malcolm Sparrow suggested (1990), policing is not rote; it is in fact a very dynamic undertaking. As many modern police managers now understand, virtually everything is in flux; the sands seem to be continually shifting under our feet. The one thing certain is change. Police managers do not have the luxury of blindly following policies, procedures and practices that were utilized in the past and have been passed down over the years. Rather, they must remain one step ahead of changing conditions in both the internal and external work environments. In other words, they need to have a plan.

Interestingly, most American police departments did not utilize effective multiyear strategic plans until quite recently. Typically, in the absence of a formal written strategic plan, the department's budget becomes the plan. This is quite common in American policing. State and national accrediting bodies such as CALEA often required departments to have a plan, however most departments produced rather simplistic products that looked more like a glorified shopping or "to do" list. When asked to submit proof of a strategic plan,

DOI: 10.4324/9781003396437-12

many departments simply submitted one- or two-page documents that listed such "strategic objectives" as "to obtain additional storage space for bulk property" or "to purchase new radios." These documents were typically prepared quickly and casually by the chief and perhaps the executive command staff. They certainly were not jointly developed by a committee of civilians and uniformed members of the service of various ranks. As a result, line officers and first-line supervisors were typically unaware of these plans and their objectives, or they simply rejected them outright, as they were never properly vetted and there was little or no attempt to obtain buy-in from the individuals who would, ultimately, be the ones doing the work.

This brings us to an extremely important point; selection of the people who will develop the strategic plan is just as important (perhaps more so) as the contents and later execution of that plan. This is a group process. If the chief intends to develop this plan alone, or merely with two or three members of senior command staff, it is best not to even begin.

First Things First

A critically important first step is to expend a considerable amount of time in determining who the members of the strategic planning committee will be. It is also critically important to formally establish a strategic planning committee. They should consist of approximately 10 to 12 individuals from within and outside the department. While the department's chief should certainly participate in this committee, he/she should not be designated as chair. Another member of the committee should do so, preferably one who has experience with the strategic planning process. A typical committee would consist of representatives from the various ranks within the department, the department's senior command staff, the local fire chief, non-sworn personnel (such as a dispatch supervisor); community representatives such as local business leaders, members of the school board, representatives from homeowners associations, an administrator from the local hospital, clergy, etc. Once this committee is formed, the project timeline should be established with specific performance milestones. It is vitally important that the planning process be concocted and completed within a specific timeframe.

If there is difficulty in identifying people for this committee, you must ask yourself a very fundamental question: "Are we ready for a real strategic plan?" This is a very important point. Some departments want a plan merely to appease critics. They need something in writing that looks impressive and conveys the impression that the department's leadership knows what they are doing. They do not actually intend, however, to commit to a specific course of action and its concomitant obligations to have to follow through on these stated promises.

This issue pertains to the municipality and its leaders as well. The choice of undertaking a *real* strategic plan is analogous to the decision one makes in his/her personal life to accept responsibility and be accountable for one's actions and decisions.

In recent years, accreditors, public officials, and members of the public alike all demand a more authentic effort to far more robust plan for moving the department forward. Rather than simply issuing annual reports at the end of the year that serve simply as a tally of work performed (i.e., how many arrests were made; how many traffic accidents were handled; how many community outreach events were attended, etc.), police departments began to be held accountable for identifying specific and measurable operational goals at the commencement of the year. For example, rather than simply reporting that a department handled 580 vehicle accidents last year, a forward-thinking chief should, at the beginning of the year, publicly state that it is an important operational goal of his/her agency to "reduce vehicle accidents with injuries by 10%." Once such a performance target has been articulated that chief must then explain exactly how members of that department will accomplish that goal (e.g., by directed enforcement activities such as radar enforcement in locations known for high numbers of vehicle crashes, increased parking enforcement to reduce double parking and increase the flow of vehicular traffic, engaging in community outreach and public education programs, etc.). This is the essence of strategic planning.

Today, American police chiefs have become far more accustomed to this method of management. Strategic planning has been demystified and has become a far more approachable and more effective method of managing police organizations.

The strategic planning process is rather straightforward (Rogers et al., 2020). Most competent managers already have an intuitive and rudimentary understanding of the practice of gap analysis. That is, they understand that an accurate "as is" assessment of the organization is a necessary first step for any plan of action. You simply cannot plan where it is that you want to go with your organization until you thoroughly understand where you are at present. This certainly makes sense. But this assessment cannot be performed solely by the chief and his or her "inner circle" (i.e., senior command staff). If the chief attempts to do so, and fails to engage individuals throughout the entire organization, he/she is literally wasting the time and energies of all those individuals who are involved in the planning process, and they are all due for a major disappointment. No plan for moving the organization forward will be embraced unless there is sufficient "buy in" from the rank-and-file members of the organization. Also, additional perspectives and opinions should be solicited to avoid tunnel vision or an unrealistically rosy picture of reality. For this reason, it is critical that the chief engage other members of the department, both sworn and unsworn, to provide their personal assessments of where the department currently is. We call this process *internal stakeholder* analysis.

Step 1 – Members of the department from various ranks and units must be engaged in the process of formulating an accurate assessment of where the department is right at this moment. This must be a brutally honest assessment, one that includes the organization's weaknesses as well as its strengths. For this reason, it is necessary that individuals outside the organization be involved as well. Members of the wider community must be engaged in this process, to properly examine the department from a variety of different perspectives and viewpoints. Police departments that intend to develop a thoughtful and comprehensive strategic plan must solicit the assistance of *"external" stakeholders*, such as local business owners, school administrators, homeowners, youth, clergy, commuters, etc. These are individuals who indeed have a "stake" in the success of the department. They are the ones who will be directly and negatively affected by the department's failure or will share in its success moving forward. Their perspectives will no doubt vary somewhat from those of members of the department. Nevertheless, it is these outside viewpoints that will offer a true and usually honest perspective regarding the department's current operations.

Police officers and their supervisors might think that a particular department is performing quite well, but the parents of local schoolchildren or advocates for the homeless might have an entirely different view. Knowledge is power. If a department intends to move forward, it must have an accurate assessment of the current situation.

Unfortunately, American police departments rarely engage members of the wider community (i.e., external stakeholders) when they are preparing their strategic plans. As a result, most strategic plans fail.

If a particular department understands the importance of internal and external stakeholder analysis and does so properly, what next?

Step 2 – Once the department knows the current "as is," the next logical step is to determine "the desired state." In other words, the department simply must ask the question "where exactly do we want to be?" Management gurus refer to this as the "desired state." It simply means that the department needs to envision what its operations and accomplishments would look like if things were proceeding optimally. Another way of understanding this is, "what exactly would success look like?"

This question is somewhat more difficult than it seems. It entails an honest evaluation of the organization's mission statement. Unfortunately, few American police departments place much emphasis upon the development of an accurate and useful mission statement. Instead, thousands of police departments merely repeat some version of "to protect and serve …" which is vague and merely inspirational. Frankly, it is nothing more than a motto. It certainly will not provide the clarity necessary to direct and guide the organization.

Many other departments simply have mission statements that are woefully out of date and out of touch with the current work environment. A critical initial step in the strategic planning process is therefore to review and refine the existing mission statement or develop an entirely new one. This entails an authentic attempt to "figure out what your value system is. Decide what your [department] stands for" (Peters and Waterman, 1982, p. 227).

A clear, direct, and understandable mission statement must be crafted so that specific organizational goals can be drawn from it and directly linked to the overriding mission. Field personnel and managers should never need to ask, "why exactly are we doing this?" It should always be clearly understood by all. This ensures that the performance management system that is ultimately developed within the department has validity and the support of all members of the organization. It also ensures that all subsequent goals and performance measures will be linked directly and logically to the organizational mission.

Step 3 – Once you have determined the as is, and have identified the desired state, all that is required is to perform a "gap analysis." That is, simply look at the distance between the current state of the department and the desired state and attempt to close the gap. When you begin to outline the deficiencies and the steps that are going to be required for closing this gap, you are essentially identifying the department's goals and objectives for the next several years. You are creating a plan of action, a plan for success.

Granted, this is indeed a simplification of the process, but it includes the essential steps of the strategic planning process (Ugboro et al., 2011; Poister, 2010). Certainly, most police managers can understand this process and should be encouraged to attempt this in their own departments. The key is to do so thoughtfully, carefully, transparently, and inclusively.

The process itself is rather straightforward. Every effort should be made to simplify the process as much as possible in order to ensure that all members understand and embrace the process. Granted, other management experts can and do offer more sophisticated strategic planning processes but they are simply not needed in the field of policing.

Therefore, let's review the three basic steps:

1) The very first step of strategic planning is to perform an accurate and honest "as is" assessment of the department. Ideally this is performed by both internal (i.e., members of the department) and external stakeholders (i.e., members of the wider community such as public officials, business leaders, community organizers, members of homeowner's associations, school administrators and parent associations, clergy, youth advocates, etc.). The purpose here is to gain a wide range of perspectives from individuals who are both familiar with and invested in the operations of the police department. Participants should be asked to provide their own personal SWOT analysis of the department. That

Figure 12.1 Strategic Plan Direction.

is, these individuals should be asked to identify the department's current strengths, weaknesses, and, looking forward, opportunities and threats to the operations of the department. These observations should be recorded, coded, and carefully analyzed to identify any major trends that emerge from these conversations. The strategic planning committee should give these observations great weight when considering the department's relative position.

2) The next step would be to identify the "desired state." In other words, internal and external stakeholders would be asked to describe what, in a utopian or ideal world, the department would look like. While it is likely that a wide variety of opinions will emerge, it is even more likely that general trends will be identified. For example, if a particular department is experiencing a problem such as low morale, it is likely that it will be repeatedly identified during discussions with internal stakeholders and will very likely be identified by external stakeholders as well. When this occurs, members of the strategic planning committee can be sure that morale is a central issue for this agency going forward.

3) The last step of the strategic planning process is rather straightforward; it is called gap analysis. Once internal and external stakeholders have identified both the as is and desired state of the agency, members of the strategic planning committee must begin the process of connecting the dots. In other words, the committee must attempt to identify those concrete action steps that will serve to move the department forward towards its desired state. It is important to note that gap analysis should generally be performed by the strategic planning committee, not by members of the stakeholders' groups. This process entails a great deal of thoughtful work and will typically extend over several weeks. Once the strategic planning committee has identified a variety of specific action steps several broad objectives for the agency will emerge. This in essence will serve as the game plan for moving the department forward over the next several years.

Closing the Gap

- Current State (From Internal and External SWOT Analyses).
- Future State (From Vision).
- Identify the Specific performance gap(s) to close.
- Identify Specific Goals and Strategies for closing the gap.

Identifying Goals and Objectives

Goals and strategies will flow naturally from the gap analysis, if it is performed honestly, and the results are conveyed accurately. Police professionals know their business well. It is likely that the department's goals and strategies for the next three years will be easily identified. Solutions will suggest themselves after a thoughtful review of the problem(s).

Unfortunately, many strategic planning efforts lose traction and fail at this point. This is particularly true if a timeline has not been established in advance. It is critical to keep the process moving. Research and common experience show that failure to carry through on plan implementation will result in a loss of employee commitment (Kalyal et al., 2020). The next steps should be accomplished relatively quickly after the stakeholders' analyses have been completed and analyzed. We suggest the following process:

1) Ideally, a moderator or outside consultant will be used to guide the work of the strategic planning committee.
2) Once the results of the stakeholder analyses have been reviewed, specific ideas for closing the performance gap should be solicited from all members of the strategic planning committee. These ideas should be recorded and shared among the group. The committee should meet in a classroom setting. Ideas for closing the performance gap should be written on the board for all to see.
3) Each member of the committee should be given an opportunity to provide several different suggestions for "closing the gap." Additional time should then be provided for committee members to review the suggestions of the entire group. The committee should attempt to be as thorough as possible.
4) Each member of the committee should then be provided with three stickers or post-its that can be placed on the board.
5) Committee members should then be directed to indicate what they personally believe to be the three most important objectives by placing one sticker/post it next to each suggestion listed on the board that they strongly agree with.
6) Once every member has done so, the group should be directed to review and discuss the results of this exercise and to identify any clustering that has occurred. Those suggestions that received the most votes should then be identified as the department's most important goals and objectives.

This represents a critical juncture for the organization. In many respects, the most important decisions are made at this point in the process. Everything else is merely execution, measurement, and adjustment. The strategic planning committee should take as much time as is required to articulate and refine the department's goals and objectives.

Ideally, a strategic plan for a police department would last for a period of three (3) years. Any shorter period would entail too much work as new plans would perpetually be being developed. Similarly, strategic plans for five or more years run the risk of tying the department into a specific course of action for too long of a period. The three-year plan seems to be ideal and is most common in American police departments.

Perhaps the best way to practice strategic planning skills is to employ them in a hypothetical police department. The following section describes a typical American police department, the Millwood P.D. Assume that you are one of Millwood's patrol sergeants and you have been assigned to serve as a member of the department's strategic planning committee. As part of the internal stakeholders' assessment, you have been asked to provide your own personal SWOT analysis of this agency:

Millwood Police Department – Case Study

Millwood has a population of approximately 24,000. The demographic mix is predominantly white (71%), followed by African-American (16%) and Hispanic (13%).

The economy is vibrant, having experienced double digit annual economic growth over the past five years, fueled by the tech industry. Over the past six months, however, tax revenue has flattened and there is talk of an upcoming layoff at the largest tech employer.

Millwood PD has the following mission statement: "To protect and Serve the People of Millwood." The department has no strategic plan.

Chief Waters has been with the department for 29 years and has no current plans for retirement.

The Millwood Police Department (MPD) has a total of 49 sworn officers (authorized level = 51 sworn) and four civilian personnel (records, property manager, etc.). The department last hired an officer two years ago.

The department is staffed by:

1 – chief
1 – captain (executive officer)
2 – lieutenants (operations and support)
7 – sergeants
1 – detective sergeant (squad commander)
6 – detectives (including one permanently assigned to a regional narcotics task force; doesn't "catch cases" or maintain a general caseload in Millwood; only works cases in Millwood if they are narcotics-related)
31 – police officers (includes two (2) K-9 officers and two SRO's)

Dispatch is performed by the county. Code enforcement is performed by two non-sworn code enforcement officers who are not department employees.

Violent crime has not traditionally been a problem in Millwood, reported UCR Part 1 crimes have always been quite low. The last murder occurred three years ago and it occurred in connection with a domestic incident.

Millwood has one high school, a middle school, and three elementary schools (two public, one private). The department's K-9 officers had performed narcotics sweeps in the high school building, but this practice was discontinued last year after several complaints from School Board members and some parents of students. The department's two SROs are assigned to the High School and Middle School. They backfill patrol positions (and take their vacations) when school is not in session.

The department's records management system (RMS) was originally purchased in 2010. The prior chief was the person responsible for its selection. The department's civilian records administrator received one week of training at the headquarters of manufacturer, and she was tasked with training all other members of the department. Patrol officers are currently able to input data in the field via MDTs in their patrol units but are frequently seen in the squad room preparing reports on desk top computers as it is apparently "a lot easier" to do so in this manner. Patrol units frequently put themselves out of service during a shift to engage in routine report writing. The RMS contains specific modules for investigative case management, internal investigations and property and evidence management, but these modules are not being used due to a general lack of familiarity with the system. These functions are all conducted in hard copy or on separate excel spreadsheets.

A large university abuts Millwood, and many of its students frequent the downtown bars and have off-campus housing within Millwood. Weekends at these bars and student apartments are always loud, and quite often violent. Patrol response times increase considerably on weekends. There have already been 17 felony assaults that have taken place in and around the downtown college bars and apartments this year, two sexual assaults (which are still under investigation) and an arson of a motor vehicle (apparently connected to a fraternity hazing incident). The local newspaper has been running a series on the overall poor level of "town and gown" relations in Millwood and a local homeowner's group has recently formed an informal alliance with downtown business owners (ones that don't cater to the college crowd). This group, known as "Take Back Millwood Now," has recently served the MPD's Chief (Waters) with a list of 25 demands which include "#17- Driving out the slumlords who enrich themselves by allowing five or more students to a bedroom" in these off-campus units.

Two major interstates run through the community and the town has a busy downtown commercial area which contains a major transportation hub (regional commuter rail, Greyhound bus terminal). Theft of cellphones, computers, and tablets from autos is a persistent problem in the large commuter parking lots. Larcenies of this type have been tracking up approximately 15% each year, for the past three years.

Several years ago, MPD detectives regularly attended monthly "Investigators' meetings" that were held in the county Sheriff's Office. All police departments in the county sent representatives, as well as the Departments of Probation and Parole, and the State's Attorney's Office. In recent years, the detectives have not attended these meetings as various electronic bulletins and list servers have "taken the place" of formal investigations meetings.

"Command staff meetings" are held weekly and are attended by the Chief, the Captain and the two lieutenants. In addition, "Supervisors Meetings" (for Sergeants and above) are scheduled quarterly but have not been held within the past eight months due to "several very high-profile incidents" that have "consumed a lot of the time" of the senior command staff. MPD detectives hold their own meetings.

Several years ago, the MPD had a separate "Community Policing Unit" which was an overlay to patrol operations. That unit has since been disbanded (since several grants have now expired) and the unit's officers and supervisor have backfilled patrol positions. The department's last annual report (which was prepared and published 2½ years ago) states that community policing is now being performed by "all members of the patrol division, who have thoroughly adopted and embraced the community policing philosophy." There is no separate "traffic unit." One officer is assigned as "traffic officer." Millwood residents continually complain of speeding in virtually all residential neighborhoods. The "community affairs officer" has recently been promoted to sergeant and that position remains vacant.

Millwood just experienced its first fentanyl overdose case of the year, a 16-year-old high school sophomore. This is the sixth to have occurred in the county over the last six months.

In addition to mandatory re-certifications, MPD officers receive a good amount of in-service training (delivered offsite and in-house). The department's training officer (a sergeant) serves as the training "coordinator" and schedules training, oversees the training budget, maintains certificates, etc. There are several other sergeants, police officers and detectives who are certified instructors (general topics, as well as many specialized topics). Several of the department's certified trainers are frequently called upon to teach at the regional police academy. Many of the MPD's in-service programs are open to officers from other departments in the county. The MPD has developed a reputation as a regional leader in the field of in-service training delivery. The department's two certified firearms instructors have developed a tactical firearms training course that is now being offered at the regional police academy.

The parking lot of the local "big box" store has become a congregation point for 'day laborers' seeking employment. Local contractors have only made matters worse by driving by each morning before 9am and picking up men for 'off the books' construction and handyman jobs. The local chapters of the plumbers and carpenters' unions have begun a local media blitz and have been putting pressure on the MPD to stop "this obviously illegal activity." Chief Waters was quoted in the papers as referring to the day laborers as "mostly undocumented illegal aliens" and has recently been characterized as being "completely insensitive to the plight of Latinos in [Millwood]" by a prominent civil rights leader. Last month, a 46-year-old female resident (a former member of the Town Council) was assaulted at the transportation center; she was punched in the face and her cell phone was taken. She described her assailant to the police as an "apparently drunken Hispanic male" in his early thirties. This incident (described by the media as "The bus station incident") has created quite a public stir and has been the source of frequent letters to the editor, as well as several emails and letters to the department and Town Council calling for "immediate action to provide for the safety of commuters and residents." No arrest has been made and the investigation is continuing. One member of the Town Council has publicly asked for Chief Waters' resignation.

All patrol units carry AED's. A patrol officer made a rescue of a 39-year-old woman with one three months ago.

The department has not scheduled a "Medal Day Ceremony" within the past six years.

Relations between the Town and the police officers' collective bargaining unit are generally described as "good." There have been two union grievances each of the past two years. There have been no significant (i.e., founded) IA investigations over the past three years.

The department's operating budget has increased incrementally over the past ten years. Historically, Millwood's tax base has been quite good. There have never been layoffs in the MPD.

Question: Do you see any issues here? As a patrol sergeant would you be able to identify any opportunities or threats for this department?

An as-is assessment is necessary before any goals or objectives are set.

If the as-is assessment is thoughtfully and honestly prepared by an individual who clearly has a stake in the organization, the resulting work product would have great utility in terms of identifying major goals and objectives for the department. It is likely that the patrol sergeant from the Millwood P.D. would produce something like this:

As you can see, specific goals and objectives for Millwood P.D. can certainly be derived from stakeholder assessments such as this. A strategic planning committee would solicit and review similar responses from individuals both within and outside the department. A robust collection of data (i.e., thoughtful suggestions and recommendations from a wide range of participants) would inform the work of the strategic planning committee, provide necessary direction for their work, and ensure buy-in for the resulting plan (Kurz, 2000).

Specific goals and objectives are nothing other than plans for organizational success. Once they are identified, the next step will be to develop a means of measurement. It is extremely important to identify meaningful performance measures that can track the department's relative degree of success in achieving its goals. Taking the case of Millwood for example, the department would likely assign fixed or mobile patrols at the transportation center to deter crime and disorder. But simply tallying the aggregate number of patrol hours is

Strength	Weakness
• Violent crime has not traditionally been a problem in Millwood, reported UCR Part 1 crimes have always been quite low. • Relations between the Town and the police officers' collective bargaining unit are generally described as "good." There have been two (2) union grievances each of the past two years. • The department's operating budget has increased incrementally over the past ten years. There have never been layoffs in the MPD. • All patrol units carry AED's. A patrol officer made a rescue with one three months ago.	• The department's civilian records administrator received one week of training at the headquarters of manufacturer, and she was tasked with training all other members of the department. • Patrol officers are currently able to input data in the field via MDTs in their patrol units but are frequently seen in the squad room preparing reports on desk top computers as it is apparently "a lot easier" to do so in this manner. Patrol units frequently put themselves out of service during a shift to engage in routine report writing. The RMS contains specific modules for investigative case management, internal investigations and property and evidence management, but these modules are not being used due to a general lack of familiarity with the system. These functions are all conducted in hard copy or on separate excel spreadsheets. • The department's records management system (RMS) was originally purchased in 2010. The prior chief was the person responsible for its selection. • The department has no strategic plan. • The department has not scheduled a "Medal Day Ceremony" within the past six years. • Theft of cellphones, computers and tablets from autos is a persistent problem in the large commuter parking lots. Larcenies of this type have been tracking up approximately 15% each year, for the past three years. • Code enforcement is performed by two non-sworn code enforcement officers who are not department employees. • Dispatch is performed by the county. • There is no separate "traffic unit." One officer is assigned as "traffic officer." Millwood residents continually complain of speeding in virtually all residential neighborhoods. • Other than mandatory re-certifications, MPD officers receive very little in-service training. The department's training officer serves chiefly as the training "coordinator" and schedules training, oversees the training budget, maintains certificates, etc. The department's two certified firearms instructors do provide training to MPD officers, but no other in-service training is delivered by members of the department. • Chief Waters has been with the department for 29 years and has no current plans for retirement.

Figure 12.2 SWOT Analysis.

Strategic Objective	Rapid Response to High Priority Calls
Performance Indicators	Benchmarks
911 Response Time	50% decrease in "Priority 1" 911 response time from [#AsIs minutes] to # minutes] over a three-year period Minimum annual decrease in response time Year 1: 25% Year 2: 15% Year 3: 10%
Citizen Satisfaction Survey	80% citizen satisfaction rate on annual survey and random audit of service calls Year 1: Year 2: Year 3:
Non-emergency/non-Officer required calls.	Reduce overall rate of non-emergency/" non-officer required" calls for service by ___ % Year 1: Year 2: Year 3:

Figure 12.3 Performance Goals and Objectives.

insufficient. We return once again to the distinction between measuring organizational outputs and outcomes (Chapter 1). Are these additional patrols making any difference at all? How do we know?

The Millwood PD must do more than simply describing how much work it has done. Town officials and community members, as well as police supervisors, also need to know how well the work was performed and whether anyone is better off in these efforts. These simple questions: *1) how much? 2) how well? and is anyone better off?* form the basis of the management method known as results-based accounting (RBA) (Freeman, 2015). In addition to reporting on the total number of additional patrol hours expended at the transportation center, the Millwood police chief should be able to report to town/city officials and community members that:

- The total number of reported crimes and calls for service originating in and around the transportation center have fallen by over 15%.
- Police response times for calls originating in and around the transportation center have dropped by 20%.
- A weekly census of homeless people lingering within the transportation center indicates that the numbers are dropping.
- Although initially the number of arrests and summonses issued in and around the transportation center spiked, that number has dropped considerably.
- A bimonthly random survey of commuters conducted in conjunction with the local community college indicates that respondents generally feel safer and believe that the transportation center and parking areas have become cleaner and more secure.

It is also imperative to identify and effectively communicate the following regarding each strategy that is formulated by any police department:

1) Specific action steps.
2) The responsible party(-ies).

3) Timeline for completion (with specific performance milestones).
4) Resources.
5) Costs.

There is a saying attributed to Albert Einstein that suggests, "not everything that can be counted, counts – and not everything that counts, can be counted." The selection of useful performance measures requires much thought and honest reflection that the organization's core business and obligations.

Once again, we believe that police officers know their business extremely well. Once they become familiar with this method of performance measurement, they will identify the measures that are most appropriate for their community.

It is critically important for all American police departments to engage in this type of strategic planning process. No modern police department should currently be operating without a multi-year strategic plan. Police organizations, like all other organizations, need to understand, embrace, and engage in a proactive form of strategic management that entails, "assessing strengths and weaknesses, identifying opportunities and threats, determining where the organization should be going, and then establishing goals, strategies, and tactics for getting there" (Kissler et al., 1998, p. 353). They must be able to anticipate where their resources will be needed (i.e. hotspot policing techniques) or, at the very least, react immediately with an effective intervention or response.

Unfortunately, as Edward Maguire (2004) notes, police agencies:

> Many other public agencies are often unable to state with any degree of precision how their performance has changed over time or how it compares with that of their peer agencies, particularly those situated in similar community contexts.
>
> (p. 1)

The Compstat system of performance management adequately addresses this problem. We believe that all American police departments should currently be utilizing a Compstat-like performance measurement (PM) system or be engaged in the process of developing one. (Chapter 3 examines the operations of such a system in detail.)

The public now demands accountability from the police. This entails providing credible explanations in response to continuous inquiries such as what was done? Was it effective? How do we know? And how much did it cost? Police officials no longer have the luxury of merely shrugging their shoulders as crime rates and costs continue to rise. They are now rightly expected to justify their efforts and expenditure.

Today, "police forces are increasingly accountable to government at various levels and to the community at large for various aspects of their performance and are expected to communicate with government and the public about what they are doing" (Collier et al., 2004, p. 458). They need to demonstrate that they have a plan; that the plan is sound; that the plan is being followed; and whether their efforts are having any measurable effect.

All managers, particularly police managers, must explore why things aren't working within their organizations. Managers need to look for trouble and determine what the root causes are. For too long, police managers have concentrated on the "whats?" instead of the "whys?"

Ideally, even when things are going as planned, there is still much work to be done. Managers should be critically examining all operations to learn what exactly this success is attributable to. Good management equals continuous learning and assessment. This is what is meant by "transformative learning," developing new forms of learning, new methods, and habits.

Everyone within the organization needs to know what their roles are, and their responsibilities are. Every police department therefore needs to have clear and comprehensive job descriptions for all sworn and un-sworn positions. There should be no instances where a necessary task goes undone because of a lack of clarity concerning whose responsibility it was to do so.

You need to have a clear and well thought out workplan, an idea of who is going to do what and when. A multi-year strategic plan with specific goals and objectives will include this information and will provide guidance and direction for all employees. Necessary adjustments can be made during ongoing monthly Compstat meetings.

References

Collier, P. M., Edwards, J. S., & Shaw, D. (2004). Communicating knowledge about police performance. *International Journal of Productivity and Performance Management*, 53(5), 458–467.

Freeman, M. (2015). *Turning Curves: An Accountability Companion Reader*. Parse Publishing.

Kalyal, H., Huey, L., Blaskovits, B., & Bennell, C. (2020). If it's not worth doing half-assed, then it's not worth doing at all. Police views as to why new strategy implementation fails. *Police Practice and Research*, 21(2), 117–133.

Kissler, G. R., Fore, K. N., Jacobson, W. S., Kittredge, W. P., & Stewart, S. L. (1998). State strategic planning: Suggestions from the Oregon experience. *Public Administration Review*, 58(4), 353–359.

Kurz, D. L. (2000). Strategic planning and police-community partnership in a small town. *The Police Chief*, 6 (12), 28–36.

Maguire, E. R. (2004). *Police Departments as Learning Laboratories*. The Police Foundation. www.policinginstitute.org/wp-content/uploads/2015/06/Maguire-2004-Police-Departments-as-Learning-Laboratories.pdf

Peters, T., & Waterman, R. (1982). *In Search of Excellence*. Harper and Row.

Poister, T. (2010). The future of strategic planning in the public sector: Linking strategic management, and performance. *Public Administration Review*, 70(December, supplement), 246–254.

Rogers, Z., McIntyre, M. L., & Caputo, T. (2020). Gold strategic plans: How well do Canadian police services do?, *Police Practice and Research*, 2(3), 210–226.

Sparrow, M. K. (1990). *Beyond 911*. Basic Books.

Ugboro, I., Obengand, K., & Spann, O. (2011). Strategic planning as an effective tool of strategic management in public sector organizations: Evidence from public transit organizations. *Administration and Society*, 43(1), 87–123.

Chapter 13

Future Considerations and Alternative Service Delivery Models

Introduction

Since the summer of 2014, and amplified in the summer of 2020, the police in the United States are facing a crisis of legitimacy (Walker and Katz, 2021). The images of Eric Garner dying in police custody, pleading to the officers that surrounded him that he couldn't breathe, and the shocking nine-minute video of George Floyd being murdered by a Minneapolis police officer sent shock waves through the foundation of American policing.

In the wake of the incidents in 2014, President Obama empaneled The Presidential Task Force on 21st Century Policing. The hundreds of recommendations issued by that Task Force under the six Pillars of Building Trust and Legitimacy, Policy and Oversight, Technology and social media, Community and Crime Reduction, Training and Education, and Officer Wellness and Safety, challenged police leaders to rethink and reimagine the way police services are provided (Office of Community-Oriented Policing Services, 2015).

After the George Floyd murder, cries of "defund the police" could be heard across the country. The City of Burlington Vermont decided that there would be a unilateral reduction in the police personnel headcount of 30% and that no new police officers would be hired for two years to have time to shrink the department and reinvent itself (Siegel and Rappleye, 2021). Although the movement to reduce the police in the U.S. did not materialize with great force, the message seemed clear: policing needed to reform.

In New York, Governor Cuomo ordered every police department in the state to engage in a comprehensive reform process. New York State Executive Order #23 was signed in August 2020 and required every locality in New York State with a police department to adopt a plan for reform by April 2021 to be eligible for future state funding. The New York State Police Reform and Reinvention Collaborative was established as a resource for local departments and as a clearinghouse for the submitted plans (New York State, 2020).

This book is aligned with the overall philosophy of police reform, not from an irrational "defund the police" approach, but from a rational approach, with the mindset that effective policing requires sound management. The chapters in this text provide some of the tools needed for effective management. In fact, the approach advocated for in this book is one of continual assessment and improvement across all operational and administrative elements in a police department. We believe that to do that important work properly, departments need a solid understanding of the conceptual framework of policing and how they fit into it with their community. With this understanding, departments then need to consider how to manage the demand for police services and the supply of resources needed to meet that demand. And finally, all of this must be considered in the context of a balanced approach ensuring communities and police employees are satisfied. To strike this balance, we offer

DOI: 10.4324/9781003396437-13

several recommendations that are consistent with best practices and the prevailing views on policing best practices.

Conceptual Framework

Police departments provide their communities with a full range of services, including responding to emergencies and calls for service (CFS), performing directed activities, and solving problems. Most departments strike a balance between law enforcement and service, and most strive to provide a high level of service to their community. In most departments, this law enforcement and service mandate manifests itself into an operational philosophy where every call for service from the public gets a police response and almost every criminal case gets investigated. This book was designed to counter this everything-for-everyone approach and challenge police managers and leaders to examine their departments more critically. Recent events make this critical assessment even more important, and the outcome of these candid assessments should look at providing policing services more efficiently and effectively. More effective and efficient police service means that alternatives to the current service delivery models should be explored and that a more balanced approach should be taken with respect to providing these alternatives. In other words, there needs to be a more robust and holistic understanding of not only the services that the police provide, but the way they provide it, or maybe not provide at all. And this understanding should integrate various managerial perspectives that include mission-critical dimensions as well as the satisfaction of the community, and well-being of the employees, both sworn and civilian.

Where Do We Go From Here?

When we consider the services any police department provides, we need to consider the department's mission and the demands from the community. The main concern in this area is essentially "mission creep." Over the years the police in general have become the stopgap, or the catch-basin, for a wide variety of social services that have little to do with the mission of the police. Research has shown that more than 70% of all CFS handled by the police are "service" calls, meaning they have little or no relevance to the police mission of crime reduction (Walker and Katz, 2021). Similarly, over the years, the police have become involved in a wide variety of order maintenance and other non-police related services.

Police response to CFS about the mentally ill, homelessness, family disputes, and prostitution, are examples of the public leveraging police resources to respond to social problems. And then there are whole categories of calls for service where the police have shouldered the responsibilities where other sectors of the economy left voids, such as reporting traffic crashes, responding to private alarms, executing warrants for the court. The police are doing these things because they are available 24x7x365 and are a readily available resource to apply to just about any problem facing a community.

There is a classic statement by renowned policing scholar Egon Bittner that describes police work in terms of situations involving "something-that-ought-not-to-be-happening-and-about-which-someone-had-better-do-something-about-now!" (Bittner, 1970). Requesting the response of an armed police officer to most service CFS, is the equivalent of summonsing an Emergency Room Physician to a simple medical issue in your home. The only common denominator is that there is always one on-duty at any given time. However, the police bring the capacity to use deadly force in those situations.

Most times, the police response to these incidents is routine. On the rare occasion things go wrong and the police are called "on the carpet" to explain their actions. The perceived use of excessive force in dealing with people with mental illness is a good example of this. The core of the police role in our society is the justified use of force. We expect them to use this force wisely, and mainly to counter crime and the unlawful force that is used against us.

Mentally ill people can sometimes be violent. If the police are present, this violence and use of force by the mentally ill person is generally countered with force by the police. The use of force in these situations might be legally justified, but in some cases probably not necessary. We have seen numerous examples in recent months that clinical psychological care would have been far superior to the police use of force. The police are well-trained in one area, but not sufficiently in the other.

So, we put demands on the police, and expect them to be the catch-basin for a wide range of social problems, but do not give them the resources and training to deal with those problems. Then we criticize them when things go wrong, not appreciating the fact that the criticism probably should be directed elsewhere. This is the dilemma facing contemporary policing, and police officers stand at the forefront of this dilemma. They need our support, and they need an organization that can give them the tools, and the leadership, to deal with this dilemma.

The chapters in this text provide the reader with a foundation for understanding the performance of their police department. However, an important part of that process is coming to an understanding about what (and how) the police should be doing in the first place. What are the philosophical and strategic foundations of the police? How should they go about achieving their mission? The chapter on strategy in this text provides an outstanding primer on strategic planning and management, and this chapter challenges the reader to arrive at a better understanding of the role of the police in their community; consider alternatives to current operations; and broaden the mission of the police from just crime, disorder, traffic, etc. to include the satisfaction of the community and well-being of the employees. To accomplish this, it's important to understand the policing landscape with regards to philosophic and strategic approaches in policing.

Philosophical and Strategic Approaches

Modern police departments will undoubtedly have Mission Statements. The NYPD Mission Statement for example "is to enhance the quality of life in New York City by working in partnership with the community to enforce the law, preserve peace, protect the people, reduce fear, and maintain order" (NYPD, 2023b). The LAPD has a similar statement: "to safeguard the lives and property of the people we serve, to reduce the incidence and fear of crime, and to enhance public safety while working with the diverse communities to improve their quality of life" (LAPD, 2023). Both share similar characteristics involving crime reduction and working in partnership with the community.

Essentially, when we think of crime control and reduction, we think of the police. Crime is caused by many factors. Over the past century, theories of crime have abounded, and there are many perspectives and schools of thought regarding the nature of crime and why it happens. The use and sale of drugs, availability of guns, gangs, poverty, unemployment, poor education, high residential turnover, poor housing, cultural conflict, and dysfunctional families, have all been associated with crime. One prominent theory, called social disorganization theory, has received much acclaim and controversy over the last thirty years and it is relevant to the strategic management of the police. The police have little to do with poverty,

Table 13.1 Continuum of Disorder

Physical Disorder	Social Disorder	Serious Crime
Low Seriousness	*Medium Seriousness*	*High Seriousness*
Graffiti	Public Drinking	Violent Crime
Derelict Cars	Noise	Property Crime
Abandoned Property	Traffic	
Litter	Prostitution	
	Illicit Drugs	

education, unemployment, etc., and cannot control family dysfunction, cultural conflicts, or poor housing stock. However, they can exert control over public places and do something about incidents of social disorder prevalent in communities.

Social disorganization theory suggests that serious crime is a function of social and physical disorder present in a community. First advanced by University of Chicago sociologists Shaw and McKay, social disorganization was defined as low socioeconomic status, high residential mobility, high cultural diversity, poor housing stock, and dysfunctional families (Shaw and McKay, 1942). The concept has evolved to define disorder on a continuum, with low-level physical disorder on one end and serious criminal disorder on the other end of the continuum.

Serious crimes, therefore, are not isolated events; they are part of a continuum of disorder and part of the fabric of a community. The most well-known articulation of this perspective is the "broken windows" metaphor described by James Q. Wilson and George L. Kelling. Wilson and Kelling's article "Broken Windows" appeared in a 1982 edition of *Atlantic Monthly*, and it argued that crime and the fear of crime are products of "broken windows" in a community. Literally, when a property has a broken window and it is not repaired, the broken window sends a signal to people in the community that no one cares about the property and invites the breaking of more windows and further disrepair of the property. This in turn invites more frequent and serious disorder, inviting people to "hang-out," drink alcohol, use drugs, make noise, be disorderly, and the like because no one oversees the area. Eventually, this combination of physical and social disorder will lead to serious criminal activity (Kelling and Wilson, 1982).

Broken windows are used in the "metaphorical" sense, where any signs of community disorder are the equivalent of a "broken window." If the disorder is left unaddressed, it signals to the community that there is a lack of control and sends an invitation for further disorder and serious crime. Thus, from a community perspective, "broken windows," or signs of both physical and social disorder, are important and visible precursors to serious criminal activity. If left unrepaired, the literal and metaphorical broken windows contribute in an indirect way to crime and the fear of crime in a community.

The implications of the concept of disorder from a police perspective is that the situation calls for renewed and strategic management and strategic planning directed at fulfilling the fundamental purpose of the organization. The police mission is to reduce crime and the fear of crime and provide a safe community. These efforts must be backed with the use of appropriate performance measures, proper organizational alignment, and effective tactics.

Crime and disorder are not alone for the mission of the department. Now, more than ever, rebuilding trust between the department and the community is critical. Events over the last few years have shown that the relationship between the police and some segments of the community are frayed. This reality must put this into a strategic context as well and issues of trust and community satisfaction need to be managed more rigorously. To manage these sometimes-competing issues, police organizations generally resort to one or more of the following approaches.

Performance Measures

This strategic focus demands that appropriate measures be developed and tracked to ensure that plans, policies, and programs are effective in achieving the goals of the department. Moore and Braga (2004), in their article "Police Performance Measures," argue that six general measures are appropriate to evaluate the performance of a police agency.[1] According to Moore and Braga, a police department should: 1) reduce crime; 2) hold offenders accountable; 3) reduce the fear of crime and promote security; 4) encourage public-centered crime defense programs; 5) improve traffic safety; and 6) provide essential emergency services. From a strategic management perspective, each of these six broad areas of police responsibility should be part of the police mandate, each of these measures should be measured, and plans and tactics must be created to achieve success in each area.

It is recommended that police departments establish measures for each of these six categories and that community leaders hold the police department accountable for making improvements in each area. While there is no exact measure for each area, it is suggested that the following data be used to track performance:

These areas of performance become, therefore, the strategic focus of the department. All programs, plans, tactics, and efforts are directed at improving the measures in these areas. Frequent and regular reporting of this information is critical, as is strict accountability for achieving the desired results.

This approach has been referred to by several different titles. It is commonly known as the "S.A.R.A." model in community policing (scanning-analysis-response-assessment), or the COMPSTAT model developed in New York City (timely intelligence-effective tactics-rapid deployment-relentless follow-up), or the policy model from the public administration arena (problem identification-policy development-policy implementation-policy evaluation).

Regardless of what this approach is called, it is essentially a strategic approach, articulating the mission of the organization into quantifiable and measurable terms and using those measures to drive the efforts and performance of the entire organization. It begins with identifying the problem. For example, if the problem is aggravated assault as measured by UCR crime counts, a thorough analysis of these crimes is necessary, determining where, when, how, and why they were committed and by whom. Armed with this information,

Table 13.2 Performance Measures

Performance Domain	Measure
Crime Reduction	UCR Part I crime rate
Holding Offenders Accountable	Crime Clearance Rate
Fear of Crime	ICMA National Cities Survey
Public-centered crime defense	Crime prevention programs
Traffic Safety	Traffic Accidents and Injuries
Providing Emergency Services	CFS Response time and Saturation Index

officers can be deployed, programs initiated, and occurrences tracked to determine the impact of the police efforts.

If the analysis of where-when-how-why indicates that domestic violence is the source of a high number of aggravated assaults, then domestic violence reduction must become the focus of the department's efforts. If the analysis reveals that certain business establishments are related to a high number of aggravated assaults, then the efforts of the department must be directed at closing these locations or bringing them under control to stop the violence.

Problem-Oriented vs. Strategic-Oriented

Problem-oriented policing is an approach to policing in which discrete pieces of police business, whether crime or acts of disorder, are subject to examination in order to learned about the problem in order to create a more effective strategy for dealing with it (Goldstein, 1979). Within a strategic approach, problem-oriented policing becomes one of the main tactics brought to bear on crime, fear of crime, traffic safety, and other areas, and is the principle vehicle for identifying problems and creating workable solutions.

The problem-oriented approach works within the strategic framework and is not an isolated police approach to community problems. In other words, the emphasis is on results – the measures of the six categories identified by Moore and Braga – and the police department is responsible and held accountable for success in these areas. Focusing on just a problem-oriented approach would narrow the focus on problems and their solutions, and not necessarily whether those solutions had any connection to the overall mission in the first place. In other words, the police can be very effective at addressing problems, but unless the result of that problem solving has an impact on improving one of the six areas of strategic focus, then the effort is wasted. It is not problem solving for its own sake, but problem solving with an overall purpose.

The overall purpose is "create and maintain a safe community." It is recommended that the six performance domains listed above be utilized to track whether this mission is being achieved, and it is further recommended that the performance measures be used to monitor police effectiveness, and to hold the department accountable for success in these areas.

These efforts should not be in a vacuum, however. They must be integrated with an active engagement with the community. Police departments have engaged different approaches to work with the community to be co-producers of public safety. Chapter 10 of this book provides a comprehensive review of community engagement and several of the main areas of this approach are reviewed here.

Community Policing

Community policing in the U.S. has a rich history. Beginning in the 1960s police scholars recognized that the prevailing model of delivering police services was ineffective. Much like today, the civil unrest during the 1960s and 1970s exposed serious shortcomings in police operations. The early empirical work with the Kansas City Preventative Patrol Experiment and the foot patrol experiments in Newark, NJ laid the groundwork for a new strategic approach for the police. Community policing has three key components: partnerships, organizational transformation, and problem solving. The police department acts as the "quarterback" with local organizations and stakeholders to build trust, reduce crime and disorder, and co-produce public safety (Office of Community Oriented Policing Services, 2014). Police departments are challenged to think differently about the conventional "crime-fighting" strategies, and routine responses to 911 CFS, and explore community partnerships and alternatives to the conventional approaches.

Community policing is not easy to implement. Over the last 50 or more years police departments have struggled to balance the community's needs with the typical service demands placed upon them. Most police departments refer to themselves as a "community policing department" but only scratch the surface when it comes to engaging in community policing as it is conceptualized.

Twenty-first-Century Policing

The President charged the task force with identifying best practices and offering recommendations on how policing practices can promote effective crime reduction while building trust. The following recommendations, known as the Six Pillars, were offered by the task force (COPS, 2015):

Building Trust and Legitimacy

> Building trust and nurturing legitimacy on both sides of the police/citizen divide is the foundational principle underlying the nature of relations between law enforcement agencies and the communities they serve.

Policy and Oversight

> If police are to carry out their responsibilities according to established policies, those policies must reflect community values. Law enforcement agencies should collaborate with community members, especially in communities and neighborhoods disproportionately affected by crime, to develop policies and strategies for deploying resources that aim to reduce crime by improving relationships, increasing community engagement, and fostering cooperation. To achieve this end, law enforcement agencies should have clear and comprehensive policies on the use of force (including training on the importance of de-escalation), mass demonstrations (including the appropriate use of equipment, particularly rifles and armored personnel carriers), consent before searches, gender identification, racial profiling, and performance measures – among others such as external and independent investigations and prosecutions of officer-involved shootings and other use of force situations and in-custody deaths.

Technology and Social Media

> The use of technology can improve policing practices and build community trust and legitimacy, but its implementation must be built on a defined policy framework with its purposes and goals clearly delineated. Implementing new technologies can give police departments an opportunity to fully engage and educate communities in a dialogue about their expectations for transparency, accountability, and privacy.

Community Policing and Crime Reduction

> The importance of community policing as a guiding philosophy for all stakeholders. Community policing emphasizes working with neighborhood residents to coproduce public safety. Law enforcement agencies should, therefore, work with community residents to identify problems and collaborate on implementing solutions that produce meaningful results for the community. Specifically, law enforcement agencies should develop and adopt policies and strategies that reinforce the importance of community engagement in managing public safety.

Training and Education

> Focuses on the training and education needs of law enforcement. To ensure the high quality and effectiveness of training and education, law enforcement agencies should engage community members, particularly those with special expertise, in the training process and provide leadership training to all personnel throughout their careers.

Officer Wellness and Safety

> The wellness and safety of law enforcement officers is critical not only for the officers, their colleagues, and their agencies but also for public safety. Pillar six emphasizes the support and proper implementation of officer wellness and safety as a multi-partner effort.

It is essential, before any reforms are developed or implemented, that the community think carefully about the philosophical and strategic approach that they want their police department to embrace. This is not a police department decision. It must be made in collaboration with the elected officials, community stakeholders, organized community groups, and the department. Clearly it won't be business as usual, but what will the future of the department look like? Will it be a full community policing organization? Will it embrace the Six Pillars identified by the Task Force? What performance measures and problem-solving strategies will the department engage? The following discussion about the demand and supply of police services can help provide the answers to these questions. However, the threshold question must be answered first: what is the mission of the department? How do we measure it and know it's being achieved? What mechanisms do we put in place to hold people accountable for achieving the mission? What mix of services will the department provide?

The next sections of the chapter revisit information in previous chapters in this book and put them into context with the over-arching theoretical approach to policing.

Demand-Side

Next is leveraging the available data to understand and triage the service demands placed on the department. Chapter 2 in this book goes into extensive details about how to determine workload and staffing levels. It is important to preserve scare police resources for crime and public safety requires a diligent effort on the part of police managers to prevent 9.1.1. from becoming that catch-basin for public complaints. Decisions regarding the demand of police services is a political decision. The determination of many officers to staff on patrol, and to determine what tasks they perform, defies an exact calculus must be made through a series of informed, and sometimes difficult choices.

Then, with the types of CFS and service demands properly identified, officers should be provided with the training, resources, and support to handle them efficiently and effectively, meaning with as little force as possible, promptly, professionally, and at the lowest possible expense. Complimenting the demand analysis is a "supply-side" analysis. How will the department provide the resources (supply) to meet these demands? Departments must ensure that police resources are available during the times of the day when they are most needed. This is accomplished by the design of shift schedules that meet demands appropriately, as well as supplying enough officers during the times they are needed. In addition, the department should explore different combinations of personnel and units, both sworn and civilian members, in imaginative and creative ways.

And finally, the department needs to develop and implement strategic plans designed to engage the community, understand their needs, and regain the trust that is essential for policing. Communities request police to respond to incidents that are not police emergencies or even police matters. Careful consideration should be given to certain categories of calls and calls where there is the greatest potential for operational dysfunction. The following broad call categories are good places to start as the department looks to preserve scare resources and minimize emergency responses to non-emergency calls: Alarms, Automobile Accidents Traffic Enforcement, Assist Citizen/Miscellaneous, Suspicious Person/Vehicle.

At a minimum, police departments should be examining their response to these categories of calls and seek to either eliminate them from their job tasks, and/or monitor them in a way to ensure that officers are both efficient and effective in handling them.

Supply-Side

This section discusses the "supply-side" of police service delivery. After the philosophical and strategic framework is considered, in context with the appropriate service demands, departments can explore various supply models to provide these services. The discussion here focuses on a two-prong approach to staffing supply.

Chapters 2 and 3 go into extensive detail about patrol allocation, deployment, and operations. This section is not designed to repeat information in those chapters. However, it is important to note that there is a very strong connection between the demand for police services, the philosophical and strategic dimensions the department embraces, and the "supply-side" of police resources to address all those competing issues. In general, the supply-side of police management involves the allocation and deployment of officers on patrol to meet the demands of the community, and this perspective has several main components:

Allocation

Uniformed patrol is considered the "backbone" of American policing. The Bureau of Justice Statistics indicate that more than 95 percent of police departments in the U.S. provide uniformed patrol. Officers assigned to this important function are the most visible members of the department and command the largest share of resources committed by the department. Proper allocation of these resources is critical to have officers available to respond to calls for service and provide law enforcement services to the public.

Again, this is where the first prong of the Rule of 60 comes into play. Accordingly, the department needs to balance the allocation of personnel in patrol and non-patrol functions. Strategically allocating resources in patrol and non-patrol enforcement functions would assist the department to achieve its public safety goals more readily and enhance service delivery. The following discussion and recommendations seek to balance staffing allocation appropriately and create other positions that could further the mission of the department.

Deployment

Allocation refers to the amount or ratio of how personnel resources are distributed in a department. Deployment means the way in which they are used: What do they do? When do they work? How are they assigned? This is where the second prong of the Rule-of-60 comes into play and the subject of extensive discussions in earlier chapters. The point here is to put deployment into the philosophical and strategic framework of policing. What the officers are doing, when and where, is as much a philosophical question as it is an efficiency question.

There are no ready-made population benchmarks for understanding police deployment. We strongly suggest that the department examines this concept with respect to the actual workload experienced. Of course, this workload needs to be examined and triaged as discussed above, but what's left requires an efficient and economical supply of officers. We also strongly suggest that this workload not constitute more than 60% of the available time (as measured by number of officers available to work), which is the second prong of the rule. Therefore, departments need to calculate workload as a percentage of available officers and ensure that there is at least 40% (even more sometimes) of the time "uncommitted" to work, or not assigned or having ample "discretionary" time.

This Rule of 60 for patrol deployment does *not* mean the remaining 40 percent of time is downtime or break time. It reflects the extent that patrol officer time is saturated by calls for service. The time when police personnel are not responding to calls should be committed to management-directed operations. This is a more focused use of time and can include supervised allocation of patrol officer activities toward proactive enforcement, crime prevention, community policing, and citizen safety initiatives. It will also provide ready and available resources in the event of an emergency.

In total, the workload demands and the supply of personnel to meet those demands need to be balanced appropriately between committed and non-committed time. The first step in achieving this balance is to understand the ratio between these two broad categories. The next step is to design a shift schedule to meet supply and demand effectively.

Schedule and Staffing

Taking into consideration the demand for police services and the concept of saturation index, appropriate levels of patrol staffing can be determined. The optimal level of patrol staffing will lead to the modeling of patrol schedules and act as the foundation for the staffing of the entire department.

The available literature on shift length provides no definitive conclusions on an appropriate shift length. A recent study published by the Police Foundation examined 8-hour, 10-hour, and 12-hour shifts, and found positive and negative characteristics associated with all three options (Amendola et al., 2011). The length of the shift is secondary to the application of that shift to meet service demands.

The 12-hour shift poses advantages and disadvantages. On the positive side, the 12-hour shift requires fewer work appearances for officers and supervisors. Presumably, fewer appearances translate into a higher quality of life away from work. From an operational perspective, the 12-hour shift results in a greater percentage of officers working on any given day, thus more officers deploy toward crime, traffic, disorder, and community issues at any one time. This shift also affords a tight unity of command with supervisors and officers working together each shift. This promotes better supervision and better esprit de corps among employees.

On the other hand, a 12-hour shift configuration with four equally staffed squads results in a constant and fixed level of patrol staffing throughout the day. However, service demands vary, peaking in the evening hours and waning in the early morning hours. With a constant supply of personnel and a variable demand for their services, there will be a continual cycle of either a surplus or shortage of patrol resources. Also, with a four-squad configuration a "silo" effect is often created. The natural rotation of this shift configuration creates four separate squads that do not interact often; this creates personnel silos. Similarly, it is difficult to communicate between the silos and between the squads and the executive management of the department. Lastly, shifts configured with two 12-hour shifts meet face-to-face but do not have any overlap. This creates problems, particularly in the evening when CFS volume is high. One shift stops taking CFS near the end of their deployment, and the oncoming shift delays taking CFS on the start of theirs. This creates gaps in patrol coverage.

Twelve-hour shifts are also long. An officer working 12 hours per day, plus commuting time, will not have much time remaining in the day for recreational, leisure, or family activities. Fatigue is also a factor. Working too many consecutive 12-hour shifts will create fatigue, which will compromise an officers' driving ability, cognitive reasoning, and reaction time. The Revere Police Department, with four consecutive 12-hour shifts, likely pushes the envelope on officer fatigue, particularly at the end of a set of four workdays.

The 10-hour shift is very popular in policing in the U.S. This shift offers the advantages of not being as taxing physically as the 12-hour shift, and still offers an extra day off compared to the standard 8-hour work week. The study cited above also presented evidence that the 10-hour shift had the most positive work- and personal-related benefits compared to the other shifts studied.

The major disadvantage with this shift length is that it is difficult to schedule. Ten is not a factor of 24, so organizing the 10-hour shift into a 24-hour day presents challenges. Using the conventional three-shift patrol model creates 30 hours of shift time. Similarly, 10-hour shifts present challenges with scheduling days off. Providing police service requires around-the-clock coverage. Eight- and 12-hour shifts feature natural opportunities to create rotating days on/off to adapt to the 24x7 service demands. Ten-hour shifts are cumbersome to schedule. For a standard work week for an enterprise that is closed on weekends, there are no real challenges, but when applied to seven-day coverage the problems arise and days off get "shoe-horned" into place with no natural combinations available.

Eight-hour shifts also offer advantages and disadvantages. Like the 12-hour shift, an 8-hour shift lends itself to a natural and consistent rotation of days off and divides equally into the 24-hour day. It is easy to implement and follow for the officers working it. The main disadvantage is that officers are required to work an extra day each week, or 52 times more per year.

Shift schedules should be designed with several (often competing) criteria in mind. The first important criteria for shift scheduling are that the supply of officers available for work closely matches the workload demands placed on the department. This means that shift schedules should be designed to meet the demands of the community and ensure that officers are assigned to work when they are needed the most, and that there is a continuous, uninterrupted supply of them. The second is that the shift schedule addresses other operational and administrative needs of the department, including training, overtime control, etc. Third, the shift schedule must consider the quality of work–life of the officers working it. Shift design must account for the desire of officers to have time off to rest and enjoy free time with their families and friends. A rested and satisfied officer is an asset for any department. Lastly, shift planning must consider the obligations a department has under any Collective Bargaining Agreements that are in effect at the time.

Service Alternatives

In addition to altering the shift plan to provide patrol coverage in a different fashion, departments should consider several different alternatives to providing service to the community. These alternatives represent opportunities for the department to improve already existing services or reform their operations to include other services that the community requires. The following is a discussion of potential in this area.

Community Engagement

Departments should consider community engagement as an essential part of their strategic planning process. Alongside crime, traffic, and disorder, community engagement and "customer" satisfaction should be considered "mission-critical" perspectives. This is a more granular approach than the philosophical dimensions discussed earlier in the report and addresses more strategic and tactical areas of community engagement. For example, it is one thing to claim that the police department has a community policing philosophy, but what does that translate into from an operational perspective? The following are recommendations that could be considered to develop a community engagement strategic plan.

- Citizen's Police Academy – This is a program designed to acquaint community residents that are not police officers with the activities of their local department. The programmatic elements vary by department, but generally feature topics such as the use of force, constitutional law, patrol, investigations, special investigations, organizational structure, and functions. Essentially, community members get a better understanding of their police department and police work in general (NYPD, 2023a).
- People's Police Academy – This is the opposite of the Citizen's Police Academy (Meminger, 2016). This type of program orients officers into the community that they are serving. This novel reform effort was pioneered in New York City by the Reverend Que English. She developed a community-led academy too help police officers, that don't live or hail from the community, transition into the community they serve through training and orientation. Local civic leaders, politicians, business owners, clergy, residents, etc. all meet with the officers as when they get assigned to the department and provide them with an understanding about neighborhood dynamic. This type of program could be developed and be delivered periodically throughout an officer's career. The idea is to promote understanding and dialogue and provide an opportunity not involving police emergencies for the officers to see the community as people.
- Police-Community Liaisons – every community is the U.S. has a plethora of active civic associations. These organizations have a mission, function, structure, and leadership, and almost all could benefit from a sound working relationship with the police department. We recommend that departments conduct a census of these organizations in the city and develop a plan to interact with them on a regular basis. The city of Rockville, MD, for example, identifies every community organization within its geographic confines and assigns a ranking officer to be the liaison between the police department and the civic organization. In addition, the city's website has an interactive mapping feature that allows the catalogues of each organization and provides contact and meeting information (Rockville, MD, 2023).
  o Designate a police–community liaison, in the rank of sergeant or above, and assign one to each community group.

o Require the liaison, or designee, to attend organization meetings.

o Develop a system to solicit, record, process, and report on issues that are raised by the organizations. For example, if the organization reports a crime or traffic condition to the liaison it is his/her responsibility to record it and develop a plan to address the condition and report back to the community organization about the efforts to address it.

o Present crime prevention and traffic safety lectures

- Departments should develop feedback mechanisms to better measure and understand community satisfaction.

o A satisfaction survey should be developed and administered at regular intervals. The results of the survey should be posted publicly on the website.

o Officers should carry business cards and distribute them during encounters with members of the public. The cards should contain information about how to contact the department as well as how to conduct the satisfaction survey.

o The department should develop a notification protocol where community stakeholders are notified about police-related events in the community. These notifications could be general crime and/or traffic alerts, or specific notifications that involve their specific community.

Technology

Departments need to explore technology as a way of improving efficiency and providing better service to the public. High-tech, low-touch, methods of police–community interactions also improve the ability of the police to engage the public in non-confrontational ways. There are two categories of technology that the department could explore in this area.

Web-based or Deferred Reporting

Communities around the country have had some success with permitting members of the public to make police reports through the department's website. Non-serious incidents and minor crimes can potentially be reported to departments without the response of an officer. Like the web links currently on their website used by the city for members of the public to request reports and services, departments could enable a web-based crime/incident reporting system. The use of this reporting mechanism is an excellent use of available technology. However, industry experience suggests that citizens still prefer the response of a "live" officer to lodge their complaints. Web-based reporting is not a panacea for reducing non-emergency responses, but an excellent tool, nonetheless. As the public becomes more "tech-savvy" this feature could be used more rigorously.

In addition to the web-based reporting, departments could consider staffing a telephone response program to various categories of CFS. The telephone response or differential response function could deal with past crimes and routine inquiries, thus eliminating the response of a sworn officer. Nonemergency calls, such as past crimes, minor property damage, and harassment, as well as building/area checks, and city ordinance CFS, can be handled by this program. Instead of dispatching an officer to these types of calls, the information is deferred (delayed) until a staff member becomes available to respond to the call, or CSO deployed, or another enforcement unit responds as appropriate. Dispatchers can record reports for certain categories of nonemergency incidents over the telephone. This process could divert nonemergency calls from the patrol units, and thus provide officers with more time to engage in proactive and directed patrols or traffic enforcement duties (Bouchrika, 2023).

LPR and CCTV Deployment

Police departments around the world are leveraging license plate readers (LPR) and closed-circuit television (CCTV) to improve operations. Perhaps the most famous use of this technology is in London and New York where those communities created a so-called "ring of steal" to combat terrorism and improve public safety (Greenemeier, 2011). Even smaller communities like the Village of Southampton in New York, a beach community of about 3,000, deploy these devices effectively. Obviously, most departments do not need to create a ring or steel or traffic Condron to prevent terrorism, put strategically sited LPRs and CCTVs could improve public safety.

We recommend that officers refrain from making random traffic stops and instead focus on high-risk crash locations and high-risk drivers. Similarly, crime is not randomly distributed in the community, but concentrated in specific locations, or hot-spots. Information about high crash locations and crime hotspots could be used to deploy LPRs and CCTVs to help combat these conditions. Also, the LPRs can be programmed to identify vehicles with suspended registration or insurance (at-risk drivers) and make the police job more effective at targeting these motorists. Instead of the police stopping people at random and opening themselves up to allegations of profiling, the technology would identify the at-risk motorist and eliminate any perceived motivations by the police.

Locating LPRs and CCTVs at strategic locations, as well as others, would provide communities with tools to improve both traffic safety and investigate crime more effectively.

Body-Worn Cameras

Body-Worn Cameras (BWCs) are an essential part of an officer's duty equipment, and as critical as their firearm and radio. The use of BWC video recordings offers an enormous upside potential to improve police operations and community relations.

Observing police–community interactions on film offers several opportunities. First, it would allow departments to identify good and bad tactics used by officers and provide them with video evidence to include in training to make the job safer for all involved. The MTA Police Department in the New York Metro region, for example, collects BWC video that illustrates exemplary officer conduct and stores those videos in an "electronic library" for other officers to reference (Police Executive Research Forum, 2023).

Second, monitoring BWC videos would allow departments to identify problematic officers that engage in poor performance when dealing with the public or handling CFS. And lastly, and where the greatest potential exists, BWCs record an enormous amount of positive and professional interactions between the police and the community. The videos also record the difficult and dangerous job the police do every day. The videos are essentially recorded evidence of police work and should be used to demonstrate to the community the good work (and the bad) that officers perform (Braga et al., 2022).

We bear witness to the sometimes-shocking police use of force seemingly daily. Masked by these accounts are the millions of professional interactions that occur. Departments could use these recordings to educate and inform the public about the realities of police work and showcase good performance.

Social Media

Police departments need to leverage social media platforms to promote positive police–community interactions. Many departments use Facebook as an informational and educational platform, but that is just one small medium to use in this space, and departments need to consider using social media in a way that transcends its conventional uses in policing and consider the marketing potential that social media possesses.

One of the critical tasks facing police departments is to restore trust with the community. Social media could be a useful tool at re-establishing that trust and promoting the excellent work that is done every day by officers. Departments need to develop and implement a community engagement strategy and leverage social media to promote that strategy and amplify the message that the department is engaging the organized community differently (Beshears, 2017).

The bottom line for the police is that there needs to be a bridge built between the police and the community that permits a better understanding of the issues facing both sides. Social media can help facilitate communication that will be essential to fostering that understanding. Using social media in a way that "humanizes" the officers and illustrates the positive contributions they make to the community are important. Similarly, using social media as a way of understanding the concerns of the community is important too. All police departments should continue their work developing social media on both sides of this spectrum.

Community Service Officers

Police departments around the U.S. are deploying non-sworn, uniformed, CSOs to support patrol operations. This position is not necessarily viewed as a support or administrative one, but one that is integrated with patrol officers to provide efficient and effective service. In general, departments that experience the greatest benefit from the CSO position embed them in patrol squads and task them with handling non-emergency police CFS. Typically, officers on patrol will respond to a heavy volume of non-emergency CFS, and these types of CFS could easily be shifted to a CSO. In addition, CSOs could respond to reports of past crimes where no suspects are present, and the emergency has passed. "Cold" thefts, vandalism, etc. could all be handled by a properly trained CSO. For example, when a member of the public responds to department headquarters to report a past theft, administrative personnel at the facility call for the officer on patrol that covers the headquarters beat to come into the facility to take the report. This is inefficient. Instead of pulling an officer from patrol, a CSO, either assigned to headquarters, or already embedded in the day shift could relieve the officer of that responsibility (Blackmore, 1979).

Departments that leverage CSOs effectively deploy them in marked vehicles without emergency lights or sirens and distinguish them from the typical police cruiser. CSOs also wear distinctive uniforms, and most importantly they receive extensive training and are compensated as full-time employees.

Communities should still carefully examine the service demands and look to minimize them to the greatest extent possible. However, there will still be a need for non-emergency police services to be provided and CSOs could be a cost-effective and operationally efficient way of meeting those demands.

Crisis Intervention Team (Co-Response Models)

Police departments should consider deploying officers to coordinate crisis intervention teams and hire qualified professionals to partner with to deal with people experiencing crisis in the community. These team would then be responsible for training officers on dealing with people in crisis, developing the appropriate policies in this area, recording, and tracking incidents, and collaborating with the local medical, psychological, and advocate communities to develop a fulsome response to these issues.

Police officers deal with people experiencing mental crises every day. In addition, communities around the country are grappling with the issue of pervasive homelessness. Creating the capacity to deal with these issues in a holistic and comprehensive way, that involves collaboration with key stakeholders, with a de-emphasis on the use of force and arrest, is an opportunity that departments should embrace.

The National Alliance on Mental Illness estimates that approximately 2,700 police departments in the U.S. have created connections with local mental health providers, hospital emergency services, and individuals with mental illness and their families, to implement Crisis Intervention Teams. The Bureau of Justice Assistance also has a Police-Mental Health Collaboration (PMHC) toolkit available online for police departments to access as they begin developing this capacity within their departments (Bureau of Justice Assistance, 2023a) This is an excellent resource that the departments could avail themselves to begin a Crisis Intervention Team in the department. Furthermore, the BJS identifies two police departments that are implementing programs that could act as models.

The Madison, WI police department began their Mental Health Liaison Program in 2004 (Bureau of Justice Assistance, 2023b). Currently, the program is supervised by a sergeant and has six sworn officers assigned. Each of these officers is responsible for one of the six patrol districts in Madison and they engage in a problem-oriented approach to addressing the underlying conditions that generate encounters between the police and people experiencing mental crises.

The Pasadena, CA police department has a similar CIT unit that has an expanded mission dealing with homeless outreach (Pasadena, 2023) The Homeless Outreach – Psychiatric Evaluation Unit (HOPE) is a collaborative team that provides emergency response and follow-up to those in need of mental health, housing, and related social services. HOPE is a co-responder model where a sworn officer is partnered with and works alongside a clinician from the Department of Health. They are first responders to mental health CFS and perform proactive enforcement and counselling for targeted populations. This model could be an effective one to deal with people experiencing mental health crises.

The approach taken will be unique to each community, however, a co-response or CIT model could resemble either of the above models or any number of other effective ones that exist across the country. The model embraced should be specifically tailored for the needs of the specific community and be as inclusive as possible. The essential elements of this program should include many, if not all, the following:

- Hiring a trained clinician to co-respond with the assigned officer to mental health CFS. These two individuals would be the core of the free-standing CIT.
- Training – all sworn personnel participate in training. In addition, the Crisis Intervention Team should be tasked with developing effective in-service training for police officers, dispatchers, and other critical groups involved in mental health crisis responding.

- CIT should respond to CFS involving mental health crises when they are available.
- Document and report mental health related CFS.
- Coordinate follow-up with individuals to ensure they access needed resources.
- Attend meetings as needed to collaborate with medical organizations, advocacy groups, and families.

Research has shown that an effective response by the police with individuals experiencing mental health crises can reduce the risks to police officers and patients, reduce the use of force by the police, reduce the number of repeat CFS responses, and deliver better services to the community. All departments should consider developing greater capacity in this area and deploy a Crisis Intervention Team to manage these important issues.

Conclusion

During the last decade there have been several events that question the legitimacy of the police and foster the need to reform. Although "defunding" police departments didn't materialize along with the rhetoric, the message was clear that the police need to change. This chapter explores the theoretical approaches to policing, and the different ways to evaluate police performance. We believe this is an important first step. Understanding how your police department operates can't be done in a vacuum, it needs to be done by looking through an historical and community lens. Once these issues are considered, then police and municipal managers can develop a better understanding of the operational performance of their department. Recommendations and examples are offered that have shown to be effective. Emulating these models, and aligning them within the strategic framework of the department is the approach that should be taken to achieve the police mission and provide sound public safety services to the community.

Note

1 www.tandfonline.com/doi/abs/10.1080/0731129X.2004.9992156

References

Amendola, K. L., Weisburd, D., Hamilton, E. E., Jones, G., & Slipka, M. (2011). *The Shift Length Experiment: What We Know about 8-, 10-, and 12-Hour Shifts in Policing*. National Policing Institute. www.policinginstitute.org/publication/shift-length-experiment/

Beshears, M. L. (2017). Effectiveness of police social media use. *American Journal of Criminal Justice*, 42, 489–501.

Bittner, E. (1970). *Functions of the Police in a Modern Society*. NIMH.

Blackmore, J. (1979). CSOs (Community Service Officers) – Tedious work but good training. *Police Magazine*, 2(3), 50–54.

Bouchrika, I. (October 10, 2023). *20 Best Police Records Management System in 2023*. Research. com. https://research.com/software/best-police-records-management-system

Braga, A., MacDonald, J. M., & McCabe, J. E. (2022). Body-worn cameras, lawful police stops, and NYPD officer compliance: A cluster randomized control trial. *Criminology*, 60(1), 124–158.

Bureau of Justice Assistance. (August 2023a). *Police – Mental Health Collaboration (PMHC) Toolkit*. BJA. https://bja.ojp.gov/program/pmhc

Bureau of Justice Assistance. (August 2023b). *Law Enforcement – Mental Health Learning Sites: Madison, WI*. BJA. https://bja.ojp.gov/sites/g/files/xyckuh186/files/media/document/lawenforcement-mentalhealthlearningsites_madison.pdf

Goldstein, H. (1979). Improving policing: A problem-oriented approach. *Crime and Delinquency*, 25, 236–258.

Greenemeier, L. (September 11, 2011). The apple of its eye: Security and surveillance pervades post-9/11 New York City. *Scientific American*, 305(3). www.scientificamerican.com/article/post-911-nyc-video-surveillance/#

Kelling, G. L., & Wilson, J. Q. (March 1982). Broken windows: The police and neighborhood safety. *The Atlantic*, 29–38.

Los Angeles Police Department (August 2023) *Mission Statement*. LAPD. www.lapdonline.org/mission-statement/#:~:text=The%20Mission%20Statement%20of%20the,improve%20their%20quality%20of%20life?>.

Meminger, D. (March 28, 2016). "People's Police Academy" aims to help officers better understand the people they police. *Spectrum News: NY1*. https://ny1.com/nyc/bronx/criminal-justice/2016/03/28/-people-s-police-academy--aims-to-help-officers-better-understand-the-people-they-police

Moore, M., & A. Braga (2004). Police performance measurement: A normative framework. *Criminal Justice Ethics*, 23, 3–19.

New York City Police Department. (August 2023a). *Citizens Police Academy*. NYPD. www.nyc.gov/site/nypd/bureaus/administrative/training-citizens-police-academy.page

New York City Police Department. (August, 2023b). *Misson Statement*. NYPD. www.nyc.gov/site/nypd/about/about-nypd/mission.page

New York State Exec. Order No. 203. (2020). New York State Police Reform and Reinvention Collaborative. www.governor.ny.gov/sites/default/files/atoms/files/EO_203.pdf

Office of Community Oriented Policing Services (2014). *Community Policing Defined*. Office of Community Oriented Policing Services.

Office of Community Oriented Policing Services (2015). *The President's Task Force on 21st Century Policing Implementation Guide: Moving from Recommendations to Action*. Office of Community Oriented Policing Services.

Pasadena Police Department (August 2023). *Patrol Division: Homeless Outreach – Psychiatric Evaluation (HOPE)*. City of Pasadena. www.cityofpasadena.net/police/divisions-and-sections/patrol-division/#homeless-outreach

Police Executive Research Forum. (February 25, 2023). *MTA Police Chief John Meuller Is Creating a "Body-Worn Camera Video Library" to Showcase Good Policing*. www.policeforum.org/trending25feb23

Rockville, MD (August 2023). *City Maps*. City of Rockville, MD. www.rockvillemd.gov/683/City-Maps

Shaw, C. R., & McKay, H. D. (1942). *Juvenile Delinquency and Urban Areas*. University of Chicago Press.

Siegel, E. R., & Rappleye, H. (2021). Burlington decided to cut its police force 30 percent. Here's what happened next. *NBC News Online*. www.nbcnews.com/news/us-news/burlington-vermont-defunded-police-force-s-happened-rcna8409\

Walker, S., & Katz, C. M. (2021). *The Police in America*. McGraw- Hill.

https://mascontext.com/issues/surveillance/ring-of-steel/

Index

For Product Safety Concerns and Information please contact our EU
representative GPSR@taylorandfrancis.com
Taylor & Francis Verlag GmbH, Kaufingerstraße 24, 80331 München, Germany

www.ingramcontent.com/pod-product-compliance
Lightning Source LLC
Chambersburg PA
CBHW080131270326
41926CB00021B/4431